THE BLUEPRINT

MW01101060

Conservative Parties and Their Impact
on Canadian Politics

In this collection, J.P. Lewis and Joanna Everitt bring together a group
of up-and-coming political scientists as well as senior scholars to explore the recent history of the Conservative Party of Canada, covering
the pre-merger period (1993–2003) and both the minority and majority
governments under Prime Minister Stephen Harper.

The contributors provide nuanced accounts about the experience
of conservatives in Canada that reflect the contemporary evolution
of Canadian politics in both policy and practice. They challenge the
assumption that Harper's government was built upon traditional
"Toryism" and reveal the extent to which the agenda of the CPC was
shaped by its roots in the Reform and Canadian Alliance parties.
Organized thematically, the volume delves into topics such as interest
advocacy, ethno-cultural minorities, gender, the media, and foreign
policy. *The Blueprint* showcases the renewed vigour in political studies in Canada while revealing the contradictory story of the modern
Conservative Party.

J.P. LEWIS is an assistant professor in the Department of History and
Politics at the University of New Brunswick.

JOANNA EVERITT is a professor and Dean of the Faculty of Arts at
the University of New Brunswick.

The Blueprint

*Conservative Parties and
Their Impact on Canadian Politics*

EDITED BY J.P. LEWIS AND JOANNA EVERITT

UNIVERSITY OF TORONTO PRESS
Toronto Buffalo London

© University of Toronto Press 2017
Toronto Buffalo London
www.utppublishing.com
Printed in the U.S.A.

ISBN 978-1-4875-0182-2 (cloth)   ISBN 978-1-4875-2168-4 (paper)

Printed on acid-free, 100% post-consumer recycled paper
with vegetable-based inks.

Library and Archives Canada Cataloguing in Publication

The blueprint : conservative parties and their impact on Canadian politics/
edited by J.P. Lewis and Joanna Everitt.

Includes bibliographical references and index.
ISBN 978-1-4875-0182-2 (hardcover). – ISBN 978-1-4875-2168-4 (softcover)

1. Conservative Party of Canada.   2. Conservatism – Canada.   3. Canada –
Politics and government – 1993–.   I. Everitt, Joanna Marie, 1964–, editor
II. Lewis, J.-P. (Jon-Paul), 1978–, editor

JL197.C75B58 2017   324.27104   C2017-901034-4

This book has been published with the help of a grant from the Federation
for the Humanities and Social Sciences, through the Awards to Scholarly
Publications Program, using funds provided by the Social Sciences
and Humanities Research Council of Canada.

University of Toronto Press acknowledges the financial assistance to its
publishing program of the Canada Council for the Arts and the Ontario Arts
Council, an agency of the Government of Ontario.

Canada Council   Conseil des Arts
for the Arts   du Canada

ONTARIO ARTS COUNCIL
CONSEIL DES ARTS DE L'ONTARIO
an Ontario government agency
un organisme du gouvernement de l'Ontario

Funded by the   Financé par le
Government   gouvernement
of Canada   du Canada

Canadä

Contents

THE BLUEPRINT

Conservative Parties and Their Impact
on Canadian Politics

1 Introduction

J.P. LEWIS AND JOANNA EVERITT

In his 2006 election night victory speech, Stephen Harper argued, "Our national identity was not forged by government policy. It does not flow from any one program, any one leader or any one party. Our Canada is rooted in our shared history, and in the values which have and will endure" (Harper 2006). Harper's statement seemed to imply that the new Conservative government would be building upon past government traditions and styles; however, in reality the party was driven by an agenda that represented a new approach to political policies and practices in Canada. Indeed, although pundits, journalists, and politicians frequently referred to the Conservative Party of Canada (CPC) as "Tories," they had more in common with the former Reform and Canadian Alliance (CA) parties than they did to the former Progressive Conservatives (PC). While often downplayed to reassure voters that this new party was not too extreme, the agenda of the CPC was closely linked to its Reform and CA roots and served as a blueprint for substantial institutional, policy, and procedural change in Canadian politics.

However, like any blueprint or initial draft, not all ideas and goals are carried to fruition, and this too was the case for the conservative agenda that drove the right during the 1990s and early 2000s. In examining the journey of the federal conservative parties of the right (PC, Reform, CA, and finally the Conservative Party of Canada) from opposition to minority government to majority government we uncover insights into how internal and external political pressures affect the policy positions and temper the core ideologies and goals of political parties.

While not all aspects of the conservative agenda were accomplished during the Harper government's term in office, as the result of institutional constraints or electoral pressures, the last twenty years of federal conservative parties have had a clear impact on the way politics are practised in Canada. In some instances these alterations build on pre-existing institutional trends (such as strong party discipline and the concentration of power in the hands of the prime minister); in others they involve new legacies of the Conservative Party (including strict communications management, permanent campaigning, and neoliberal pragmatism). Although the lasting effects of this shift will not be fully understood for years, and may indeed be eradicated by a new government taking new approaches, our contributors show how certain significant changes, regardless of their subtlety, appear to have taken place. The deviations from the past discussed in this book are not to be confused with the thesis that Canadians themselves are becoming more conservative, as argued by Bricker and Ibbitson in their book *The Big Shift* (2013). Rather, we argue that, despite constraints that often make it difficult to reform politics or procedures, traditional Canadian political institutions and groups were approached in new ways by the Conservative government, and this had the effect of restructuring our governmental practices and processes. Evidence of these changes is found in the Conservative government's impact on three central features of Canadian politics – political processes (elections, political parties), political actors (advocacy groups, ethnocultural minorities, gender, Quebec, Indigenous peoples, mass media), and political institutions (Constitution, Parliament, the executive, federalism). As well, consideration of the government's approach to foreign policy provides a further measure of the impact of these changes and is significant as a result of the emphasis the Conservative government and Harper placed on international affairs.

This book seeks to illustrate how the experience of conservative parties in Canada since 1993 reflects the contemporary evolution of Canadian politics in both policy and practice. By focusing on conservative parties pre- and post-merger we find how new and old political ideas and approaches survive, and how others are rejected. In doing so, we aim to highlight the contradictory story of the Conservative Party of Canada – a party and government that was both pushed by political ideology and pulled by political strategy.

Contemporary Canadian Conservatives and Theoretical Understandings of Canadian Politics

This book outlines the impacts of policy and political process since the end of the third-party system in 1993 (Carty, Cross, and Young 2000), the decline of the version of conservatism known as "Toryism," and the emergence of a new national political vehicle in the form of the Conservative Party of Canada. As Bittner and Koop (2013, 2) note in the introduction to their 2013 collection on political parties and elections in Canada, "Longitudinal accounts of Canadian politics ... have always grappled with issues of continuity and change." Our contributors provide an important elaboration of the continuity and change of politics and government from the perspective of conservative parties in government and opposition over the last two decades. While identifying continuity, this book attempts to highlight the change that has occurred, both to the parties and the political system as Canadian conservatives assumed more power and influence, and hints at the impact that this will have on future governments. More specifically, the chapters offer evidence of change to two formative theories of Canadian politics: (1) the evolution of the Canadian federal party system, and (2) the idea of a Tory-touched liberal political culture.

The federal election results of 1993 are significant when viewed within the context of Canadian party politics as a whole. That election witnessed the beginning of the end of the Progressive Conservative Party and the electoral emergence of the Reform Party (Carty, Cross, and Young 2000). By adopting this time frame (1993–2015) for their chapters, our contributors provide historical and contextual analyses of the influence of the last two decades of federal conservative parties on Canadian politics, while in opposition (Progressive Conservative/Reform/Canadian Alliance/Conservative) and in government (Conservative). As one of the goals of each chapter, the authors attempt to demonstrate how approaches and perspectives towards political institutions, processes, and actors changed from pre-merger of the federal conservative parties (the Progressive Conservative Party, the Reform Party/Canadian Alliance [1993–2003]) to post-merger (the Conservative Party [2003–15]). In this way, the collection allows the reader to better understand Canadian politics, focused not on the "shared history" that Harper mentioned in his speech, but on the new paradigms his party has created.

On the transition from a splintered opposition to a new Conservative party and government, common trends are found throughout the chapters. The new Conservative government changed positions on a number of Reform's founding ideals and objectives (parliamentary reform, immigration reform, recognition of Quebec, multiculturalism policy) and left behind a number of beliefs traditionally associated with the Progressive Conservatives (strong national programs, activist executive federalism, soft power/moderate approach to foreign policy). On the basis of these departures, the Conservative Party under Stephen Harper may have disappointed many former Reform/CA/PC partisans, but these pragmatic, electorally driven policy positions helped the CPC build a solid national base of voter support, which increased from one election to the next.[1] Even in 2015 when the party lost its majority in Parliament, it received only slightly fewer than 200,000 votes than it had in 2011. This suggests that its election loss was due to an influx of new voters voting for the Liberals rather than a dramatic shift of votes from the Conservatives.

One driving factor in this change in the party system is a weakening of the role that Toryism played in new conservative values. In the past, the original Conservative Party of John A. Macdonald, Robert Borden, and R.B. Bennett, and then the Progressive Conservative Party, was the home of "Toryism." The four central tenets of Toryism are (1) *tradition*, (2) *sense of community*, (3) *order over liberty*, and (4) *politics over economics*. The new Conservative Party rejected two of these tenets outright: *sense of community* and *politics over economics*. Meanwhile, the other two tenets, *tradition* and *order over liberty*, have been retained, less out of allegiance to a traditional form of Toryism (which saw social democratic ideas and liberalism converging) than as a product of the new Canadian political environment, which the Conservatives helped create. This new environment was exemplified by market-driven policies delivered through targeted and branded politics. *Tradition*, as found in the prevalence of the monarchy, families, and the church, was adopted by the Conservative Party to accentuate party brand and appeal to median voters. *Order over liberty* was adopted less as an interpretation of societal order and more as a neoconservative view of the modern world. The once widely acclaimed "Tory touch," which helped explain the moderating forces in the defunct federal Progressive Conservative Party, was in retreat within the new party.

Evidence that Toryism is in decline among Canadian conservatives is found throughout this book. This argument is most clear in chapter 2, which concludes that the new Conservative Party reflects the changeable and encompassing nature of conservative ideology that has reoriented the party into a "new brokerage" party. Building upon the theoretical contributions of the recent Farney and Rayside (2013) volume, which

---

1   Popular vote: 2004 – 29.6 per cent; 2006 – 36.3 per cent; 2008 – 37.7 per cent; 2011 – 39.6 per cent; 2015 – 31.9 per cent.

argues for a varied and broad interpretation of Canadian conservatism, we believe that the Conservatives have been successful by adopting a big-tent ideological approach that is equal parts neoliberalism, neoconservatism, populism, moral conservatism, and economic conservatism. Less present in this mix is the traditional Tory touch that was found in the former Progressive Conservatives. The manifestation and dominance of these diverse strains reflects the political imperatives or institutional constraints confronting the party at any given time.

Evidence that the new Conservative Party has been able to broker these diverse conservative values can be found in election study data that demonstrate convergence between Reform/Canadian Alliance partisans and Progressive Conservatives after the merger on most social and constitutional issues, with some difference remaining on economic and moral traditional issues (chapter 3) – again, more continuity and change. The Conservatives' most explicit change can be seen in how the new party engages with external actors – favouring private economic interests over public interest groups (chapter 4); rejecting direct efforts to engage in gender politics by positioning women's issues under crime, justice, or family policy umbrellas (chapter 6); abandoning the electoral courtship of Quebec after initial and modest electoral success and in doing so rejecting decades of traditional brokerage between English-Canadian and French-Canadian interests (chapter 7); discarding pre-existing Indigenous rights in favour of pan-Canadian visions of citizenship (chapter 8); and adopting an ideologically driven foreign policy approach that departed from historically moderate and measured approaches to global affairs (chapter 14).

However, in other political and policy areas there was a mix of continuity and change driven by Conservatives' goals of winning and keeping office or by institutional constraints that limited the extent to which they could implement a new ideological agenda. For example, the Conservatives followed the Liberal Party in courting immigrants, but with less focus on policy inclusion and more on political and electoral inclusion (chapter 5). In government, parliamentary pressures of maintaining support of two party bases led the Conservatives to adopt a less ideological and more strategic approach to traditional Canadian political institutions such as the Constitution, the executive, and the legislature (chapters 10, 11, and 12). And finally, Stephen Harper as prime minister adapted federalism to better meet his policy and political goals through a form of calculated "individualized executive federalism" (chapter 13).

How do these observations contribute to our theoretical understanding of Canadian politics? The experiences of Canadian conservative parties in government and opposition provide evidence that the dominant theme of continuity *and* change endures, even in an era of political and policy evolution and upheaval. The key element of this argument is that, while the conservative story of the last two decades presents change in the process and policy of Canadian politics, common institutional themes continue – political parties continue to court diverse interests, executives still dominate legislatures, and ideologies, regardless of how liberating or threatening, are still tempered by the moderating Canadian political climate.

The journey from opposition to government has been an evolution for federal conservative parties. Parties and politicians once deemed too "scary" (Reform/Canadian Alliance) or irrelevant (Progressive Conservative) were able to find a way to form government and stay in power long enough to have a significant political and policy impact. Not unexpectedly, many of the authors in this book suggest that much of the process has been an unpredictable mix of politics and pragmatism. As Stephen Harper noted in 2008, "Two things you have to do. One thing you do is you have to pull conservatives, to pull the party, to the centre of the political spectrum. But what you also have to do, if you're really serious about making transformation, is you have to pull the centre of the political spectrum toward conservatism" (Wells 2008, 18). This volume explores the extent to which Stephen Harper has pulled Canadian politics into terrain advantageous to the Conservative Party following three election wins and almost ten years in government.

The chapters of this book cover the period up to and including the 2015 federal election, and it is important to note the significance of the campaign and its results. First, the campaign itself reflected the Conservative Party's approach to electoral politics. The new approach, which the party honed over the last three elections, includes a tightly scripted, highly branded, and leader-dominated campaign. Stephen Harper was front and centre, routinely appearing alone at campaign events. While this approach has been adopted by past parties, the Conservatives brought it to new levels in Canadian politics with increased reliance on negative political advertising, micro-market research polling and strategizing, and, most significantly, a full embrace of the permanent campaign that blurs the lines between partisan government and the non-partisan public service (Delacourt 2013). In the weeks leading up to the dropping of the writ for the 2015 election, Conservative members of Parliament and ministers crisscrossed the country making funding

announcements and re-announcements in an unprecedented exploitation of the powers of incumbency and government. In the end, it would
be all for naught; the Conservative Party won 99 seats (down from 159)
and the Liberal Party won 184 seats, enough to form government in
the new 338-seat Parliament. While it is too early to tell how much of
the party's policy and political imprint will be permanent, the last two
decades provide enough evidence to at least explore the initial impact.
It is our hope that this book will initiate an investigation that will continue into the coming decades.

This introduction sets the stage by providing an overview of the main
themes found throughout the chapters: (1) economic individualism, (2)
pragmatic electioneering, (3) adversarial politics, and (4) institutional
disdain. These themes identify approaches to policy and politics. While
appearing to be a departure from previous Canadian governments and
parties, the approaches have been cloaked in a level of moderation and
incrementalism that distracts many from what may actually be revolu-
tionary changes. As Peter Russell suggests in the concluding chapter
of this book, what the authors tell is a story of moderation. A common
narrative of the chapters is of a party moderating certain political actions, policy positions, and institutional ideas to gain and hold power.
However, this moderate turn should not be confused with a turn to
the centre of the political spectrum. What we see instead is electorally
opportunistic behaviour – a party holding onto ideological positions
while focused on the ends of securing enough voter support to form
government. Before discussing the four themes in more detail, it is important to review the literature on the federal conservative parties in
opposition and in government since 1993 to provide a sense of what
has been previously explored and to suggest additional sources for the
keen reader.

This book is an attempt to fill a gap in the academic literature on
federal conservative parties. Previous work on this topic can be divided
into three parts, with a focus on: (1) conservatives in opposition, (2)
conservatives in government, and (3) Stephen Harper himself. Despite
different approaches or styles, the shared narrative running through
most of the work matches that of this book: the right-of-centre was split
in 1993 with a strong ideological strain, which was eventually tempered
to achieve electoral success. Even amidst this moderation, conservative
policy positions and competitive political practices were observed.

The emergence of the Reform Party, breaking through the decades-
long Liberal/Progressive Conservative hegemony, created a bevy of
academic interest. Much of this work attempted to explain the party's

rise to power (Barney 1996; Flanagan 1995; Harrison 1995; Harrison and Krahn 1995; Laycock 1994, 2002; Sharpe and Braid 1992) and identify who was supporting this new federal party (Archer and Ellis 1994; Harrison, Johnston, and Krahn 1996; Nevitte et al. 1998). Scant academic attention was paid to the federal Progressive Conservative Party from 1993 to 2003, and this is reflected in the chapters of this book as well. However, much more attention was paid to the Progressive Conservatives once the parties merged to "unite the right." For more background on the merger there are a number of popular political books (Plamondon 2006; Segal 2007; Wells 2007; Carson 2014) and academic works (Bélanger and Godbout 2010) worth consulting.

Once the Conservative Party formed government in 2006, academic attention turned to a number of political and policy sub-topics now affected by a new government after years of Liberal rule. Research and writing has focused on the prowess of the Conservative electoral campaign machine (Flanagan 2007, 2014), the historical/comparative place of the Conservative government (Behiels 2010; Cody 2008; Malloy 2009; Snow and Moffitt 2012), twenty-first-century conservatism in Canada (Farney and Rayside 2013), federalism (Caron and LaForest 2009), citizenship and immigration (Chapnick 2011) and conservatism and the Americanization of Canadian constitutional culture (Schneiderman 2015). Other more general works have focused on the last two decades of Canadian parties and elections where conservative parties had a distinct place (Bittner and Koop 2013; Kanji, Bilodeau, and Scott 2012).

While the previous literature contributes significantly in the specific areas listed, this book draws on a number of diverse areas of Canadian politics to present a cohesive and comprehensive narrative. For example, there has been special attention to electioneering and ideology (Bittner and Koop 2013; Farney and Rayside 2013; Flanagan 2007; Flanagan 2014; Malloy 2009), but less attention to the process of governing, a theme that crops up throughout this book (see chapters 10, 11, 12, and 13 in this volume). As well, moving beyond a focus on the means (Behiels 2010; Snow and Moffitt 2012), our volume addresses the ends – impacts of Conservative political and policy approaches (see chapters 4, 5, 6, 7, and 8). As well, some chapters (see chapters 5 and 13) build on earlier work that covered specific areas of interest such as multiculturalism and federalism (Caron and LaForest 2009).

The most recent and notable academic contribution to our understanding of conservatism and Canadian politics is Farney and Rayside's edited collection *Conservatism in Canada*. In the book's comprehensive exploration of conservative ideology in Canada, the editors argue that their collection "illustrates the varieties of conservatism at play in contemporary Canadian politics" (2013, 4). Farney and Rayside's position that the "conservative" label in Canada is used in a variety of ways and includes notions of neoliberalism, populism, and moral conservatism is reflected in the descriptive narratives and evidence of this book. From the Conservatives' approaches to groups (women, Indigenous peoples, ethnocultural minorities) to institutions (Parliament, Cabinet, the Constitution), big-tent conservatism is found as contemporary Canadian federal conservative parties have shifted between market-driven small-government positions to populist electorally targeted behaviour. Implicitly, the idea that the Canadian conservative parties are driven by big-tent conservatism can be found in every chapter, whether it is the Conservative government's neoliberal favouring of economic themed interest groups (as discussed in chapter 4) or the Reform/Canadian Alliance populist beliefs in the processes of government (as discussed in chapters 11 and 12). More explicitly, in chapter 2, Farney and Koop address the Conservative Party and government's ideological commitments, noting the neoliberal turn in approaches to market and economic policy. As Bélanger and Stephenson note in chapter 3, in the 2004 election, the newly incarnated Conservative Party attempted to shed its controversial moral conservatism roots in favour of a moderate brand of electorate-ready neoliberal ideas; these observations reflect Steve Patten's thesis that argues for the "triumph" of neoliberalism in the new Conservative Party (2013). Kate Puddister and James Kelly take up the idea of neoliberal influence in chapter 7, which makes the case that the Conservative government's approach to Quebec is influenced by a neoliberal view of small government, in turn committing to watertight compartments within the féderation. Finally, while certain elements of hard-line social conservatism examined by Farney (2012) are found here to be downplayed through media and legislative strategies (see chapters 9 and 11 in this volume), as Shaun Narine argues (see chapter 14 in this volume), many point to the Conservative government's foreign policy to find its true stripes in its neoconservative approach to Canada's role on the world stage. In aggregate, the specific political and policy topic–based chapters of this book fit well alongside an ideological and theoretical contribution such as Farney and Rayside's (2013). In a manner similar to the way the contributors to that collection navigate the philosophical agreements and disagreements of Canadian conservatism, our contributors examine the commonalities and contradictions of the policies, practices, and politics of Canadian conservatism.

Not surprisingly, with over two decades in public life and almost ten years as prime minister, Stephen Harper was regular fodder for political authors in Canada, starting with William Johnson (2005). The treatment of Harper ranged from moderate explorations of his political success (Hébert 2007; Ibbitson 2015; Wells 2007, 2013) to stinging indictments of his legacy (Bourrie 2015; Engler 2012; Gutstein 2014; Harris 2014; Martin 2010; Nadeau 2011). Many of these recent treatments build on the˙common theme of Harper as a controlling, commanding, and win-at-all-costs political actor. While the authors of this collection do not explicitly attempt to prove or disprove these characterizations, the chapters offer a nuanced and grounded exploration of the federal conservatives through traditional Canadian political science topic areas, in an effort to produce a comprehensive account. In the following section, we briefly outline the four themes of federal conservative policy positions and political practice that animate this volume.

Economic Individualism

With a view to seeking broader voter support, a number of key policy positions from the Reform Party's 1993 election platform were abandoned by Canadian federal conservative parties over time. There was a turn away from Reform's early opposition to multiculturalism and some components of official bilingualism, as well as a more open approach to immigration. In combination with other abandoned populist institutional ideas (more free votes, removing power of the party leader to sign candidate nomination papers, use of referendum and recall initiatives), the 2015 Conservative Party shared little resemblance to its Reform origins. However, as our authors note, while the party and government may have tempered or dropped certain moral, social, and political/democratic ideals, the ideology of the neoliberal economic platform was largely intact. Regardless of efforts to attract new blocs of voters or explore new terrain in pragmatic bouts of cooperation, the Conservative Party of Canada still advanced a program that promotes economic individualism supported by decreased regulation and promotion of a free market.

In their chapter on political parties and federal conservatives, Royce Koop and Jim Farney (chapter 2) argue that, while the merger of the parties moderated or softened some of the social conservative views associated with the former Reform and Canadian Alliance parties, the neoliberal free market approach remained consistent over two decades. Farney and Koop also suggest that the new Conservative Party of Canada represents a "new brokerage" party that does not rely on the Canadian tradition of brokering major regions of the country (e.g., Ontario and Quebec) and instead brokers specific interests through new directed approaches to political market research and political messaging.

Similar nuance is found when considering conservative voters in Éric Bélanger and Laura Stephenson's chapter (chapter 3). Here, the authors track the attitudes of Reform/Canadian Alliance/Progressive Conservative voters pre-merger and weak/strong Conservative partisans post-merger. The authors are interested in how conservative voters reacted to the merger and if there was an ideological consolidation on the right of the spectrum in the Canadian electorate. Bélanger and Stephenson assess the changing attitudes of voters concerning economic, social, and constitutional issues. They find that pre-merger there was agreement between Reform/Canadian Alliance and Progressive Conservative voters on economic issues and disagreement on social and constitutional issues. Surprisingly, consolidation of voter attitudes did not happen after the post-merger between weak and strong conservative voters, suggesting that unification of the right is still in progress.

Some of the volume's authors suggest that specific groups in Canada are affected by the emphasis on economic individualism. In her chapter on women and federal conservative parties (chapter 6), Melanee Thomas argues that the parties have dismissed equality of outcome for equality of opportunity – an approach rooted in a strong belief in individualism. Thomas notes that the idea of "women's issues" was rejected as a component of the parties' strong commitment to individualism and market/economic conservatism. Another group of Canadians for whom federal conservative parties have espoused a strong view of economic individualism is Indigenous Canadians. In chapter 8, Michael McCrossan argues that federal conservative parties and the Conservative government championed Indigenous policy that was based in self-interest and individualism, where integration of Indigenous people will happen through a "freely competitive market economy." A similar economic emphasis was the inspiration for the Conservatives' approach to immigration as they concentrated their attention on skilled migrants, temporary foreign workers, and those who fill identified labour market needs (chapter 5). Furthermore, in his chapter on foreign policy (chapter 14), Shaun Narine suggests that part of the Conservative government's approach to other countries was based on a desire to sell Canadian natural resources and place Canadian economic interests ahead of all other considerations when making foreign policy decisions. Yet it should be noted that the Conservative dogmatic approach to economic policy has been tempered by a pragmatic streak, reacting to political (minority governments) or economic (2008 recession) realities. Another theme that is found throughout the chapters of this book is the federal conservatives' embrace of pragmatic electioneering.

Pragmatic Electioneering

Successful Canadian political parties have a long tradition of adopting pragmatic approaches to economic, social, and political issues in an effort to attract different groups and create a broad electoral base. Until 1993, the Liberal and Progressive Conservative parties did their best to occupy a place near the centre of the ideological spectrum. While most would argue that the CPC did not lead a centrist government, there are a number of instances where unexpected policy positions were adopted in the interest of winning elections. The Conservatives did not adhere to pragmatic decision-making because they are pragmatists, but rather adhered to pragmatic decision-making because in Canadian politics this approach works. The authors in this volume provide a number of examples to support the notion of pragmatic electioneering. Farney and Koop (chapter 2) agree with Tom Flanagan's depiction of the CPC as a "garrison party," argue that the CPC is the "most tightly disciplined party in Canadian history," and discuss the permanent campaign mode into which the Conservatives settled. But the nature of the Conservative Party's actions is not the only evidence of this permanent and pragmatic competition – the party's approach to certain groups and issues also reflects this illustration.

Pragmatic approaches to particular groups in Canada are discussed in chapters 5 (on ethnocultural minorities) and 7 (on Quebec). In her chapter on federal conservative parties and ethnocultural minorities, Erin Tolley suggests that Canadian conservatives came a long way from the early days of the Reform "restrictionist immigration stance and anti-multiculturalism rhetoric" to a Conservative government and party that has built a reputation for reaching out to Canadians of various ethnic backgrounds. However, as Tolley suggests, this ethnic outreach can be interpreted as a political strategy concerned with broadening the party's voter base and positioning the party further away from its xenophobic Reform roots. While Tolley admits this tactic is adopted by other parties, the Conservative approach is unique in its marriage of "politics, policy, and electioneering" and the unapologetic overtness of this orientation.

In their chapter on federal conservative parties and Quebec, Kate Puddister and James Kelly suggest that there was an initial courtship of Quebec voters, which included the Conservative government's support of a Bloc Québécois motion recognizing Quebec as a nation within Canada, and the prime minister's commitment to "open federalism" and devolution of powers to the provincial government. In her chapter on federal conservatives and federalism (chapter 13), Anna Esselment further describes the Conservative government's incomplete attempt at "open federalism." Similar to other ideological positions abandoned by Harper in the interest of pragmatic, electoral gains, we see a departure from a hard-line division of powers; Harper and his government followed an open federalism approach to complete one-off agreements with provinces (auto sector bailout) or encroach in provincial jurisdiction on economic matters (national security regulator, labour market training). Yet Puddister and Kelly contend that after a brief period, the new Conservative Party returned to its Reform roots by ignoring or opposing the wishes of the majority of Quebeckers. After peaking in the 2006 federal election with ten seats, the CPC stalled in both 2008 and 2011 with five seats each and appeared to have stopped its deliberate wooing of Quebec through previous acts of devolution and symbolic recognition before winning a somewhat surprising twelve seats in 2015. During the 2015 campaign, when the Conservatives raised the campaign issue of women wearing the niqab at the ballot box it was perceived as an attempt to attract voters in Quebec where support for the ban was particularly popular. While the niqab debate would end up hurting the NDP the most, the electoral strategy reflected some of the Conservative Party's continued willingness to find wedge issues to exploit politically in Quebec.

In his chapter on federal conservatives and the Constitution (chapter 10), Emmett Macfarlane outlines the strategic and pragmatic approach of the Conservative government to constitutional and Charter issues. Macfarlane stresses the electoral need for Harper to adopt a moderate approach to previously problematic rights issues and an informal approach to difficult constitutional change. The Conservative government adopted strategic approaches (by pushing to not reopen them) on two key moral issues – abortion and same-sex marriage – in a balancing

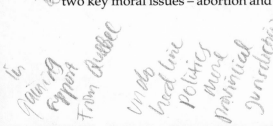

effort to placate its social conservative base while not alienating social progressive/fiscal conservatives who may otherwise be attracted to the party. Much of this strategy appears to have been in reaction to the "hidden agenda" accusations that dogged the party under Preston Manning and Stockwell Day. Macfarlane suggests that on rights issues, the Conservative government demonstrated its true nature more on "law and order" and national security issues (e.g., Insite, Omar Khadr, mandatory minimums).

In his chapter on foreign policy, Shaun Narine argues that much of the Conservative government's foreign policy was based on domestic political considerations. The Conservative government used foreign policy positions abroad to build multi-ethnic voting blocs at home. In adopting this approach, the Conservative government was able to maintain a more moderate domestic policy agenda while pursuing an ideologically oriented foreign policy.

As the ensuing chapters suggest – especially those on Indigenous Canadians, women, foreign policy, and the executive and Parliament – pragmatic politics can act as a Trojan Horse, distracting observers from any divisive tactics that the Conservative government has adopted. Like the Liberal Party before them, the Conservative Party was quick to hasten an aggressive partisan path that leaves brokerage politics behind for a system of picking winners and losers. The third recurring theme of this book is the practice of adversarial politics.

Adversarial Politics

The new Conservative Party developed a reputation for playing somewhat fast and loose with electioneering. Between the "in and out" scandal of 2006, the Dean Del Mastro trial related to spending infringements in 2008, and the "robocalls" affair in 2011, the Conservatives have kept both feet in the grey area of election campaigning. When Stephen Harper asked for the dissolution of Parliament in August 2015, creating one of the longest election campaign periods in Canadian history (eleven weeks), it was seen by some as a way for the Conservative Party to benefit from their fundraising advantage over the Liberals and New Democrats, as a longer campaign doubled the spending cap to almost $50 million. The move was also seen as another Conservative government action based solely on election strategy and not prudent public policy. However, certain tricks of the electoral trade are nothing new in Canadian politics – a hyper-competitive, rule-bending electoral campaign was not the invention of the new Conservative Party. As well, the tradition of soliciting as many interests as possible to produce nationwide electoral support was replaced by the Conservatives with a sophisticated, micro-targeted permanent campaign of matching diverse interests (Flanagan 2007). While the Conservative Party of Canada found a way to gain enough electoral support to form a majority government, the party was clear in picking political winners and losers, in turn heightening the already adversarial environment of Canadian politics. Some of the adversarial battles outside of the typical partisan strife are found with Conservatives and interest groups, the media, and Indigenous Canadians.

In her chapter on interest groups (chapter 4), Nicole Goodman argues that both in opposition and in government, federal conservative parties demonstrated an affinity to certain types of interest groups. Before the merger, the Reform and Canadian Alliance parties made strong connections to conservative populist groups such as the National Citizens Coalition and Canadian Taxpayers Federation. In government, Goodman argues that the Conservatives were selective in favouring private interest groups focused on banking and resource development while running aggressive campaigns against environmental groups or, as Conservative finance minister Joe Oliver described them, "radical groups." Another group the Conservatives engaged in conflict with was the media.

In her chapter on the federal Conservatives and the media (chapter 9), Andrea Lawlor highlights the adversarial relationship that developed between the two camps. While conflict between the press and political parties is not new to Canadian politics, the Prime Minister's Office escalated this divide by blocking access to Cabinet (see chapter 12 in this volume) and the Conservative caucus, and bypassing traditional media outlets. Lawlor notes that the Conservative government adopted practices such as targeting specific media outlets, especially local or ethnic, for providing access to government officials. While the Conservative government's approach was met with much pushback from the Ottawa press corps, it reflects another politically strategic choice of the government.

Where we find more evidence of ideological influence on policy is the Conservative government's approach to Indigenous peoples and Indigenous politics. While they praised him for extending an official apology on the experience faced by many Indigenous Canadians in the residential school system, most observers found Stephen Harper's approach to Indigenous policy a relic of Reform Party policy. As Michael McCrossan argues in his chapter (chapter 8), the Conservative government and Reform/Canadian Alliance parties adopted "pan-Canadian visions of citizenship and territory in such a way that pre-existing Indigenous rights to land, sovereignty, and governance are conceptually excluded and discounted from policy consideration." Similar to the response the Liberal government's White Paper received in the late 1960s, the Conservative government's approach to economic growth mobilized Indigenous Canadians to action, with 2013's "Idle No More" movement representing this common front against the Conservatives. While the Conservatives picked fights with certain political groups, they also found conflict within the institutions where they practise politics. The following and final theme is the disdain that was found in the Conservatives' approach to many Canadian political institutions.

Institutional Disdain

While some of the Conservative Party's actions demonstrated moderate approaches to Canadian political institutions, a growing narrative supports the view that the anti-establishment views of the former Reform Party were not far from the surface. As the authors in this collection suggest, the Conservative government showed increasing disdain or contempt for institutions such as Parliament (Malloy), the Supreme Court (Macfarlane), Cabinet (Lewis), federalism (Esselment), and the Charter of Rights and Freedoms (Macfarlane). As Malloy argues (chapter 11), the Conservative government continued on the path of previous governments of emphasizing the House of Commons as a body of governance, focused on providing power to the executive, instead of a body of representation, focused on members as representatives of their constituents. This approach was a clear departure from the direct democracy advocated in the early years of the Reform Party that was shaped by American examples (Schneiderman 2015).

The Senate was also an institution of contention for the Conservative government, especially considering the party's history of proposing reform. Starting with the Reform Party's "Triple-E (Elected, Equal, Effective)" Senate proposals in the early 1990s, the Conservative Party promised Senate reform in every one of its election platforms. Ironically, it has been the Senate where the Conservative government found its greatest political scandals. First of all, the party and government experienced a political crisis with the revelations of expense abuses by three high-profile senators – Pamela Wallin, Mike Duffy, and Patrick

Brazeau. Following this, the Prime Minister's Office was embroiled in the revelation of Stephen Harper's Chief of Staff Nigel Wright's offer to personally pay for Duffy's expense errors. While Harper was not implicated, Wright resigned in an embarrassing episode for the government, and the Mike Duffy fraud trial was a significant distraction during the first weeks of the 2015 election campaign.

In the months following the initial activity of the Senate scandal, the Conservative government sent five reference questions to the Supreme Court on the constitutionality of unilaterally reforming or abolishing the Senate. The court ruled against unilateral action, including the implementation of term limits, requiring the provinces' consent through the general amending formula. Harper's response was to not fill any of the nineteen Senate vacancies before the 2015 election, which was followed by an announcement on the campaign trail that he would cease appointing any senators at all.

The prime minister also faced political scandal for his use of prorogation and dissolution of Parliament. Discussed in detail elsewhere (Aucoin, Jarvis, and Turnbull 2011; Russell and Sossin 2009; Schneiderman 2015), Harper's prorogation in December 2008, to avoid a vote of non-confidence, and December 2009, when critics suggested he was avoiding investigations into the treatment of Afghan detainees, and dissolution of Parliament in 2008, forcing an election even though the Conservative government's own fixed election date law did not call for an election until October 2009, were seen as actions that were subverting Canadian political institutions and practices. Harper was not the first prime minister to use conventions to his political advantage, but in aggregate the actions are telling of a certain cynical approach to Canadian politics.

In addition to trying the patience of Canadian parliamentary experts, the Conservative government also had its fair share of controversial dealings with the courts. Less controversial, but definitely in keeping with Reform-era criticisms of the role of the Charter of Rights and Freedoms was the cancellation of the Courts Challenge Program that provided funds for Charter-based challenges to legislation. More controversial was the prime minister's dispute with Chief Justice Beverley McLachlin over phone calls made concerning the failed court appointment of Marc Nadon. In this case, institutional disdain and discredit appeared to border on institutional disrespect (Schneiderman 2015).

Another area where the Conservative government faced criticism was the prime minister's approach to communicating and meeting with premiers. In her chapter on federalism (chapter 13), Anna Esselment describes Harper's unilateral approach (with only one first ministers' meeting in nine years) as "individualized executive federalism" – an approach that allowed Harper to avoid the politicized nature of previous first ministers' meetings led by prime ministers such as Pierre Trudeau and Brian Mulroney. Another group of political leaders that were marginalized under the Conservative government were Cabinet ministers. As J.P. Lewis describes in his chapter (chapter 12), the combination of new styles of communications management and hyperpartisan politics led to a bevy of no-name Cabinet ministers with only a handful having any public profile. In his chapter on foreign policy, Shaun Narine argues that the Conservative government took a radical approach to foreign policy, reflecting a strong rejection of past approaches based on multilateral institutions and international law and adopted a moralistic ideological stance on foreign affairs.

Still, in light of this list of institutional attitudes that attracted the attention of Canadian political scientists, the electoral and political ramifications were not fully realized until the electorate's rebuke in 2015. The Harper voting base – depicted throughout this collection in different ways, whether it is suburbanite families or small-business-minded new Canadians – seemed less troubled by political institution debates and more concerned with bottom-line, personal finance policy issues. The Conservative popular vote and number of seats in 2015 (31.9 per cent and ninety-nine respectively) matched those of their first election as a new party in 2004 (29.6 per cent and ninety-nine) and they actually received over 1,500 more votes in 2015. Taken together, the chapters in this volume present the initial success of the Conservative government's agenda on a diverse range of Canadian politics topics. This is complex story in which the Conservative Party and government held on to some of the formative ideals of its predecessor political parties (Reform/Canadian Alliance/Progressive Conservative) while letting others go for the sake of broadening their national political base.

We have titled this book *The Blueprint: Conservative Parties and Their Impact on Canadian Politics* because we argue that at this point in history the impact of the new Conservative federal party is not that of a fully formed legacy, nor is it simply the impression left by a passing interlude. Instead it is a blueprint – a plan that serves as a potential model for future directions that, depending upon how much structural change has been achieved, may or may not guide Canadian politics into the future. The 2015 election brought to an end the near-decade of Conservative government and installed a new Liberal government under Justin Trudeau that appears keen to take approaches to politics very different from those of their predecessors. However, the degree to which they will be successful will be affected by actions and practices put into place by the previous Conservative government.

It is too soon to tell whether the Conservative government's decade in office was just one more of the many previous conservative interludes that have interrupted Liberal dynasties in the past (Clarkson 2005; LeDuc et al. 2010). In this book we do not try to predict how long the Conservative Party will be in opposition, nor do we attempt to assess how influential their decade in power will be on future governments. Instead we have tried to present a story of how the Conservative government arrived at their approaches to Canadian political institutions and policy areas through their varied history as parties in opposition (1993–2006) as well as their experience in leading minority and then majority governments (2006–15). In doing so we draw attention to the themes of Canadian politics with a specific focus on the political era and actors, identifying how Conservative actions and decisions may have altered Canadian public policy and political practice, and demonstrating how these changes are reflections of traditional strands of conservative ideology and contemporary trends in strategic politicking.

REFERENCES

Archer, Keith, and Faron Ellis. 1994. "Opinion Structure of Party Activists: The Reform Party of Canada." *Canadian Journal of Political Science* 27 (2): 277–308. http://dx.doi.org/10.1017/S0008423900017364.

Aucoin, Peter, Mark Jarvis, and Lori Turnbull. 2011. *Democratizing the Constitution: Reforming Responsible Government*. Toronto: Emond Montgomery.

Barney, Darin David. 1996. "Push-button Populism: The Reform Party and the Real World of Teledemocracy." *Canadian Journal of Communication* 21 (3): 381–413.

Behiels, Michael D. 2010. "Stephen Harper's Rise to Power: Will His 'New' Conservative Party Become Canada's 'Natural Governing Party' of the Twenty-First Century?" *American Review of Canadian Studies* 40 (1): 118–45. http://dx.doi.org/10.1080/02722010903545418.

Bélanger, Éric, and J.F. Godbout. 2010. "Why Do Parties Merge? The Case of the Conservative Party of Canada." *Parliamentary Affairs* 63 (1): 41–65. http://dx.doi.org/10.1093/pa/gsp041.

Bittner, Amanda, and Royce Koop, eds. 2013. *Parties, Elections, and the Future of Canadian Politics*. Vancouver: UBC Press.

Bourrie, Mark. 2015. *Kill the Messengers: Stephen Harper's Assault on Your Right to Know*. Toronto: Patrick Crean Editions.

Bricker, Darrell, and John Ibbitson. 2013. *The Big Shift: The Seismic Change in Canadian Politics, Business, and Culture and What It Means for Our Future*. Toronto: HarperCollins.

Caron, Jean-Francois, and Guy LaForest. 2009. "Canada and Multinational Federalism: From the Spirit of 1982 to Stephen Harper's Open Federalism." *Nationalism & Ethnic Politics* 15 (1): 27–55. http://dx.doi.org/10.1080/13537110802672370.

Carson, Bruce. 2014. *14 Days: Making the Conservative Movement in Canada*. Montreal and Kingston: McGill-Queen's University Press.

Carty, R. Kenneth, William Cross, and Lisa Young. 2000. *Rebuilding Canadian Party Politics*. Vancouver: UBC Press.

Chapnick, Adam. 2011. "A 'Conservative' National Story? The Evolution of Citizenship and Immigration Canada's *Discover Canada*." *American Review of Canadian Studies* 41 (1): 20–36. http://dx.doi.org/10.1080/02722011.2010.544853.

Clarkson, Stephen. 2005. *The Big Red Machine: How the Liberal Party Dominates Canadian Politics*. Vancouver: UBC Press.

Cody, Howard. 2008. "Minority Government in Canada: The Stephen Harper Experience." *American Review of Canadian Studies* 38 (1): 27–42. http://dx.doi.org/10.1080/02722010809481819.

Delacourt, Susan. 2013. *Shopping for Votes: How Politicians Choose Us and We Choose Them*. Madeira Park, BC: Douglas & McIntyre Publishing.

Engler, Yves. 2012. *The Ugly Canadian: Stephen Harper's Foreign Policy*. Black Point, NS: Fernwood Publishing.

Farney, James. 2012. *Social Conservatives and Party Politics in Canada and the United States*. Toronto: University of Toronto Press.

Farney, James, and David Rayside, eds. 2013. *Conservatism in Canada*. Toronto: University of Toronto Press.

Flanagan, Tom. 1995. *Waiting for the Wave: The Reform Party and Preston Manning*. Toronto: Stoddart.

– 2007. *Harper's Team: Behind the Scenes in the Conservative Rise to Power*. Montreal and Kingston: McGill-Queen's University Press.

– 2014. *Winning Power: Canadian Campaigning in the Twenty-First Century*. Montreal and Kingston: McGill-Queen's University Press.

Gutstein, Donald. 2014. *Harperism: How Stephen Harper and His Think Tank Colleagues Have Transformed Canada*. Toronto: Lorimer.

Harper, Stephen. 2006. "Our Great Country Has Voted for Change." *National Post*, 25 January.

Harris, Michael. 2014. *Party of One: Stephen Harper and Canada's Radical Makeover*. Toronto: Viking.

Harrison, Trevor. 1995. *Of Passionate Intensity: Right-Wing Populism and the Reform Party of Canada*. Toronto: University of Toronto Press.

Harrison, Trevor, Bill Johnston, and Harvey Krahn. 1996. "Special Interests and/or New Right Economics? The Ideological Bases of Reform Party Support in Alberta in the 1993 Federal Election." *Canadian Review of Sociology* 33 (2): 159–79. http://dx.doi.org/10.1111/j.1755-618X.1996.tb00193.x.

Harrison, Trevor, and Harvey Krahn. 1995. "Populism and the Rise of the Reform Party in Alberta." *Canadian Review of Sociology and Anthropology / Revue canadienne de sociologie et d'anthropologie* 32 (2): 127–50. http://dx.doi.org/10.1111/j.1755-618X.1995.tb00765.x.

Hébert, Chantal. 2007. *French Kiss: Stephen Harper's Blind Date with Québec*. Toronto: Alfred A. Knopf Canada.

Ibbitson, John. 2015. *Stephen Harper*. Toronto: Signal.

Johnson, William. 2005. *Stephen Harper and the Future of Canada*. Toronto: McClelland and Stewart.

Kanji, Mebs, Antoine Bilodeau, and Thomas Scott. 2012. *The Canadian Election Studies: Assessing Four Decades of Influence*. Vancouver: UBC Press.

Laycock, David. 1994. "Reforming Canadian Democracy? Institutions and Ideology in the Reform Party Project." *Canadian Journal of Political Science* 27 (2): 213–47. http://dx.doi.org/10.1017/S0008423900017340.

– 2002. *The New Right and Democracy in Canada: Understanding Reform and the Canadian Alliance*. Don Mills, ON: Oxford University Press.

LeDuc, Lawrence, Jon Pammett, Judith McKenzie, and Andre Turcotte. 2010. *Dynasties and Interludes: Past and Present in Canadian Electoral Politics*. Toronto: Dundurn.

Malloy, Jonathan. 2009. "Bush/Harper? Canadian and American Evangelical Politics Compared." *American Review of Canadian Studies* 39 (4): 352–63. http://dx.doi.org/10.1080/02722010903319079.

Martin, Lawrence. 2010. *Harperland: The Politics of Control*. Toronto: Viking Canada.

Nadeau, Christian. 2011. *Rogue in Power: Why Stephen Harper Is Remaking Canada by Stealth*. Toronto: Lorimer.

Nevitte, Neil, Andre Blais, Elisabeth Gidengil, Richard Johnston, and Henry Brady. 1998. "The Populist Right in Canada: The Rise of the Reform Party of Canada." In *The New Politics of the Right: Neo-Populist Parties and Movements in Established Democracies*, edited by Hans-Georg Betz and Stefan Immerfall, 173–202. New York: St Martin's.

Patten, Steve. 2013. "The Triumph of Neoliberalism within Partisan Conservatism in Canada." In *Conservatism in Canada*, edited by James Farney and David Rayside, 59–78. Toronto: University of Toronto Press.

Plamondon, Bob. 2006. *Full Circle: Death and Resurrection in Canadian Conservative Politics*. Toronto: Key Porter Books.

Russell, Peter, and Lorne Sossin, eds. 2009. *Parliamentary Democracy in Crisis*. Toronto: University of Toronto Press.

Schneiderman, David. 2015. *Red, White, and Kind of Blue: The Conservatives and the Americanization of Canadian Constitutional Culture*. Toronto: University of Toronto Press.

Segal, Hugh. 2007. *The Long Road Back: The Conservative Journey, 1993–2007*. Toronto: HarperCollins.

Sharpe, Sydney, and Don Braid. 1992. *Storming Babylon: Preston Manning and the Rise of the Reform Party*. Toronto: Key Porter.

Snow, Dave, and Benjamin Moffitt. 2012. "Straddling the Divide: Mainstream Populism and Conservatism in Howard's Australia and Harper's Canada." *Commonwealth and Comparative Politics* 50 (3): 271–92. http://dx.doi.org/10.1080/14662043.2012.692922.

Wells, Paul. 2007. *Right Side Up: The Fall of Paul Martin and the Rise of Stephen Harper's New Conservatism*. Toronto: Douglas Gibson Books.

– 2008. "Harper's Canadian Revolution." *Maclean's* 17 (September).

– 2013. *The Longer I'm Prime Minister: Stephen Harper and Canada, 2006–*. Toronto: Random House Canada.

2 The Conservative Party in Opposition and Government

JAMES FARNEY AND ROYCE KOOP

While other chapters in this volume explore the effects of the movement of Canadian conservatives from opposition to government on a range of aspects of Canadian government and politics, in this chapter we turn our view inward and explore the consequences of success for the Conservative Party itself. Exploring the effects of time while in government or opposition on political parties has a long history in the study of Canadian politics. In his book *The Government Party*, Reginald Whitaker (1977) describes the process of inward organizational deterioration and stagnation as the Liberal Party – highly successful throughout the twentieth century – both invaded and was invaded by the state at the end of their great, lengthy terms in office. In his equally important book, *The Tory Syndrome*, George Perlin (1980) told a similar story from the perspective of the opposition, documenting how long periods of time out of favour nurtured an equally destructive lack of discipline in that party.

The instability of the last twenty years in Canadian politics makes it difficult to describe the Liberals clearly as the Government Party or to describe the challenges of being in opposition as solely a *Tory Syndrome*. It is at this point – at the conclusion of just under a decade with Stephen Harper as prime minister and his party's defeat in the 2015 election – that it is important to assess the Conservative Party from a medium-term historical perspective. We do so by exploring three themes:

1 The *commitments* of the party;
2 The *orientation* of the party; and,
3 The *organization* of the party.

The first theme is the ideological commitments of the party, especially the commitment of the party to the free market. Many commentators note the strong commitment of the Conservative Party to the free
market (e.g., Pitsula 2007, 375). But it has not always been so, as the
Conservative Party succeeded under John A. Macdonald in part by advocating the system of tariffs included in his National Policy, and party
leader Robert Stanfield was a strong advocate of wage and price controls in the 1970s. In keeping with the party's more recent free-market
commitments, Harper's first instinct was to dismiss the recent economic downturn as a simple "correction," but he soon accepted and subsequently embraced the role of the state in providing stimulus to the
faltering economy. The role of Keynesian-inspired policies likely did
not come naturally for the University of Calgary–educated economist,
but Harper's actions here demonstrate that he cannot be wholly dismissed as neoliberal in his orientations. While exercising a more or less
moderated commitment to the free market, the party also contains important groups committed to populism and social conservatism. One
part of both winning and holding office, it seems, has been convincing
these groups to downplay their ideological preferences in pursuit of
practical policies and the winning of office.

By orientation, we refer to the party's ideology and approach to societal interests. This theme relates to the crucial distinction between
ideological parties and brokerage parties. Brokerage parties – parties
committed to papering over major societal divisions in order to avoid
fracturing the state as a whole – are a major feature of the Canadian
literature. According to Meisel (1963), brokerage parties exist in Canada because leaders recognized that exploiting the division between
Quebec and English Canada (and all the cleavages this distinction en-
tails) threatened the state as a whole. In this account – which remains
very much the scholarly standard – Canada's big brokerage parties were
the crucial integrating actors in Canadian politics and long dominated
national politics.

But there is doubt as to whether brokerage parties continue to dominate Canadian politics, or whether they ever really did. Scholars writing from a political economy perspective, for example, reject the view
of the Liberal and Conservative parties as brokers. Instead, they argue that these parties are ideological, consistently protecting owners
rather than workers (Clarke et al. 1996). The shake-up of the Canadian
party system, beginning in the 1993 federal election, similarly questioned the prospect of brokerage politics, as the two new parties in the

system explicitly rejected brokerage in their turn to ideological, plebiscitarian, democracy (Young and Cross 2002). More recent accounts of brokerage politics cast doubt on whether the parties continue to function in this manner (Carty 2013). We argue here that the Conservatives refashioned themselves as a "new brokerage party," using the advantages offered by demographic change and technological advances in campaigning to operate across emerging cleavages in Canadian politics in an electorally advantageous and (relatively) ideologically consistent way.

The final theme is the organization of the party. It was long recognized that brokerage parties required strong leaders to both personify the party in the eyes of the public and lord over the party in public office. The organizations that Canadian parties developed to accommodate both the demands of discipline in Parliament and the needs of a societally very diverse country were what Carty (2004) refers to as franchise parties, characterized by divisions of power between the leader and the party organizations in the constituencies. This "franchise bargain" gave the leader free rein over policy formulation while the constituency associations retained their ancient right to select candidates. The result was a stratarchical style party, with strong leaders combined with devolved locations of power.

While the franchise model can accommodate significant push and pull between different components of party organizations, there is evidence that the franchise bargain specified by Carty is breaking down or, at the very least, is under strain. Along with the transformation of the party system in 1993 came willingness of parties to "do politics differently" and consult members on policy matters. More importantly, leaders have increasingly disregarded the rights of local party members to select (and deselect) their nominees for office. This comes in three forms. First, party leaders maintain the right to decline to sign the nomination papers of candidates, thereby reserving the final say over who will represent the party in any given riding (Cross 2011, 54–5). Second, party leaders have used the minority Parliaments that existed between 2004 and 2011 to justify shielding incumbent MPs from renomination challenges. Finally, the willingness of leaders to "parachute" candidates into ridings means that local members are not only deprived of the right to choose personnel but may have an unpopular candidate foisted on them (Koop and Bittner 2011). All this suggests that the franchise bargain that Carty maintains characterizes Canadian parties is in significant flux and a near-constant state of renegotiation.

The Commitments of the Party

One of the striking features of the current Conservative Party is the diverse ideological heritages that the party's adherents draw on. It includes a very few Red Tories, a substantial number of populists, a significant contingent of social conservatives, and a majority committed primarily to the free market and reducing the size of the state. Put into contrast with other politically active Canadians, proponents of each of these positions deserve to be called conservative. There is, though, the potential for significant disagreement and tension between each of these commitments – disagreements that blew the Canadian right apart in the 1990s (Carty, Cross, and Young 2000). One distinguishing feature of the present-day CPC is that the party has managed to both minimize such disagreements between devotees of different aspects of conservatism and, in government, to progressively minimize ideology as an aspect of its identity (Farney and Malloy 2011). There are tendencies, preferences, and appeals to be sure, but little by way of a clear ideological program. Instead there is a fundamental orientation to a particular ideological base and, perhaps, a consistent view of federal-provincial relations that is congruent with, but not a necessary part of, conservative ideology (see chapter 13 in this volume).

While we argue that much of the party's downplaying of ideology has been driven by the imperatives of winning and holding office, some of the change can also be explained if we recognize that the 1980s and 1990s were a uniquely fertile period of ideological debate among Canadian conservatives. The current period – where the party and movement seem not overly concerned about ideology – represents a return to a historical norm rather than a departure from it.

This fertile ground had been prepared by the events of the 1970s and 1980s, which destabilized the post-war ideological consensus. The stagflation crisis, repeated oil shocks, and rising unemployment of the late 1970s and early 1980s had largely discredited the Keynesian post-war economic consensus, and conservatives, like other political actors, were trying to sort out what came next. For many Canadian conservatives (generally called Blue Tories at the time), the answer came in embracing economic neoliberalism, reducing the size of the state at home, and pursuing free trade abroad. Red Tories – who were attracted to Keynesian economic planning and a fairly sizeable welfare state out of a sense of noblesse oblige – were seldom enthusiastic about this shift, though most who retained any political prominence at all (e.g., Joe Clark, Hugh Segal, and Peter MacKay) made their peace with the change (Segal 1997).

In addition to these economic questions, the debate over reforming the Canadian Constitution posed two deep questions for Canadian conservatives. The first was over what it meant to be Canadian: Was it engaging multiculturalism, bilingualism, and a Bill of Rights? Or was it retaining the British connection, parliamentary supremacy, and Common Law? What was the place to be granted Quebec: An equal province? Asymmetry? Affiliated nation status? Should federal or provincial governments be pre-eminent in public policymaking? With such existential questions on the table, it was perhaps natural that questions of institutional reform also engaged conservatives. Here, the preferred form of the Senate was the most notable flashpoint, but the whole process of constitutional reform came in for severe questioning, as did core Canadian political institutions like party discipline. The twinned questions of the meaning of "Canadian" and the proper operation of our democratic institutions were the bright line splitting populist Reformers from Progressive Conservatives and those members of the Bloc Québécois who had formerly been conservatives of from what soon became the rump of the PCs.

A final cross-cutting set of ideological disagreements among conservatives concerned how to react to the considerable social change that Canada had undergone. Immigration has never been as contentious in Canada as in Western Europe or the United States, but there certainly were elements in the Reform Party who wanted an assimilationist agenda pursued, with opposition to the wearing of turbans by RCMP officers being the most visible. A more lasting division has been between social conservatives – who see changing sexual norms, definitions of family, and abortion as issues that demand a political response and pose a very significant threat to Canada – and other conservatives who either see such matters as secondary or, and Joe Clark would be an the example here, are generally on the progressive side of the debate. While the Liberals also had a sizeable contingent of socially conservative activists and MPs, social conservatives had more of an influence in Reform and the Canadian Alliance (Farney 2012).

These old and new divisions in Conservative ideology, brought to prominence by pressing political events, created a fragmented – but very creative – ideological space on the Canadian right as various journals, news magazines, and think tanks all tried to identify the ideological path forward for the party. The ideological differences also overlapped with and reinforced regional, leadership, and party fractures after the 1993 election. The Reform Party's populist appeals, friendliness to social conservatives, and calls to dramatically reduce the size of the state found its strongest support in Western Canada (Ellis 2005). Reformers found the PCs – whether led by Mulroney, Campbell, Charest, or Clark – far too focused on Quebec, insufficiently fiscally conservative, and too socially liberal. They questioned whether the pragmatic change advocated by the Tories inside the PC party rendered them only Liberals under a different party label. From the other side, PCs, with their strength in Ontario and Atlantic Canada, responded that Reformers were seeking an unconservative rupture in Canada's governing traditions, were attempting to undercut policies that protected national identity, and had a simplistic vision of the benefits the free market would bring (Segal 1997).

By 1999, when Manning successfully moved the United Alternative process through the Reform Party's convention, the political question on the Canadian right was how to weave these organizationally disparate ideological fragments back together (Plamondon 2006). As described above, pursuing this goal saw first the Reform Party transformed into the Canadian Alliance, and then, in 2003, merge with the Progressive Conservatives to form the Conservative Party of Canada. Stephen Harper was successful at building a workable position for a party created out of a union between the Canadian Alliance – first led by the socially conservative and ardently populist Stockwell Day – and the PCs, led in the late 1990s and early 2000s by Red Tories like Joe Clark and Peter MacKay.

The glue that bound these disparate groups together was a shared commitment to winning office and the centralized organizational form of the new party that downplayed ideology (Flanagan 2007, 2013). At the same time, there was a remarkable ideological coalescence as the different groups in the party found agreement in a rhetorical commitment to a small state and free market (one that, in policy terms, is often washed out by a desire to intervene in support of specific businesses or to encourage resource-based development), to (undefined) middleclass families, and to a view of federalism that pushed the provinces forwards as political actors in place of the federal government.

An important part of the party's commitments when it was formed was the inclusion and legitimization of social conservatives. While Harper himself is probably best described as a Christian libertarian on such matters as abortion and same-sex rights (Johnson 2005), it is clear that he positioned the party as firmly opposed to gay marriage during the 2005 debates in Parliament and, somewhat less clearly, in the 2006 election. This also attracted a sizeable number of pro-life activists to the party (Farney 2012). Their failure to stop gay marriage and, it seems, the failure of social conservatism as a bridge to new Canadian voters, has reduced their standing in the party. While the party continues to include a sizeable contingent of social conservatives, as demonstrated by debates in 2012–13 over abortion, those same debates showed that social conservatives were opposed by the bulk of the Cabinet. It may also be that the movement shifted at least its language and perhaps its strategy to be less conservative in recent years (Saurette and Gordon 2013).

The party's commitment to populism faded after it won office, continuing a trend that began when Reform's first group of MPs entered Parliament in 1993. The first piece of legislation the government passed, the Accountability Act, was a response to populist demands for more accountability and transparency in government. But it struggled with the implications of these reforms in government and largely failed to implement other parts of its democratic reform agenda. Senate reform was an important issue, but the government's efforts were blocked by the Supreme Court, and the party did little to reduce party discipline, offer more voice to parliamentarians, or resolve the problems of centralized power that so exercised Reformers. Indeed, when it comes to party organization, the Conservatives have created perhaps the most tightly disciplined party in Canadian history (Flanagan 2013).

Social conservatism and populism fell largely by the wayside as both ideological commitments and electoral appeals since 2006. What has remained visible is a distinctive view of what Canadian federalism ought to look like. Sometimes called "open federalism" (Harmes 2007), this view seeks to minimize the role of the federal government in areas of provincial jurisdiction (see chapter 13 in this volume). Perhaps most stridently expressed in the "firewall" letter of 2000, in which Stephen Harper and a number of other prominent conservatives advised Alberta Premier Ralph Klein to pursue maximum possible autonomy from national public policy, this vision of federalism seeks a return to the division of jurisdiction outlined in Sections 91 and 92 of the 1867 Constitution Act, reduced use of federal spending power, and greater acceptance of policy experimentation by the provinces (Harper et al. 2001).

Economic policy is a more complicated story. While balanced budgets, limited government interference in the market, and the pursuit of self-sufficiency through labour market participation remained central commitments, the party's policies in office could be better understood as "business-friendly" government. That is, it was not laissez-faire principles that guided the government, but the growth and promotion of the Canadian business community. This meant the government would step in to prevent business failure, as it did in the 2009 auto bailout, when conventional free market thinking might suggest that the bankruptcy of at least one of the big three automakers was acceptable. Like in many Western countries, the very substantial stimulus measures the government undertook, and the resulting deficits, actually increased the size of the federal government. The party preferred business over labour and seemed to ensure a mobile and relatively cheap labour force through changes to Employment Insurance rules that encourage recipients to move in search of work, and through the increased prominence of the employer immigrant nominee program, which gives preference to those immigrants coming to Canada with a job in hand. The government pursued free trade agreements vigorously and shifted Canadian aid policy to be more closely tied to the interests of Canadian businesses operating abroad, but it also intervened to prevent the sale of Canadian economic champions (as with the BHP Billiton potash buyout proposal). It also found tax expenditure as an efficient and relatively inexpensive way to garner electoral support from particular groups. Such market-distorting interventions would have been abhorrent to Stephen Harper as leader of the National Citizens Coalition.

In its ideological commitments, then, the party retained a commitment to free market solutions (Patten 2013), but also tilted towards ensuring the success of Canadian business (especially in the resource sector). It has pursued populism only in relatively weak ways and signalled its amiability to social conservatives more often than it has acquiesced to their policy demands. On federalism, its agenda seems to have been more vigorously pursued. This dilution of ideology is a feature of the traditional brokerage model of Canadian politics, where parties identify and seek to satisfy multiple groups of supporters by downplaying their ideological positions. While operating within this traditional model, we argue that the CPC has embraced its modification in important and novel ways.

The Orientation of the Party

Over the last twenty years, the conservative movement in Canada has struggled to find a way to work together because there are significant ideological differences among its members. Its success has been based on the premise that all members of the conservative coalition favour winning office over advancing their particular ideological desire. This commitment to winning office marks a return to the historical goal of Canada's conservative parties, but the country's diversity and the historical location of the Liberal Party has traditionally made that goal a difficult one. Since it won government, we would argue that demographic shifts in the Canadian population – as well as the party's change in focus – have made the party's future success more likely. It also suggests, however, that Canada may be entering a transitional period. Canada's political history is one of "old brokerage" politics. This form of brokerage required that our major parties (or at least the more successful one in each party system) hold together coalitions that included Quebec and some significant part of English Canada while obscuring the differences between the two groups (Carty 2015). Carty's examination of the twentieth century suggests that only the Liberals were consistently a brokerage party. This debate is one we pass over here too quickly, but we do suggest that the last fifteen years have seen the Conservatives transition more clearly into a "new brokerage" style of politics where parties pursue minimum winning coalitions (Flanagan 2007) that are geographic patchworks built upon the micro-targeting of carefully defined societal and economic groups in swing ridings in ways that, as with old-fashioned brokerage, minimize the divides between these groups and tempers ideology. To understand the extent of this transition requires understanding the history of old brokerage that, for the century after 1896, made it very difficult for the Conservatives to win office.

The Liberal Party's dominance of twentieth-century Canadian politics was based on a number of factors. As the consistent party of government, they were able to wield the power of patronage to ensure support. This consistency also made it easy for them to attract able activists and candidates. In many provinces – at least until the 1960s – they enjoyed the support of powerful provincial Liberal machines. In the second and third party systems, they enjoyed the support of Roman Catholics and immigrants, as well as of Canadian big business. All of this was wrapped in a geographic distribution of support reasonably well insulated from the regional tensions that periodically affect Canadian life. Though weak in Western Canada from the 1920s onwards, the Liberals could count on most of Ontario and Quebec, as well as solid support in Atlantic Canada, from election to election. These advantages peaked mid-century, but they remained sufficiently strong that the Liberals were still viewed as Canada's "natural governing party" at the end of the 1990s. Moreover, this was a distribution of support that allowed the Liberals to broker the major divides in Canadian politics – French-English, Quebec–Rest of Canada, Protestant-Catholic, and urban-rural – effectively while minimizing disagreement over class (Johnston 2008).

This put the Conservatives in a very difficult situation. For most of the century, their base tilted more rural, more western (after 1957), more Canadian-born, and more Protestant than that of the Liberals. They did receive business support, but it tended to be small business, rather than St James or Bay Street, that supported the party. They did catch up provincially, and powerful provincial Tory machines in Ontario and Alberta did lend important support to the federal party. Finally, as the opposition party, the Conservatives had trouble attracting the same quality of candidate or distributing the same amount of patronage as their Liberal competitors (Perlin 1980). As Johnston (2008) has pointed out, their only hope for electoral victory was for circumstances to dislodge some part of the Liberal coalition from its natural home. Usually, this dislodging was done by regional tensions, and usually it was a co-alition of Quebec and the West (along with a smattering of Ontario and Maritime seats) that was available to Conservative strategists. This was an inherently unstable coalition, and one that never lasted more than two elections, even though it did produce stunning landslides under Diefenbaker and Mulroney.

The 1993 election was the most catastrophic breakdown of such a West-Quebec coalition. It saw the Progressive Conservative party reduced from majority government to two seats, the official opposition formed by the Bloc Québécois (which contained many disaffected former Tories from Quebec), and the Reform Party dominate Western Canada. In a highly regionalized party system, the 1993, 1997, and 2000 elections seemed to prove there was room for only one national party.

The Unite the Right movement, which transformed Reform into the Canadian Alliance and then saw the merger between the Progressive Conservatives and the Alliance, did reunite the Canadian right. Under MacKay, Day, and – until 2008 – Stephen Harper, it seems that the basic strategy of the party was a variation on the traditional brokerage one. Assured of the support of the West and most of rural Ontario, what the party desperately needed to form the government was a substantial block of Quebec seats. Even in the aftermath of the sponsorship scandal, the Conservatives were unable to break through in Quebec in a significant way in the early and mid-2000s, though they won enough seats to form a minority government in 2006 and held onto a core of support in the province in 2008 and 2011.

Between 2006 and 2008 a significant shift in strategy took place. Some of this might be attributable to being in government, but much of it should be seen as the party's response to Canada's changing demography and seat distribution, the availability of new campaign technology, and a change in direction of a key member of the Conservative leadership – Jason Kenney (Marwah, Triadafilopoulos, and White 2013). Kenney – despite his position on the ideological right of the party – typified the new form of brokerage by bridging the urban-rural and new-old Canadian divides that are now as deep as the French-English ones. Even before the 2013 seat redistribution, this was a brokerage that was able to happen mostly in English (and languages like Punjabi and Mandarin) allowing the Conservatives to form a government with a coalition that did not include a large number of Quebec seats. It is something other than a catch-all party, because it operated not in ideological space but on changed, yet familiar, ground of ethno-national divides that Johnston (2008) has identified as the second axis of competition in Canadian politics.

The demographic change underpinning this shift can be summed up as urbanization, diversification, and Westernization. Urbanization, on the face of it, ought to hurt the Conservatives, given their traditional strength in rural and small-town Canada. However, prior to the most recent election they proved adept at winning in the suburbs around Vancouver and Toronto (unsurprisingly, they also did well in Calgary and Edmonton). And it is in these suburbs that most of Canada's urbanization is happening. These are also the areas where Canada's population is diversifying the most quickly. While political scientists are still trying to sort out the causal factors behind the change, it is clear that the historical Liberal advantage among new Canadians and Catholics had weakened in the 2000s, and it is left to be seen whether the Liberals' success in 2015 reflects a true return to traditional patterns of support of these portions of the population. Finally, the Canadian population is shifting west of the Ottawa River into areas where the Conservatives have traditionally been strong.

While these changes favoured the Conservatives, they were also faster to adapt to them than the other major parties. The Liberals, until the selection of Justin Trudeau as leader, were deeply divided by infighting between Chrétien and Martin loyalists, preoccupied with national unity, and increasingly caught up in the sponsorship scandal. The NDP, under Jack Layton, was successfully responding to these changes but from the other end of the ideological spectrum and working with the resources of a minor party.

The key change that the party undertook was a shift from a strategy focused on regional brokerage to building a stable minimum winning coalition facilitated by the precise identification of swing voters in winnable ridings (Flanagan 2013). These strategies were made possible by low-cost polling and direct-dial technology, as well as the information management capacity provided by the Conservative Information Management System (CIMS). They pushed the party away from targeting regions of the country and focused its appeals on specific demographic groups in geographically spread out, but demographically similar areas of the country. Some of these profiles were precise enough, for example, to hinge on the difference between minivan- and sedan-driving families. These technological shifts were available to all parties, but the Conservatives had a lead in profiling their supporters and took more advantage of it.

A particularly important implication of these changes was that the Conservatives were able to use these tools to add new Canadian voters to their coalition. This strategic shift was personified in Jason Kenney. Though Kenney's early activism was in the Canadian Taxpayers Federation and the Reform Party, he had deeper links than many in those groups to social conservatives, especially the pro-life movement. During the debate over gay marriage, he was seen as the most senior social conservative in the party and garnered visibility attending events and reaching out to ordinary social conservatives. As one part of this activity, he was tasked with using social conservatism as an ideological bridge to new Canadians, who the party hoped might identify with its family values message. Social conservatism seems not to have provided the bridge, but Kenney and other Conservative strategists did identify that the party's commitment to small business and low taxes could. As immigration minister, he turned the role into a powerful political position, spearheading an impressive and sustained outreach to community associations and ethnic groups across the country. Supported by an increasingly diverse Conservative caucus, Kenney's outreach personified an impressive transition for the party (see chapter 5 in this volume).

Whether these changes will solidify to reflect a new pattern of brokerage, and whether Quebec can so easily be cast aside, remains to be seen. Certainly Justin Trudeau's 2015 victory suggests that other demographic combinations and other styles of appealing to the electorate are certainly possible. Nevertheless, the extent to which the CPC has successfully campaigned in this new environment suggests that, at least on the right, an important shift has occurred.[1] Just as a relative downplaying of ideology helped facilitate this transition, so too did the development of a powerful and flexible, if highly centralized, organization, which we turn to next.

The Organization of the Party

Under Harper's leadership, the organization of the Conservative Party saw a sharp redefinition of power relationships between different actors within the party. This redefinition had two forms, which reflect both change and continuity since the creation of the new Conservative Party. First, power within the party was centralized, to the benefit of the leader and his staff. This is a substantial change from the situation within the old Progressive Conservative Party, the Reform Party, and the Canadian Alliance, and thus commands most of our attention in this section. Second, the party organization continued to be flat, with virtually no intermediary organizations between the leader and the constituency associations. This is a continuation of the organizational template of the Reform Party, which constantly eschewed regional and auxiliary organizations, and contrasts strongly with the other parties, which are characterized by mass-style auxiliary and regional appendages. The result of party organizational changes under Harper was the development of a sleek, centralized, and electorally focused organization.

There have been three impetuses for centralization of the party organization. The first, and perhaps most important, are the experiences and the inclinations of Harper himself. When he assumed the leadership of the Canadian Alliance in 2002, the party had been through a fractious period of rebellion, with many MPs leaving the caucus (see chapter 11 in this volume). Furthermore, Harper inherited a party national council that appeared to be hostile to the leader. Harper found himself embroiled in a lengthy but little publicized power struggle that strengthened his resolve to free himself from the Reform Party conception of a party governing body. As Flanagan (2013, 85) argues of this power struggle, "It convinced him [Harper] that he, as party leader,

---

1 Despite losing the 2015 election, the Conservatives garnered only 200,000 fewer votes than they did in 2011 and almost 400,000 more than they did in 2008.

should never again be subject to a governing council and led, I believe to many features of the constitution adopted by the Conservative Party of Canada after the 2003 merger."

Second, the "permanent campaign" (Flanagan 2013) that existed throughout Canada's most recent period of minority Parliaments clearly drove centralization of the party organization. Canadian parties, with the exception of the NDP, have traditionally been understood as cadre parties, which come together to fight elections but maintain little organizational existence between elections. This has changed substantially during a period when first Liberal Paul Martin's and then Harper's minority governments faced the constant threat of defeat and being thrown into an election campaign. The danger of re-election campaigns placed a strong emphasis on the constant campaign but also empowered the party leader and his staff, leading to the development of what Flanagan calls the garrison party: the fusing of party and campaign organization.

Finally, the centralization of powers under Harper was aided and abetted by the acquiescence of other party actors. In large part, this relates to the permanent campaign: other party actors were willing to sacrifice voice for the good of the wider party. These actors were found in the party in public office (ministers and MPs), central office (employees of the party), and local office (constituency association members, activists, and members). Minority Parliaments also drove intense partisanship among party MPs (see, e.g., Blidook and Byrne 2013), which reinforced their acquiescence to their leader.

Centralization has manifested itself in the Conservative organization in three ways. First, power has been centralized through the subordination of intra-party agencies to the party leader and his staff. Second, intra-party agencies are of particular note in this respect. The Reform Party vested significant independent power in a party management body, the Executive Council. In contrast, the equivalent body in the Conservative Party, the National Council, has few executive powers, its role having been revised mostly to mediate the relationship between the party in Ottawa and the party in the constituencies. As a less powerful body, the new council offers few opportunities for activists to challenge the leader. In addition, Harper's power struggle with the party's council in 2002 resulted in the selection of Don Plett to the presidency, a position that he would occupy for several years as a Harper loyalist.

The second and arguably more important intra-party agency to have seen centralization is the Conservative Fund Canada. As noted many times, the financial supremacy of the party has been key to its electoral success since 2006, and the party owes much of this success to the management of the fund's long-time chair, Harper loyalist Irving Gerstein. Crucially, the power to appoint members to the small cadre that directs the fund was transferred from the National Council to the leader, giving Harper significant influence over one of the most crucial functions of the contemporary party. Flanagan (2013, 87) does not mince words on the consequences of this power for Harper: "The reality is that the leader controls the party through the fund, especially its chairman."

The third way that organizational power has been centralized in the Conservative Party is through the leader's dominance over policy and the "message" of the party. While it is the ancient right of leaders in Canada under the franchise bargains to retain control over policy, this tendency accelerated under Harper. This is a notable reversal, given that providing ordinary members with a significant say in policy development was a central commitment of the Reform Party. Indeed, this trend in the party more clearly resembles the pattern of the Progressive Conservative Party, which provided leaders with greater freedom from the policy wishes of party members.

Perhaps more importantly, the extent to which Cabinet ministers experienced message control in Harper's governments was remarkable (see chapter 12 in this volume). From the beginning, a centralized party apparatus extended its reach into the party in public office, demanding that Cabinet ministers vet communications through the PMO and not participate in freelancing discussions with journalists (Wells 2013). It would, however, be a mistake to assume that ministers were simply well whipped, as it appears that self-discipline played a significant role in the remarkable consistency of Cabinet communications.

The same was true for caucus, as MPs, following a long period in the political wilderness and a new period of minority Parliaments, were willing to trade political wins for strict message control. A useful yardstick for the extent to which caucus MPs disciplined themselves was how the social conservative wing of the party behaved in the years following the party's first win in 2006. Social conservatives in the caucus were reluctant to speak out, instead preferring to follow the prime minister's claim that discipline in a minority Parliament would lead to a majority government. But the party leadership also disciplined members of caucus. A good example of such discipline in caucus meetings was the one-minute rule, whereby MPs could speak but were forced to limit themselves to a minute.

Finally, centralization of power within the Conservative organization has been achieved in personnel selection. Under the Canadian parties' franchise agreements, the right to select personnel is reserved for party members in the ridings in nomination races organized by the local constituency associations. While this right has been chipped away in all parties, this has been particularly pronounced in the Conservative Party.

Centralization of power over personnel selection takes place in two ways. The practice under the Reform Party was to submit incumbent MPs to renomination contests in the lead-up to election campaigns, thereby ensuring that local members would choose candidates in each election. This was traditionally true in the other parties, including the Progressive Conservative Party, with the result that prior to each election some incumbent MPs would be defeated for the nomination and thus lose their right to run for their parties. Under the Conservative Party, however, the party leader either renominated incumbents through his control of the National Council or provided for an easily passable mechanism to ensure that incumbents would not be challenged. The result was that incumbent MPs owed their renominations to the prime minister, not local party members.

The second way in which the party leader centralized control over party nominations was by either appointing candidates outright or by manipulating nomination contests to favour certain candidates. Unlike the Liberal Party, the Conservative Party does not publicize its appointed candidates, so it is sometimes difficult to know who has been appointed – one exception is the parachuting of federal government whistle-blower Allan Cutler into the riding of Ottawa South prior to the 2006 election. What is clear, however, is that party members have frequently complained about central party office manipulation in nomination contests, with the result that local members are given no choice of candidates in nomination campaigns. Such manipulations necessarily take place via the National Council and the party president, Don Plett. In this way, the long reach of the leader could extend directly into the constituencies.

While there have been important organizational changes in the development of the Conservative Party, where the party has retained its Reform-style structure is in its flat overall organization. While the NDP and Liberal Party have maintained auxiliary organizations and, in some cases, formal organizational linkages with provincial parties, the Conservative Party has resisted calls to adopt such additions to its structures.[2] The continuation of a flat organization complemented Harper's centralizing and dominating tendencies, as a simple organization structure presents fewer obstacles to the centralization of power. Furthermore, the absence of distinctive intra-party locations of power such as auxiliaries ensured that no dissidents or challengers to his leadership would be able to construct bases of opposition to his power.

As mentioned earlier, the result, according to Flanagan, is a garrison party, a unique structure in which the permanent organizational structure of the party is fused with its campaign apparatus. The predominant organizational features of this arrangement are centralization and simplicity. This garrison structure makes sense as the organizational form favoured by the Conservative party's only leader, Harper, and was uniquely adapted to the period of minority Parliaments that characterized Canadian politics from 2004 to 2011. The garrison that surrounded Harper, however, may have isolated him and contributed to his eventual downfall in 2015.

Conclusion

This chapter has primarily explored the transformation in the party after it crossed the threshold from the opposition to the government benches in 2006 and from minority to majority government in 2011. We use this final section to explore whether we can expect the changes of the 2006–15 period to be sustained after the Conservatives lost the 2015 election and Harper resigned as leader.

At the level of ideological commitments, there is little reason to believe we will see a significantly different orientation towards federalism or economic policy from the party. Social conservatism, though, is more problematic for the party in this new electoral environment. As we have seen, Harper was aided in his attempts to minimize the prominence of this faction of Conservative supporters by the minority Parliaments and the seeming acquiescence of his MPs. But the party's majority government removed the threat of immediate defeat, and social conservative MPs were more active after 2011, despite their leader's preferences on issues such as abortion and same sex-marriage. The

---

2   The one exception is the Quebec wing of the party.

party's loss in 2015 means that the social conservatives' opportunity to bring their agenda to government has passed for the time being. Their defeat at the party's convention in the spring of 2016 on the question of whether or not the party platform ought to continue to espouse a heterosexual definition of marriage suggests that their influence within the party has waned. The question is whether, even as a minority, they will once again discipline themselves to attain power, or whether their lack of policy influence during the course of Harper's time in power will convince them that an alternate – perhaps more rambunctious – strategy is more appropriate.

In contrast, the orientations of the party towards the electorate are unlikely to change in the years ahead, simply because of its continued commitment to winning office requires it to respond to Canada's changing demographic reality. In particular, the party's outreach to new supporters in "new Canadian" communities will continue to pay dividends in future re-election campaigns. The party has never successfully embraced the role of broker, as the Liberal Party did in the past. Even when the party lost in 2015, it did not face catastrophe, and party members seem convinced that they are well prepared to win in the future on the basis of their orientations to the electorate. Its attitude towards the electorate will also help determine whether Canadian conservatives engage with the emergent nativism that underpinned Donald Trump's campaign in the United States or the Brexit campaign in the United Kingdom. Canada's high levels of diversity – and the legacy of Jason Kenney – would suggest there are only very limited gains to be made through such appeals here. But it is also clear that some candidates for the party's leadership think otherwise.

Finally, we expect to see alterations in the organization of the Conservative Party in this new party system context, although any changes to such a sticky organization are likely to be slow. One important change may be in personnel selection: local activists and members are unlikely to accept continued interference in local nominations. Such interference was perhaps seen as necessary in the context of the minority Parliaments when it was necessary for the prime minister to protect incumbent MPs from time-consuming renomination challenges and recruit star candidates to assist the party as a whole. While members and activists appeared unlikely to continue to accept such interference in the wake of the 2011 election, the 2015 election saw the return of substantial central control, as Harper expelled several candidates over the course of the campaign as their foibles made national headlines. The

Conservative Party, it seems clear in the face of a resurgent Liberal Party, can never be comfortable in power, and so the characteristics of Harper's disciplined garrison party may now be institutionalized as the party enters a new phase of its evolution.

REFERENCES

Bittner, Amanda, and Royce Koop, eds. 2013. *Parties, Elections, and the Future of Canadian Politics*. Vancouver: UBC Press.

Blidook, Kelly, and Matthew Byrne. 2013. "Constant Campaigning and Partisan Discourse in the House of Commons." In Bittner and Koop, *Parties, Elections and the Future of Canadian Politics*, 46–66.

Carty, R. Kenneth. 2004. "Parties as Franchise Systems: The Stratarchical Organizational Imperative." *Party Politics* 10 (1): 5–24. http://dx.doi.org/10.1177/1354068804039118.

– 2013. "Has Brokerage Politics Ended? Canadian Parties in the New Century." In Bittner and Koop, *Parties, Elections and the Future of Canadian Politics*, 10–23.

– 2015. "Brokerage Parties, Brokerage Politics." In *Parties and Party Systems: Structure and Context*, ed. Richard Johnston and Campbell Sharman, 13–30. Vancouver: UBC Press.

Carty, R. Kenneth, William Cross, and Lisa Young. 2000. *Rebuilding Canadian Party Politics*. Vancouver: UBC Press.

Clarke, Harold D., Jane Jenson, Lawrence LeDuc, and Jon H. Pammett. 1996. *Absent Mandate: Canadian Electoral Politics in an Era of Restructuring*. 3rd ed. Toronto: Gage.

Cross, William. 2011. *Political Parties*. Vancouver: UBC Press.

Ellis, Faron. 2005. *The Limits of Participation: Members and Leaders in Canada's Reform Party*. Calgary: University of Calgary Press.

Farney, James. 2012. "Canadian Populism in an Era of the United Right." In Farney and Rayside, *Conservatism in Canada*, 43–59.

Farney, James, and Jonathan Malloy. 2011. "Ideology and Discipline in the Conservative Party of Canada." In *The Canadian Federal Election of 2011*, ed. Jon Pammett and Christopher Dornan, 247–71. Toronto: Dundurn.

Farney, James, and David Rayside, eds. 2013. *Conservatism in Canada*. Toronto: University of Toronto Press.

Flanagan, Tom. 2007. *Harper's Team*. Montreal, Kingston: McGill-Queen's University Press.

– 2013. "Something Blue: The Harper Conservatives as Garrison Party." In Farney and Rayside, *Conservatism in Canada*, 79–94.

44   The Blueprint

Harmes, Adam. 2007. "The Political Economy of Open Federalism." *Canadian Journal of Political Science* 40 (2): 417–37. http://dx.doi.org/10.1017/S0008423907070114.

Harper, Stephen, Tom Flanagan, Ted Morton, Rainer Knopf, Andrew Crooks, and Ken Boessenkool. 2001. "Re: The Alberta Agenda." *National Post*, 26 January.

Johnson, William. 2005. *Stephen Harper and the Future of Canada*. Toronto: McClelland and Stewart.

Johnston, Richard. 2008. "Polarized Pluralism in the Canadian Party System." *Canadian Journal of Political Science* 41 (4): 815–34. http://dx.doi.org/10.1017/S0008423908081110.

Koop, Royce, and Amanda Bittner. 2011. "Parachuted into Parliament: Candidate Nomination, Appointed Candidates, and Legislative Roles in Canada." *Journal of Elections, Public Opinion, and Parties* 21 (4): 431–52. http://dx.doi.org/10.1080/17457289.2011.609297.

– 2013. "Parties and Elections after 2011: The Fifth Canadian Party System?" In Bittner and Koop, *Parties, Elections, and the Future of Canadian Politics*, 308–31.

Marwah, Inder, Phil Triadafilopoulos, and Steven White. 2013. "Immigration, Citizenship, and Canada's New Conservative Party." In Farney and Rayside, *Conservatism in Canada*, 95–119.

Meisel, John. 1963. "The Stalled Omnibus: Canadian Parties in the 1960s." *Social Research* 30 (3): 367–90.

Patten, Steve. 2013. "The Triumph of Neoliberalism within Partisan Conservatism in Canada." In Farney and Rayside, *Conservatism in Canada*, 59–78.

Perlin, George C. 1980. *The Tory Syndrome: Leadership Politics in the Progressive Conservative Party*. Montreal, Kingston: McGill-Queen's University Press.

Pitsula, James M. 2007. "The Mulroney Government and Canadian Cultural Policy." In *Transforming the Nation: Canada and Brian Mulroney*, ed. Raymond B. Blake, 357–80. Montreal, Kingston: McGill-Queen's University Press.

Plamondon, Bob. 2006. *Full Circle: Death and Resurrection in Canadian Conservative Politics*. Toronto: Key Porter.

Saurette, Paul, and Kelly Gordon. 2013. "Arguing Abortion: The New Anti-Abortion Discourse in Canada." *Canadian Journal of Political Science* 46 (1): 157–85. http://dx.doi.org/10.1017/S0008423913000176.

Segal, Hugh. 1997. *Beyond Greed: A Traditional Conservative Confronts Neo-Conservative Excess*. Toronto: Stoddart.

Strom, Kaare. 1990. "A Behavioral Theory of Competitive Political Parties." *American Journal of Political Science* 34 (2): 565–98. http://dx.doi.org/10.2307/2111461.

Wells, Paul. 2013. *The Longer I'm Prime Minister: Stephen Harper and Canada, 2006–*. Toronto: McClelland and Stewart.

Whitaker, Reginald. 1977. *The Government Party: Organizing and Financing the Liberal Party of Canada, 1930–58*. Toronto: University of Toronto Press.

Young, Lisa, and William Cross. 2002. "The Rise of Plebiscitary Democracy in Canadian Political Parties." *Party Politics* 8 (6): 673–99. http://dx.doi.org/10.1177/1354068802008006003.

3 The Conservative Turn among the Canadian Electorate

ÉRIC BÉLANGER AND LAURA B. STEPHENSON

Political parties hold unique positions in democratic governments. They are the most visible symbols of electoral competition and can define the range of preferences held by the polity. For many, politics is "unthinkable" without the organizing capacity of parties (Schattschneider 1942); for others, it is "unworkable" (Aldrich 1995). As this volume is a study of conservative politics in Canada, we would be remiss if we did not consider how voters have reacted to federal conservative parties since 1993.

One of the most dramatic events in conservative politics in Canada was the 2003 merger of the Canadian Alliance (CA) and Progressive Conservative (PC) parties (see chapter 2 in this volume). The literature on political parties addresses changes in parties (see, for example, Panebianco 1988; Harmel and Janda 1994), but surprisingly little has been written about mergers of parties, possibly because they occur relatively infrequently.[1] The literature on party mergers that does exist tends to focus on why and how a merger came about, with special attention to the actions of leaders (e.g., Kim 1997; Ware 2009; Bélanger and

---

1 Electoral coalitions are much more common, especially in parliamentary proportional representation systems. For a discussion of coalitions, see Laver and Schofield (1998) and Golder (2006). Mergers tend to occur more frequently in volatile party systems, such as post-communist societies (for a discussion of party systems in such societies, see Kreuzer and Pettai 2003), although they can constitute an attractive option in two-party systems when the resources available to the parties are relatively small, they have distinctive regional bases, and the parties involved have enjoyed limited electoral success, as was the case with the CPC (Ware 2009: 114–17; Bélanger and Godbout 2010).

Godbout 2010; Marland and Flanagan 2015). The incentives for merging are often electoral – that is, a desire to improve electoral success. Nevertheless, almost no attention has been paid to voters, and so we know little about how *voters* react to party mergers.[2]

How has the merger that produced the Conservative Party of Canada affected voters? In this chapter, we consider how the attitudes of supporters of federal conservative parties evolved from 1993 to 2011,[3] focusing on whether the merger and consolidation of party options on the right side of the ideological spectrum contributed to a conservative turn in Canada. We assess how the change in federal conservative party voting options affected how citizens understood and evaluated political issues by tracking the ideology and attitudes of individuals who supported the various parties on the right side of the ideological spectrum before the merger, and of strong and weak Conservative partisans after the merger. Our assumption is that if ideological differences between those who strongly and weakly identified with the Conservative Party remained, then the merger simply forced Canadians on the right to support their only option, without actually affecting the views of the electorate; if there were few or no differences, then the merger influenced the nature of conservative attitudes in Canada.

Another related question that we investigate in this chapter is whether conservative partisans increased in numbers and/or whether they became more loyal to their party over time. Again, our assumption is that if there was indeed a shift to the right among the Canadian electorate, then we should see a significant increase in the proportion of voters identifying with the right-wing party options, and especially with the single one that remained after the merger. Likewise, we should observe a stronger correlation between conservative partisanship and conservative vote choice since the beginning of the period under study. Two important reasons that may account for the rise of the Conservative Party are that it was able to enlarge its pool of partisans and that its partisans were more loyal when casting their ballots. Such trends would constitute additional indicators that a genuine consolidation occurred on the right side of the ideological spectrum in Canada.

---

2 For an exception, see Denver and Bochel (1994). They provide an analysis of the reactions of party members (who presumably were also voters) to the merger of the Social Democratic Party and Liberal Party in Great Britain during the 1980s.
3 Data from the 2015 Canadian Election Study were not available at the time this chapter was written.

The Conservative Party of Canada gained votes and seats in the federal elections between 2004 and 2011.[4] We are interested in looking beyond the vote to examine possibly more profound changes that may have occurred under the surface. In so doing, we hope to gain some insight into the change in the party's fortunes in 2015. While we do not analyse the 2015 election, an understanding of the nature of Conservative support going into that contest is informative. For this reason, our study will focus on two main questions:

1 Conservative policy preferences: Did the rise of the Conservative Party between 2004 and 2011 affect the nature of conservative partisans' policy preferences?
2 Conservative partisan attachment: Did the success of the Conservative Party affect the nature of conservative partisanship?

The chapter begins with a brief summary of the important party system changes that happened on the right side of the Canadian political spectrum since 1993. It then discusses the possible consequences that these changes may have had for Canadian voters' attitudes and behaviours, thus generating a number of expectations. The rest of the chapter uses individual-level survey data from the Canadian Election Studies (CES) to test these expectations.

The Conservative Party of Canada: The Struggle to Unite the Right

Between 1993 and 2004, the Liberal Party of Canada was in a privileged position due to the splintering of right-wing support (Scotto, Stephenson, and Kornberg 2004). The Liberals' traditional competition, the centre-right PC Party, was weakened because voters had another conservative option, the Reform Party (Bowler and Lanoue 1996). Reform's strong social conservatism, as well as predominant Western Canadian flavour, created real divides among those on the right side of the ideological spectrum.

After vote-splitting produced another Liberal majority in the election of 1997, an attempt was made to unite the parties by the Reform Party's

---

4 It should be noted that even in 2015, when it lost seats, the Conservative Party's absolute number of votes was still higher than in any election other than 2011. In other words, although the Conservatives' proportion of the vote declined significantly, they still maintained the support of over 5.5 million Canadians in 2015.

leader, Preston Manning. His "United Alternative" assemblies brought Reformers together with members of other political parties. In January 2000, the assembly voted to create the Canadian Reform Conservative Alliance (known as the Canadian Alliance), which eventually replaced the Reform Party. However, "the federal Progressive Conservatives decided to have nothing to do with the United Alternative" (Flanagan 2001, 290). The CA's policies were not very different from those of the Reform Party, save for modifications (such as ending opposition to official bilingualism) that were engineered to improve the electoral chances of the party beyond the West (289). The party was criticized for its strong conservative social values and was seen as a magnet for radical conservatives. Conservative-minded people who saw the Reform and Alliance parties as essentially the same did not rush to abandon the PC Party to put an end to vote-splitting. Data from the 2000 Canadian Election Study reflect this – a majority of PC voters thought there was "hardly any" difference compared to about 7 per cent who felt there was "a lot" of difference between the Reform and Alliance parties. Similarly, about 30 per cent of PC voters indicated that they felt the Alliance was simply too extreme. The Canadian right remained fragmented and the Liberals once again won a majority government in 2000.

In October 2003, PC leader Peter MacKay and CA leader Stephen Harper reached an agreement to merge their parties and create a new party vehicle, the Conservative Party of Canada. The agreement (the merged party's first ideological statement) contained ideological elements from both parent parties. Some of the founding principles included a "balance between fiscal accountability, progressive social policy and individual rights and responsibilities" and a "belief that it is the responsibility of individuals to provide for themselves, their families and their dependents, while recognizing that government must respond to those who require assistance and compassion" (Harper and MacKay 2003, 1, 2). The memberships of both parties ratified the agreement in December 2003.

Bélanger and Godbout (2010) argue that the merger was practical and rooted in electoral strategy, a necessary decision to provide a united alternative to the Liberals. However, beyond this electoral motivation, the merged party's positions and ideology were not initially clear. While the merger agreement articulated several of the new Conservative Party's founding beliefs, it did not indicate how those beliefs would translate into practical policies and ideological direction. Several of the party's policy angles appeared to be moderate and familiar to former PCs, but the election of Stephen Harper as leader of the party in 2004, over former Ontario PC Cabinet minister Tony Clement and businesswoman Belinda Stronach, led to uncertainty about how and if these statements were going to be realized. Several prominent PC members expressed their displeasure with the new party and distanced themselves, some even to the extent of joining another party.[5] Former PC prime minister Joe Clark received the most publicity, remarking on television that he "would be extremely worried about Mr. Harper. I personally would prefer to go with the devil we know" (Scoffield and Fagan 2004).[6]

Although it had chosen its leader only two months earlier and had yet to articulate its full ideology, the fledgling party was forced to contest an election when Parliament dissolved in May 2004. The party's platform was carefully crafted to avoid controversial topics; as Ellis and Woolstencroft (2004, 91) state, "What was not mentioned in the policy platform was indicative of the party's attempt to present a moderate, competent, and safe choice for centrist voters." Given that the party was created to be an electoral vehicle for right-wing success, its performance was disappointing. It received 29.6 per cent of the vote for a total of ninety-nine seats. Although less than the combined support the party's predecessors received in 2000 (25.5 per cent for the Alliance and 12.2 per cent for the PCs), the Conservative Party did limit the Liberal Party to a minority government. Turcotte (2004) argues that the "merger failed to receive partisan approval" (316) and the party suffered from the desertion of former PC supporters, who were also more likely to abstain than supporters of other parties. Former Alliance support was high for the new party, at 88 per cent, compared to 68 per cent from former PC voters (320).

Following the 2004 election, and under Stephen Harper's guidance, the Conservative Party was gradually able to better define its ideological orientations and turn them into simple but clear neoliberal principles. The aim was to offer a more moderate brand to the electorate, for instance by shedding or downplaying some of the party's controversial moral stances. These efforts have been considered to be successful by most political observers and analysts (see, e.g., Bricker and

---

5   One such MP was Scott Brison, who chose to join the Liberals.

6   The new party also caused problems in the Senate, where Senators Lowell Murray, Elaine McCoy, and Norman Atkins chose to sit as Progressive Conservatives, rather than Conservative members.

Ibbitson 2013; Farney and Rayside 2013), helping the party to gain a greater number of parliamentary seats from one election to the next and ultimately win a majority government in 2011. It would seem, despite a somewhat rocky start with former PC supporters, that the Conservative brand had consolidated among voters by 2011. The rest of this chapter evaluates this impression.

Party Options and Attitudes in the Electorate

If parties organize politics for individuals, then the electoral options may influence how voters judge issues. Seen through the lenses of political parties, the options for political attitudes may be truncated or primed. One assumption of electing a Conservative government is that the Canadian public now desires more conservative politics and policies. But is that true? Many would see the Conservative Party merger as a key moment in the current success of the right in Canada because it created a single, unified political actor that voters could rally behind. However, voting for a party and allowing it to shape one's attitudes are two different things.

If citizens come to see issues through a political lens, they may change their preferences, either because they are convinced by the party's position, or because they wish to reduce the dissonance between their own views and those of the party they support. Such opinion formation may have been at work on the Canadian political right over the last two decades. The gradual ideological polarization of the Canadian party system that accompanied the rise of the Conservative Party appears to have put an end to the era of "brokerage" political parties at the federal level (Carty 2013; see also Bricker and Ibbitson 2013, as well as chapter 2 in this volume). For most of the twentieth century, the consensus understanding of federal party politics in Canada was that, as a result of the geographical spread of the country and the varied regional political interests of its population, political parties had to act as accommodating brokers, that is, build large short-term coalitions of voters in order to mobilize pan-Canadian support and win elections (Meisel 1963; Scarrow 1965; Bickerton, Gagnon, and Smith 1999). The result of this party behaviour was that the big national political parties, the Liberals and Progressive Conservatives, were both aiming at the centre of the ideological spectrum. Programmatically speaking, from election to election they thus ended up as being very similar, not much more than a slightly left-of-centre Tweedledee and a slightly right-of-centre

Tweedledum. Indeed, the party manifesto data analysed by Koop and Bittner (2013) show that for most of the post-war period the Liberal and PC parties more or less overlapped in their left-right ideological placement (although they differed in the degree to which they were willing to accommodate the interests of French Canadians, especially in Quebec). Since they were so close in their positions on most policy issues, the one characteristic that distinguished the two national parties was their leadership. Thus, the brokerage era of Canadian party politics saw the debate surrounding federal election campaigns as revolving more around the attributes, competencies, and charisma of their respective leaders than around clear and distinguishable policy propositions (Clarke et al. 1979, 1984, 1991, 1996).

Having brokerage political parties was not without its effects on the Canadian electorate. According to an influential account, it led voters to develop flexible attachments to the parties (Clarke et al. 1996). Canadian partisanship was thus construed as being flexible in the sense that voters would shift party identification from one election to the next because the parties that mobilized them did so only with a short-term goal in mind, thus discouraging Canadian voters from developing durable attachments to the parties (Stevenson 1987) along the lines of what studies of partisanship in the United States had observed (e.g., Campbell et al. 1960). As Johnston (2013, 284) aptly put it, the domination of brokerage parties not only "coexisted with a distinctively Canadian pattern of volatility – indeed, [it] was responsible for it." In addition, because of their programmatic similarities, brokerage parties did not provide voters with clear and distinctive ideological labels with which they could identify strongly, thus further weakening the meaningfulness of partisanship as a long-term socio-psychological anchor of vote choice in Canada.

This conventional view of Canadian partisanship may not be as relevant as it used to be, however. First, additional empirical work (Johnston 1992) has shown that party identification in Canada may be less flexible than initially thought, suggesting that part of its apparent volatility is an artefact of not allowing individuals to indicate non-partisanship when answering electoral surveys – although that conclusion has been challenged by Clarke, Kornberg, and Scotto (2009), who argue that a change in the wording of the party identification question does not substantially alter the level of instability. Second, and more important, the party system changes since the 1990s have started to shift the nature of party identification: partisans today appear to be more stable, more loyal, and more intense in their attachment than in the past, largely in response to the arrival of more programmatic parties in the form of the Reform Party/Canadian Alliance, the Bloc Québécois, and the new Conservative Party of Canada (Bélanger and Stephenson 2010).

From this point of view, the consolidation of the right that was achieved with the Conservative Party merger may have been a key moment. By reducing the party offerings on one side of the ideological spectrum, it may have affected Canadian voters' attitudes and behaviours in significant ways, paving the way to a right turn among the electorate. If such a "big shift" (to quote Bricker and Ibbitson 2013) indeed happened, then we would expect to observe a number of patterns. First the rise of the Conservative Party should have led to a consolidation of conservative partisans' political views, resulting in more homogeneous policy preferences within this group of voters. This process, in turn, would likely help foster more loyal (i.e., less flexible) conservative partisans, leading us to expect a stronger correlation between partisanship and vote choice on the right end of the spectrum. The Conservatives' rise is also likely to have drawn new partisans and consolidated the demographic profile of its partisan base, that is, to dampen or even eliminate some of the demographic cleavages that characterized the separate right-wing partisan groups at the beginning of the period. The next section will examine these questions in turn, starting with a look at the policy preferences of right-wing party identifiers.

Empirical Findings

To assess whether there has been a conservative shift over the last two decades, it is important to look at the policy preferences of Canadians. If there has been consolidation among voters on the right of the ideological spectrum, such that the moderate conservatism of the Progressive Conservatives lost its base with the party system changes, we should observe an increased similarity of issue positions among right-leaning partisans. If attitudes continue to show fragmentation, then it is a strong indication that no real conservative consolidation occurred in the electorate.

To assess this question, we compare the attitudes of right-wing party partisans in 1993, 1997, and 2000 (Reform or CA versus PC) and then look at the attitudes of weak and strong Conservative Party identifiers from 2004 to 2011. Two right-wing parties competed for votes in the same ideological space until the Conservative Party merger. After that time, voters had only one party they could support if they wished to express their right-wing preferences. The variation between weak and strong supporters is assessed in order to draw a distinction between committed partisans ("strong") and those who might have identified with the Conservatives only because no other party option existed ("weak"). Blais et al. (2001) have shown that weak identifiers in Canada are less loyal than strong identifiers, whether in terms of voting for their party or evaluating their party highly. Thus, we consider weak identifiers to represent a group of individuals who may be temporary, transient, or vulnerable partisans. We expect that any indication of significantly different attitudes between strong and weak partisans (post-2003) would indicate a lack of consolidation among Conservative identifiers.

We analyse questions from the Canadian Election Studies that probe attitudes about economic and political issues, as well as social groups: left-right placement, free enterprise, Canada-U.S. ties, moral traditionalism, women, outgroups (immigrants and racial minorities), Indigenous Canadians, regional alienation, Quebec (for the rest of Canada [ROC] only), and Quebec sovereignty (for Quebec only) (see the appendix for details and question wordings). Seven of these ten indicators are indices created from two or three survey questions. The responses were all adjusted to range from 0 to 1 for comparability.

Figures 3.1–3.10 plot the mean position of Progressive Conservative and Reform or Canadian Alliance partisans on each of the ten indicators. There are two things to notice. First, the progression of attitudes across the 1993–2000 elections is clear. In some cases attitudes changed little; in other cases there was important movement. Second, the relative positioning of the two partisan groups is variable across the attitude questions.

Attitudes are grouped under three themes: economic issues, social issues, and constitutional issues. The economic issues are left-right placement, free enterprise, and Canada/United States. For left-right placement, there is variation between the Canadian Alliance and PCs (2000) but not the Reform Party and PCs.[7] The results for free enterprise show no variation at all. Although there was a rightward shift from 1993, the variation between the parties is statistically insignificant. Finally, the Canada/U.S. issue reveals statistically significant

---

7 The rightward shift observed in 2000 may be an artefact of the choice set used that year (three answer options rather than a 0–10 scale). See the appendix for details.

Figure 3.1: Left-Right Placement

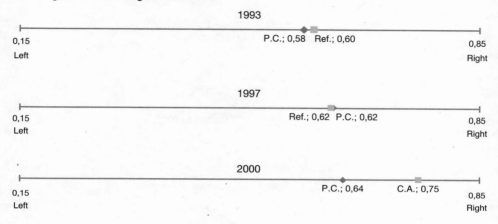

Figure 3.2: Free Enterprise

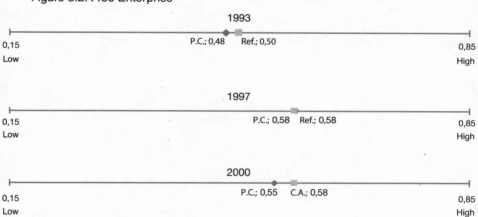

Figure 3.3: Canada/U.S. Ties

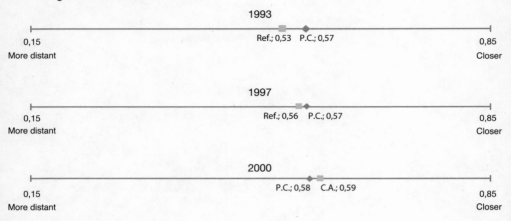

Figure 3.4: Moral Traditionalism

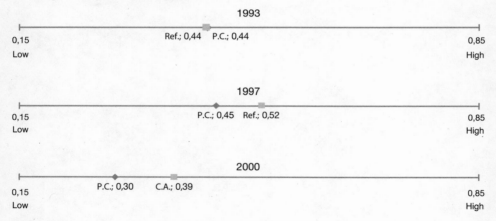

Figure 3.5: Women

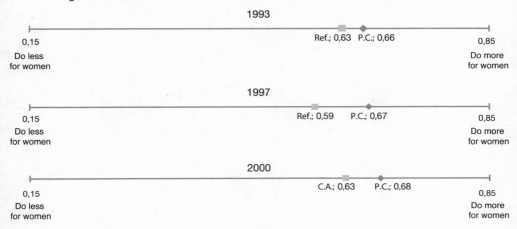

Figure 3.6: Outgroups (Immigrants and Racial Minorities)

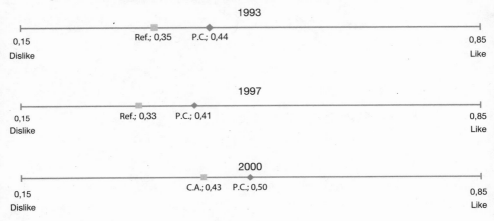

Figure 3.7: Indigenous Canadians

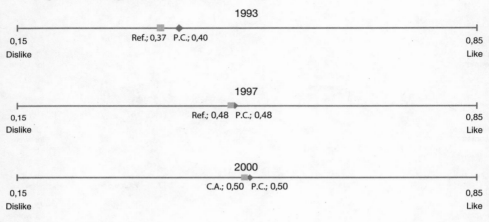

1993

0,15 — Dislike

Ref.; 0,37   P.C.; 0,40

0,85 — Like

1997

0,15 — Dislike

Ref.; 0,48   P.C.; 0,48

0,85 — Like

2000

0,15 — Dislike

C.A.; 0,50   P.C.; 0,50

0,85 — Like

Figure 3.8: Quebec (ROC Only)

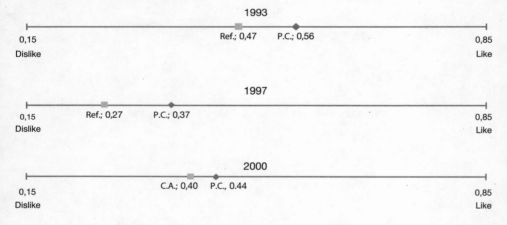

1993

0,15 — Dislike

Ref.; 0,47   P.C.; 0,56

0,85 — Like

1997

0,15 — Dislike

Ref.; 0,27   P.C.; 0,37

0,85 — Like

2000

0,15 — Dislike

C.A.; 0,40   P.C., 0,44

0,85 — Like

Figure 3.9: Regional Alienation

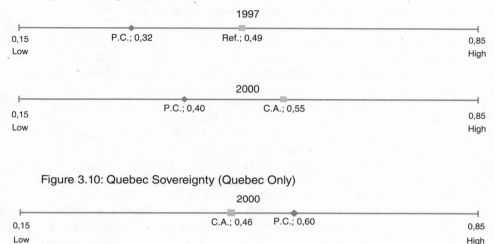

Figure 3.10: Quebec Sovereignty (Quebec Only)

variation in 1993 but not after, although there appears to be a general shift of partisans towards having closer ties with the United States. Overall, the attitudes of conservative voters on economic issues during 1993–2000 are mostly similar.

Next we consider social issues. The moral attitudes of the parties are significantly different in 1997 and 2000. Attitudes towards women vary in each election year, as do attitudes towards outgroups. Attitudes towards Indigenous Canadians, however, consolidate over time and also become more positive among both partisan groups. In general, there is more significant variation in attitudes towards social issues as compared to economic issues.

Finally, we consider constitutional issues. On the question of Quebec (how much one likes Quebec and how much one thinks should be done for Quebec), attitudes of the two partisan groups in the ROC are significantly different from each other in each year, with the PCs being more pro-Quebec. Regional alienation attitudes are also significantly different in both years the question was asked, with Reform/CA partisans clearly showing more alienation. Comparison of right-wing partisan groups on Quebec sovereignty is possible only for the 2000 election because no Reform Party supporters from Quebec are to be found in the CES surveys,[8] but in that year partisans in Quebec did not hold different attitudes.[9]

These results consider just the time prior to the Conservative Party merger. While economic attitudes were similar in the two party groups, there was variation on moral and constitutional issues. Did this change after the merger?

Figures 3.11–3.20 show the equivalent results for weak and strong[10] Conservative partisans from 2004 to 2011. For economic issues, there is no evidence of consolidation over time between the two groups of partisans. Differences are stable and significant. The two groups are significantly different on the left-right scale. The free enterprise and Canada-U.S. attitude differences between the two groups of partisans are also stable across the elections, and significant in three of the four elections. Of interest is that there was a clear shift over time in attitudes about relations with the United States in favour of closer ties, and a more recent shift away from free enterprise, but the variation between the partisan groups remained – with strong partisans systematically locating themselves more to the right, being more in favour of free enterprise, and wanting closer ties with the United States than weak partisans.

For social issues there is a similar pattern. Moral traditionalism attitudes are significantly different between the two partisan groups for three of the four elections, and there was an overall shift towards the lower end of the scale – although strong partisans always score higher on the scale than weak partisans. Attitudes towards women are more stable over time and more similar across the groups, being significantly different only in 2006. Attitudes towards outgroups and Indigenous Canadians also show similarity between the two groups of partisans. In the case of Indigenous Canadians, there was consolidation before

---

8 The Reform Party did not field candidates in Quebec during the 1993 election. It did field some in 1997, but the party received only 0.3 per cent of vote support in that province that year.

9 The lack of a statistically significant difference may be due in this case to the low number of observations ($N = 25$).

10 The category of "strong partisans" groups those in the CES who responded that their partisanship was "very strong" or "fairly strong." See Blais et al. (2001) for a thorough justification of this operationalization.

Figure 3.11: Left-Right Placement

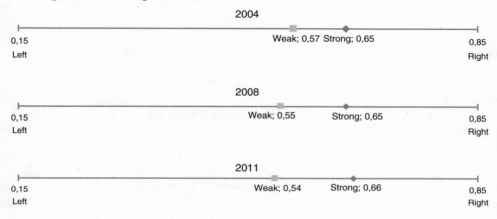

Figure 3.12: Free Enterprise

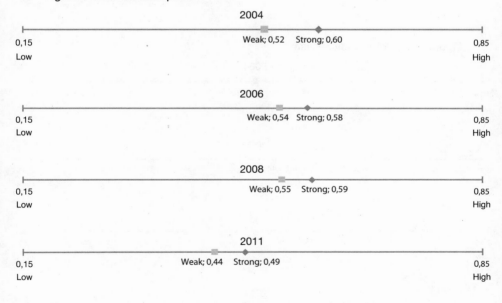

Figure 3.13: Canada/U.S. Ties

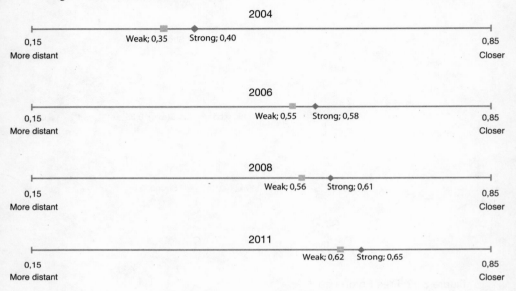

2004

0,15
More distant

Weak; 0,35   Strong; 0,40

0,85
Closer

2006

0,15
More distant

Weak; 0,55   Strong; 0,58

0,85
Closer

2008

0,15
More distant

Weak; 0,56   Strong; 0,61

0,85
Closer

2011

0,15
More distant

Weak; 0,62   Strong; 0,65

0,85
Closer

Figure 3.14: Moral Traditionalism

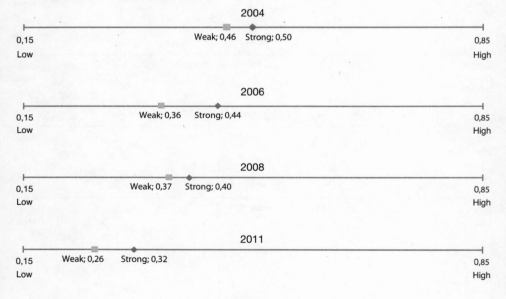

2004

0,15
Low

Weak; 0,46   Strong; 0,50

0,85
High

2006

0,15
Low

Weak; 0,36   Strong; 0,44

0,85
High

2008

0,15
Low

Weak; 0,37   Strong; 0,40

0,85
High

2011

0,15
Low

Weak; 0,26   Strong; 0,32

0,85
High

Figure 3.15: Women

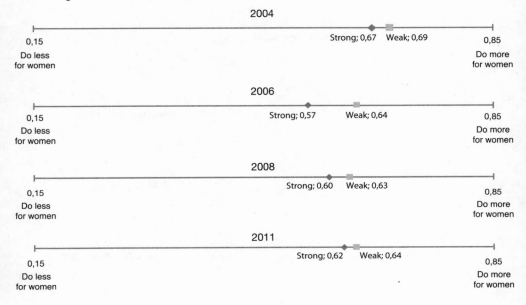

Figure 3.16: Outgroups (Immigrants and Racial Minorities)

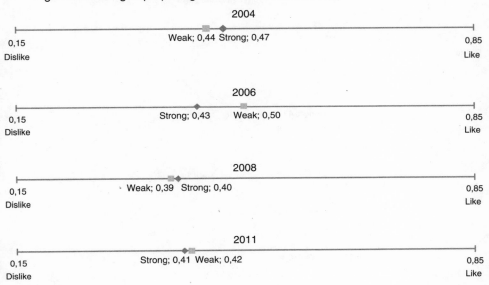

Figure 3.17: Indigenous Canadians

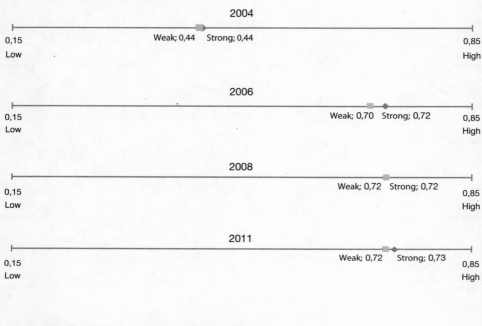

Figure 3.18: Quebec (ROC Only)

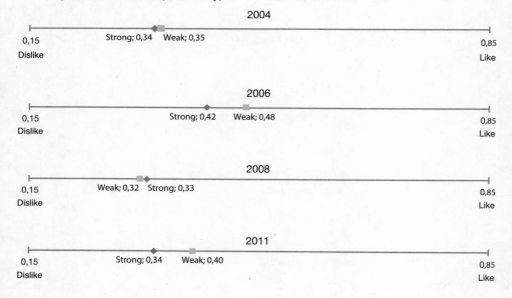

Figure 3.19: Regional Alienation

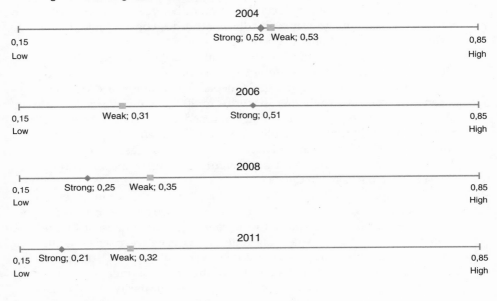

Figure 3.20: Quebec Sovereignty (Quebec Only)

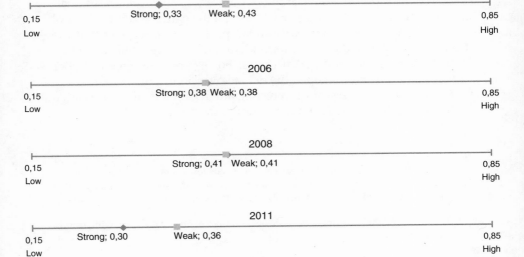

the merger, and it appears to have continued.[11] Attitudes towards out-groups, however, were significantly different between the right-wing parties. After the merger, it seems these attitudes consolidated, being significantly different only in 2006.

Finally we consider the constitutional issues. Attitudes towards Quebec were significantly different in 2011 but were not in the other three elections. Before the merger, Quebec was a point of difference; it remains to be seen whether attitudes in 2011 were outliers or part of a new trend. Regional alienation remained an issue of difference – although note that, overall, feelings of regional alienation greatly declined since the Conservative Party came to power. Last, there are no differences in attitudes about sovereignty among weak and strong Conservative partisans in Quebec.[12]

What do these results tell us about conservative attitudes in general? Table 3.1 summarizes the results presented above to aid the discussion. In the 1993–2000 period (prior to the merger), economic issues were a point of similarity between the federal conservative parties, while social and constitutional issue attitudes were substantially different. After the merger, the trends reversed. Variation on economic issues was substantial but there appears to have been more similarity on other issues. Two issues stand out, however, as distinguishing weak and strong Conservative Party supporters. Regional alienation was a point of contention. This may reflect differences between old Reformers who came to the party because of its strong Western focus and new Conservatives in other provinces. The other point of difference was moral traditionalism. As the only right-wing party, those on the extreme right on moral issues had no other major party to support, despite the fact that the Conservative Party did much to moderate its message and move to a more centrist position on such issues. For example, Stephen Harper consistently refused to reopen the debate over abortion.

These results suggest an interesting interpretation of conservative politics over the past twenty years. Prior to the merger, economic issues

---

11 Figure 3.15 seems to indicate a large shift post-2004 toward more positive views of Indigenous peoples, but this trend may be biased by the fact that the index in the last three elections is based on only one survey item, as opposed to two items in 2004.

12 Again, this might be attributable to the low number of observations (ranging from 22 to 104).

Table 3.1. Summary of Findings about Conservative Partisans' Attitudes

	PC vs Reform/CA differences (1993–2000)	Weak vs strong differences (2004–2011)
Economic issues		
Left-right placement	1/3	3/3
Free enterprise	0/3	3/4
Canada-U.S. ties	1/3	3/4
Social issues		
Moral traditionalism	2/3	3/4
Women	3/3	1/4
Outgroups	3/3	1/4
Indigenous Canadians	1/3	0/4
Constitutional issues		
Quebec (like)	3/3	1/4
Regional alienation	2/2	3/4
Quebec (sovereignty)	0/1	0/4

Note: Proportions indicate significant differences at $p <\, = 0.10$.

were a point of similarity for the right-wing parties, whereas social and constitutional issues were hurdles that delayed the merger. After the merger, the balance shifted, such that a new cleavage appeared on economic issues. As it was the only party espousing conservative policies, however, voters had little choice but to support the Conservatives, even if they disagreed with aspects of their economic policy. The new Conservative Party thus seems to have acted as more of a "big tent" on economic issues in the elections after the merger.

Another way of evaluating whether there was consolidation among conservative voters after the creation of the Conservative Party of Canada is to see whether the Conservatives were able to increase the size of their partisan base. Findings presented by Gidengil et al. (2012) for 2000–8 suggest that they were. Our own results presented in table 3.2 confirm these findings. According to the table, the actual proportion of Canadians who identified with the Progressive Conservative Party gradually declined between 1993 and 2000, from 22 per cent of the electorate down to about 4 per cent, while the proportion of citizens identifying with the Reform Party/Canadian Alliance experienced a

Table 3.2. Proportion of Conservative Partisans by Election

	1993	1997	2000	2004	2006	2008	2011
PC	22.0	16.3	4.4				
Reform	6.4	8.8					
CA			11.7				
Conservative				17.9	18.0	26.3	26.9
Strong				84.2	83.9	74.0	86.6
Weak				15.8	16.1	26.0	13.4

Note: The last two rows disaggregate strong vs weak partisans (totalling 100%).

slow but steady growth (from 6 to 12 per cent). That growth continued after the merger, with the proportion of Conservative partisans in 2004 (18 per cent) actually being slightly greater than the sum of PC and CA partisans four years prior. That proportion remained stable in the 2006 election, but increased significantly (to 26 per cent) in the first election that followed the Conservative Party's arrival into power.

Further evidence of partisan consolidation can be observed when examining the relative proportion of strong versus weak partisans within the Conservative base. These numbers are presented in the last two rows of table 3.2. Note the greater number of weak Conservative partisans in 2008, most likely a result of an influx of new identifiers that year. But the significant finding is that, while the total proportion of Conservative partisans remained stable from 2008 to 2011, the relative proportion of weak partisans decreased (from 26 to 13 per cent). This seems to suggest that voters who became new Conservative identifiers in 2008 not only stayed with the party, they also went from weak to strong partisanship in the few years between the two elections. Two points can be made about this change. First, these numbers illustrate rather clearly the extent to which the strengthening of Conservative partisanship over time was stepwise. Yet they also suggest that further growth would require an influx of new (weak) partisans. Whether the party can attract new partisans, and from where, are important questions that the 2015 election results seem to have answered. Second, the consolidation and strength of Conservative support suggests that the "right vs the rest" competition that characterized elections between 2004 and 2011 is unlikely to fade. Indeed, the 2015 election saw the continuation of this trend. Nonetheless, even if the party does not increase the size of its base, it has a substantial group of committed supporters. In addition, it seems unlikely that the two main parties to the left of the Conservatives, the Liberals and the NDP, will engage in some form of merger, especially with the Liberal Party's return to power (on this, see Godbout et al. 2015).

Thus far the data indicate that the Conservative Party became well rooted in the electorate after 2004. The party gained a relatively large partisan base, more than the Progressive Conservatives enjoyed prior to the merger, and there was some consolidation of social and consti-tutional issue attitudes among its supporters. Another way to consider whether there was a general consolidation of conservative support is to look at the demographic bases of the different right-leaning parties and partisan groups before and after the merger.

Table 3.3 shows the number of significant demographic differences between the different federal conservative parties (between 1993 and the merger) and weak and strong Conservative partisans (2004–11). According to these results, there is little indication of substantial change in the demographic bases of conservative support. Before the Conser-vative Party was formed, there were consistent significant differences between the PCs and the more conservative federal parties in gender, and in residence in the Atlantic provinces, British Columbia, and the Western provinces. After the merger the gender difference disappeared. Some regional variation was still present (but not in Atlantic Canada), as were differences in religiosity, age, and income, but the latter three are not significant in each election year.

If the more extreme federal conservative parties were supported by specific demographic groups, there was little substantial change after the merger other than eliminating the gender differences between sup-porters. This can seem like a neutral story – if one assumes that support-ers of the different federal conservative parties were transformed into strong and weak partisans of the Conservative Party, then the variation is to be expected and is of minor import. If one considers, however, that the results from 2004 to 2011 reflect individuals who aligned with the *same* party, the differences among supporters are more intriguing. The regional variation is especially interesting. In 2011, for example, the proportion of strong supporters was relatively higher than weak supporters in the West, British Columbia, and Ontario, but the reverse was true in Quebec. This suggests that Conservative support in Quebec is more vulnerable to fragmentation (see also chapter 7 in this vol-ume), although it must be noted that in the 2015 election, Quebec was the only province in which Conservative support remained stable (at

Table 3.3. Summary of Findings about Conservative Partisans' Socio-Demographic Profile

	PC vs Reform/CA differences (1993–2000)	Weak vs strong differences (2004–11)
Age	1/3	2/4
Male	3/3	0/4
University Education	1/3	0/4
Income	1/3	1/4
Religiosity	1/3	2/4
Ontario	1/3	2/4
Quebec	2/3	4/4
BC	3/3	1/4
Atlantic	3/3	0/4
West	3/3	3/4

Note: Proportions indicate significant differences at $p < = 0.10$.

17 per cent). Religiosity was another factor of difference in 2011. Strong supporters were significantly different in their religiosity than weak supporters – again, a source of potential vulnerability.

Finally, there is the issue of the vote loyalty of Conservative partisans. Did they become more loyal over time? Simple correlations between strong partisanship and vote for each of the Progressive Conservatives, the Reform Party, the Canadian Alliance, and the Conservative Party provide an answer to this question.

Table 3.4 demonstrates that vote loyalty was stronger for the more right-wing federal conservative parties than the Progressive Conservative Party in the two elections prior to the merger. After 2004, there was a further increase in loyalty towards the Conservative Party, with Pearson's coefficient of correlation reaching a high of 0.66 in the 2011 election. This suggests that those who strongly identified with the Conservatives gave their vote to the party in considerable numbers, much more so than other conservative partisans did at the beginning of the period under study. This finding is evidence of relative success by the Conservative Party in consolidating its support base.

That said, the correlations between weak Conservative partisanship and vote choice (see the bottom row of table 3.4) suggest that the increase in loyalty among Conservative supporters may have reached a

Table 3.4. Correlations between Partisanship and Vote Choice by Election

	1993	1997	2000	2004	2006	2008	2011
PC	0.43	0.42	0.23				
Reform	0.42	0.53					
CA			0.59				
Conservative				0.58	0.56	0.61	0.66
Weak				0.09	0.16	0.18	0.11

Note: The correlations all refer to "very strong/fairly strong" partisans, except in the last row (weak partisans).

ceiling in 2011. Of course partisans who declare that they identify only weakly with their party cannot be expected to display a strong relationship between their identification and their vote choice. However, the data in the table show that the correlation among weak partisans doubled between 2004 and 2008, from 0.09 to 0.18, but dropped to 0.11 in the 2011 election, which saw the Conservative Party achieve a majority government. The 2011 election shows the largest gap between correlation coefficients for strong and weak partisans. Considering that 2011 is also the election in which we found the lowest proportion of weak Conservative partisans (see table 3.2), these findings suggest that there may not be much room left for growth in partisan loyalty for the Conservative Party. Yet, even if that is true, the increase in loyalty among conservative partisans observed since the 1990s certainly signals the end of flexible partisanship in Canada, at least on the political right.

Conclusion

What do these empirical results say about the Conservative Party, especially in light of its loss of power in the 2015 election? We suggest there are two points that should be considered carefully. First, while the Conservative Party's support in Canada is substantial and is reflected in the 31.9 per cent of voter support it received in 2015, whether the electorate on the right side of the ideological spectrum became unified since the simplification of the party system is not certain. There are some indications that this is the case – for example, the consolidation of most social and constitutional attitudes between 2004 and 2011.

However, economic attitude differences remained in 2011, as did some demographic relationships and attitudes on moral traditionalism. The "type" of conservatism in Canada was not uniform, despite a single party representing all of the interests. The Conservative Party thus appears to have transformed into more of a big tent on these specific attitudes, an indication perhaps that partisan consolidation on the ideological right remained incomplete after 2011. While the Conservative merger happened over a decade ago, it is possible that more time is needed for the consolidation to be completed. However, it is also possible that the differences observed among supporters in 2011 are part of the reason for the party's 2015 loss. Perhaps there is no more room for consolidation. If so, then these findings about the size and loyalty of the Conservative partisan base are even more relevant. How the party will fare under a new leader is an important question for future research.

Our results suggest that seeing the success of the Conservative Party as an indication of a conservative shift in the electorate may be premature. There remained significant differences between weak and strong Conservative supporters in 2011, and these suggest that some of the moderate conservatism (sometimes referred to as "red Toryism") that characterized the Progressive Conservative Party may still resonate in the Canadian electorate. Until a full study of vote choice in 2015 is conducted, we cannot know whether weak Conservatives deserted the party, or whether the Liberal victory was a result of coordination among left-wing voters. Nonetheless, the results presented here, as well as the outcome of the 2015 election, suggest that the Conservative Party went far, but not all the way, towards uniting right-wing support among Canadians between 2004 and 2011.

REFERENCES

Aldrich, John H. 1995. *Why Parties? The Origin and Transformation of Political Parties in America.* Chicago: University of Chicago Press. http://dx.doi.org/10.7208/chicago/9780226012773.001.0001.

Bélanger, Éric, and Jean-François Godbout. 2010. "Why Do Parties Merge? The Case of the Conservative Party of Canada." *Parliamentary Affairs* 63 (1): 41–65. http://dx.doi.org/10.1093/pa/gsp041.

Bélanger, Éric, and Laura B. Stephenson. 2010. "Parties and Partisans: The Influence of Ideology and Brokerage on the Durability of Partisanship in

Canada." In *Voting Behaviour in Canada*, edited by Cameron D. Anderson and Laura B. Stephenson, 107–36. Vancouver: UBC Press.

Bickerton, James, Alain-G. Gagnon, and Patrick J. Smith. 1999. *Ties That Bind: Parties and Voters in Canada*. Don Mills, ON: Oxford University Press.

Bittner, Amanda and Royce Koop, eds. 2013. *Parties, Elections, and the Future of Canadian Politics*. Vancouver: UBC Press.

Blais, André, Elisabeth Gidengil, Richard Nadeau, and Neil Nevitte. 2001. "Measuring Party Identification: Britain, Canada, and the United States." *Political Behavior* 23 (1): 5–22. http://dx.doi.org/10.1023/A:1017665513905.

Bowler, Shaun, and David J. Lanoue. 1996. "New Party Challenges and Partisan Change: The Effects of Party Competition on Party Loyalty." *Political Behavior* 18 (4): 327–43. http://dx.doi.org/10.1007/BF01499092.

Bricker, Darrell, and John Ibbitson. 2013. *The Big Shift*. Toronto: HarperCollins.

Campbell, Angus, Philip E. Converse, Warren E. Miller, and Donald E. Stokes. 1960. *The American Voter*. New York: Wiley.

Carty, R. Kenneth. 2013. "Has Brokerage Politics Ended? Canadian Parties in the New Century." In Bittner and Koop, *Parties, Elections, and the Future of Canadian Politics*, 10–23.

Clarke, Harold D., Jane Jenson, Lawrence LeDuc, and Jon H. Pammett. 1979. *Political Choice in Canada*. Toronto: McGraw-Hill Ryerson.

– 1984. *Absent Mandate: The Politics of Discontent in Canada*. Toronto: Gage.

– 1991. *Absent Mandate: Interpreting Change in Canadian Elections*. 2nd ed. Toronto: Gage.

– 1996. *Absent Mandate: Canadian Electoral Politics in an Era of Restructuring*. 3rd ed. Toronto: Gage.

Clarke, Harold D., Allan Kornberg, and Thomas J. Scotto. 2009. *Making Political Choices: Canada and the United States*. Toronto: University of Toronto Press.

Denver, David, and Hugh Bochel. 1994. "Merger or Bust: Whatever Happened to Members of the SDP?" *British Journal of Political Science* 24 (3): 403–17. http://dx.doi.org/10.1017/S0007123400006918.

Ellis, Faron, and Peter Woolstencroft. 2004. "New Conservatives, Old Realities: The 2004 Election Campaign." In Pammett and Dornan, *The Canadian General Election of 2004*, 66–105.

Farney, James, and David Rayside, eds. 2013. *Conservatism in Canada*. Toronto: University of Toronto Press.

Flanagan, Tom. 2001. "From Reform to the Canadian Alliance." In *Party Politics in Canada*, 8th ed., edited by Hugh G. Thorburn and Alan Whitehorn, 280–91. Toronto: Prentice-Hall.

Gidengil, Elisabeth, Neil Nevitte, André Blais, Joanna Everitt, and Patrick Fournier. 2012. *Dominance and Decline: Making Sense of Recent Canadian Elections*. Toronto: University of Toronto Press.

Godbout, Jean-François, Éric Bélanger, and Frédéric Mérand. 2015. "Uniting the Left? The Potential for an NDP-Liberal Party Merger." In *Reviving Social Democracy: The Near Death and Surprising Rise of the Federal NDP*, edited by David Laycock and Lynda Erickson, 257–79. Vancouver: University of British Columbia Press.

Golder, Sona N. 2006. *The Logic of Pre-Electoral Coalition Formation*. Columbus: Ohio State University Press.

Harmel, Robert, and Kenneth Janda. 1994. "An Integrated Theory of Party Goals and Party Change." *Journal of Theoretical Politics* 6 (3): 259–87. http://dx.doi.org/10.1177/0951692894006003001.

Harper, Stephen, and Peter MacKay. 2003. "Agreement-in-Principle on the Establishment of the Conservative Party of Canada." Ottawa.

Johnston, Richard. 1992. "Party Identification Measures in the Anglo-American Democracies: A National Survey Experiment." *American Journal of Political Science* 36 (2): 542–59. http://dx.doi.org/10.2307/2111490.

– 2013. "Situating the Canadian Case." In Bittner and Koop, *Parties, Elections, and the Future of Canadian Politics*, 284–307.

Kim, HeeMin. 1997. "Rational Choice Theory and Third World Politics: The 1990 Party Merger in Korea." *Comparative Politics* 30 (1): 83–100. http://dx.doi.org/10.2307/422194.

Koop, Royce, and Amanda Bittner. 2013. "Parties and Elections after 2011: The Fifth Canadian Party System?" In Bittner and Koop, *Parties, Elections, and the Future of Canadian Politics*, 308–31.

Kreuzer, Marcus, and Vello Pettai. 2003. "Patterns of Political Instability: Affiliation Patterns of Politicians and Voters in Post-Communist Estonia, Latvia and Lithuania." *Studies in Comparative International Development* 38 (2): 76–98. http://dx.doi.org/10.1007/BF02686269.

Laver, Michael, and Norman Schofield. 1998. *Multiparty Government: The Politics of Coalition in Europe*. Ann Arbor: University of Michigan Press. http://dx.doi.org/10.3998/mpub.8290.

Marland, Alex, and Tom Flanagan. 2015. "From Opposition to Government: Party Merger as a Step on the Road to Power." *Parliamentary Affairs* 68 (2): 272–90. http://dx.doi.org/10.1093/pa/gst015.

Meisel, John. 1963. "The Stalled Omnibus: Canadian Parties in the 1960s." *Social Research* 30 (3): 367–90.

Pammett, Jon H., and Christopher Dornan, eds. 2004. *The Canadian General Election of 2004*. Toronto: Dundurn.

Panebianco, Angelo. 1988. *Political Parties: Organization and Power*. New York: Cambridge University Press.

Scarrow, Howard A. 1965. "Distinguishing between Political Parties: The Case of Canada." *Midwest Journal of Political Science* 9 (1): 61–76. http://dx.doi.org/10.2307/2109214.

Schattschneider, E.E. 1942. *Party Government*. New York: Rinehart.

Scoffield, Heather, and Drew Fagan. 2004. "Clark Slams Harper, Calls Him Dangerous," *Globe and Mail*, 26 April.

Scotto, Thomas J., Laura B. Stephenson, and Allan Kornberg. 2004. "From a Two-Party-Plus to a One-Party-Plus? Ideology, Vote Choice, and Prospects for a Competitive Party System in Canada." *Electoral Studies* 23 (3): 463–83. http://dx.doi.org/10.1016/S0261-3794(03)00054-4.

Stevenson, H. Michael. 1987. "Ideology and Unstable Party Identification in Canada: Limited Rationality in a Brokerage Party System." *Canadian Journal of Political Science* 20 (4): 813–50. http://dx.doi.org/10.1017/S0008423900050423.

Turcotte, André. 2004. "Canadians Speak Out." In Pammett and Dornan, *The Canadian General Election of 2004*, 314–37.

Ware, Alan. 2009. *The Dynamics of Two-Party Politics: Party Structures and the Management of Competition*. New York: Oxford University Press. http://dx.doi.org/10.1093/acprof:oso/9780199564439.001.0001.

Appendix: CES Survey Questions Used to Create Attitudinal Variables

(Note: CPS stands for "campaign period survey," PES for "post-election survey," and MBS for "mail back survey.")

Left-Right Placement

Where do you place yourself in politics on a scale from 0 to 10, where 0 is left and 10 is right?
(In 2000, the question only had three answer options: left, right, or centre.)
MBS was used in 1997, 2004, 2008, and 2011, while CPS was used in 2000 and the Referendum survey in 1993 (not available in 2006).

Free Enterprise

People who don't get ahead should blame themselves, not the system.

PES was used for all elections except in 1993, where MBS was used.
When businesses make a lot of money, everyone benefits, including the
    poor.
PES was used for all elections except in 1993, where MBS was used.

Canada-U.S. Ties

Using the same scale, how do you feel about the United States?
PES was used for all elections.
Do you think Canada's ties with the United States should be much clos-
    er, somewhat closer, about the same, much distant, or much more
    distant?
*CPS was used for the 1993, 2004, and 2006 elections, and PES was used for
    the others.*

Moral Traditionalism

Do you think it should be very easy for women to get an abortion, quite
easy, quite difficult, or very difficult?
PES was used for all elections except in 1993, where CPS was used.
Society would be better off if more women stayed home with their
    children.
CPS was used for all elections except in 2008 and 2011, where PES was used.
Only people who are legally married should have children.
*CPS was used for the 1993 and 1997 elections, and MBS was used for the
    others (not available in 2006).*

Women

How much do you think should be done for women?
*CPS was used for the 1993, 2000, and 2004 elections, and PES was used for
    the others.*

Outgroups (Immigrants and Racial Minorities)

Should Canada admit more or less immigrants?
CPS was used for all elections except in 2008 and 2011, where PES was used.
How do you feel about racial minorities?
PES was used for all elections (not available in 2000).

What should be done for racial minorities?
CPS was used for all elections except in 2008 and 2011, where PES was used.

Indigenous Canadians

Do you think that Indigenous Canadians are better off, worse off than, or about the same compared to other Canadians?
CPS was used in 1997 and 2000, and PES was used in 2004 (not available in the other four elections).
How do you feel about Indigenous Canadians?
PES was used for all elections.

Regional Alienation

In general, does the federal government treat your province better, worse, or about the same?
CPS was used for the 1997, 2000, 2004, and 2006 elections, and PES was used for the others (not available in 1993).

Quebec (ROC Only)

How do you feel about Quebec?
PES was used for all elections.
How much should be done for Quebec?
CPS was used for all elections except in 2008 and 2011, where PES was used (not available in 1993).

Quebec Sovereignty (QC Only)

Do you think the French language is threatened in Quebec?
CPS was used in 1993; PES was used in 1997, 2000, and 2006; MBS was used in 2011 (not available in 2004 and 2008).
If Quebec separates, the situation of French in the province will get better, get worse, or stay the same?
PES was used for all elections (not available in 1993).
There is no reason to have a sovereignist party in Ottawa.
PES was used in 1997, 2000, and 2011, and CPS was used in 2004, 2006, and 2008 (not available in 1993).

4 Private over Public: A Conservative Approach to Interest Advocacy

NICOLE GOODMAN

There are numerous ways for citizens to exert their voices politically in a democratic society. Many of these are individual acts such as voting or writing a letter to an elected official; others, however, are collective actions by groups of individuals seeking to bring about change. Some groups are concerned with the enactment of specific legislative or policy change, whereas others take the shape of movements seeking broader attitudinal change. Whatever their end goal, groups are an important component of civil society. They work to advance specific interests of societal groups and serve as intermediaries between the state and civil society. Although Parliament and Cabinet represent the traditional instruments of policymaking, the content of policy is often influenced by the lobbying efforts of specific "interest" groups. The amount of influence groups wield over the development and content of policy, however, largely depends on the political context and the government of the day. This chapter examines the topic of interest groups and the relationship between these organizations and federal conservative parties since 1993. Specifically, it evaluates which groups win and which ones lose based on the electoral fortune of conservatives parties. Generally, the Canadian polity has seen groups with private economic interests succeed in influencing policy under the leadership of the Conservative government, while groups that advocate for collective goods have been far less successful in realizing their policy goals.

A number of questions are raised in the literature regarding the influence of interest groups. This chapter examines the relationship of interest groups with Canada's federal conservative parties since 1993. Specifically, it addresses key questions posed by academics, practitioners, and the media that relate to the following three themes:

1 Opportunities for political participation: Have conservative parties been open to interest group interaction, or closed off from it?
2 Legislation and policy frameworks: Who is heard? Which groups win and which ones lose? Whose voice exerts an influence on policy and which ones are left out? What tactics do private and public interest groups employ to influence policy?
3 Implications for Canadian democracy: What does the unequal influence of some groups in policymaking mean for Canadian democracy and the representation of interests?

Many of these questions are more easily answered since the party took power in 2006, but the historical relationship between the Reform and Canadian Alliance and interest groups is important, since certain groups helped facilitate Stephen Harper's rise to power. The history also highlights a telling conflict between private and public interests, and what constitutes a "special interest."

Interest Groups

Groups that wish to advance their interests by influencing public policy without seeking to govern, or taking responsibility for the management of government, are referred to synonymously in the literature as pressure groups (Key 1964; Pross 1975, 1992), advocacy groups (Young and Everitt 2004), and interest groups (Berry 1978; Montpetit 2009; Newman and Tanguay 2002; Thorburn 2007). This chapter refers to these groups as *interest groups*, given that they seek to advance or advocate for a particular interest or set of interests. Some of these interests serve a selective group in society, whereas others deliver collective goods. In this way, the classification of interest groups can be further broken down into the categories of private and public.

Private groups are composed of individuals who seek economic benefits for a select group. These groups strive to influence policy to achieve *selective benefits*, which means that the benefit derived is often exclusively for their membership alone. Economic or professional associations are typically characterized as groups representing private interests and are usually well organized (Berry 1978; Olson 1965). Examples include the Canadian Association of Petroleum Producers, whose goal is to advance the interests of the Canadian petroleum industry, and the Canadian Bankers' Association, which advocates for the interests of Canadian banks.

Public groups, by comparison, typically do not have an economic self-interest and advocate for policy changes that benefit people outside their immediate membership. These are often referred to as *diffuse benefits*, since they result in advantages for the wider community (Berry 1978; Olson 1965). An example of a public interest group is Mothers Against Drunk Driving, an organization that creates awareness about driving under the influence and encourages people to not consume alcohol and drive. Although in some cases the interests of private- and public-oriented groups may overlap, generally the private/public distinction is a helpful categorization to understand whether the beneficiaries of advocacy fall outside of group membership or exclusively within it. This is particularly important for understanding whose voices are heard in the policymaking arena.

Aside from trying to influence policy and provide an outlet for citizens to express their opinions, interest groups have several functions. Groups often serve as an important source of technical and political information for government. They seek to affect electoral outcomes by providing endorsements and political donations, and helping to mobilize voters for candidates who support their cause. They also work to shape public opinion on specific issues through information campaigns and other outreach efforts. Finally, interest groups can play a role in organized protest, and sometimes litigation (Dyck 2011).

Generally, these functions present a number of benefits for society, namely the role interest groups play as a mechanism for collective expression. Groups can serve as a participatory channel when there is not one and can provide a vehicle for points of view that are not reflected in conventional institutions. They can also facilitate more comprehensive public policy, and their presence can improve government responsiveness to citizen interests. Lastly, a plethora of diverse interest groups is a sign of a healthy democratic culture (Young and Everitt 2004).

Yet while interest groups can be beneficial and enhance democracy in Canada, they can also hinder democratic debate, particularly if they have unequal resources. A group with greater financial support, for example, has an advantage over a group with less money and might have a better chance of gaining access to government. Other considerations such as the size of a group, its cohesiveness, organizational skills, the nature of the issue it is advancing, and its leadership can also improve or diminish a group's chances of gaining access to government. Unequal access can be problematic if groups advocating for selective benefits are being included in policy discussions and those speaking for collective ones are left out. If only certain interest groups have a say in policy debates, these discussions can become limited to a particular perspective, leaving out other critical voices. If some interest groups have a disproportionate say in the development of public policy, it can raise questions about whether policymaking is being informed largely by elected members or unelected officials.

Have Federal Conservative Parties Been Open to Interest Group Interaction, or Closed Off from It?

1993–2006: Interest Groups and the Conservatives in Opposition

The story of the Conservatives prior to forming government does not neatly apply to the questions guiding this chapter, but it sets the stage for future interactions between interest groups and the political party. Some groups played significant roles in conservative parties' formation, party leadership races, and electoral success. In the case of the Reform Party, interest groups were crucial to the party's establishment, guiding its constitution, and developing its agenda. Moreover, groups played an important role in uniting the right and supporting Stephen Harper's pursuit of the Canadian Alliance leadership. This support continued through the merger of the Alliance and the Progressive Conservatives in December 2003 and creation of the Conservative Party of Canada, and the federal elections of 2004 and 2006 when the party formed a minority government.

The Reform Party had an important, yet antagonistic relationship with interest groups. On the one hand the party was founded on interest advocacy, and its constitution and much of its duration rested on interest group support. On the other hand, the party was wary of other special interests and their influence (see chapter 10 in this volume). Part of its identity was in fact rooted in attacking these groups and their interests. From its beginning the Reform Party was never meant to be a long-standing political party, but was created to serve an immediate political goal – to advocate for Western interests. As Tom Flanagan (1995, 23) observes, the temporary nature of the Reform Party is evident from the phrasing of the party's constitution, which stipulates, "This Constitution shall become null and void, and the Party shall cease to exist, on November 1st, 2000 A.D., unless this Constitution is re-enacted in its present or amended form by a two-thirds majority of the delegates to a Party Assembly held before that date." According to founder Preston

Manning, the party was based on a particular method, a populist approach designed to advocate for the interests of a specific geographic group, and not on ideology (ibid.).

Many of the party's ideals were founded on the "reform tradition" in Canadian politics, which the party constitution cites as being represented by Western protest groups, interest groups, and other protest initiatives that sought to remedy injustices and inequities in the West and elsewhere (Flanagan 1995, 21). The origins of the tradition emerged from reform parties and groups in Nova Scotia and Upper and Lower Canada in the early 1800s that fought against elite control and pushed for government institutions that were more representative and responsible (ibid.).

While the party's constitution and guiding principles came from a tradition forged by smaller parties and groups dedicated to promoting these interests, its agenda was as much a product of challenging other "special interests." This speaks to the Reform tradition and the "social antagonism between two groups, identified as 'the elites' and 'the people'" (Laycock 2002, 56). Developed by the Reform Party, and carried on by the Canadian Alliance, this special interest category included groups that accepted state subsidies to fund their activities. Reformers believed that government should not financially support "special interests" and that instead the resources and opportunities available to these groups should be left to the vagaries of the free market. According to David Laycock (57) this encompassed "feminist lobby groups, Native organizations, ethnic and cultural minority groups, state-aided arts and cultural organizations, providers of state-subsidized legal assistance to the poor and traditionally disadvantaged, the management and employees of virtually all Crown corporations and state agencies, and all public sector unions."

Reform Party members further believed that the voices of many of these groups should be excluded from public policy. Ironically, it was seen as acceptable for groups that worked to benefit the party, such as the National Citizens Coalition and the Fraser Institute, a right-wing think tank, to play a role in shaping public opinion on key issues. Attacks on "special interest" groups became a permanent feature of the party's approach and messaging, and was largely a factor in the successful Canadian Alliance leadership campaign of Stockwell Day in 2000. The strategy to protest interests characterized the new right and may have set the tone for the current Conservative Party of Canada's tendency to favour private interests over public ones. Overall, voices representing interests that the Reform Party and Canadian Alliance opposed were left out, while those of groups supporting big business were included.

While the notion of "special interests" has framed conservative development since 1993, certain interest groups have played an important role in bringing the Conservatives to power, especially providing the media messaging and financial wherewithal for Stephen Harper's path from president of the National Citizens Coalition to prime minister of Canada. Serving as a Reform MP, Harper became disillusioned with the party and decided not to run again in 1997. Instead, he took up a position leading the National Citizens Coalition (NCC), a conservative interest group that represents free market principles. Harper was able to use the group to create roadblocks for Reform party leader Preston Manning when the two did not agree on the creation of a united party of the right. The NCC also provided Harper with the support necessary to defeat Stockwell Day as leader of the Canadian Alliance.

In 1999, when Preston Manning sought to replace the Reform Party with a united alternative, the NCC spent $20,000 on a poll to show that party factions were deeply divided. The group strategically released this information to the media a few days before party members were to meet and vote on creating a new party. A new party was eventually formed in 2000, however, and the Reform Party became the Canadian Alliance, which was a blend of reform and progressive conservative principles. In 2001, amidst internal and external pressures pushing Stockwell Day out, Harper left his position at the NCC to run for the Alliance leadership. After his departure the NCC became a Stephen Harper "leadership machine" producing supportive propaganda and fundraising mail-outs (Nicholls 2009, 120–5). Despite the fact that the NCC was supposed to be a non-partisan interest group, it became a pseudo headquarters for Harper volunteers. As Tom Flanagan (2007, 46) points out, money was the biggest issue for Harper's leadership contest. In response, the NCC mobilized and issued a series of fundraising letters, raising over one million dollars in political donations and solving the financial woes of the Harper campaign (Flanagan 2007; Nicholls 2009).

Support from the NCC continued into the 2004 federal election. Legislation introduced by the Chrétien government made this election the first where spending limits on political advertising were imposed on third party groups such as the NCC – specifically, non-party entities. Groups were required to register with Elections Canada prior to releasing any ads. The NCC opposed the new "gag laws" and navigated around the legislation by taking advantage of the fact that many Canadians do not distinguish between federal and provincial political parties. The group issued an ad targeting Ontario Premier Dalton McGuinty and asked Canadians to "Send the Liberals a Message" – a strategic manoeuvre to rally support for Harper. By finding a loophole to the federal law, the NCC hoped to translate voter disdain for McGuinty provincially into votes for Harper federally.

The NCC, however, was not the only group to support Harper and his rise to power. The Canadian Taxpayers Federation (CTF) and Citizens Centre for Freedom and Democracy contributed either by providing direct support or through favourable media. At times throughout Harper's leadership campaign, officials at the CTF were instrumental in providing strategic advice (Flanagan 2007). Observing what happened to group members when they spoke out against decisions of the party starkly illustrates the allegiance of these groups to the conservatives.

In 2006, the NCC responded to the Conservative budget unfavourably, openly suggesting it was more a product of Liberal or NDP principles than Conservative ones. After a series of negative comments about the budget and the party in the press, the NCC vice-president and author of the comments, Gerry Nicholls, was fired from the organization without an explanation after twenty-two years of service (Nicholls 2009, 155). While there is no conclusive evidence confirming that Nicholls's critical assessments cost him the position, shortly after his departure the NCC took a much more moderate stance on the budget and the party's legislative business.

During the rest of their time in government, Conservative policy diverged from many of the more right-wing principles advanced by the NCC, but this was a manoeuvre largely to secure power. According to former party strategists like Flanagan, the Conservatives' policy plan is one of incrementalism, whereby the party slowly makes inroads on selective items in the conservative agenda. Despite the incremental approach, the party catered to the interests of big business and resource development while occupying a majority in Parliament. One notable example is the conflict between the advocacy efforts of environmental groups and oil and gas associations and lobby groups. Preferential treatment for private groups is also well illustrated through the Conservatives' interaction with the Canadian Bankers' Association and affinity for evangelical Christian organizations. Efforts geared at the marginalization of public groups, by comparison, can be seen through the

Conservatives' treatment of Indigenous groups, women's groups, and groups advocating for Canadian content in broadcasting.

2006–2015: Interest Groups and the Conservatives in Government

Hugh Thorburn (2007) observes that the lobbying relationship between interest groups and government in Canada has historically favoured private interests, regardless of political stripe. He argues that except for the United States, the power of business lobby groups over the Canadian state is greater than other industrialized countries. The Conservative Party in government (2006–15) maintained this tradition. Their election was accompanied by a political climate in which certain private interest groups experienced unequal access to government and had their voices disproportionately reflected in public policy. Public groups, by contrast, were mostly relegated to the periphery, some even further marginalized by structural impediments introduced by the Conservative government in an attempt to weaken their voices in the public arena. This trend became more pronounced when the party formed a majority government in 2011. Interest advocacy focused on oil and gas development, banking, and mining was favoured, while groups representing environmental protections and equality issues such as Indigenous rights and women's issues were marginalized. The open favouritism of oil and gas groups over organizations that seek to protect and sustain Canada's natural environment characterizes the Conservative government's approach to public groups.

Who Is Heard? Whose Voice Exerts Influence on Policy and Which Ones Are Left Out?

Private Groups

In January 2013, documents accessed through an Access to Information Request revealed a letter addressed to Minister of the Environment Peter Kent and Natural Resources Minister Joe Oliver written by several oil and gas lobby groups.[1] The letter pointed to key pieces of environmental

---

1   These groups include the Canadian Association of Petroleum Producers, the Canadian Energy Pipeline Association, the Canadian Fuels Association, and the Canadian Gas Association. Together, they formed a combined energy lobby called the Energy Framework Initiative.

legislation and regulatory guidelines that describe the approval process of energy projects as outdated or prohibitive for energy development. Six pieces of legislation were identified as requiring modification because they advanced a philosophy of prohibiting harm "rather than enabling responsible outcomes," including the Canadian Environmental Assessment Act, the National Energy Board Act, the Species-at-Risk Act, the Fisheries Act, the Migratory Birds Convention Act, and the Navigable Water Protection Act (Energy Framework Initiative 2011). Within ten months of receiving the letter the Conservative government introduced legislation to either repeal the acts or considerably weaken their environmental protections.

Many of these proposed changes came into force as a result of the omnibus budget bill C-38, otherwise known as the Jobs, Growth, and Long-term Prosperity Act.[2] Despite unanimous opposition to the bill in the House of Commons from other parties and public disapproval, the Conservative majority passed the bill, significantly altering the Environmental Assessment Act, National Energy Board Act, and Fisheries Act. Changes to the Environmental Assessment Act, for example, eliminated the requirement for many smaller environmental assessments, shortened the time for assessments, and downloaded additional assessment requirements to the provinces and territories (Hemmera 2013).

The bill also made specific modifications to the National Energy Board (NEB), the federal agency that oversees and approves international and intergovernmental energy projects in Canada. Changes were made to restrict public participation in the NEB's hearing of proposed projects, to shorten the timelines in which projects could be reviewed, and to shift decision-making power for larger projects from the agency to Cabinet. With respect to public participation, for example, before Bill C-38 any Canadian citizen or group could write a Letter of Comment to express an opinion in an NEB hearing. Amendments to the legislation, however, required that any party wishing to participate, even by letter, must complete a twelve-page application to be vetted by the NEB, who is responsible for approving participation of suitable applicants. Furthermore, changes no longer required the NEB to hold a public hearing for proposed pipeline projects less than forty kilometres long. Finally, adjustments to the decision-making process shifted power

---

2 Nearly six months later, the Conservatives introduced another omnibus bill, Bill C-45, which weakened provisions in the Navigable Waters Protection Act.

from the agency to Cabinet for energy projects over forty kilometres in length at a time when many large energy projects were about to be brought before the board, such as the Northern Gateway proposal.

Though members of the Conservative Party claimed these changes were part of a program to achieve responsible resource development, a 2012 report produced by the Polaris Institute revealed that since 2008 there had been a 463 per cent increase in meetings between government and oil and gas lobbies than with environmental organizations. Not all of these meetings were held with industry associations or groups themselves. Some were convened with lobbyists – individuals hired to influence the government to design, introduce, and pass legislation that is favourable for the individual(s) who engaged the lobbyist. The disparity in the number of meetings suggests private groups had unequal access to government compared to their public counterparts. Furthermore, the fact that specific legislative and policy changes requested by industry interest groups were put into place less than a year after they were solicited raises questions about the influence and power of private groups over decision-making.

The frequency with which government met with officials representing private interests, however, was not restricted to oil and gas. The banking industry, through the Canadian Bankers Association, had the second-most encounters with politicians and bureaucrats in 2012, at 169 meetings (Vongdouangchanh 2013). Banks received special treatment under the Conservative government through an unpublicized bailout of $114 billion dollars between September 2008 and August 2010 to offset the impact of the 2008 recession. In the 2013 budget a special "bail-in" provision was also written in for banks. In the event that important banks experienced a worrisome depletion of capital, they would be able to convert liabilities (such as customer deposits) into capital. Legally, this provides banks with the option of drawing upon citizen savings when levels of capital are low (Macdonald 2012). This change is a legal measure many would argue is not in the "public" interest.

While there is no established link between the frequency of meetings with government and the outcomes listed here, the large number of meetings that were accommodated by government officials, and the fact that some significant policy decisions favouring industry were made, supports the theory that the Conservatives have an affinity for business interests. It also suggests that the legislative and policymaking system is characterized by unequal access to government, which produces unequal policy outcomes.

Aside from the interests of business, Conservatives forged a relationship with other special interests, namely fundamentalist Christian organizations. Stephen Harper appointed many former Christian evangelical lobbyists to top positions in his government. In 2009, for example, controversy stirred over the presence of Christian organizations in the PMO when Harper promoted Darrel Reid, former head of Focus on the Family Canada, as his deputy chief of staff, and filled the post of director of policy with Paul Wilson, former executive director of Trinity Western (a Christian-focused university in British Columbia) (Diebel 2009). In addition to the hiring of political staffers from the ranks of these organizations, other appointments were given to evangelical faithfuls. Jason Kenney, for example, appointed the former director of public policy for the Evangelical Fellowship, Douglas Cryer, to the Immigration and Refugee Board; while Preston Manning and others were given appointments on boards responsible for shaping science policy. In her analysis of the rise of Christian nationalism in Canada, Marci McDonald (2011, 46–8) explains how the Conservative government provided the religious right with historic access to Ottawa. One example is the allocation of $26 million in funding to private Christian colleges, which was unheard of. This relationship raises questions about the separation of church and state and private interest influence on the Conservative government. Conservative actions that marginalized groups advocating for public interests reinforces the importance of asking these questions.

Public Groups

The Conservatives' time in government was characterized by an antagonistic relationship with groups representing public interests, particularly environmental groups and those advocating for equal rights. In addition to passing legislation considered unfavourable for these groups, or cutting public funding in their specific areas, the government attempted to marginalize many of them and cast doubt on their credibility. In February 2012, for example, Conservative Senator Nicole Eaton launched a formal inquiry into donations to environmental groups from non-domestic sources, claiming "interference of foreign foundations in Canada's domestic affairs" (Raj 2012). The language used by Conservative members in the House of Commons and Senate framed the issue of Alberta oil development as a Canadian process and decision that should be free from foreign involvement, yet the inquiry did not contest money invested in Canadian oil and gas interest groups by offshore oil companies or other interested foreign parties. Tax returns filed with the Canada Revenue Agency (CRA) reveal that only one of the ten Canadian organizations that reported receiving the most foreign donations is a conservation group, Ducks Unlimited. The others included groups focused on international aid such as Care Canada and World Vision International, and universities (Canadian Press 2012).

In addition, Bill C-38 imposed provisions that granted the Canada Revenue Agency greater powers to enforce the spending limits of charitable organizations, primarily to ensure that groups did not use more than 10 per cent of their budget for political activities such as protests. Amidst economic recovery and cuts in funding to government programs, the Conservatives committed an additional $8 million in the 2013 budget to help facilitate enforcement. Although this provision applies to all groups with charitable status, the Conservatives were particularly vocal about the importance of enforcement for environmental groups, given their public protest of bitumen extraction in Alberta and public challenges to changes in environmental legislation. The goal of the inquiry, and expanded CRA powers, was to limit environmental groups' eligibility for charitable donations and call their legitimacy into question during a time of public debate regarding environmental protection and energy development. It was also a strategic move that allowed certain voices to set the agenda and frame the energy policy debate.

A final effort to marginalize environmental groups was the alleged attempt of the Prime Minister's Office (PMO) to cut the funding of the Canadian group ForestEthics while it was a legally registered intervenor in the NEB's hearing of Enbridge's proposed Northern Gateway project.[3] In January 2012, an employee of ForestEthics, Andrew Frank, came forward as a whistle-blower. In a sworn affidavit, Frank claimed that the PMO had threatened Tides Canada, a funding agency of Forest-Ethics, stating that if donations to the group were not cut there would be consequences, notably that the government would challenge the status of Tides as a charitable organization. In addition, the PMO expressed the view that ForestEthics could be considered both "an enemy of the Government of Canada" and "an enemy of the people of Canada" (Frank 2012).

---

3 This was the last energy project reviewed under the old provisions. The Line 9B pipeline is the first project under the new changes.

Aside from strategic attempts to publicly dampen the concerns of environmental organizations, the Conservatives made similar efforts with Indigenous and women's groups. As part of the Idle No More movement, for example, there were calls for the government to revisit the living conditions of Indigenous communities and the changes to land provisions included in the 2013 budget bill. Much of this debate centred on Attawapiskat Chief Theresa Spence, who went on a hunger strike in protest to obtain a meeting with the prime minister and governor general. Just days before the meeting was to take place, however, financial audits were leaked by the Department of Aboriginal Affairs and Northern Development, which alleged mismanagement of finances in Attawapiskat. The release of these documents changed the tone of the debate and shifted the focus away from the actual issues Indigenous communities were experiencing to headlines suggesting the RCMP (and not Stephen Harper) should be visiting chiefs (Levant 2013).

Another example is the Conservative government's refusal to launch an inquiry into the more than 1,100 Indigenous women who have gone missing or been murdered since 1980. Despite repeated efforts by human rights groups to put pressure on the Conservatives to investigate this problem further, Harper publicly stated that the government felt the matter had been studied sufficiently and denied social elements may be at play (Chase and Galloway 2014). In their pre-election budget (2015) the government did allot $25 million towards stopping violence against Indigenous women and girls, though this financial commitment did nothing to address the murders themselves or the causes of violence and appeared to be a political strategy for the 2015 election (Rennie 2014).

Finally, the Conservative government's treatment of women's groups can also be characterized as unfavourable. In its first year in office the government ended the Court Challenges Program, which funded litigation by minority groups that challenged discriminatory laws. The national childcare program, which had been fought for by women for years, was also eliminated. In addition, in the spring of 2010, funding was cut to fourteen women's organizations as part of a $5 billion reduction to Status of Women Canada programs. Many of the affected groups had publicly spoken out against the government's anti-abortion comments in the months prior, and accusations were made that the reduction in funding was in retaliation. Furthermore, when groups criticized the government's decision to not fund abortion as part of foreign aid,

Conservative Senator Nancy Ruth publicly advised them to keep quiet or risk government "backlash" (Delacourt 2010). The women's group, Ad Hoc Coalition for Women's Equality and Human Rights, referred to the government's actions as an "attack on democracy in Canada" (Brennan 2010). Other groups, such as the Canadian Research Institute for the Advancement of Women, accused the government of trying to silence women's interests (ibid.) In her analysis of progress achieved by women's groups in Canada, Sylvia Bashevkin (2012, 1) argued that under the Conservatives' "crucial equality markers" were moved "backward in a deliberately under-the-radar manner." Though there was not the same open effort to discredit women's organizations as with environmental and Indigenous groups, significant changes were made that counter women's advocacy efforts for equality.

Taken together, these actions fostered a culture of intimidation among groups and citizens for speaking out against government business or political priorities. Many organizations advocating for public issues that were not clearly represented at the political level were quieted. With respect to political priorities, the Conservatives used an array of tools to weaken or oppose critical viewpoints with the goal of controlling the narrative of key policy topics. These examples further illustrate that the Conservatives went beyond merely closing themselves off from the interests of these groups. In some cases the government raised questions regarding group legitimacy and enacted structural measures to harm their credibility. In many ways, the Conservative Party sought to frame these groups as radical or irresponsible to discredit their agendas and reframe the debate to focus on controversy with the organizations themselves, rather than on the issue at hand. The Conservatives' time in government can be characterized by the facilitation of an unequal opportunity structure for private and public interests, providing industry groups with disproportionate access to government and an unequal impact on public policy.

What Tactics Do These Groups Employ?

Looking specifically at the interactions of oil and gas groups and environmental associations with the Conservatives in government, two specific strategies advanced the interests of private groups. These include the more frequent institutionalized participation of private groups, and the creation of a non-profit organization aimed at reframing the oil debate and shifting public opinion. These techniques allowed oil and gas groups to target both the internal ecosystem of government and the broader external environment.

Private groups are more likely to be registered as lobbyists or to work with hired lobbyists. The frequency with which oil and gas groups and their agents used formal channels outnumbered environmental groups by 80 per cent. According to the Office of the Commissioner of Lobbying of Canada's *Registry of Lobbyists*, eight industry associations and twenty-seven oil and gas companies, or their representatives, registered 2,733 communications with the government from July 2008 to November 2012. The most active group during this period was the Canadian Association of Petroleum Producers (CAPP) with 563 communications. Environmental groups, by contrast, had a more limited formal presence. Only eleven environmental groups were listed as formally registered (seven of which were active from November 2011 to November 2012) and there were 485 logged communications during the four years. To put this into perspective, CAPP logged 563 communications during this period, while the Climate Action Network, one of the biggest Canadian environmental organizations, registered only 6 (Cayley-Daoust and Girard 2012).

Further analysis of these communications reveals that private oil and gas groups and lobbyists had better access to senior bureaucrats and elected officials, especially ministers with key portfolios such as Finance, Immigration, Natural Resources, and the Environment. Better access to high-level officeholders indicates that these groups had more opportunities to influence government priorities and policy, and raises questions regarding whether the system favoured these private groups. During the Conservative majority government, the frequency of meetings between elected officials and private interest groups increased dramatically. In fact, many oil and gas associations and corporations doubled their formal interactions with government between 2010 and 2011 (Cayley-Daoust and Girard 2012). This suggests that oil and gas groups were inclined to interact with government through institutionalized mechanisms. It also implies an asymmetry in access to government.

Part of this disparity may be explained by the fact that private groups are often better organized and are part of business and professional networks that have deeper pockets. Certainly in this instance, with lobbying efforts being sponsored by some of the largest and most profitable companies in the world, inequality in financial backing is a consideration. Seven of the oil and gas companies represented by

Canadian interest groups occupy spots in the top 10 of *Fortune* magazine's 500 largest global companies. In 2012, the seven companies reported combined revenues of $2.534 trillion, a sum that is greater than the GDP of Russia (Cayley-Daoust and Girard 2012, 3). While registry data indicate that private companies make use of formal channels more frequently and often have advantages in access, the efforts and success of the oil and gas lobby dwarf those of other private associations representing prominent industries such as mining, the automotive industry, and forestry. Abundant financial resources, the fact that many oil and gas companies sought to expand and develop new projects, and a party willing to listen likely explain this pattern.

Aside from participation through institutionalized mechanisms, private groups also sponsored a bold campaign to reframe Canada's oil development and exportation through the creation of a registered non-profit called EthicalOil (EO). By doing this, they took a debate that was about selective benefits and sought to make it about collective benefits by focusing on morality. The notion of "ethical" oil comes from a book by Canadian lawyer, lobbyist, and former *Sun* news correspondent Ezra Levant, *Ethical Oil: The Case for Canada's Oil Sands*. Levant makes the argument that we should exploit oil development in Canada and export it to other countries since Canada is not responsible for widespread human rights abuses, as are many other countries that are large producers of oil. The book garnered a lot of attention, and EthicalOil was subsequently created to help spread the message. Immigration Minister Jason Kenney's former communications director, Alykhan Velshi, left his position with the government to write a blog and provide content to the EO website to promote the organization and attract attention to its cause (Nikiforuk 2011). EO took part in media discussions framing the decision to exploit Canada's bitumen reserves as a Canadian one and not something that "foreign-funded [environmental] radicals" should have a say in. Not only was the exploitation of bitumen framed as a "Canadian choice," it was positioned as being akin to the production of fair trade coffee – both are political labels intended to elicit a particular response.

In the spring and summer of 2012, EthicalOil focused the debate on the development of the Northern Gateway pipeline, a project that proposed to ship bitumen from Alberta to British Columbia, where it was to be taken by tankers and exported to China. The project was widely denounced by a majority of the public, especially in British Columbia. A plebiscite held in Kitimat (the community where the bitumen would transfer from pipeline to tanker) in April 2014 showed opposition from

58.4 per cent of the town, while 41.6 per cent supported development. The rationale for Northern Gateway, according to EO proponents, was its focus on oil development in Canada instead of purchase from foreign countries. Production in Canada is considered more "ethical," given that human rights abuses are not an issue. Ironically, the Northern Gateway proposal was to ship the extracted bitumen to China, a country that has a record for human rights abuses.

At the critical time when public evaluations of the project were forming, EO was responsible for a myriad of messages intended to shape public opinion on the issue. Simultaneous messaging from senior government officials, namely Prime Minister Stephen Harper, Natural Resources Minister Joe Oliver, and Environment Minister Peter Kent, echoed the same language, references, and framing. The fact that the government and a non-profit, positioned to look out for the welfare of Canadians during an economic downturn, delivered the same messages served to shape the nature of the public debate to the ethics and morality behind oil development instead of the potential environmental implications. Environmental groups fought back, countering with their own messaging and social media campaigns that included letter blitzes and public petitions. They, however, did not have government echoing their communications. Although many media outlets voiced concern, they were powerless against a majority government with an agenda to support big business and relegate environmental concerns to the periphery.

It is difficult to assess how successful this approach was in shaping public opinion, but it was a strategic tactic to frame thinking and discussion regarding the development of Alberta bitumen and call the legitimacy of environmental groups into question. Together, the institutionalized lobbying and attempts by oil and gas to influence government policy on the inside, while also seeking to set the agenda and shape public opinion on the outside, was a powerful strategy to ensure selective interests were represented in policymaking.

Conservatives Leaving Government

Ironically, the October 2015 election campaign, which culminated with the Conservatives being unseated as the ruling party and the Liberal Party led by Justin Trudeau forming government, was guided largely by many of the interest groups discussed in this chapter. First, many of the groups that saw themselves or their issues of interest as being oppressed or ignored under the Conservative tenure worked hard to see a different party form government. Some groups pooled resources to form larger entities to fund negative Conservative advertising. Engage Canada, for example, funded by more than thirty unions and centre-left interest groups, formed months before the campaign to run pre-election advertising against Stephen Harper (Radwanski 2015). A total of 112 groups, including an Indigenous advocacy organization, also registered individually as third parties with Elections Canada to advertise, many of them hoping to influence voters to support a Conservative opponent in the 2015 federal election (Postmedia News 2015). Second, leaders of groups (such as chiefs of First Nations) encouraged members not to support the Conservative Party and formed new groups to mobilize electors, or to promote strategic voting (Galloway 2015). Rally the First Nations Vote, Leadnow's Vote Together campaign, and Strategic Voting are some of the groups that advocated voting to unseat the incumbent government. On the other hand, some groups that were negatively affected by the Conservative regime stayed quiet during the election, notably environmental groups. Legislation passed by the Conservative government that permits charities to spend a maximum of 10 per cent of their time on non-partisan political activities caused many of these groups not to overtly engage in the campaign to avoid compromising not-for-profit status.

In support of the Conservative Party, one major group called HarperPAC formed, but dissolved soon after its emergence, given that it had not sought permission from the party. While the Conservatives preferred donations to go through the party directly, the theme of special interests played a role in party strategy. In an attempt to win votes near the end of the campaign, for example, Stephen Harper publicly warned that Liberal leader Justin Trudeau was an elitist who would prioritize special interests over the needs of "ordinary Canadians" (Chase 2015). The irony of this argument is that the Conservative approach while in government was also focused on special interests. Though it is unclear the extent to which interests influenced the election outcome, groups certainly played a role in attempting to mobilize and influence voters.

Conclusion: What Are the Democratic Implications for the Canadian Polity?

During their time in government (2006–15) the Conservatives favoured private interests, most notably oil and gas groups, corporations, and their hired lobbyists. The legacy of support for big business may have been inherited from the Reform Party. It could also be, however, that favouring selective interests is part of the tradition of Canadian politics. While the influence of private groups in the political and economic context may have been particularly strong at the time (e.g., oil and gas), previous examinations of interest group relations with government cite similar findings, regardless of the political stripe of the governing party. Hugh Thorburn's (2007, 405–6) analysis of interest group interaction between the Mulroney government (1984–93) and Chrétien and Martin governments (1993–2006) also notes that "big business-dominated interest groups and their hired guns" led the activity. Regardless of the origins of the pattern, such schemes present problems for the quality of democracy in Canada.

For one, the Conservatives' openness to interaction with private interest groups and reluctance to engage in relations with public-oriented associations points to an asymmetry in access to government. This resulted in less inclusive policy consultation, left a range of public voices unrepresented in the setting of political priorities, and raises questions about representativeness. Also worrisome were the deliberate attempts of the Conservatives to marginalize the voices of these groups through legislative action, a Senate inquiry, media framing and messaging, leaked financial information, and intimidation and threats. These tactics prompt concern about the extent to which the Canadian government governs in the democratic interests of the people. Shutting out these groups can have negative impacts on citizen trust and public grasp of government responsiveness. Negative attitudes contribute to unfavourable perceptions of the political environment and can discourage political participation, creating a less active citizenry and compounding democratic malaise (Goodman 2012).

The conclusion that business groups had unequal access to, and influence on, policymaking is further supported by the absence of checks on interest groups during the Conservative tenure. The strong Canadian executive characteristic of the Westminster system is cited as a mechanism that can work to prevent groups from impeding the government's will. The presence of social democratic parties such as the New Democratic Party and the Bloc Québécois are also noted as checks on interest group influence (Thorburn 2007). Both of these checks, however, are rather ineffective in a scenario where government favours the selective interests of business-oriented groups over public ones, and holds a majority of the seats in the House of Commons. During the Conservatives' final mandate, the Bloc had a low seat count, which limited its ability to check government power. At the same time, the NDP experienced growing pains as it formed the official opposition for the first time and adapted to a larger legislative presence. The absence of these checks reinforced an asymmetrical relationship between government and interest groups, resulting in disproportionate outcomes.

With respect to interest group tactics, institutionalized lobbying seems to have been an effective technique under the Conservative government. This raises questions about access and the disparity in informational, organizational, and financial resources between private and public groups. The fact that government and interest groups aligned their messaging was a powerful force to shape the debate on oil development in Canada. In this way, private groups had better access to government behind closed doors, and the two actors coordinated externally to shape public opinion in support of their mutual interests. These "interests" represent a selective segment of society and overlook collective interests that could deliver long-term benefits to the broader Canadian polity.

Interest groups have played an important role in the politics of federal conservative parties since 1993. They were instrumental in forming the ideological basis for the emergence of the Reform Party and were a key feature of its agenda and that of its successor party, the Canadian Alliance. Groups also provided an important source of support for Stephen Harper to pursue and win the leadership of the Canadian Alliance and eventually win the 2006 federal election. While the out-of-government conservatives advocated for certain interests, the parties benefited most from the support that interest groups provided. The transition to government, however, produced a more reciprocal relationship, as the party held the power of the public purse and the legislative authority to politically address the needs of specific groups. In government, the Conservatives continued the tradition of focusing on the interests of big business, especially while forming a majority government (2011–15). The limitations placed on public groups during this period raise concerns for representation, equality, fairness, inclusiveness, responsiveness, and trust in the Canadian political system.

Looking to the future, what does the new political reality mean for federal governance and democracy in Canada? It is too soon to tell. Oil and gas groups seem to be receiving less publicized favourable treatment, but this may have more to do with lower oil prices and the economic climate than Liberal politics. The Liberal government appears more willing to engage with Indigenous communities, as evidenced by the immediate response to the Attawapiskat youth suicide crisis, removal of Canada's objector status to the UN Declaration on the Rights of Indigenous Peoples, national inquiry into missing and murdered Indigenous women, and willingness to meet with communities such as the File Hills Qu'Appelle Tribal Council to improve relations with the federal government. However, only time will tell what a Trudeau government means for interest advocacy in Canada. The historical relationship between interest groups and the governing Liberals has been characterized by the considerations of private groups. With the Conservatives serving as the official opposition, Canadians can hope the asymmetrical treatment of some groups will become more balanced, but if history is any indication of future trends, it is likely special interest access and influence will remain an issue in Canadian politics.

REFERENCES

Bashevkin, Sylvia. 2012. *Regress Trumps Progress: Canadian Women, Feminism and the Harper Government*. Washington, DC: Friedrich Ebert Foundation.

Berry, Jeffrey M. 1978. "On the Origins of Public Interest Groups: A Test of Two Theories." *Polity* 10 (3): 379–97. http://dx.doi.org/10.2307/3234414.

Brennan, Richard J. 2010. "Tories Accused of Culture of Intimidation." *Toronto Star*, 4 May. http://www.thestar.com/news/canada/2010/05/04/tories_accused_of_culture_of_intimidation.html.

Canadian Press. 2012. "Environmental Charities Don't Top List of Foreign Funded Groups." CBC News, 10 May. http://www.cbc.ca/news/politics/environmental-charities-don-t-top-list-of-foreign-funded-groups-1.1247417.

Cayley-Daoust, Daniel, and Richard Girard. 2012. *Big Oil's Oily Grasp: The Making of Canada as a Petro-State and How Oil Money Is Corrupting Canadian Politics*. Ottawa: Polaris Institute.

Chase, Steven. 2015. "Harper Attacks 'Liberal Special Interests' as Campaign Nears End." *Globe and Mail*, 18 October. http://www.theglobeandmail.com/news/politics/harper-attacks-liberal-special-interests-as-campaign-nears-end/article26864560/.

Chase, Steven, and Gloria Galloway. 2014. "Harper Continues to Resist Calls for Missing Aboriginal Women Inquiry." *Globe and Mail*, 17 December. http://www.theglobeandmail.com/news/politics/harper-continues-to-resist-calls-for-missing-aboriginal-women-inquiry/article22133991/.

Delacourt, Susan. 2010. "Aid Groups Advised to 'Shut the F— Up' on Abortion." *Toronto Star*, 3 May. http://www.thestar.com/news/canada/2010/05/03/aid_groups_advised_to_shut_the_f_up_on_abortion.html.

Diebel, Linda. 2009. "Boom Times for PMO's God Squad." *Toronto Star,*
19 December. http://www.thestar.com/news/insight/2009/12/19/
boom_times_for_pmos_god_squad.html.

Dyck, Rand. 2011. *Canadian Politics: Critical Approaches. Concise.* 5th ed.
Scarborough, ON: Nelson College.

Energy Framework Initiative. 2011. Letter to Ministers Peter Kent and Joe
Oliver, 12 December. http://www.greenpeace.org/canada/Global/canada/
pr/2013/01/ATIP_Industry_letter_on_enviro_regs_to_Oliver_and_Kent.pdf.

Flanagan, Tom. 1995. *Waiting for the Wave: The Reform Party and Preston
Manning.* Toronto: Stoddart.

– 2007. *Harper's Team: Behind the Scenes in the Conservative Rise to Power.*
Montreal and Kingston: McGill-Queen's University Press.

Frank, Andrew. 2012. "Whistleblower's Open Letter to Canadians." Scribd.,
24 January. http://www.scribd.com/doc/79228736/
Whistleblower-s-Open-Letter-to-Canadians.

Galloway, Gloria. 2015. "Chiefs Urge Aboriginal People to Vote against Harper
Government." *Globe and Mail,* 7 July. http://www.theglobeandmail.com/
news/national/trudeau-to-roll-out-plan-to-bolster-funding-for-aboriginal-
education/article25334759/.

Goodman, Nicole. 2012. "Reconceptualizing Civic Duty: A New Perspective
on Measuring Civic Duty in Voting Studies." PhD diss., Carleton University.

Hemmera. 2013. "Bill C-38: A Changing Environmental Assessment Process."
http://hemmera.com/bill-c-38-changing-environmental-assessment-process.

Key, V.O. 1964. *Politics, Parties, & Pressure Groups.* New York: Crowell.

Laycock, David H. 2002. *The New Right and Democracy in Canada: Understanding Reform and the Canadian Alliance.* Don Mills, ON: Oxford
University Press.

Levant, Ezra. 2011. *Ethical Oil: The Case for Canada's Oil Sands.* Toronto:
McClelland & Stewart.

Levant, Ezra. 2013. "Audit Nightmare: The RCMP, Not Harper Should Be
Meeting with Chief Spence. *Toronto Sun,* 7 January. http://www.torontosun
.com/2013/01/07/audit-nightmare-the-rcmp-not-harper-should-be-meeting-
with-chief-spence.

Macdonald, David. 2012. *The Big Banks' Big Secret: Estimating Government
Support for Canadian Banks during the Financial Crisis.* Ottawa: Canadian
Centre for Policy Alternatives.

McDonald, Marci. 2011. *The Armageddon Factor: The Rise of Christian Nationalism
in Canada.* Toronto: Random House Canada.

Montpetit, Éric. 2009. "Are Interest Groups Useful or Harmful." In *Canadian
Politics,* 5th ed., edited by James Bickerton and Alain G. Gagnon, 265–82.
Toronto: University of Toronto Press.

Newman, Jacquetta, and A. Brian Tanguay. 2002. "Crashing the Party: The Politics of Interest Groups and Social Movements." In *Citizen Politics: Research and Theory in Canadian Political Behaviour*, edited by Joanna Everitt and Brenda O'Neill, 387–412. Toronto: Oxford University Press.

Nicholls, Gerry. 2009. *Loyal to the Core: Stephen Harper, Me and the NCC*. Jordan Station, ON: Freedom Press Canada.

Nikiforuk, Andrew. 2011. "Five Falsehoods about Ethical Oil." *Tyee*, 29 September. http://thetyee.ca/Opinion/2011/09/29/Ethical-Oil-Falsehoods/.

Olson, Mancur. 1965. *The Logic of Collective Action; Public Goods and the Theory of Groups*. Cambridge, MA: Harvard University Press.

Postmedia News. 2015. "More Than Two Dozen 'Third Parties' Registered in Hopes of Influencing Federal Election." *National Post*, 19 August. http://news.nationalpost.com/news/canada/more-than-two-dozen-third-parties-have-registered-in-hopes-of-influencing-federal-election.

Pross, A. Paul. 1975. *Pressure Group Behaviour in Canadian Politics*. Toronto: McGraw Hill Ryerson.

– 1992. *Group Politics and Public Policy*. Toronto: Oxford University Press.

Radwanski, Adam. 2015. "Unions, Centre-Left Interests to Begin Ad Campaign Attacking Harper's Tories." *Globe and Mail*, 11 June. http://www.theglobeandmail.com/news/politics/unions-centre-left-interests-to-begin-ad-campaign-attacking-harpers-tories/article24924913/.

Raj, Althia. 2012. "Nicole Eaton: Green Charities Using Foreign Cash to Fight Oil Sands Development, Argues Tory Senator Launching Inquiry." *Huffington Post*, 28 February. http://www.huffingtonpost.ca/2012/02/28/nicole-eaton-green-charity-oil-sands-canada_n_1307440.html.

Rennie, Steve. 2014. "Senators Offer Legal Arguments for Missing, Murdered Women Inquiry." *Huffington Post*. 20 November. http://www.huffington-post.ca/2014/11/20/missing-murdered-aboriginal-women-liberals_n_6191962.html.

Thorburn, Hugh G. 2007. "Interest Groups, Social Movements, and the Canadian Parliamentary System." In *Canadian Parties in Transition*, edited by Alain G. Gagnon and Brian A. Tanguay, 385–410. Toronto: University of Toronto Press.

Vongdouangchanh, Bea. 2013. "Oil, Banking, Mining Top Three Lobbying Issues in 2012: Lobbying Registry." *Hill Times*, 2 February. http://www.hilltimes.com/2013/02/02/issue-01-07-2002-32/23569.

Young, Lisa, and Joanna M. Everitt. 2004. *Advocacy Groups*. Vancouver: UBC Press.

5 Political Players or Partisan Pawns? Immigrants, Minorities, and Conservatives in Canada

ERIN TOLLEY[1]

For decades, the Liberal Party garnered a reputation as the country's most immigrant-friendly party. Recognizing that attracting immigrant and minority voters[2] was crucial to forming government, the Conservative Party worked hard to earn their affections. They reminded Canadians that it was John Diefenbaker's Tories who introduced Canada's first Bill of Rights and Brian Mulroney's government who enshrined official multiculturalism in law. They noted that it was the Progressive Conservatives who offered redress for the country's internment of Japanese Canadians during the Second World War. The first member of Parliament of Chinese descent was a Progressive Conservative, and so was the country's first Black member of Parliament. Even so, sceptics were undeterred, pointing to the anti-immigrant rhetoric spouted by the party's predecessors, the Reform Party and Canadian Alliance, as proof of the Conservatives' latent right-wing racism and xenophobia.

Throughout their time in government, the Conservatives were dogged by accusations of prejudice and "hidden agendas," even though xenophobic and anti-immigrant sentiments were largely silenced as the

---

1 I am grateful to John Biles and Antoine Bilodeau, who provided important feedback on an earlier version of this chapter. Thanks are also extended to the volume editors and anonymous reviewers whose comments improved the analysis.

2 I use the term *racial minority* to refer to those who are non-white and non-Caucasian in race or colour; this mirrors Statistics Canada's "visible minority" category. *Immigrant*, meanwhile, is used to refer to those Canadians who were born outside of this country. Terms like *minority*, *diverse*, and *cultural community* are used when the precise sub-population, whether immigrant or racial minority, is either unknown or not well defined.

party worked to carve out a policy space that appealed to an alliance of rural and Western Canadian–based populists and the country's largely suburban immigrant and minority communities. The Conservative government undertook a massive overhaul of immigration and multiculturalism policy and pinpointed so-called ethnic voters as an important constituency. However, as this chapter argues, symbolic gestures often stood in place of a principled policy agenda. This is emblematic of the pragmatism that is one of the hallmarks of the Conservative approach, a theme identified in the introduction to this volume. The engagement of ethnic voters, the appointment of immigrants and minorities to the Senate, and senior officials' frequent appearances at cultural events are not insignificant measures, but they are in some ways symbolic. In fact, they may placate the public, lulling them into thinking that substantive measures are being taken to address inequality and discrimination when really very little is being done in this regard (Edelman 1964). In assessing the Conservatives' approach to immigration, multiculturalism, and the engagement of minorities in politics, we should think not just about the outward actions but also about the apparent motivations. In this light, the Conservatives' efforts, while substantial, often appear to be less about inclusion and altruism and more about instrumentalism and electioneering. Nowhere was this more apparent than during the 2015 federal election campaign.

Immigrants and Ethnocultural Minorities in Canadian Politics

The notion that Canada is a country of immigrants is a central theme in the national narrative. However, just as the sociologist John Porter (1965) observed in his classic work, *The Vertical Mosaic*, wealthy and predominantly white men continue to control the country's key political institutions (Andrew et al. 2008), a trend that mirrors the electoral under-representation of women, Indigenous peoples, and other marginalized groups in Canada (see chapters 6 and 8 in this volume). There is good reason to examine the intersection between Canada's immigrant and minority communities and the country's electoral politics. First, immigrants and minorities are increasingly important electoral players, although their presence in elected bodies has often fallen short of their presence in the general population (Black 2013). Second, one's status as an immigrant or minority can exert an important influence on one's electoral and political behaviour. Whether it is voter turnout, political interest, or vote choice, researchers have found important differences between new immigrants and more established Canadians as well as between white and racial minority voters and candidates (Anderson and Black 2008; Tolley and Goodyear-Grant 2014; Bilodeau and Kanji 2006). Finally, although immigration and multiculturalism figure prominently in our national mythology, the relevant policy questions have largely been articulated separately from those related to electoral politics. Nonetheless, as the population diversifies and parties increasingly adopt sophisticated voter segmentation strategies, socio-demographic characteristics are likely to become more salient in electoral politics and policy.

This chapter brings these areas together. It focuses on Canada's conservative parties – the Reform Party, Canadian Alliance, Progressive Conservative Party, and Conservative Party of Canada – from 1993 to 2015 and examines three broad themes:

1 Policy framework: How have policies on immigration and multiculturalism evolved under federal conservative parties since 1993?
2 Political participation: How have federal conservatives engaged immigrants and minorities as voters?
3 Electoral involvement: To what extent have immigrants and minorities participated as federal conservative party members and parliamentary office-holders?

I argue that the merged Conservative Party shifted immigration and multiculturalism policy to align with the party's broad emphasis on efficient administration, economic prosperity, law and order, and a narrative that centres on Canadian values. The movement was gradual, beginning with the party's distancing of itself from the clearly restrictionist and anti-multicultural orientation of the Reform Party to a more open, but measured policy space that appeals to specific groups of immigrant and minority voters, while not alienating the party's traditional base. This was an essential part of a concerted strategy to attract new blocs of voters to the Conservative fold. Although some pundits and party officials posited that the Conservatives pulled the rug from under the Liberals' feet and "captured the ethnic vote," the results of the 2015 federal election show that this conclusion was perhaps premature. Certainly the party found success in some immigrant communities, but many racial minority voters remained staunchly Liberal. Meanwhile, while in government, the Conservative front bench was almost entirely white; parliamentarians with racial minority backgrounds were given very few positions of real influence or power, leaving the party open to accusations of pandering and self-interest.

From Get Out, Stay Out to Come In, Welcome

The period from the 1990s onward was one of widespread changes in global approaches to migration, integration, citizenship, and multicul-turalism. More affordable and accessible travel facilitated increased mobility, while more progressive social attitudes encouraged govern-ments to adopt policy frameworks that would not discriminate – explic-itly or implicitly – against qualified entrants from particular countries or racial backgrounds. As a result, so-called destination countries like Canada were forced to balance the desire for a steady stream of work-ready immigrants against sometimes isolated but influential fears about the influx of new, diverse citizens-in-waiting. During this peri-od, Abu-Laban (1998) summed up the Liberals' strategic positioning as "welcome/STAY OUT." The party continued to identify itself as open and inclusive but simultaneously emphasized economic immigration. The Liberal government handpicked skilled immigrant workers and transformed the party's historical attachment to multiculturalism into a discourse about integration into Canada.

The Conservative government went to great lengths to differentiate itself from its Liberal predecessor – branding itself as "Canada's New Government" – but the two parties actually converged in their eco-nomic framing of immigration policy. As is outlined in more detail below, the Conservatives focused on the selection of economic immi-grants, with more immigrants chosen by the provinces to fill local la-bour market needs, as well as those working in so-called in-demand occupations. This was accompanied by reductions in humanitarian in-take, including refugees and family class immigrants, as well as steps to inject a more law-and-order approach into immigration processing. The Conservatives' immigration policy aligned squarely with both its eco-nomic and crime agendas, but it also contained echoes of the approach implemented by the Progressive Conservatives in the 1990s. Indeed, in-creased immigration levels were initially pitched to Brian Mulroney's Cabinet because "more immigrants would provide a new source of vot-ers supportive of the Conservative party" (Abu-Laban 1998, 193). The Progressive Conservatives proposed revisions to the Immigration Act, while downgrading the Department of Multiculturalism into a program and cutting its budget. Some observers suggested that the overhaul was intended primarily to head off gains that had been made by the Reform Party, which was pitching significant changes in this policy field (Abu-Laban 1998).

In its 1988 platform and statement of principles, the Reform Party proposed an immigration system focused on economics that would include restrictions on family immigration and provide Parliament with greater control over entry into Canada (Reform Party of Canada 1988). They advocated the use of referenda for "major changes to immigration," while invoking inflammatory language about alleged "immigration abuses," "bogus refugees," "improper selection of immigrants," and "ghettoized minorities" (23–4). The party's restrictionist immigration stance was reiterated in its 1990 statement of principles and policies, which also called for the abolition of the federal government's multiculturalism program. The document outlined an individualistic stance on cultural preservation and advocated state assistance only in the integration of "ethnic cultures into the national culture" (Reform Party of Canada 1990, 23). In 1995 the party advocated a return to the "tap on, tap off" approach to immigration, specifying that immigration levels should be adjusted to reflect the national unemployment rate, with a cap of 150,000 newcomers per year anytime unemployment exceeded 10 per cent (Reform Party of Canada 1995, 22). The document called for the "acceptance and integration of immigrants to Canada into the mainstream of Canadian life" and stated the party's opposition to the "current concept of multiculturalism and hyphenated Canadianism." It reiterated the need to abolish state support for multiculturalism (Reform Party of Canada 1995).

Throughout the party's official documents, emphasis was placed on reduced government interventions, personal responsibility, and a "Canada first" discourse. Among party members, the messaging often veered in an even more strident direction. For example, in 1988, Doug Collins was acclaimed as a Reform Party candidate. Collins was a journalist who had publicly stated his support for caps on the entry of racial minority immigrants to Canada. He was dropped as a candidate after he refused to sign a pledge indicating he supported the party's opposition to racism, with party officials noting the action was needed "to fight the perception of extremism and racism" (Bellett 1988; Walkom 1988). Six years later, while speaking to a reporter following a parliamentary debate on amendments to the Human Rights Act, Bob Ringma, a Reform MP, said he thought businesses should be permitted to fire or reassign "ethnics" and gay or lesbian employees whose presence offended customers. Ringma and his colleague Dave Chatters, who publicly endorsed the comments, were suspended from caucus, but both were applauded by Reformers on the floor of the party's annual convention just two months later (Henton 1996).

That said, on some fronts, the Reform Party was not that far from other parties. Indeed, as Reformers gained electoral traction, the Liberal government's immigration policy also shifted, with decreases in annual immigration levels and a changed emphasis towards economic immigration (Abu-Laban 1998). The Liberals' 1993 Red Book pledged to raise immigration levels to 1 per cent of the population – about 290,000 newcomers per year – but levels actually fell from 256,641 in 1993 to a low of 174,195 in 1997, after which they gradually increased, although never reaching that 1 per cent goal under the Liberals (Citizenship and Immigration Canada 2014). The focus also moved to economic immigration, a position that meshed with the party's emphasis on fiscal restraint and responded to a growing body of research on increasing wage gaps between immigrants and the Canadian-born (Picot and Hou 2003).

With the rebranding of the Reform Party as the Canadian Alliance, observers wondered whether the party would change its stance on some of the more restrictionist aspects of its immigration and multiculturalism policies. The party's 2000 election platform noted that the Alliance would welcome immigrants, while keeping criminals out (Canadian Alliance 2000). There was a commitment to retaining existing immigration levels and no mention of restricting family class immigration or abolishing the multiculturalism program, although the party did promise to repeal employment equity legislation. Nonetheless, during the actual election campaign, the party "hardly raised the [immigration] issue" (Blais et al. 2002, 146). Controversy erupted, however, when an Alliance candidate, Betty Granger, argued that Canadian students were being denied admission to university programs in Victoria and Vancouver because of an influx of foreign students. She called it an "'Asian invasion' and suggested that 'what was coming off these boats was not the best clientele you would want for this country'" (Alberts 2000). Granger eventually resigned as a candidate. Later in the campaign, a fundraiser for an Alliance candidate in British Columbia was fired after he suggested that immigrants from China and Hong Kong might engage in fraudulent voting practices (Mickleburgh 2000). The new party was portrayed as racist and "scary" (Matas 2000) and failed to make inroads in the 2000 election. It was disbanded in 2003 when the Canadian Alliance and Progressive Conservative Party merged to form the Conservative Party of Canada.

Recognizing the limitations of the positions taken by the Reform Party and Canadian Alliance, the Conservative Party put forward policy positions that were attractive to immigrant and minority voters from urban areas but did not alienate its Western and conservative base. Adopting a "buffet style" approach (Black and Hicks 2008, 248), the Conservatives pursued policies that were both expansionist and restrictionist. As far back as 1991, Stephen Harper cautioned against a "culturally phrased" immigration policy. He instead advocated an immigration policy framed in economic terms, arguing that anything else "'would be politically too dangerous – it would be too easy for the other parties to attack as veiled racism'" (qtd in Marwah, Triadafilopoulos, and White 2013, 105).

Under the Conservative government, immigration rose to its highest level in almost fifty years (Citizenship and Immigration Canada 2014), with the focus placed squarely on specific economic immigrants. Such an approach is consistent with public opinion, which shows a strong connection between citizens' support for immigration and their belief that newcomers contribute to the economy (Reitz 2012). Under the Conservatives, provinces, employers, and labour market demands drove the selection of newcomers, with particular attention paid to immigrants who speak one official language and have Canadian work experience. This emphasis was evident under the Liberals but arguably became more entrenched under the Conservatives. The Conservatives also worked with the provinces to improve recognition of foreign credentials and allocated funding to assist newcomers in entering the job market. The number of temporary foreign workers admitted annually more than doubled under the Conservatives, a move that curried favour with employers, particularly in Alberta where unemployment rates were at record lows.

The length of temporary work permits was increased, and measures were taken to make it easier for employers to hire foreign workers. However, the movement towards temporary migration halted somewhat in 2014 when evidence of program abuse came to light, including allegations that qualified Canadian applicants were being turned away in favour of foreign workers. Invoking "Canada first" language and promising to penalize abusers, the government worked to toughen rules and ensure Canadian workers would be treated fairly (Canadian Press 2014). In addition to all of these changes, there were policy overhauls to streamline processes, reduce administrative backlogs, and increase the ability of the immigration minister to exercise policy discretion – measures that were broadly consistent with the Conservatives' efforts to reduce inefficiencies. Moreover, referring to the right of landing fee as a "head tax," the government cut this amount in half, a move that not only fit with their reputation as tax-cutters but also appealed to immigrant voters (Black and Hicks 2008).

Simultaneously, the Conservatives decreased the number and proportion of newcomers entering as family class immigrants. However, as is shown in figure 5.1, this decrease was also evident when the Liberals took office in 1993 following a brief period of high levels of family class immigration. Nonetheless, in 2011, under the guise of addressing long wait times, the Conservative government placed a two-year moratorium on applications for the sponsorship of parents and grandparents and introduced a multi-entry "super visa." The super visa allows parents and grandparents of Canadian permanent residents to visit the country for up to two years, but it does not give access to government services nor offer any potential of permanent residency and citizenship. This move responded to demands from immigrants wanting to sponsor family members while also addressing concerns that older immigrants were entering Canada to benefit from social programs to which they had not contributed. The government also introduced conditions on the sponsorship of spouses and partners in an effort to address what it characterized as immigration marriage fraud.

There was a progressive movement away from refugees with government discourse targeting perceived queue-jumpers, "bogus" asylum claimants, human traffickers, deportees, and others who "abuse Canada's generosity" (Conservative Party of Canada 2013), positioning that was consistent with the government's law-and-order approach. At times, the framing appeared mean-spirited or out of step with public sentiment. During the 2015 federal election campaign, Minister of Citizenship and Immigration Chris Alexander appeared intemperate when questioned by a journalist about the refugee crisis as a photograph of a two-year-old boy who drowned while attempting to flee from Syria with his family made international headlines. As public support mounted, and grassroots campaigns were launched to sponsor Syrian refugees, the government was accused of inaction and callousness. The *Globe and Mail* reported that the Prime Minister's Office had halted the processing of Syrian refugee claims for several weeks in 2014, pending an "audit" to ensure the integrity of the refugee system and the "screening out [of] threats to Canada" (Friesen 2015). The conflation of refugee flows with security concerns is a hallmark of Conservative discourse in this policy area.

Figure 5.1: Distribution of New Immigrants, by Entry Category, 1988–2014

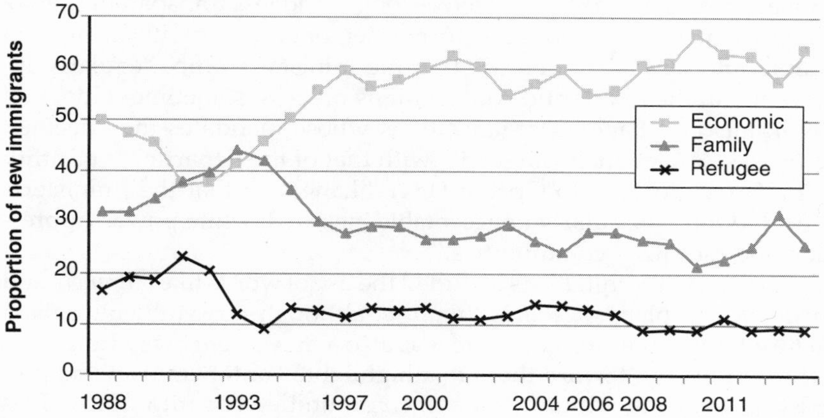

Source: Citizenship and Immigration Canada (2014)

On the citizenship front, the Conservatives revised the Canadian citizenship study guide, working to reframe conceptions of Canadian identity in ways that reflect the party's values (Chapnick 2011) while showing their convergence with those of newcomer and minority communities. Advancing the view that Canada made it too easy for newcomers to obtain citizenship, the Conservatives tightened language requirements, and the citizenship exam was made more difficult; unsurprisingly, failure rates increased (Griffith 2013). In 2014, the government amended the Citizenship Act in an effort to make citizenship "harder to get and easier to lose"; critics argued that the provisions effectively created two classes of citizens, by distinguishing between native-born and naturalized Canadians and allowing for the revocation of the latter's citizenship (Griffith 2015a). When the Liberals came to power in 2015, they repealed a number of the changes that the Conservatives made to citizenship.

While, on the surface, the Conservative government championed multicultural initiatives through its engagement with cultural communities, there was in some ways also a retreat during their time in office. For example, although funding for multiculturalism had been on the decline since the Liberals first introduced cuts in the 1990s, the Conservatives continued that erosion, opting to not even spend nearly

40 per cent of the funds annually allocated to such programs; the approval process was also criticized as longer and less transparent (Levitz 2013). An insider's account by a former senior official at Citizenship and Immigration Canada confirms that the minister's office regularly intervened in the grants and contributions process, sometimes Googling applicants and flagging organizations whose mandates they deemed to not be "'directionally aligned'" with that of the department (Griffith 2013, 36). According to Griffith (154), "Language that the [minister's office] found particularly unacceptable included: white power, oppression and racialized communities."

Other semantic initiatives included the use of words like *pluralism* and *integration* in place of *multiculturalism*, although the Multiculturalism Act itself went untouched. There was also a movement away from anti-racism initiatives toward those that highlighted anti-Semitism and pre-existing tensions within minority communities (Griffith 2013). This was emphasized in the 2013 Speech from the Throne, which did not mention racism or prejudice explicitly but instead asserted that the Conservative government would "not hesitate to uphold the fundamental rights of *all Canadians* whenever they are threatened" (emphasis added). This rhetorical sleight of hand downplayed the significance of prejudice experienced by minorities, instead casting the issue as one that affects everyone.

There were also administrative "resets," including the shifting of responsibility for multicultural programming from the Department of Canadian Heritage to the Immigration Department (Griffith 2013). Instead of having a minister responsible for the multiculturalism file, this program area was but one of three – immigration, citizenship, and multiculturalism – that fell under a single portfolio. This move diluted the time, attention, and visibility previously accorded to the multiculturalism policy file (Griffith 2013) and also symbolized the Conservatives' contention that multiculturalism is not about all Canadians but instead about those with immigrant backgrounds. When they came to power in 2015, the Liberals shifted the multiculturalism file back to the Department of Canadian Heritage but, diverging from past practice, did not name a separate minister responsible for this policy area.

Other policy decisions were more targeted, often appealing to groups that cynics claim are among those the Conservatives wished to attract to their base. These included redress for the Chinese head tax and an apology for the government's 1914 turning away of Sikhs aboard the *Komagata Maru*. An inquiry into the Air India tragedy, the designation of an ambassador for religious freedom, the recognition of Macedonia's independence, the admission of stateless Vietnamese refugees from Thailand and the Philippines, the lifting of visa requirements for visitors from Poland and the Czech Republic, the recognition of the Armenian genocide, and the designation of the fourth Saturday in November as Ukrainian Famine and Genocide Memorial Day are other examples of this approach. These initiatives were popular within the communities that they targeted, a development that Griffith (2013, 73) points out helped "to pave the way for more ambitious and controversial immigration and related reforms. It was easier for the government to tighten immigration and refugee policy when they acknowledged the excessive restrictions of the past." While a principled stance may have underpinned each of these announcements, there was nonetheless an electoral orientation. For example, the historical recognition settlement offered to Ukrainian Canadians was far more generous than that offered to Italian Canadians, even though both communities had been subjected to comparable wartime internment measures; some observers suggest that this was a result of the minister's reading of the political benefits that might accrue as a result (Griffith 2013).

Looking strictly at policy concerns, the Conservatives did not differ significantly from the Liberals who preceded them; both placed a strong emphasis on integration, the acquisition of Canadian citizenship, and respect for diversity within a framework of Canadian laws and values. In other words, it is not so much on the goals that there is divergence between the parties, but rather on the evidence – often political – that was used to justify decisions, the overall strategy and messaging, and a predilection for political calculus to inform all of these. One columnist characterized the Conservatives' approach as "the politics of slice and dice, of small ball as they say in baseball, of saying one thing but doing another, of preaching restraint while practising the imperative of targeted spending at portions of the electorate central to the Conservatives' core" (Simpson 2013).

This type of politics was perhaps what was at the core of the Conservative government's 2011 ban on the wearing of the niqab, or facial veil, during the taking of the citizenship oath. Zunera Ishaq, a devout Muslim, challenged the ban saying that while she would remove her veil in private, she would not do so in a public citizenship ceremony. In 2015, a federal court judge ruled that the policy was unlawful, but the Conservatives were undeterred and launched an appeal. Noting that covering one's face is "not how we do things here," Prime Minister

Harper argued that "it is offensive that someone would hide their identity at the very moment where they are committing to join the Canadian
family" (Quan 2015a). Conservative MP Larry Miller was even more
pointed, telling a radio call-in show that women who wish to wear the
niqab during a citizenship ceremony should "stay the hell where you
came from" (Edmiston 2015). Miller later apologized, but the comment
was reminiscent of the xenophobia his party had worked so hard to
rid itself of. In a column about the government's position, Margaret
Wente wryly observed, "Never mind the Constitution and all that. This
is about politics, not principles" (Wente 2015).

The niqab emerged again when, in the midst of the 2015 federal election campaign, the federal court denied the government's appeal of their
earlier decision. The Conservatives sought leave to appeal the decision
to the Supreme Court and requested a stay of the decision, a move that
would deny Ishaq from taking the oath and exercising her right to vote
on election day (Quan 2015b). The court rejected the government's application for a stay in the ruling, but by this time the Conservatives had
doubled down, noting that upon re-election they would introduce legislation to ban face coverings during citizenship ceremonies and would
consider banning the niqab within the federal bureaucracy. Polling suggested that the niqab is unpopular among most Canadians, but particularly within the traditional Conservative base and in Quebec, a region
in which the Conservatives could stand to make inroads (Loewen 2015;
Anderson and Coletto 2015). Late in the campaign, the government announced it would create a tip line so that Canadians could report "barbaric cultural practices," a move that many believed unfairly targeted
Muslim Canadians. As discussed below, the Conservatives have consistently had weak support among Muslim voters and therefore were unlikely concerned about alienating them. However, the tactic may have
had an unintended consequence, one that eroded the perception of the
Conservatives as an immigrant-friendly party that is open to diversity.
The legislative agenda was a tool, one that would be wielded unspar-
ingly to win votes among identified pockets of voters. This was at the
heart of the Conservatives' ethnic outreach strategy.

Engaging "Ethnic Voters" in Canada's Conservative Movement

Conservative ethnic outreach is in no way a new phenomenon. Under
John Diefenbaker, the Tories pursued policies that appealed to immigrant and minority voters. Tory MPs created street-by-street files on

ethnic communities and built personal relationships at lunches and weddings. Christian Champion (2006) – a historian who later served as a citizenship policy advisor to Jason Kenney, a Conservative minister under Harper – argues that it was the Conservatives' early efforts to lure immigrants and minorities to their parties that actually inspired the Liberals' later outreach strategies.

By contrast, although the Reform Party initiated a "bridge-building" strategy, its main focus was to increase the party's name recognition within cultural communities and to encourage immigrants and minorities to become members. According to one party insider, the "best solution to the party's [public relations] problem on ethnic issues was to attract members of visible minority groups to the cause" (Madan 1998). One way that the party did this was to highlight the presence of racial minority members in caucus and on the candidate slate; this was evident in a 1997 campaign video, "A Fresh Start for Canadians," which featured five Reform candidates; two of them, Rahim Jaffer and Janice Lim, have racial minority backgrounds. These measures aside, organizers in the Reform Party and Canadian Alliance tended to concentrate their efforts on their Western Canadian base, with an eye towards eventually attracting voters in Ontario or Quebec. Nonetheless, there was a sense among some that a different strategy might be in order. Tom Flanagan (2009, 2011) suggests that Stephen Harper first sowed the seeds of the Conservatives' ethnic strategy in 1996 when he argued in a speech that to form a majority government, federal conservatives would need a tripartite electoral coalition similar to the ones assembled by Brian Mulroney and John Diefenbaker before them. At the time, Harper pegged Western Canadian and rural Ontario populists, traditional Ontario and Atlantic Canadian Tories, and francophone nationalists in Quebec as the most likely members of the coalition. Flanagan (2009) later dubbed these the "three sisters." The merger of the Progressive Conservative and Canadian Alliance parties brought together two of the sisters – the populists and traditional Tories – but the Québécois proved more elusive, as was made abundantly clear in the 2006 election. Although the Conservatives won, they failed to make their breakthrough in Quebec and were left with a minority government (see chapter 7 in this volume).

Building on initial gains that had been made with ethnic communities in the debates on same-sex marriage – an issue to which many immigrant and minority Canadians were opposed – the Conservatives redoubled their efforts to attract this segment of the population to their cause. This included some of the policy reforms noted above, as well as efforts to build relationships with immigrants, minorities, and ethnic community leaders. As Flanagan (2011, 106) points out, "The underlying assumption of the Conservative outreach was that many ethnic voters 'ought' to be voting Conservative rather than Liberal. Many new Canadians are socially conservative, believing in stable traditional families rather than the lifestyle obsessions of Liberal elites. Most are religious; a surprising number, especially among Chinese, Vietnamese, Koreans and Filipinos, are Christian. Many are economically conservative and entrepreneurial ... In other words, many immigrants look like Conservative core voters, except that they may have a different skin colour and mother tongue."

The Conservatives set out to show new Canadians that they were open and tolerant and to demonstrate that "your values are our values" (Martin 2010, 227). By 2008, Jason Kenney, at the time the secretary of state for multiculturalism and Canadian identity, claimed that he had attended more than 500 ethnic community events since the party had taken office two years earlier. A page from one day of his itinerary includes interviews with a Korean-language newspaper and a multicultural radio station, an appearance on a Punjabi radio call-in show, meet-and-greets at three different Jewish synagogues, two fundraisers (one with Indo-Canadians and another with Armenian Canadians), separate round tables with Chinese Canadian and Persian Canadian community leaders and subsequent media availability, a ball sponsored by the Mississauga Board of Chinese Professionals and Business, and, to cap it all off, a major Hindu festival at 10:30 p.m. (Rana 2008). Although members of other parties also attended community events, arguably no one was more vigorous – or visible – than Mr Kenney. Conservatives have also made themselves readily available to the so-called ethnic media while limiting the Parliamentary Press Gallery's access to the prime minister and his Cabinet (Persichelli 2011; see also chapters 9 and 12 in this volume). During the 2011 election, Conservatives reportedly spent close to $2 million on ethnic media monitoring (Cheadle and Levitz 2012), while in 2015 they ran ads in the Chinese- and Punjabi-language media that suggested the Liberals would legalize marijuana and put brothels in communities.

The Conservatives' approach to ethnic engagement is in no way scattershot but premised on forging alliances and targeting their policy agenda at key demographics. A 2007 strategic blueprint leaked to the media indicated that as many as one-fifth of Canada's ethnic groups would not be "accessible" to the party, and efforts would focus else-where with targeted mail-outs, direct voter contact, personal meetings at "major ethnic events," and the development of voter databases with information on immigrant and minority Canadians (Leblanc 2007). A leaked internal document highlighting the Conservatives' "very ethnic riding" strategy bluntly summed up the essential point: "There are lots of ethnic votes. There will be quite a few more soon. They live where we need to win" (Conservative Party 2011). While Conservatives denied that they were explicitly targeting specific communities, media reports suggested that Canadians with Korean, South Asian, Persian, Polish, Jamaican, Filipino, Vietnamese, Jewish, and Chinese (particularly Can-tonese) backgrounds had been given special attention (MacCharles 2008). Data compiled by a former senior official at Citizenship and Im-migration Canada suggest that a disproportionate number of Minister Kenney's official statements and speeches were directed at Jewish and Chinese Canadian communities (Griffith 2013).

Advertisements produced by the party for the 2011 federal election reinforced the perceived convergence of values between Conservatives and specific minority communities. One ad featured Nina Grewal, a member of Parliament of Sikh faith. Accompanied by images of Indo-Canadians arriving in Canada, the voice-over notes, "For over 100 years, Indo-Canadians have worked hard to build Canada. Things haven't al-ways been fair for us, but the Conservatives have always recognized our history and our community's sacrifice." The ad included a photo of Stephen Harper outside a gurdwara, his head covered by an off-white handkerchief, as is customary when visiting a Sikh temple. The voice-over continues, "The Conservatives fight for our values: belief in hard work, respect for tradition, and the importance of family," and the cam-era then pans back to Grewal. With a photo of her family visible in the background, the MP says, "That's why I'm a Conservative. Isn't it time to vote our values?" Other ads with similar messaging and visu-als featured MPs Alice Wong and Tim Uppal, as well as Harry Tsai, a candidate with links to the Taiwanese Canadian community.

Following the 2011 election, Conservative officials claimed that the party captured "42 percent of the ethnic vote and 24 of 25 suburban ridings" (MacCharles 2008). The party's own internal polling is said to have suggested that well over half of Cantonese-speaking voters in sub-urban ridings in Toronto and Vancouver intended to vote Conservative (Bricker and Ibbitson 2013, 25). Although these efforts to "court the ethnic vote" have been highly touted, some research suggests that the success of this strategy may be more urban legend than reality (see also chapter 3 in this volume). One reason for the apparent disconnect between the rhetoric and the research is the nebulous notion of an "ethnic" voter, a label that could encompass many disparate segments of the population, including Canadians of non-French or non-British ancestry, those with racial minority backgrounds, those with immigrant origins, or any combination of these. Contrary to conventional wisdom, the Conservatives did not forge a "rainbow coalition," nor was the party's 2011 majority government wholly a result of their increased appeal among a wider and more diverse swathe of voters (Soroka et al. 2011). Rather, racial minorities were, in the aggregate, still strongly attached to the Liberals, with the Conservatives' "ethnic" support coming primarily from white immigrants, particularly those with Italian, Polish, and German backgrounds (Harell 2013; Chignall 2015).[3] The Conservatives' "ethnic" engagement strategy appears to have been much narrower than the narrative implied. That conclusion is underscored when one examines the presence – and power – of immigrants and minorities in the Conservative Party and as parliamentary office-holders.

Immigrants and Minorities in the Party and Parliamentary Office

When characterizing the Reform Party, adjectives often include *WASPy* or the more derisive *redneck*, descriptors owing to its Western Canadian origins and the stereotypes that accompany such a lineage. One columnist notes that the party tried to overcome this perception when at its 1991 convention it "paraded around a potential British Columbia candidate of Oriental [*sic*] heritage as if to prove its inclusiveness," but the membership profile remained largely white (Simpson 1997). Moreover, unlike other parties that established women's commissions, youth wings, or multicultural advisory boards, the Reform Party and Canadian Alliance both explicitly rejected such approaches, viewing them as "special interest" politics (Cross 2004).

---

3 One shortcoming of the data that Harell uses is that there were an insufficient number of racial minority respondents to allow for an analysis of diversity within that category. This is important because single-member district plurality systems do not require parties to capture the support of *all* racial minority voters, but merely a large enough number of those who reside in geographically concentrated areas. The Conservatives capitalized on this feature of our electoral system by strategically targeting ridings with large pockets of those communities with whom they felt there were natural affinities.

Consistent with the profile of other parties, most of the Reformers elected in the 1993 election were white men with Anglo-Saxon and Christian origins. However, the fifty-two-member Reform caucus did include Keith Martin, a racial minority of Iranian heritage who was born in England, as well as six MPs with birthplaces in the United States, United Kingdom, Austria, and Germany (Parliament of Canada 2012). By 1997, the caucus had diversified further with the election of five (26.3 per cent) of the nineteen racial minority MPs in the House of Commons (Black 2000). Among these were Rahim Jaffer and Deepak Obhrai, respectively the country's first Muslim and Hindu MPs, as well as Gurmant Grewal, who claims to have made the fastest ascent from immigrant to MP in Canada, securing elected office just five years and eight months after first arriving in this country (Jetha 2002). Following the 2000 election, the newly formed Canadian Alliance also boasted five racial minority MPs (Black 2008). Although the gains in Parliament were small, the face of conservatism in Canada was changing.

In 2000, William Cross and Lisa Young surveyed more than 3,800 members of Canadian political parties, including those in the Canadian Alliance. The questionnaire included items on the members' ethnic origins, place of birth, and mother tongue. As is shown in table 5.1, while there were variations in origins and ethnocultural make-up of the major parties, one that stands out as the least diverse is not the Canadian Alliance, but rather the Progressive Conservative party, which had the largest number of members with British ethnic origins and the smallest proportion of immigrants. The Canadian Alliance attracted a substantial number of immigrants (although those they have attracted are more likely to have originated from Britain than immigrants in any of the other parties), and it was also home to a number of members whose mother tongue was neither English nor French (Cross and Young 2002).

It was following the formation of the new Conservative Party, however, that we witnessed a real demographic transformation on the right side of the ideological spectrum. This was no more evident than when the party presented its candidates. In 2004, the Conservatives nominated proportionately more racial minority candidates than any other party (Black and Erickson 2006). As is shown in table 5.2, of the 308 candidates who ran under the Conservative banner in this election, 10.7 per cent had racial minority backgrounds, a number that bested both the NDP and Liberals. Black and Hicks (2006) posit that putting forward a more multicultural face was one attempt to delegitimize the perception of racism that had dogged the Reform and Canadian Alliance parties. Nonetheless, two years later in 2006, when the party felt it

Table 5.1. Ethnocultural Origins of Political Party Members in Canada, 2000 (%)

	Liberal	NDP	Canadian Alliance	Progressive Conservative
Born outside Canada	13.9	22.1	13.9	11.7
Top three countries of origin if not Canada	Britain (14.0) India (10.9) Italy (9.3)	Britain (26.0) USA (23.6) Scotland (5.5) Netherlands (5.5)	Britain (43.3) USA (12.2) Germany (12.0)	Britain (35.9) USA (12.4) Netherlands (8.2)
Lived in Canada entire life	84.2	77.5	84.6	87.5
Mother tongue other than English or French	11.3	11.9	11.3	7.4
British ethnic origins	53.5	30.4	51.3	70.1

Source: Cross and Young's (2002) mail-back survey of political party members.

Table 5.2. Racial Minorities as a Proportion of Candidates, by Party, 2004–2015

	2004	2006	2008	2011	2015
Conservative	10.7	8.1	9.8	10.1	13.0
Liberal	8.4	11.0	9.8	9.1	16.2
NDP	9.4	7.8	10.7	10.4	13.0
Bloc Québécois	6.7	7.8	10.7	8.0	2.8
All candidates	9.3	9.0	10.1	9.7	13.2

Sources: Black (2011, 2013); Black and Hicks (2006); Griffith (2015b); author's own calculations.

had a realistic chance of forming a minority government, the number of racial minority Conservative candidates fell by 8, although there was a slight rebound in the 2008 and 2011 elections. In 2015, when thirty new seats were added to the House of Commons – many in ethnically diverse ridings in the Greater Toronto Area – racial minority candidates made up 13 per cent of the Conservative slate, but the Liberals nonetheless outpaced them, with 16 per cent of their candidates coming from racial minority groups.

We have also witnessed fluctuations in the number and proportion of racial minority MPs. As is shown in table 5.3, the number of racial minorities elected to Parliament as members of a federal conservative

Table 5.3. Racial Minority Members of Parliament, by Party, 1993–2015

		1993	1997	2000	2004	2006	2008	2011	2015
Reform / Alliance / Conservative[a]	% caucus	1.9	8.3	7.8	7.1	5.8	5.6	7.2	6.1
	(n)	(1)	(5)	(5)	(7)	(6)	(8)	(12)	(6)
Liberal	% caucus	6.8	8.4	7.0	9.6	11.7	11.7	5.9	20.2
	(n)	(12)	(13)	(12)	(13)	(12)	(9)	(2)	(39)
NDP	% caucus	–	4.8	–	–	3.4	2.7	13.9	4.5
	(n)	(0)	(1)	(0)	(0)	(1)	(1)	(13)	(2)
Bloc Québécois	% caucus	–	–	–	3.7	7.8	6.1	25.0	–
	(n)	(0)	(0)	(0)	(2)	(4)	(3)	(1)	(0)
All MPs	%	4.4	6.3	5.6	7.1	7.5	6.8	9.4	13.9
	(n)	(13)	(19)	(17)	(22)	(23)[b]	(21)	(28)	(47)

[a] The Progressive Conservative Party did not elect any racial minority MPs between 1993 and 2000, the last election in which it ran its own candidates. As a result, it has been excluded from the table.

[b] Ève-Mary Thaï Thi Lac, a Bloc Québécois MP, was elected in a by-election in 2007; she has not been included in the results for 2006. Thi Lac was the first Canadian of Vietnamese origin elected to the House of Commons.

Sources: Black (2000, 2002, 2008),Crawford (2011), Center for Research-Action on Race Relations (2006), Parliament of Canada (2013), Tolley (2015); author's own calculations.

party gradually increased, from one in 1993 to twelve in 2011, although the proportionate presence of racial minority MPs in the Conservative caucus has hardly budged since its first members were elected under the new banner in 2004. Moreover, the absolute number plummeted in 2015, when just six racial minority MPs were elected as Conservatives.

In the period under study, the proportion of the Canadian population with a racial minority background has also increased dramatically, and none of the parties have kept pace with these demographic changes. In 2011, racial minorities made up 19.1 per cent of the population, while among Canadian citizens – those who have a right to vote and run for office – 15 per cent were racial minorities. Against both metrics, the presence of racial minorities in the population far exceeds the presence of racial minorities in the Conservative caucus. To be fair, no Canadian political party has a make-up that truly reflects the country's demographics. Even the Liberals, whose post-2015 caucus included a record number of racial minority MPs, saw the election of very few Black,

Asian, and Latin American MPs. However, the diversity gap is particularly notable among the Conservatives, given how much attention has been devoted to the party's ethnic engagement strategies.

The Conservative Party's enthusiasm for diversity is even somewhat less apparent when we look at its upper echelons. As one Conservative Party strategist told me in an interview, "What limited minority representation [the government] has, has really not important positions. Many of them have no positions" (personal interview, 30 August 2012; qtd in Tolley 2016, 217n10). When the Conservatives first formed government in 2006, just two racial minority members of Parliament were named to Cabinet: Bev Oda and Michael Chong. Less than ten months later, Chong resigned from Cabinet after the prime minister reportedly failed to consult him on a Conservative motion to recognize the Québécois as a nation within a united Canada. For nearly the next five years, Oda was the only racial minority member of the Harper ministry. She was joined in 2011 by three more ministers with racial minority backgrounds, although all served in junior positions: Bal Gosal as minister of state for sport, Tim Uppal as minister of state for democratic reform, and Alice Wong as minister of state for seniors.

After a Cabinet shake-up in July 2013 – billed as a rebranding exercise – the three racial minority Cabinet ministers were left in low-profile portfolios. As the new Cabinet was sworn in, one columnist observed that it was the "blond-haired, blue-eyed duo of [Chris] Alexander and [Michelle] Rempel" whom Prime Minister Harper sent out "as the generational change couple" (Harper 2013). While the proportions of racial minorities and immigrants in the Conservative Cabinet are actually slightly higher than those in the party's caucus,[4] a historical perspective suggests that the Liberals have been somewhat more committed to elevating racial minority MPs to Cabinet and placing them in positions of power. Not only did the proportion of immigrant and minority appointees to the Cabinets of Jean Chrétien and Paul Martin exceed that of immigrants and minorities sitting in the Liberal caucus, these ministers occupied a much broader and more influential range

---

4 Following the 2013 Cabinet shuffle, 7.8 per cent of those occupying Cabinet seats had racial minority origins, compared to 7.2 per cent in the Conservative caucus. Similarly, while 10.3 per cent of Cabinet ministers were born outside of Canada, 9.0 per cent of caucus members were foreign-born.

of posts, including Natural Resources, National Revenue, Health, and Veterans Affairs.[5] In 2015, much was made of Justin Trudeau's diverse and gender-balanced Cabinet, which showcased racial minorities in key portfolios, including National Defence, Infrastructure, and Innovation, Science, and Economic Development.

Although few racial minority MPs were promoted to Cabinet under the Conservatives, the party did make an active effort to showcase immigrant and racial minority Canadians in more symbolic positions, a strategy that was particularly evident in the Senate. During his tenure, Stephen Harper made fifty-nine appointments to the Senate. Of these, eight had racial minority backgrounds (13.6 per cent of all appointments). All eight of the Conservatives' racial minority appointments were born outside Canada (in Pakistan, the Philippines, India, Korea, Jamaica, Singapore, and Vietnam), as was Doug Finley, who was born in England and raised in Scotland. The appointments included Salma Ataullahjah, the first senator of Pakistani heritage; Tobias Enverga, Jr, the first senator of Filipino descent; Yonah Martin, the first Korean-Canadian senator; Thanh Hai Ngo, the first senator with Vietnamese origins; and Vim Kochar, the first senator of Indian origin. These appointments were no accident; the nominations were deliberate, and one senator with whom I spoke said that they were partly a result of the prime minister's interest in diversity (personal interview, 6 November 2012). Certainly, efforts to diversify the upper chamber and provide immigrant and minority Canadians with representation in Parliament are laudable. It remains to be seen, however, what real influence they can exercise from unelected seats in an institution with declining public and political legitimacy.

---

5 Under Stephen Harper, sixty-seven individuals were appointed to Cabinet. Of these, five (7.5 per cent) had racial minority backgrounds, while eight (11.9 per cent) were born outside Canada. When Jean Chrétien was in office, he appointed seventy-three members to his Cabinet. Of these, six (8.2 per cent) had racial minority backgrounds, while twelve (16.4 per cent) were born outside Canada. Under Paul Martin, fifty Cabinet appointments were made; of these, five (10 per cent) had racial minority backgrounds and eight (16 per cent) were born outside Canada. When Justin Trudeau took office in 2015, he appointed thirty individuals to Cabinet. Of these, five (16.7 per cent) had racial minority backgrounds, and three (10 per cent) were born outside Canada.

Conclusion

Over time, the federal Conservative Party moved away from the re-strictionist immigration stance and anti-multiculturalism rhetoric of its Reform Party predecessor. It positioned itself within a careful policy space that emphasized economic immigration, while tightening up the refugee and family streams and showing little sympathy for those who might abuse the system. Senior Cabinet ministers made themselves highly visible at cultural events and within the ethnic media, but substantive action on multicultural and anti-racism initiatives was significantly curbed. The government targeted its policy and legislative agenda at initiatives that would appeal to ethnocultural communities that they believed to have "natural" Conservative leanings, a strategy that extended to the party's intense focus on ridings with particular ethnocultural compositions.

Certainly the Conservatives are not alone in trying to attract immigrant and minority voters to their fold; the Liberals have been doing it for decades. Other parties have forged their entire electoral fortunes by exploiting a regional base, and senior citizens have been an important voting bloc for all parties. Electoral segmentation is thus neither uniquely Conservative nor exclusively ethnic. If it can be said that there is something different about the Conservatives' approach, it is perhaps in their overt and unapologetic linkage between politics, policy, and electioneering. Party officials made little secret of the ways in which the government tied its public policy agenda to its political goals. Government resources were even used to political ends (Cheadle and Levitz 2012). Again, this is not uniquely Conservative. What is different is not the blind or unyielding pursuit of power, but rather the frankness with which this party has pursued those ends. Broad public policy objectives were frequently obscured by wanton electioneering, with Bricker and Ibbitson (2013, 271) aptly characterizing the government's approach as "resolutely principled, when convenient." A scan of the Conservative caucus drew this observation into stark relief, with racial minority MPs having received symbolic roles but few positions of real power or influence throughout the government's tenure. I would argue that immigrant and minority Canadians were used instrumentally. The Conservative Party pandered to them with piecemeal offerings that conveniently appeased them without alienating core supporters elsewhere.

The 2015 election challenged this approach, with the Conservatives struggling to stem the tide of Liberal support. The government's proposed ban on the niqab – opposed by both the Liberals and the NDP – was part of the Conservatives' undoing. The NDP criticized the move and watched its fortunes in Quebec fall. The Conservatives picked up some of these seats, but voters elsewhere, sensing a shift, threw their support behind the Liberals. The Conservatives attempted to employ wedge politics; nowhere were the results of this gamble more evident than in the Greater Toronto Area, where the so-called ethnic battlegrounds went almost entirely Liberal.

While in office, the Conservatives walked a tightrope, hoping to appeal to racial minority and immigrant voters while still retaining the affections of their rural and Western base. The 2015 election illustrated how the relationship between Conservatives and their immigrant and minority supporters could be damaged by tactics that vilified Muslims, refugees, and dual citizens. Moreover, Conservatives struggled to gain a foothold with large numbers of racial minority voters. With this racial minority population making up an increasing proportion of many ridings, the party effectively saw its edge evaporate. At the time of writing, Conservatives were engaged in selecting a new leader. Some of the candidates, including Kellie Leitch and Stephen Blaney, advocate tightening immigration policy. Leitch has proposed to screen potential immigrants for "Canadian values," while Blaney has suggested he would invoke the Charter's notwithstanding clause in order to prohibit niqabs from citizenship ceremonies. How these policies would help to resuscitate the party's fortunes is unclear.

As they pick up the pieces following their 2015 defeat, the Conservatives might be well advised to peer into the past. The Liberal Party's dramatic implosion in 2011, while surprising, had in some ways been foreshadowed by the unrest of voters and party members who felt ignored and taken for granted. The Liberals' long affinity with immigrant and minority voters was partly a result of relationships that were sown, cultivated, and nurtured. These relationships are the basis of trust, and that trust can draw voters closer, while its absence can push them away. Certainly, in an increasingly diverse country, political parties are remiss if they are not at least somewhat responsive to the needs and concerns of Canadians with immigrant and minority backgrounds. When part of a coherent and consistent policy framework, such responsiveness is good for Canadian democracy. That said, the alarm must be sounded when concerns are tokenized, ignored outside of elections, or largely heeded in a Hail Mary pass to invigorate party fortunes. When attempting to retain power, no party appears immune to such temptations.

REFERENCES

Abu-Laban, Yasmeen. 1998. "Welcome/STAY OUT: The Contradiction of Canadian Integration and Immigration Policies at the Millennium." *Canadian Ethnic Studies* 30 (3): 190–211.

Alberts, Sheldon. 2000. "Dumped Alliance Candidate Fires Back at Day." *National Post*, 21 November.

Anderson, Bruce, and David Coletto. 2015. *The Niqab, Hijab, Anxiety & Accommodation*. Ottawa: Abacus Data.

Anderson, Christopher G., and Jerome H. Black. 2008. "The Political Integration of Newcomers, Minorities and the Canadian-Born: Perspectives on Naturalization, Participation, and Representation." In *Immigration and Integration in Canada in the Twenty-First Century*, edited by John Biles, Meyer Burstein, and James Frideres, 45–75. Montreal and Kingston: McGill-Queen's University Press.

Andrew, Caroline, John Biles, Myer Siemiatycki, and Erin Tolley, eds. 2008. *Electing a Diverse Canada: The Electoral Representation of Immigrants, Minorities and Women*. Vancouver: UBC Press.

Bellett, Gerry. 1988. "Decision to Reject Collins Made for Party, Reform Chief Says." *Vancouver Sun*, 20 October.

Bilodeau, Antoine, and Mebs Kanji. 2006. "Political Engagement among Immigrants in Four Anglo-Democracies." *Electoral Insight* 8 (2): 43–9.

Black, Jerome H. 2000. "Ethnoracial Minorities in the Canadian House of Commons: The Case of the 36th Parliament." *Canadian Ethnic Studies* 32 (2): 105–14.

– 2002. "Ethnoracial Minorities in the House of Commons: An Update on the 37th Parliament." *Canadian Parliamentary Review* (Spring): 24–8.

– 2008. "The 2006 Federal Election and Visible Minority Candidates: More of the Same?" *Canadian Parliamentary Review* 30 (3): 30–6.

– 2011. "Visible Minority Candidates and MPs: An Update Based on the 2008 Federal Election." *Canadian Parliamentary Review* 34 (1): 30–4.

– 2013. "Racial Diversity in the 2011 Federal Election: Visible Minority Candidates and MPs." *Canadian Parliamentary Review* 36 (3): 21–6.

Black, Jerome H., and Lynda Erickson. 2006. "Ethno-Racial Origins of Candidates and Electoral Performance: Evidence from Canada." *Party Politics* 12 (4): 541–61. http://dx.doi.org/10.1177/1354068806064733.

Black, Jerome H., and Bruce Hicks. 2006. "Visible Minority Candidates in the 2004 Election." *Canadian Parliamentary Review* 29 (2): 26–31.

– 2008. "Electoral Politics and Immigration in Canada: How Does Immigration Matter?" *Journal of International Migration and Integration* 9 (3): 241–67. http://dx.doi.org/10.1007/s12134-008-0069-5.

Blais, André, Elisabeth Gidengil, Richard Nadeau, and Neil Nevitte. 2002. *Anatomy of a Liberal Victory: Making Sense of the Vote in the 2000 Canadian Election*. Peterborough, ON: Broadview.

Bricker, Darrell, and John Ibbitson. 2013. *The Big Shift: The Seismic Change in Canadian Politics, Business, and Culture and What It Means for Our Future*. Toronto: HarperCollins.

Canadian Alliance. 2000. *A Time for Change: An Agenda of Respect for All Canadians*. Calgary: Canadian Alliance.

Canadian Press. 2014. "Jason Kenney on Hot Seat as Controversy Rages over Temporary Foreign Workers." CBC News, 29 April. http://www.cbc.ca/news/politics/jason-kenney-on-hot-seat-as-controversy-rages-over-temporary-foreign-workers-1.2625377.

Center for Research-Action on Race Relations. 2006. "The 2006 Federal Election Result: Visible Minorities Still Under-represented in the House of Commons." News release. Montreal: CRARR.

Champion, Christian P. 2006. "Courting 'Our Ethnic Friends': Canadianism, Britishness, and New Canadians, 1950–1970." *Canadian Ethnic Studies* 38 (1): 23–46.

Chapnick, Adam. 2011. "A 'Conservative' National Story? The Evolution of Citizenship and Immigration Canada's *Discover Canada*." *American Review of Canadian Studies* 41 (1): 20–36. http://dx.doi.org/10.1080/02722011.2010.544853.

Cheadle, Bruce, and Stephanie Levitz. 2012. "Ethnic Media Monitored for Kenney's Image." *Globe and Mail*, 14 November.

Chignall, Selina. 2015. "Immigrants Are Not a Monolithic Voting Block." *iPolitics*, 22 September. http://ipolitics.ca/2015/09/22/immigrants-are-not-a-monolithic-voting-block/.

Citizenship and Immigration Canada. 2014. *Facts and Figures – Immigration Overview: Permanent and Temporary Residents*. Ottawa: Minister of Public Works and Government Services.

Conservative Party. 2011. "Breaking Through: Building the Conservative Brand." Internal party document.

Conservative Party of Canada. 2013. Immigration. Accessed 1 October 2012, http://www.conservative.ca/?page_id=1414.

Crawford, Kyle. 2011. "Diversity in the 41st Parliament Ottawa." Samara. Accessed 8 August 2013. http://www2.samaracanada.com/blog/post/Inside-the-41st-Parliament-NDP-now-most-diverse-Liberals-least-diverse.aspx.

Cross, William. 2004. *Political Parties*. Vancouver: UBC Press.

Cross, William, and Lisa Young. 2002. "The Study of Canadian Political Parties." Survey data. Sackville, NB.

Edelman, Murray. 1964. *The Symbolic Uses of Politics*. Urbana, IL: University of Illinois Press.

Edmiston, Jake. 2015. "Tory MP Larry Miller on Women Wearing Niqabs at Citizenship Ceremonies." *National Post*, 17 March. http://news.nationalpost .com/news/canada/canadian-politics/tory-mp-larry-miller-on-women-wearing-niqab-at-citizenship-ceremonies-stay-the-hell-where-you-came-from.

Flanagan, Tom. 2009. *Harper's Team: Behind the Scenes in the Conservative Rise to Power*. 2nd ed. Montreal and Kingston: McGill-Queen's University Press.

– 2011. "The Emerging Conservative Coalition." *Policy Options* (June–July): 104–8.

Friesen, Joe. 2015. "PMO Ordered Halt to Refugee Processing." *Globe and Mail*, 8 October.

Griffith, Andrew. 2013. *Policy Arrogance or Innocent Bias*. Ottawa: Anar.

– 2015a. *Canadian Citizenship: "Harder to Get, Easier to Lose."* Canadian Bar Association. https://multiculturalmeanderings.files.wordpress.com/2015/05/citizenship-cba-8-may-2015-final.pdf.

– 2015b. "Visible Minority Candidates in the 2015 Election: Making Progress." *Policy Options*. http://policyoptions.irpp.org/2015/10/17/visible-minority-candidates-in-the-2015-election-making-progress/.

Harell, Allison. 2013. "Revisiting the 'Ethnic' Vote: Liberal Allegiance and Vote Choice among Racialized Minorities." In *Parties, Elections and the Future of Canadian Politics*, edited by Amanda Bittner and Royce Koop, 140–60. Vancouver: UBC Press.

Harper, Tim. 2013. "PM Pushes Youth but Relies on the Old Guard." *Toronto Star*, 16 July.

Henton, Darcy. 1996. "Seeing the Light on Reform's Dark Side." *Toronto Star*, 3 July.

Jetha, Inayat. 2002. "Linking Party, Riding and Community: Ethnic Minority Politicians in Canada." Master's thesis, University of Calgary.

Leblanc, Daniel. 2007. "Tories Target Specific Ethnic Voters." *Globe and Mail*, 16 October.

Levitz, Stephanie. 2013. "Multiculturalism Funding: Feds Allowing Millions to Go Unspent Each Year." *Huffington Post*, 5 July.

Loewen, Peter. 2015. "Support for Niqab Bans Is Deep and Wide." *Ottawa Citizen*, 10 October.

MacCharles, Tonda. 2008. "Travelling Tory Woos Ethnic Voters." *Toronto Star*, 23 February.

Madan, Richard. 1998. "Building Bridges with Ethnic Voters: The Reform Party Wants to Bring Visible Minorities under Its Wing." *Ottawa Citizen*, 1 November.

Martin, Lawrence. 2010. *Harperland: The Politics of Control*. Toronto: Viking.

Marwah, Inder, Triadafilos Triadafilopoulos, and Stephen White. 2013. "Immigration, Citizenship and Canada's New Conservative Party." In *Conservatism in Canada*, edited by James Farney and David Rayside, 95–119. Toronto: University of Toronto Press.

Matas, Robert. 2000. "'Scurrilous' Ads Enrage Alliance." *Globe and Mail*, 24 November.

Mickleburgh, Rod. 2000. "Alliance Fundraiser Fired for Comments." *Globe and Mail*, 17 November.

Parliament of Canada. 2012. "Members of the House of Commons Born outside Canada." Library of Parliament. http://www.parl.gc.ca/Parlinfo/Compilations/Parliament/BornOutsideCanada.aspx?Menu=HOC-Bio&Show=MP.

Parliament of Canada. 2013. "Parlinfo." http://www.parl.gc.ca/Parlinfo/

Persichelli, Angelo. 2011. "Soudas Helped Kenney Change His Approach with Ethnic Media." *Hill Times*, 6 June.

Picot, Garnett, and Feng Hou. 2003. *The Rise in Low-Income Rates among Immigrants in Canada*. Ottawa: Minister of Industry.

Porter, John. 1965. *The Vertical Mosaic: An Analysis of Social Class and Power in Canada*. Toronto: University of Toronto Press. http://dx.doi.org/10.3138/9781442683044.

Quan, Douglas. 2015a. "Harper Vows to Appeal Court Ruling Allowing Women to Wear Niqab during Citizenship Oath." *National Post*, 12 February. http://news.nationalpost.com/news/niqab-court-ruling-appeal.

– 2015b. "Ottawa Urges Court to Prevent Muslim Woman from Taking Oath before Election." *National Post*, 30 September.

Rana, Abbas. 2008. "Tories Set Sights on Winning 30 More Ridings in Next Election." *Hill Times*, 28 July.

Reform Party of Canada. 1988. *Platform and Statement of Principles*. Calgary, AB: Reform Party of Canada.

– 1990. *Principles and Policies*. Calgary, AB: Reform Party of Canada.

– 1995. *Principles and Policies*. Calgary, AB: Reform Party of Canada.

Reitz, Jeffrey G. 2012. "The Distinctiveness of Canadian Immigration Experience." *Patterns of Prejudice* 46 (5): 518–38. http://dx.doi.org/10.1080/0031322X.2012.718168.

Simpson, Jeffrey. 1997. "Reform's Visible-Minority Members Support Its Line on Equality." *Globe and Mail*, 2 October.

– 2013. "Slice-and-Dice Politics, Conservative Style." *Globe and Mail*, 23 February.

Soroka, Stuart, Fred Cutler, Dietlind Stolle, and Patrick Fournier. 2011. "Capturing Change (and Stability) in the 2011 Campaign." *Policy Options* 32 (6): 70–7.

Tolley, Erin. 2015. "Visible Minority and Indigenous Members of Parliament."
   In *Canadian Election Analysis: Communication, Strategy, and Democracy*, edited
   by Alex Marland and Thierry Giasson, 50–1. Vancouver: UBC Press.
– 2016. *Framed: Media and the Coverage of Race in Canadian Politics*. Vancouver:
   UBC Press.
Tolley, Erin, and Elizabeth Goodyear-Grant. 2014. "Experimental Evidence
   on Race and Gender Affinity Effects in Candidate Choice." Paper presented
   at the annual meeting of the Canadian Political Science Association,
   St Catharines, ON, 29 May.
Walkom, Thomas. 1988. "Running a Campaign on Race." *Globe and Mail*,
   31 October.
Wente, Margaret. 2015. "Why Stephen Harper Is Playing Niqab Politics." *Globe
   and Mail*, 21 February. http://www.theglobeandmail.com/globe-debate/
   why-stephen-harper-is-playing-niqab-politics/article23117749/.

6 Equality of Opportunity but Not Result: Women and Federal Conservatives in Canada

MELANEE THOMAS

As essential as it is for democracy, the concept of equality is highly contested. Asking whether or not a person or group is "equal" in politics raises the question, equal in what? Some might say that the best way to measure political equality is to focus on outcomes or results. This view typically examines groups and sees equality as a collective outcome. Others might contend that the presence of equal opportunities or the absence of barriers better measure equality in politics. This view emphasizes individual results over collective or group-based results.

Those who focus on equality of outcome or result may examine Canadian women's position in politics and argue that, because women are not included in political institutions at the same rates as men, gender equality does not yet exist in Canadian politics. By contrast, those who ascribe to equality of opportunity might note that there are no formal restrictions on women's participation in the political process and use this to conclude that there is gender equality in Canadian politics. Indeed, how a party reacts to political groups such as women, as well as the policy positions and actions typically associated with these groups, depends a great deal on the view of equality that a party subscribes to.

Parties and advocacy organizations that lean to the political left, such as the New Democratic Party (NDP) or advocacy organizations such as Equal Voice, argue that women will not be equal in Canadian politics until they achieve political outcomes that are on par with men's (Cross 2004; Equal Voice 2009). However, federal conservative parties since 1993 have taken a different approach, emphasizing equality of opportunity. From the outset, the Reform and Canadian Alliance parties, and to some extent the merged Conservative Party, have rejected the existence of group-based politics and "women's issues" (see chapter 10 in this volume). Any issue that might relate to gender and/or women is instead folded under a broader policy domain, such as crime and justice, or the family. Any public effort to engage women voters *as women* was, and continues to be, routinely rejected by these parties. Their stance may be due, in part, to an assumption or understanding that women in the conservative parties' rank and file also hold these fundamental individualist views; it may also be due to a reluctance to make public any internal equity efforts engaged in by the party. As a result, the current (public) Conservative approach to women is much more consistent over time than is their approach to visible minorities (see chapter 5 in this volume). Conservative efforts directed at visible minorities, though instrumental and strategic, are still directed at them as a *group*. By contrast, Conservatives simply do not engage with women as a political category.

This chapter argues that the concepts of individualism and equality of opportunity provide a useful lens with which to evaluate how women are integrated in Canada's federal conservative parties – the Progressive Conservative Party, the Reform Party, the Canadian Alliance, and the Conservative Party of Canada – from 1993 to 2015. This evaluation contains three planks and asks three questions:

1 Public policy: How have individualism and the rejection of traditionally defined "women's issues" shaped conservative parties' policy?
2 Electoral involvement: To what extent have women participated in internal party democracy as candidates for election and parliamentary office holders?
3 Political participation: How has conservative parties' rejection of women as a political group structured their engagement with women as voters? How have women voters responded to this approach?

Consistent with the overall theme of this volume, this chapter argues that between 1993 and 2015, federal conservative parties shifted the Canadian policy agenda to the right. In so doing, they have redefined the options now offered by *all* federal parties on some issues, such as child care. Similarly, collectivist elements of the Progressive Conservative Party that may have been open to engaging with women as a political group in the 1980s and 1990s appear to have been muted or jettisoned during the merger. Thus, we need to understand how (and which) women were integrated into the Reform Party and the Canadian Alliance if we are to understand why the Conservative Party of Canada rejects gender-based politics.

"We want to say there aren't any women's issues"

The late 1980s and early 1990s marked a period of social change and political contention in Canada. Social issues such as abortion and euthana-
sia were challenged in the courts and in Parliament, and the meaning of
gender equality was contested through mega-constitutional processes,
including the failed Meech Lake and Charlottetown Accords.[1] These issues, when coupled with an economic downturn, highlight this period
as one of "social-cultural, economic and political turmoil" (Sigurdson
1994, 261–2).

The Reform Party reacted to this context using moral (Judeo-
Christian) traditionalism as a foundation for a unified Canadian culture
that emphasizes law and order, and free enterprise (Sigurdson 1994,
261–2). This combined emphasis on social and economic conservatism
produced a considerable emphasis on the power and role of the individual. Indeed, much of Reform's economic and social policy was predicated on individuals knowing what is best for themselves; the extension
of this idea was that individuals should be free from government interference or regulation to do what they want (ibid.). This was echoed in
much of the policy of the merged party and the Harper government's.

This yearning for economic freedom did not, however, include a desire for greater individuality in social or political life. Instead, Reform's
emphasis on individuality "also represents an open hostility to the individual promoted by cultural changes that threaten to overturn traditional patterns of society" (Sigurdson 1994, 275–6). This was manifested
in the Reform Party as a rejection of equality of result, affirmative action, and "women's issues." For example, a 1996 Reform Party Task
Force on the Charter of Rights and Freedoms contended that equality
rights have "been interpreted by the courts as guaranteeing equality of
outcome, rather than equality of opportunity … To end this tendency
in the interpretation of Section 15(1), we have added the words 'equality of opportunity" to the Section" (Reform Party of Canada 1996, 20).

The task force report further stated, "There is no part of the Charter
more repugnant to mainstream Canadian values than Section 15(2)," the
section that defines affirmative action programs as permissible under

---

1 As many as five provinces initially agreed to a gender-equal Senate reform proposal
   forwarded by the National Action Committee on the Status of Women (NAC),
   where half the Senate seats would be reserved for women (Rebick and Day 1992).

the Canadian constitution (Reform Party of Canada 1996, 21). Thus, the party's proposed changes to equality rights under the Charter would have made it unconstitutional to enact legislation to ameliorate the "conditions of disadvantaged individuals or groups" (22). According to this task force report, the only appropriate way to introduce legislation to ameliorate the condition of disadvantaged individuals or groups of Canadians was through a majority vote in a referendum (ibid.). Though critics might baulk at using majority rule to restrict or remove minority rights, individuals subscribing to Reform's view may argue this concern is removed when equality is defined only in terms of opportunities rather than results.

A similar view underpinned Reform's rejection of Section 27 of the Charter. This section requires that the Charter be interpreted in a manner consistent with Canada's multicultural society. Reform rejected this on the grounds that Section 27 "has the potential for group-specific rights to be 'read in' to the Charter" (Reform Party of Canada 1996, 23). In both cases, any barrier to "equal" competition was identified as problematic. For the Reform Party, this included any provision or mechanism designed to assist historically and/or systematically disadvantaged groups, as such provisions and mechanisms are perceived to be an unfair advantage for "people who have not proved they deserve it" (Dahlerup 2007, 75). Placing such strong emphasis on individualism and individual rights led the Reform Party, and those conservative parties that came after it, to reject group politics.

Rejecting group politics has specific consequences for women, as clearly seen in the Reform Party of Canada Women's Work Group meeting in November 1990 (Reform Party of Canada Records, 1990). Three expert speakers were invited to address the group on economic issues, domestic violence and legal issues, and health. No formal report was generated from this meeting; instead, the invited speakers and the question and answer period that followed were video recorded; that video was subsequently donated to the University of Calgary archives.[2]

The recording includes several questions from the floor that are illuminating, particularly for understandings of how women are integrated

---

2 Following each presentation and question and answer period, the participants gathered in small groups to discuss the material and make policy recommendations for the Reform Party, focusing on how each proposal reflected "economic, social, and populist" concerns. The event appears to be chaired by Sandra Manning.

within the Reform Party. The women present rejected equality of result and embraced radical individualism in a manner consistent with the task force on the Charter highlighted above. For example, the expert presenter on economic issues noted that pay equity – ensuring that women are paid the same as men for work of the same value – could overcome the portion of the gender pay gap that economists attribute to outright bias against women in the workplace. In response, a participant commented, "I have a bit of a problem with the whole affirmative action thing. I think that if you say, 'I'm going to hire you because you're a woman, as opposed to you because you're a man,' then that's just going to increase the resentment, and say, 'Well you know really, like you're incompetent and we hired you because you're a woman and we had to, we were forced to.'" This comment suggests that rather than acknowledging the bias or discrimination women may systematically face in the workplace, the women participating in this Reform Party event assumed these policies would be used instead to unjustifiably favour women over men, as though women who may need pay equity provisions have not really "earned" it. Similarly, the fear appeared to be that instead of rewarding them for their individual merit, policies designed to support women as a group may actually penalize individual women.

The most pointed question about group politics and women was directed to the expert speaker on domestic violence, in part because the speaker's presentation clearly indicated that patterns of spousal and child abuse are strongly gendered: this expert stated that women are overwhelmingly more likely than men to be victims of domestic violence, while the perpetrators of that violence are almost always men. The first question from the floor directly questioned how the Reform Party appeared to be addressing this kind of social pattern: "From what you're saying, would you then agree with this statement: that you think it is socially irresponsible for political leadership party to … not take a proactive position on issues that are pertinent specifically to women, *even if we want to ignore the fact and we want to say they aren't women's issues*? You have told us that battered women affect women, that wage inequity affects women. Is it [pause] socially responsible for a party to [pause] accept their responsibility to be proactive on these issues, and actually promote the changing of these issues?" (emphasis added).

The speaker responded, "Calling [domestic violence] a woman's issue, I think, is not terribly productive." The rationale for rejecting the label "woman's issue" is multifaceted but includes the notion that identifying issues as those that disproportionately affect women makes it

easier for such issues to be ignored or omitted from the political agenda. Though this may be true, it helps show the bias against women and
gender issues in politics at the time. This reinforces the idea that equality of opportunity –that women compete equally with men for political
attention and policy – may not exist, especially if Canadian politics is
dominated by men. Beyond the participant's question, this connection
between women's issues and problems with equality of opportunity
was not made explicit at the Reform Party event.

Other participants' comments did not reflect such clear rejections of
group politics. Some noted that men on their constituency association
executives were upset that men were not invited to the event. They
reported that these men said, "This constituency should deal with violence against women, and it's our problem as men." The participant
concluded from this conversation with her constituency association executive, "Dealing with what we perceive, or are supposed to perceive as
a woman's issue, and excluding the cause of the issue is our mistake."

Several insights stem from this early Reform meeting. First, it was
discussed and broadly accepted by the participants that women within
the Reform Party wanted to say that there "aren't any women's issues"
(see also Flanagan 2009). This can be interpreted as an endorsement of
equality of opportunity and individualism from the party's rank and
file. That said, this view was openly questioned, suggesting that even
from the outset, at least some Reform Party members were interested in
addressing issues that disproportionately affect women. Nevertheless,
when issues such as pay equity are raised, there is a strong perception
that policies to address them undermine meritocracy by potentially
disadvantaging other individuals who may or may not be part of the
group(s) motivating those policies.

Finally, the video suggested that the views expressed at the event
mattered for Reform's early policies, and that women and traditionally defined women's issues were not a priority for the Reform Party.
In the early 1990s, a meeting like the one in the video outlined above
would have carried weight with the Reform Party, as it is a quintes-
sential example of grassroots, populist policymaking. This was the
heart of Reform's notion of "doing politics differently." A comparable
event in more established parties, such as the Liberal or Progressive
Conservative Party, would have been more easily dismissed because
there were large gaps between the parliamentary and extra-parliamentary wings of the parties. However, this video is the *only* part of the Reform
Party archive that directly addresses women. Therefore, it is especially

telling, though not surprising, that grassroots women were not nurtured as women in the party beyond a single event in 1990. This suggests that women were neither integrated into the party at the same rate or scope as men at that time, nor were they into the future.

How has the emphasis on equality of opportunity translated into conservative parties' policy positions on issues that are traditionally defined as "women's issues"? Three are examined here: childcare, pay equity, and Status of Women Canada.

Childcare

Federal conservative parties' positions on childcare changed dramatically between 1988 and 1993. In 1988, the governing Progressive Conservative Party proposed a $6.4 billion childcare strategy to create a national childcare system to help women access the labour market (Progressive Conservative Party of Canada 1988). The party abandoned this policy during the economic recession in the early 1990s; subsequent childcare policies from all federal parties have been shaped by the Reform Party's 1993 statement on childcare (although some more quickly than others). The Reform Party opposed a public childcare system, instead advocating that the government subsidize "financial need, not the methods, institutions, or professionals who supply child care. Let parents decide what's right for their child" (Reform Party of Canada 1992). By 2000, the Progressive Conservatives were proposing to increase the Child Tax Credit to $1176 per child per year (Progressive Conservative Party of Canada 2000). The Canadian Alliance's proposal increased the amount to $3000 per child per year (Canadian Alliance 2000). The policy that was ultimately introduced by the Conservative government in 2006 was a $1200 per year "Choice in Child Care Allowance" for each child under the age of six (Conservative Party of Canada 2006).

Though the Conservative Party's recent platforms attacked left-leaning political parties for continuing to propose a national childcare program, it is worth noting that even the social democratic New Democratic Party of Canada (NDP) advocated for increasing the amount of non-taxable funding provided through the child tax benefits (NDP 2011, 2015). This suggests that federal conservative parties' positions on funding childcare through tax credits has acted as a policy contagion, even for parties that continue to advocate for public childcare programs. Indeed, by 2015, both the Conservatives and Liberals were speaking about childcare only in terms of tax credits (Conservative Party of Canada

2015; Liberal Party of Canada 2015). Any discussion of childcare as a social program was absent from the Conservative platform, while the Liberals made reference to childcare in both 2011 and 2015 without providing program or policy details outside of tax credits (Liberal Party of Canada 2011, 2015). Only the NDP campaigned on creating a national system of childcare in these recent elections (NDP 2015).

Pay Equity

On the recommendation of the Royal Commission on the Status of Women, women workers in Canada have the right to equal pay for work of equal value through the Canadian Human Rights Act (Pay Equity Task Force 2004, 1; Canadian Human Rights Act 1985). This speaks both to the legal and popular understanding of pay equity and its focus on the value of the work or tasks performed. Pay equity is not the same as equal pay; though both are covered by statute, equal pay legislation covers women and men employed in the same or similar jobs. By contrast, pay equity evaluates whether the remuneration in different jobs that require comparable levels of skill, effort, and responsibility are equivalent. Only those employed in jobs traditionally held by women can make a pay equity claim (Ontario Pay Equity Commission 2012). This emphasis on value means that what constitutes pay equity is broader than what constitutes equal pay.

The view taken by federal conservative parties after 1993 is narrower. The Conservative Party of Canada argued, "Individuals should only be judged on skills, qualifications and merits. Women must be entitled to equal pay for equal work" (Conservative Party of Canada 2014, 29). This is an endorsement of equal pay, as well as a tacit rejection of pay equity and group-based politics. This view is not surprising, given the resistance to the legal and economic definitions of pay equity provided to the Reform Party's Women Work Group noted above.

This resistance may be rooted more in economic conservatism than in a rejection of group-based politics. It seems plausible, for example, that an economic conservative would reject pay equity as a concept by arguing that if the work performed in different jobs was of equal value, the market would recognize this value, and those employed in those different jobs would be paid comparable salaries. Two implications stem from this argument. First, the systematically lower wages found in traditionally feminine occupations relative to traditionally masculine occupations reflects a "real" difference in value, rather than stereotypes or bias that undervalues women's work. If the work was of equal value, the market would recognize this, and there would be no pay gap. Second, individuals or groups that use legal remedies to seek pay equity do so without justification because the market does not deem their work to be meritorious.

The difficulty with this market argument is that it is tautological: if the market is always assumed to assess the value of work fairly, as it is by some forms of economic conservatism and ideology, then there is no possible interpretation of real wages in a market that would determine work is undervalued. This is perhaps why several pay equity cases that largely feature a systematic gender gap in pay for men over women have legal merit (see, for example, *Public Service Alliance of Canada v Canada Post Corp* 2011).

Status of Women Canada

Shortly after forming government in 2006, the Conservatives announced three key changes to Status of Women Canada (SoW).[3] First, its budget was to be cut by $5 million, resulting in the closure of twelve of sixteen regional offices (Canada 2007b). Second, its Policy Research Fund – originally designed to "support independent, nationally relevant forward-thinking policy research on gender issues" – was eliminated (7). Third, the mandate of SoW's Women's Program was reframed around "women's economic status and violence against women" (3). Any initiative proposed by a group to engage in research, to advocate on behalf of women, or to facilitate the involvement of women and women's groups in the policy process was labelled as ineligible for funding (3–4).

This policy decision highlights the implications of defining equality by opportunities rather than results. When the Standing Committee responsible for Status of Women held hearings on the changes to SoW, a minority of witnesses, including the minister responsible for SoW, argued that the programs should target individual women who faced individual barriers, because Canadian women and men are equal *in law*. As a result, systematic advocacy or research examining gender inequality is argued to be unnecessary. However, the majority of witnesses argued

---

3 Status of Women Canada became an agency of the federal government in 1976 to coordinate policy and administer programs related to the status of women.

that there are considerable differences between equal rights under the law and equality of outcomes. One witness noted, "Legal experts now don't even talk about equality in law. They talk about equality in fact ... So, equality must be substantive, it must be real, and we must be able to measure it" (Canada 2007b, 9).

The majority of the recommendations presented in the Standing Committee's report use witness testimony to recommend that the Conservative government's policy changes to SoW be reversed (Canada 2007b, 17). The Conservative MPs on the committee dissented, arguing that "women have gained equal rights under Canadian law" (27), and that "all Canadians, women and men, are free to advocate to all levels of government and there is nothing to prevent organizations from raising money to advocate or conduct research" (28). Note how the Conservatives' view prioritizes equal competition, while simultaneously excluding any discussion of results or outcomes. By contrast, several groups that testified before the committee noted that though all Canadians might be free to approach government, relationships between government and many Canadian women, including Indigenous Canadian women, women who are poor, and living in rural or outlying areas, "are difficult, if not impossible, to cultivate" (14). This suggests that opportunities to address the government are not equal. Nevertheless, the government's response to the committee report highlighted economic initiatives, framing the issues raised as about "economic security and violence," rather than about women's issues (Canada, 2007a, 2).

Changes to the Status of Women represent some of the clearest implications of federal conservative parties' emphasis on equality of opportunity and individualism, and their rejection of equality of result. Their focus on individual opportunity led directly to policy changes that prevented women from using a government agency to make group-based equity claims, or even research whether policy outcomes systematically affect women and men in dissimilar ways. This view persists despite community and academic reports presented directly to the government through a parliamentary committee documenting gender-based inequalities of outcome.

Two broad conclusions can be drawn from these policy examples. First, when federal conservative parties appear to be ignorant or dismissive of women's issues, that may be more the result of a strong commitment to assumptions about politics. When politics is seen to be about individuals rather than groups and when the market is seen to be infallible in assigning value to work, it narrows the scope of the parties' preferred policy options. Though these options can be fairly evaluated as anti-feminist and resistant to gender equality (Bird and Rowe 2013), discussions of alternatives may be unproductive. If the alternatives start with different premises about equality, individualism, and economics, the result may be "talking past" the conservative parties' proposals. This "talking past" is evident in the SoW report cited above, especially when the positions of the committee and of Minister Bev Oda are compared.

Second, the fact that federal conservative parties take policy positions on women's issues indicates they do not necessarily ignore women as a constituency (see chapter 3 in this volume). Rather, the women integrated into these parties represent a narrow, potentially homogeneous sub-population of Canadian women.[4] Like the parties themselves, these women have a strong commitment to individualism and market conservatism, they reject "women's issues," and they reject definitions of equality predicated on results. Women who disagree with these starting premises simply have not been integrated into these conservative parties.

Does the Conservative Party Actively Recruit Women Candidates?

Given the parties' emphasis on individualism and meritocracy, it should not be difficult for women in these parties to be nominated as candidates, should they wish to be. They would, in theory, simply need to demonstrate that they are the best possible candidate in a district. Yet table 6.1 demonstrates that this is likely not the case.

The most "gender equal" candidate slates for federal conservative parties appear for the Progressive Conservatives in 1993 and 1997, and in 2008 and 2011 for the Conservative Party of Canada. Here, about one in five candidates nominated by these parties is a woman. This record does not sparkle when compared to other parties – for example, 43 per cent of NDP candidates, 40 per cent of Green candidates, and 31 per cent of Liberal candidates in 2015 were women (Parliament of Canada 2015, author's calculations). Still, one in five is the most "gender equal" a conservative party's candidate slate has been since 1993. The other elections shown in table 6.1 demonstrate that outside the elections noted above, federal conservative parties typically nominate a dismally

---

4 Cross (2004) notes that Canadian Alliance Party members are a homogeneous group, being older, whiter, wealthier, and more likely to be men than the general population.

Table 6.1. Women Candidates by Party and Election

Election year	Progressive Conservative Party	Reform/ Canadian Alliance	Conservative Party of Canada
1993	67 (23%)	23 (11%)	–
1997	56 (19%)	23 (10%)	–
2000	39 (13%)	32 (11%)	–
2004	–	–	36 (12%)
2006	–	–	38 (12%)
2008	–	–	63 (21%)
2011	–	–	68 (22%)
2015	–	–	65 (19%)

Source: Parliament of Canada (2015), author's calculations.

low number of women candidates. This is especially the case for the
Reform and Canadian Alliance parties, as well as the earliest elections
conducted with the merged Conservative Party of Canada.

Why does this pattern appear both at the beginning and the end of
the period under study? In 1993, the likely reason is the Progressive
Conservative Party's imminent and expected electoral defeat. Women
candidates are more likely to be nominated in districts they are unlikely
to win, especially in times of crisis such as the imminent loss of government through general election (Thomas and Bodet 2013; Bruckmüller
and Branscombe 2010); this sacrificial lamb effect arguably affected
nomination contests for the Progressive Conservatives in 1993 and may
have continued to do so for the party in 1997 (Goodyear-Grant 2010).
Still, this cannot explain why precipitously fewer women were nominated for the Progressive Conservatives by the 2000 election.

The pattern at the end of the period is different, as the number of
women candidates nominated by the Conservative Party of Canada
nearly doubled from 38 in 2006 to 63 in 2008. Raw numbers suggest
that this jump cannot be due to a sudden increase in supply (Ashe and
Stewart 2012, 691). Every federal party in Canada was required to find
only 154 (2004–11) or 169 (2015) women to recruit as candidates to field
a gender-equal candidate slate. One way to facilitate this is to ensure
that women are elected to electoral district association (EDA) executives. EDA executives are often tasked with recruiting candidates, and
research shows that women executives are significantly more likely

to recruit women candidates (Cheng and Tavits 2011). It is implausible that Conservative women's credentials changed so dramatically between 2006 and 2008 that a new supply of qualified women was available to the party. It is equally implausible that the proportion of women on EDA executives doubled during this period. Instead, the timeline strongly suggests that there was a targeted effort to recruit more women candidates to run for the Conservative Party of Canada in 2008.[5]

If this is the case, the fact that the party does not state it publicly is telling. Instead, when advocacy organizations such as Equal Voice challenge federal parties to nominate an equal number of men and women candidates, the Conservative response highlighted how "women must have every *opportunity* to make a meaningful contribution to Canadian democracy" (Equal Voice 2009, emphasis added). As is the case with policy, conservative federal parties routinely emphasize equality of opportunity, even when their behaviour is more congruent with equality of result. Still, given the discrepancies that remain between the proportion of women nominated by the Conservative Party of Canada and other federal parties, it is reasonable to conclude that any efforts to increase women's candidacies may be less about equality of result and more about avoiding embarrassment.

Even if the Conservative Party of Canada made concerted efforts to nominate more women candidates, it does not follow that these efforts extend to ensuring these women actually win. Thomas and Bodet (2013) note that for all federal parties, women candidates are systematically nominated in ridings where their party's support is less stable over time. For the 2008 and 2011 federal elections, over one in three male Conservative candidates ran in seats that are, in effect, guaranteed victories; by contrast, fewer than one in five female Conservative candidates were placed in party strongholds. Comparable patterns are found in seats with incumbents, as well as open seats. As a result, if the Conservative Party of Canada nominated women in safe seats at the same rate that they did men in 2011, 25 per cent of the women in the House of Commons would come from the Conservative caucus alone. As it stands now, women barely comprise 25 per cent of the House

---

5 An alternative to the raw numbers approach is to assess what proportion of a group such as women seeks out nominations, and then to compare the proportion of that group that successfully secures a candidacy. This approach is more effective at assessing demand and gatekeeping of party officials (Ashe and Stewart 2012).

across all party caucuses (Parliament of Canada 2013). This analysis cannot be replicated for 2015, because the electoral boundaries were redistricted and thirty new seats were added to the House of Commons. Yet there is no evidence from the Conservatives to suggest this has changed, as they nominated fewer women as candidates in 2015 than in 2011, despite the addition of those thirty new seats. It is difficult to conclude from these results that women running as candidates for the Conservatives are given equal opportunities compared to their male peers.

Women's candidacies for federal conservative parties tell us three things. First, these parties do a poorer job at nominating women than do other federal parties. This suggests that women's integration into the more elite aspects of the party is, at best, underdeveloped. Second, table 6.1 shows that for most of the period under study, little to no effort was made to recruit women candidates for these parties. If any recruitment initiatives were undertaken, they have not been publicly disclosed; instead, the parties continue to publicly discuss this aspect of women's integration into their parties in terms of equality of opportunity alone. Third, despite the parties' rhetoric, the fact that Conservative women candidates are systematically nominated in districts they are less likely to win indicates that gender-based equality of opportunity remains a goal these parties have yet to achieve.

Engaging Steve and Heather, but Not Zoe

Federal conservative parties' emphasis on equality of opportunity, as well as their reluctance to disclose if and when they recruit women into more elite positions in the party, narrows their electoral appeal. For example, between 1993 and 2000, women were 11 percentage points less likely to vote for the Reform and Canadian Alliance parties than were men. This gender gap is identified as a key factor in the Alliance's failure to break through in Ontario (Gidengil et al. 2011). Therefore, a measure of success for the merged Conservative Party of Canada is their appeal to women voters.

Immediately after the merger, the Conservatives did better with women voters, as there was no gender gap in the party's support in 2004. However, though it is half the size it once was, the gender gap re-emerged in 2006 and has persisted since (Gidengil et al. 2011; see also McInturff 2015). Overall, the Canadian Election Studies show that though the Conservative Party expanded their support beyond the old Reform/Canadian Alliance base by gathering more votes in Ontario and suburban areas, the general constituency for the party has not grown. Conservative voters, like those who supported the Canadian Alliance and Reform Party, are more likely to be market conservatives with traditional moral values who support closer ties to the United States. Women remain considerably less likely than men to hold all these views (Gidengil et al. 2011).

Other important bases of support for the Conservatives include married voters, as well as (Protestant) Christians who believe the Bible is the literal word of God (Gidengil et al. 2011). This is reflected in voter profiles developed by Conservative Party strategists (Flanagan 2009, 223–4). To assist in understanding their base, the party developed and named imaginary supporters. Core Conservative constituents include "Steve and Heather," a Protestant, married couple in their forties with three children. Steve is reported to own his own business; the profile is silent about Heather, save for her relation to Steve. Another core voter is "Eunice," a Protestant in her seventies who lives on a modest pension, but owns her own home. "Mike and Theresa" are a Catholic couple who would be core Conservative voters if not for their religion (see also Blais 2005). Notably, "Zoe" is a caricature of a twenty-something woman who would never support the Conservatives, because she holds a bachelor of arts, does yoga, and eats organic food. Zoe's male counterpart is "Dougie," who works at Canadian Tire and is identified as a supportive voter who is difficult for the party to reach.

Though blunt, these profiles tell the same story as the Canadian Election Studies: family, religion, and gender are key socio-demographic factors that identify Conservative voters. While some women voters are integrated into party strategy, others are clearly excluded. Though the Conservatives increased their support in elections leading up to 2015, these voter vignettes suggest that the Conservative base – or at least the party's perception of its own base – has not changed much since the merger, especially with respect to women voters.

As a result, it is perhaps unsurprising the gender gap in vote choice for parties on the political right in Canadian federal elections persisted throughout the 2000s (see Gidengil et al. 2005), though it waned considerably by 2011 (Gidengil et al. 2011). Traditionally, Canadian women were more reluctant than men to support the Reform, Canadian Alliance, and merged Conservative Party of Canada, in part because women are more sceptical of market liberalism, less socially conservative, and less regionally alienated than are men (ibid.). However, by 2015, the gender gap in vote choice for the Conservative Party of Canada was considerable (again), as women were 7 percentage points less likely than men to vote for the Conservatives. Women were considerably more likely than men to hold negative evaluations of Stephen Harper and to think that it was time for a change in government. Furthermore, women broadly disagreed with the Conservative approach to issues such as how best to fund childcare, preferring a publicly funded system over direct support to parents (O'Neill and Thomas 2016). Given the role of the Reform Party in changing the national narrative on how best to address childcare in the early 1990s, this issue may have contributed to the merged Conservative's party weaker appeal to women twenty years later.

Conclusion

Canada's federal conservative parties approach women's integration through equality of opportunity and individualism: though the parties forward policy in domains traditionally identified as women's issues – including pay equity, childcare, and Status of Women examined here – they explicitly reject the "women's issues" label. The parties' emphasis on individualism and equality of opportunity also leads them to reject mechanisms designed to ameliorate systematic discrimination, whether those mechanisms exist in the Charter or in a government department such as Status of Women Canada. Unlike other groups' experiences with the parties over time (see chapter 5 in this volume), the parties' public approach to women's integration, or lack thereof, has been consistent.

That said, there is some evidence to suggest that the merged Conservative Party's closed-door approach to women's integration within the party as candidates is different. It is implausible that the supply of potential women Conservative candidates doubled between the 2006 and 2008 elections; instead, the most plausible explanation is that the party made a concerted effort to recruit women. This possibility has not been publicly disclosed, suggesting that it is more important to the party to be seen as championing individuals who through competition were identified as the best candidates – that is, equality of opportunity – instead of owning up to their efforts to ensure equality of result. It is also plausible that the party recruited women candidates because their inability to do so as compared to other parties was, and continues to be, somewhat embarrassing.

Overall, this approach to women's integration within the parties has not been especially successful. Certainly women who endorse equality of opportunity and reject group politics are present in these conservative parties. However, this does not appear to be the majority of Canadian women. The gender gap in Alliance support may have cost the party the 2000 federal election. Outside of 2004, women are considerably less likely to support these parties than are men (Gidengil et al. 2011). And when party strategists build voter profiles (Flanagan 2009), there is no evidence to suggest that they take women especially seriously as autonomous voters, save when it appears clear that they will not vote Conservative. Given that Canadian women are, on average, sceptical of market conservatism, traditional moral values, and closer ties to the United States (Gidengil et al. 2011), their support for the current Conservative Party will not likely change unless its approach to women and gender issues changes first.

It is possible that the Conservatives could expand their appeal to Canadian women without changing their commitment to equality of opportunity. Real questions remain about whether equality of opportunity actually exists in Canadian politics. Women candidates, including those who run for the Conservative Party, are disproportionately nominated in ridings they have poorer chances of winning (Thomas and Bodet 2013). The SoW report described above demonstrates that opportunities to address the government are not equal, especially for Indigenous Canadian women, poor women, and women in remote communities. Even those who reject "women's issues," such as the speaker at the Reform Party of Canada Women's Work Group, identify bias against women in politics when they observe that identifying issues that disproportionately affect women makes it easier for those issues to be ignored or omitted from the political agenda. And if international organizations identify women's political empowerment as about 20 per cent of men's (Schwab et al. 2013), it suggests equal competition for women in politics simply does not exist. Equality of opportunity can be used to generate strong arguments to address these issues.

However, to do so, group politics must be acknowledged to exist and to be legitimate. It is unlikely that the party leadership is prepared to do so publicly, in part because the ideas underpinning the parties' ideological orientations outlined above suggest that any reference to equality of result remains deeply antithetical to Conservative party elites and loyalists. Even so, maintaining this status quo appears unwise. Arguably, the Conservative majority in 2011 was produced by another party's implosion rather than by a meaningful increase to its base support. In order for the Conservatives to win again, they need to increase their base, and this includes meaningfully increasing their appeal to Canadian women. They had done neither by 2015. Though it would be ill-advised to disingenuously or unapologetically attempt to integrate any group into a political party for electoral purposes only, it does seem strategic for the Conservatives to genuinely reconsider their approach to integrating women and gender. Perhaps their best opportunity to do so is in the period following the 2015 election loss.

REFERENCES

Ashe, Jeanette, and Kennedy Stewart. 2012. "Legislative Recruitment: Using Diagnostic Testing to Explain Underrepresentation." *Party Politics* 18 (5): 687–707. http://dx.doi.org/10.1177/1354068810389635.

Bird, Karen, and Andrea Rowe. 2013. "Women, Feminism, and the Harper Conservatives." In *Conservatism in Canada*, edited by James Farney and David Rayside, 165–83. Toronto: University of Toronto Press.

Blais, André. 2005. "Accounting for the Electoral Success of the Liberal Party in Canada." *Canadian Journal of Political Science* 38 (4): 821–40.

Bruckmüller, Susanne, and Nyla E. Branscombe. 2010. "The Glass Cliff: When and Why Women Are Selected as Leaders in Crisis Contexts." *British Journal of Social Psychology* 49 (3): 433–51. http://dx.doi.org/10.1348/014466609X466594.

Canada. 2007a. Parliament. House of Commons. Standing Committee on the Status of Women. *Government Response to the Eighteenth Report of the Committee on the Status of Women*. 1 sess., 39th Parliament. http://www.parl.gc.ca/HousePublications/Publication.aspx?DocId=3077423&Language=E&Mode=1&Parl=39&Ses=1.

Canada. 2007b. Parliament. House of Commons. Standing Committee on the Status of Women. *The Impacts of Funding and Program Changes at Status of Women Canada*. 1 sess., 39th Parliament. Committee Report 18. http://www.parl.gc.ca/HousePublications/Publication.aspx?Language=E&Mode=1&Parl=39&Ses=1&DocId=2876038&File=0.

Canadian Alliance. 2000. *A Time for Change: An Agenda of Respect for All Canadians*. http://www.poltext.org/sites/poltext.org/files/plateformes/can2000all_plt_en._14112008_173717.pdf.

Cheng, Christine, and Margit Tavits. 2011. "Informal Influences in Selecting Female Political Candidates." *Political Research Quarterly* 64 (2): 460–71. http://dx.doi.org/10.1177/1065912909349631.

Conservative Party of Canada. 2006. *Stand Up for Canada: Conservative Party of Canada Federal Election Platform 2006.* http://www.poltext.org/sites/poltext.org/files/plateformes/can2006pc_plt_en._14112008_165519.pdf.

– 2014. *Conservative Party of Canada Policy Declaration.* http://www.conservative.ca/media/documents/Policy-Declaration-Feb-2014.pdf.

– 2015. *Our Conservative Plan to Protect the Economy.* http://s3.documentcloud.org/documents/2454398/conservative-platform-2015.pdf.

Cross, William. 2004. *Political Parties: The Canadian Democratic Audit.* Vancouver: UBC Press.

Dahlerup, Drude. 2007. "Electoral Gender Quotas: Between Equality of Opportunity and Equality of Result." *Representation* 43 (2): 73–92. http://dx.doi.org/10.1080/00344890701363227.

Equal Voice. 2009. "Canada Challenge 2009: Building the Momentum to Elect More Women in Canada." http://www.equalvoice.ca/challenge_09.cfm.

Flanagan, Tom. 2009. *Harper's Team: Behind the Scenes in the Conservative Rise to Power.* 2nd ed. Montreal and Kingston: McGill-Queen's University Press.

Gidengil, Elisabeth, Matthew Hennigar, André Blais, and Neil Nevitte. 2005. "Explaining the Gender Gap in Support for the New Right: The Case of Canada." *Comparative Political Studies* 38 (10): 1171–95. http://dx.doi.org/10.1177/0010414005279320.

Gidengil, Elisabeth, Neil Nevitte, André Blais, Joanna Everitt, and Patrick Fournier. 2011. *Dominance and Decline: Making Sense of Recent Canadian Elections.* Toronto: University of Toronto Press.

Goodyear-Grant, Elizabeth. 2010. "Who Votes for Women Candidates and Why? Evidence from the 2004 Canadian Election Study." In *Voting Behaviour in Canada,* edited by Cameron D. Anderson and Laura B. Stephenson, 43–64. Vancouver: UBC Press.

Liberal Party of Canada. 2011. *Your Family. Your Future. Your Canada.* http://www.poltext.org/sites/poltext.org/files/plateformes/can2011lib_plt_en_12072011_115050.pdf.

– 2015. A New Plan for a Strong Middle Class. https://www.liberal.ca/files/2015/10/New-plan-for-a-strong-middle-class.pdf.

McInturff, Kate. 2015. "Filling in the Blanks: What Do the Polls Say about Women Voters?" Behind the Numbers, 19 November. http://behindthenumbers.ca/2015/09/18/filling-in-the-blanks-what-do-the-polls-say-about-women-voters/.

New Democratic Party of Canada. 2011. *Giving Your Family a Break: Practical First Steps.* http://www.poltext.org/sites/poltext.org/files/plateformes/can2011ndp_plt_en_12072011_114905.pdf.
–   2015. *Building the Country of Our Dreams.* https://www.ndp.ca/platform.
O'Neill, Brenda, and Melanee Thomas. 2016. "Because It's 2015: Gender and the 2015 Federal Election." In *The Canadian Federal Election of 2015,* edited by Jon H. Pammett and Christopher Dornan, 275–304. Toronto: Dundurn Books.
Ontario Pay Equity Commission. 2012. *A Guide to Interpreting Ontario's Pay Equity Legislation.* Toronto: Queen's Printer for Ontario. http://www.payequity.gov.on.ca/en/DocsEN/guide_act.pdf.
Parliament of Canada. 2013. "Party Standings in the House of Commons (Unofficial)." http://www.parl.gc.ca/ParlInfo/lists/PartyStandings.aspx?Language=E&Section=03d93c58-f843-49b3-9653-84275c23f3fb&Gender=F.
–   2015. "Women Candidates in General Elections: 1921 to Date." http://www.parl.gc.ca/about/parliament/federalridingshistory/hfer.asp?Language=E&Search=WomenElection.
Pay Equity Task Force. 2004. *Pay Equity: A New Approach to a Fundamental Right.* Ottawa: Department of Justice. http://ywcacanada.ca/data/research_docs/00000052.pdf.
Progressive Conservative Party of Canada. 1988. *Politiques en bref.* http://www.poltext.org/sites/poltext.org/files/plateformes/can1988pc_plt._14112008_181252.pdf.
–   2000. *Change You Can Trust: The Progressive Conservative Plan for Canada's Future.* http://www.poltext.org/sites/poltext.org/files/plateformes/can2000pc_plt_en._14112008_173707.pdf.
Rebick, Judy, and Shelagh Day. 1992. "Why We Should Have Gender Equality in the New Senate." *Gazette,* 14 September.
Reform Party of Canada. 1992. *56 Reasons Why You Should Support the Reform Party of Canada.* http://www.poltext.org/sites/poltext.org/files/plateformes/can1992r_plt_en_12072011_125233.pdf.
–   1996. *Charter of Rights and Freedoms Task Force Final Report.* http://contentdm.ucalgary.ca/cdm4/document.php?CISOROOT=/reform&CISOPTR=7182&REC=7.
Reform Party of Canada Records. "Women's Issues – RPC Women's Work Group, 24 November 1990." Special Collections, Libraries and Cultural Resources, University of Calgary, box 19, video, 120 minutes.
Schwab, Klaus, Börge Brende, Saadia Zahidi, Yasmina Bekhouche, Annabel Guinault, Amey Soo, Ricardo Hausmann, and Laura D. Tyson. 2013. *The Global Gender Gap Report: 2013.* Geneva: World Economic Forum.

Sigurdson, Richard. 1994. "Preston Manning and the Politics of Postmodernism in Canada." *Canadian Journal of Political Science* 27 (2): 249–76. http://dx.doi.org/10.1017/S0008423900017352.

Thomas, Melanee, and Marc André Bodet. 2013. "Sacrificial Lambs, Women Candidates, and District Competitiveness in Canada." *Electoral Studies* 32 (1): 153–66. http://dx.doi.org/10.1016/j.electstud.2012.12.001.

7 With or without You: Quebec, the Conservative Movement, and the Pursuit of Majority Government

KATE PUDDISTER AND JAMES B. KELLY

The 2006 Canadian election signalled changing winds for the Conservative Party. Not only was this the first time that the party had been called to form the government within the House of Commons, it achieved this electoral success with the election of ten members of Parliament from the province of Quebec. The election of the Conservative Party to a minority government was not entirely surprising, as the previously governing Liberal Party had found itself in a weak electoral position that stemmed in part from its role in the Sponsorship Scandal (Clarke et al. 2006). What was surprising about the results from the 2006 federal election was that the Conservative Party had achieved this electoral success by gaining seats in Quebec, a province that in many ways should not be a bastion of Conservative Party triumph. Indeed, the election of ten members from Quebec was surpassed only in the 2015 federal election, with the election of twelve members. This election marked one high point in the generally precarious relationship between Quebec and the federal conservative party movement, including the Reform Party, the Canadian Alliance, and the Progressive Conservative Party. Indeed, with the exception of a brief period under Brian Mulroney, Quebec remained a Liberal stronghold for much of the twentieth century (the Progressive Conservative Party only won a handful of Quebec seats in their last three federal elections: 1993, one; 1997, five; 2000, one).

Prior to 2006, the Conservative Party and Stephen Harper ignored Quebec by rejecting special status for the province, criticizing asymmetrical relations between Quebec and Ottawa. While in opposition, when discussing constitutional amendments to recognize the distinct society of Quebec, Harper denounced such motions as an "appeasement of ethnic nationalism" (Cameron 2008). Yet in 2006, following his first election as prime minister, Harper not only supported, but sponsored a House of Commons motion to recognize the Québécois as a nation within a united Canada.[1] To be sure, this motion is consistent with the past approaches of the party, as it only symbolically recognized the distinct status of Québécois as a people and did not acknowledge a Québécois state.

The Québécois motion does, however, represent a calculated political shift by the Conservative Party in 2006 to transform its minority status into majority government, hoping to build on their electoral success in Quebec. Indeed, in 2008, Harper called the election a year before the statutorily mandated date with the possibility of increasing the party's strength in Quebec, as the Conservatives were tied with the Bloc Québécois in Quebec polls (Bélanger and Nadeau 2009). The cracks in the relationship between the Conservative Party and the province first appeared during the 2008 election and came to a head in the 2011 election, in which the party achieved a majority government without significant seat gains from Quebec.[2] It had become apparent that the Conservative Party had abandoned a Quebec strategy for electoral gain and instead produced public policy (such as the dismantling of the long-gun registry) that not only ignored the wishes of Quebec, but often directly opposed them. This chapter examines whether these inconsistencies were simply the by-product of a view of the Harper government's open federalism (see chapter 13 in this volume) or were evidence of a pragmatic electoral strategy and tactical governance of provincial-federal relations with Quebec. In assessing this we address three questions:

1 Quebec and electoral success: How did the Conservative Party
  (and its predecessors) attempt to turn a previous antagonistic
  relationship with Quebec into one of electoral success?

---

1 It is important to note that the Conservative Party's Québécois motion was introduced to counter a similar motion introduced by the Bloc Québécois that sought to acknowledge that the Québécois form a nation. However, the Conservative motion added the qualification that the Québécois form a nation *within a united Canada*, a clause absent from the Bloc motion.

2 In the 2015 election, the Conservative Party of Canada actually increased the number of members elected in the province although it still lost power to the Liberal Party of Canada.

2 Federal-provincial relations and Quebec: What were the implications of this political strategy by the Conservative government for
  federal-provincial relations and governance in relation to Quebec?
3 The Conservative Party and Quebec identity: Did the Conservative
  Party truly change its position on Quebec identity? Or was this shift
  simply symbolic and evidence of political strategy? What changes
  occurred in this relationship when the Conservative Party found
  itself in a majority government?

The Question of Quebec

A discussion of Quebec is central to any analysis of Canadian politics.
The province contains the largest proportion of francophones in the
country, and its courting is almost essential in achieving federal electoral success in Ottawa. More importantly, however, the province and
its history are fundamental to the very nature of Canada. The compact theory of Canadian Confederation holds that the foundation of
Canada was based on the compact between two founding peoples –
English and French – which implies a special protection and promotion
of French language and culture as embodied in Quebec to ensure its
survival in the face of the majority anglophone culture (Breton 1988;
McRoberts 2001; Russell 2004; Anderson 2007). Rather than a compact
of provinces, the cultural compact theory holds that Quebec deserves
special status in the Canadian federation, which at times requires an
asymmetry of powers for the province in relation to the rest of Canada,
giving the province more power over aspects of governance such as immigration policy. While the compact theory can be subject to criticism
for numerous reasons – most glaring being complete disregard for the
role of Indigenous Canadians in the founding of Canada (see chapter 8
in this volume) – it serves as a central impetus for Quebec nationalism.
    Nationalism can be understood as the culmination of the creation of
a social and political identity. A nationalist sentiment can generate a
struggle over the definition of a community, control over resources, and
individual identity. According to Breton (1988), nationalism is based on
the following: *inclusion/exclusion* – understanding of who is Québécois
and who is not; a *"national interest"* – what Québécois require to survive and prosper; *comparison* – how Québécois fare in comparison to the
rest of Canada; and *the environment* – how Canadian federalism, society, and political actors help or hinder Québécois and their interests. In
cases of sub-state nationalism as in Quebec, this struggle can result in a

separatist-sovereignty sentiment, as a means of protecting both identity and resources.

The current incarnation of Quebec nationalism was born out of the Quiet Revolution of the 1960s, in which nationalist sentiment in the province shifted from a defensive survival mechanism to an offensive doctrine of expansion of the powers of the province and a desire to become *maîtres chez nous*. This shift resulted in public policy changes such as the nationalization of Hydro-Québec, the creation of a Quebec pension plan, and the establishment of a secular education ministry. While the level of support for Quebec sovereignty has ebbed and flowed following the 1960s, it has twice resulted in a provincial referendum on Quebec independence, the first in 1980 and the second in 1995, the latter coming remarkably close to a win for the "yes" to independence vote, with 50.6 per cent voting no and 49.4 per cent voting yes.

Quebec nationalism has resulted in two failed constitutional amendment packages (the Meech Lake and Charlottetown Accords) spearheaded by the Progressive Conservative Party under Brian Mulroney, many Supreme Court of Canada cases, and public policy measures by both the federal government (such as the Clarity Act by the Chrétien Liberals) and Quebec provincial government (such as Bill 101 and the French sign law introduced by the Parti Québécois and defended by all Quebec governments, regardless of party identity) aimed at either quelling or stoking the sovereignty fires of Quebec. The centrality of Quebec to Canadian politics and society underpins our understanding of brokerage politics and means that no actor (including political parties in opposition and in government) can ignore the importance of its unique position in the federation and its nationalist sentiments.

The Reform Party, Canadian Alliance, and *La Belle Province*: An Unlikely Romance

> I've always thought that the love affair between the people of Québec and Stephen Harper made less sense than Britney Spears' first marriage. There's no durability in it. It isn't based on any long-term deep compatibility and affection. And I think that will become clear as time goes on. (Bob Rae (qtd in Wells 2006, 273))

The Conservative Party and its predecessors have had a complicated relationship with the Province of Quebec. Beyond the simple fact that there is often an ideological difference between the parties of the right and Québécois on social policy,[3] this relationship never had a high probability of being stable and successful because it was built on a flawed foundation (see chapter 3 in this volume). The position on Quebec taken by the Reform Party under Preston Manning could be characterized as both antagonistic and competitive. Its initial position was that Quebec nationalism is dangerous and the separatist movement should not be appeased since it believed that Canada could exist without Quebec. Furthermore, the party's rallying cry "The West wants in" fostered a particular vision of federalism that either overtly rejected any special status for Quebec or demanded that the asymmetries in the federal division of powers between Ottawa and Quebec be extended to the West. These positions resulted in rhetoric that was at times blatantly anti-Quebec, or at best ignored the province, suggesting that the Reform Party had abandoned brokerage politics, or was approaching it in a way very different from that of parties in the past.

While Preston Manning's western-based Reform Party was beginning to receive attention on the national stage, Prime Minister Brian Mulroney was attempting to reach an agreement on the Meech Lake Accord. This accord was focused in part on quelling separatist sentiments in Quebec, included a distinct society status for Quebec, increased powers for the provinces, and offered the ability for provinces to opt out of future federal programs with compensation. It was vocally opposed by Manning and the Reform Party whose 1988 Platform, "The West Wants In," argued that the accord would not actually promote national unity and would be "detrimental to the West and to the country as a whole" (1988, 7). The Reform Party of Canada was opposed to recognizing Quebec as a distinct society and "the granting of special status to any group or party within Canada" (Reform Party of Canada 1988). Standing out from the rest of the political parties in Canada, the Reform Party was the only one to oppose the Meech Lake Accord.

Tom Flanagan (academic and former Conservative Party strategist) identified sentiments like the ones expressed in the 1988 platform as

---

3 Hébert (2007, 120) supports this notion by examining the position of Quebec in the major social debates of the past several decades, including, for example, strong opposition to the death penalty in Quebec, the fact that the Quebec National Assembly voted unanimously to extend civil unions to homosexual couples before any other province, the greater proportion of gender equality in the provincial legislature, and the high level of state intervention in welfare in the province.

part of the party's electoral strategy to position itself as "the party of English Canada" (Flanagan 2009, 39). While the Reform Party translated its 1988 election platform into French, it did not run a single candidate in Quebec until 1997, nor was the leader bilingual. Manning and his party did not support official bilingualism; instead the party advocated for "territorial bilingualism," which involved "a recognition of French in Quebec and English elsewhere as the predominant language of work and society" (Reform Party of Canada 1988, 24–5). The Reform Party advocated that bilingualism be required only in "key federal institutions" such as Parliament and "critical federal services," and a removal of "forced" bilingualism in provincial governmental institutions. These policies reflected the Reform Party's rejection of the cultural compact foundation theory, and the position they took in "Let Quebec be Quebec. Let the West be the West."

This posturing towards Quebec was continued with the Reform Party's opposition to the Charlottetown Accord. Like the Meech Lake Accord, the Charlottetown Accord recognized a distinct society status for Quebec and provided for increased powers of provincial jurisdiction, and received strong opposition from the Reform Party. During the negotiations and debates over the Charlottetown Accord, Preston Manning argued that Canada could "live with the loss of Quebec," again demonstrating the Reform Party's unwillingness to appease separatist movements in Quebec and "a love it or leave it" attitude (Flanagan 2009). Manning attempted to promote the Reform Party as the only party that could speak for Canada outside of Quebec and could continue to speak for Canada should Quebec choose to separate. This hard-line approach against special recognition or status for Quebec was taken by Manning at the urging of his advisors, which at the time included future prime minister Stephen Harper (ibid.).

When the Reform Party was not directly opposing measures to appease Quebec and strengthen its position within the Canadian federation, the party ignored the province. Its first electoral breakthrough in the 1993 federal election was made without running any candidates from Quebec. This strategy was extremely nearsighted, as it is very difficult to achieve electoral success on the national stage without some electoral support in Quebec.

Following this early period marked largely by antagonism and at some times rejection of Quebec, the strategy of the party changed. Even though the Reform Party had achieved official opposition status following the 1997 election, it did so without any seats in Quebec. The party realized that in order to avoid being relegated to simply a western protest party, without pan-Canadian appeal, its strategy in dealing with Quebec needed to change. Still under the leadership of Manning, the Reform Party attempted to reach out to other parts of the right side of the political spectrum, hoping to capture the *bleu* strain of Quebec nationalism (but not separatism). Over time it expanded its party administration to the province, ran candidates in elections, and revealed a new-found openness towards the bolstering of provincial powers.

This shift and softening of its position on Quebec became more evident when the party transitioned to the Canadian Reform Conservative Alliance (commonly known as the Canadian Alliance) (Malloy 2003). A few years later, in March 2005, the new Conservative Party's founding convention was held in Montreal to illustrate the importance placed on securing seats in the province. Finally, under the label of the Conservative Party and the leadership of Stephen Harper, the party was able to elect ten members of Parliament in Quebec in 2006, signalling a turnaround in relations with the province and an attempt at adopting a more traditional approach to brokerage politics than taken by the Reform Party. However, this approach did not last long, and by 2011 the Conservative Party's standing in the province had declined to half its 2006 size, only to increase to twelve seats as a result of vote-splitting in the 2015 election.

Post-1993, the other right-of-centre party, the Progressive Conservatives (PCs), also struggled in its efforts to gain influence and electoral success in Quebec. Dismal election results in the 1993 election and the weak showings in subsequent elections prevented the PCs from making a substantial impact within the province. Their poor showing can be linked to the fact that relations with Quebec and the priorities of Quebeckers were either not part of PC election platforms (1993, 2000), or were mentioned only in a general discussion of federal-provincial relations (1997). With this understanding of the challenging relationship underpinning the conservative movement's relations with Quebec, our discussion now turns to an analysis of the Conservative Party's federal relations with Quebec and Stephen Harper's "open federalism."

Federal-Quebec Relations

As previously mentioned, the Conservative Party's predecessor, the Reform Party, did not provide much support for Quebec in policy on federal-provincial relations. In the early days of the party it approached relations between Quebec and the federal government in contradictory ways, either as *Quebec as comrade* or as *Quebec as competitor*. The first approach was based in the sentiment that "if it is good enough for Québec, it is good enough for the West." This position is not inherently anti-Quebec; instead it was focused on achieving an equal status with Quebec in asymmetrical power relations between the province and Ottawa. Many of the arguments made in the infamous "firewall letter" fall in this category.[4] The letter called for the province of Alberta to utilize several of its constitutional powers that have been informally assumed by the federal government. The authors explain that if Quebec can create and implement its own pension plan and provincial police force, Alberta should do the same. These arguments are grounded in what Cameron (2008) considers the neoliberal approach to federalism, that all provinces should be treated equally and that any tokens offered by the federal government to a particular province (most often Quebec) should be made available to all. This particular approach is neoliberal because it is aimed at limiting the size and scope of the federal government, while encouraging provinces to protect the powers afforded to them in the constitution (see chapter 13 in this volume). When the party articulated its opinions on Quebec and provincial powers in this way, Quebec was seen as a comrade in the fight against the overreaching, power-hungry federal government. However, it is important to note that even when the Reform Party viewed the province as a comrade, it did so without any recognition of a distinct Quebec identity or nationalism.

While some of the Reform Party's positions on federal-provincial relations can be characterized as complementary to Quebec; other positions poised the province as a competitor. Evidence can be found in the party's strong opposition to both the Meech Lake and Charlottetown Accords. In a speech to a 1989 assembly of the Reform Party, Manning argued, "If we continue to make unacceptable constitutional, economic, and linguistic concessions to Québec at the expense of the rest of Canada, it is those concessions themselves which will tear the country apart" (Flanagan 2009, 44). Moreover, in terms of fiscal relations, the

---

4 The firewall letter refers to an open letter to Alberta Premier Ralph Klein published in the 24 January 2001 edition of the *National Post*, signed by Stephen Harper and five other prominent Alberta conservatives.

Reform Party did not explicitly support equalization, while all other major federal parties were quite vocal about their support for the program (Lecours and Béland 2010). In Quebec, as a receiver of equalization payments, this lack of enthusiasm for the program would not fare well. In their competitive relations with the province, the Reform Party and Canadian Alliance rejected asymmetrical federalism because they believed that it stands as a threat to their vision of federalism and provincial-federal relations.

These two positions – Quebec as comrade and Quebec as competitor – are largely contradictory at their core, and as a result, federal and provincial relations proved to be a stumbling block to the party's attempt to achieve cross-Canadian appeal and transition away from its position as a regionalist protest party. This realization caused the party to alter its vision of federalism and adopt a new approach and rhetoric towards the province specifically, and federalism in general.

Beginning in 1993, Preston Manning began to push forward his new conception of relations with Quebec, which he referred to as "new federalism." New federalism was aimed at keeping Quebec in the Canadian federation, but did not allow for any room for sovereignty association, again reiterating his "love it or leave it" attitude with the province. Building on his belief in territorial bilingualism, Manning argued that the official bilingualism project of the federal government had failed and that it was up to Quebec to promote the French language (Manning 1993). From this position, Manning promoted what he called an equal provinces/equal citizens constitutional model, which advocated that all provinces should take advantage of their constitutionally defined powers, moving power away from the federal government. Although new federalism approached relations with Quebec in a slightly more conciliatory tone, this pitch offered no substance to Quebec and did not differ significantly from the Reform's early positions on federalism.

This approach continued throughout the history of the Reform Party. The 1999 Blue Book, the final major party policy document before the Reform Party changed into the Canadian Alliance, still refused to allow for any special status for Quebec and continued to push for an equality of the provinces model (Reform Party of Canada 1999). With the rebranding of the Reform Party as the Canadian Alliance, many of the original policy positions were softened to increase the party's cross-Canada appeal (Malloy 2003; see also chapter 2 in this volume). In this reinvention, the party dropped opposition to official bilingualism, as an attempt to bridge the divide between the party and Quebec. However, in subsequent elections, the party still failed to make significant inroads in the province, failing again to elect a single parliamentarian from Quebec in the 2000 election. During this period, the PC Party did not fare much better in Quebec, even under the leadership of the province's future premier, Jean Charest. The PC Party did not overtly support any special status for Quebec in federal-provincial relations, but did not antagonize the province either. Instead, without official party status under Charest, the party struggled to be heard by both the media and in the House of Commons, making it difficult for the party to have an impact in general and on the Quebec file specifically.

While the Reform Party and then the Canadian Alliance gradually shifted its policy and posturing to appeal to Quebec voters, the first real attempt by the conservative movement to win the support of Quebec occurred under Stephen Harper's leadership of the Conservative Party. It was during the Conservative Party's first election in 2004 that Harper unveiled his plan for open federalism (see chapter 13 in this volume), a model of federalism that respected the constitutionally defined jurisdiction of the provinces while promoting a strong central government that was focused largely on national priorities like defence and the economy (Harper 2004).

This plan of open federalism did not make waves in either Quebec or the rest of Canada until over a year and a half later, during the 2005–6 election campaign. In a pivotal speech during a campaign stop in Quebec City, Harper laid out his plan for open federalism to Quebec voters (Hébert 2007, 61). Harper continued to define open federalism as a respect for the provinces and their jurisdictional powers by the federal government, the very same arguments that he made over a year before in the *National Post*. The content of the speech was not new, but the reception by the audience was. This pitch for open federalism was different from the previous iterations, because this time, Quebec voters, weary of the Liberal Party and disinterested in the Bloc Québécois, were actually listening (ibid.). Harper and the Conservative Party were offering Quebec voters what they referred to as a new vision of federalism that would allow them more control over their own domain and for the first time in party history, the voters of Quebec were paying attention.

The push for open federalism and a promise of a Charter of Open Federalism arguably improved the Conservative Party's electoral prospects in Quebec. The party's election platform for the 2006 election, "Stand Up for Canada," contained a large section devoted to open federalism and relations with Quebec, a marked change from the strategy of its predecessor parties. The platform made specific promises regarding giving Quebec greater responsibility for protecting its cultural identity by inviting it to play a role in the United Nations Educational, Scientific and Cultural Organization (UNESCO), and more general promises regarding provincial participation in international trade policy and Canada's participation in trade agreements. The open federalism frame carried through the 2006 election and had a strong presence in the 2006 Speech from the Throne, which made specific reference to federal-provincial relations with Quebec: "The Government is committed to an open federalism that recognizes the unique place of a strong vibrant Québec in a united Canada. It will work with the government and legislature of Québec in a spirit of mutual respect and collaboration to advance the aspirations of Québecers" (Government of Canada 2006a). Unlike the rhetoric employed by Preston Manning and the Reform Party, this iteration of federalism made specific reference to the unique position of the Province of Quebec within the federation and sought to capitalize on this position.

Similarly, the UNESCO declaration made specific reference to a "spirit of a federalism of openness" and recognized that Quebec can act legitimately as the forebear of French language and culture on behalf of the rest of Canada. What is more significant about this declaration is that it specifically acknowledged that open federalism does require some form of asymmetry in application, accepting that Quebec is different from other provinces and territories, with a "unique personality" (Government of Canada 2006b). The declaration does, however, make clear that the Government of Quebec and the Government of Canada will participate in unison on the "general orientations of Canadian foreign policy," thereby precluding the delegate from Quebec from expressing an opinion that contradicts that of the rest of the Canadian delegation (ibid.). Unfortunately, the UNESCO partnership did not materialize in the way both governments had hoped, as the result of the rules of the organization itself; the implications are discussed further below.

Few observers were instantly enamoured with Harper's open federalism. Quebec scholars Caron and Laforest (2009) posit that if Quebec receives an outcome different from that of other provinces under open federalism, it is not due to the intentions of the Conservative government. Instead, the authors argue that there is a difference between "direct asymmetry of intent," which would be present in specific policies that strengthen the power of the Quebec government to control matters it deems essential for protecting their cultural identity; and "indirect asymmetry of results." The latter is a "de facto asymmetry resulting from the intended symmetry [and] is not an acknowledgement of the multinational character of the state but is, rather, based on the fundamental notion of equality of all federal partners" (47). This critique of open federalism assumes that granting distinctiveness for Quebec requires a reduced role for the federal government in Quebec. In this understanding, open federalism does not imply any grand gestures by the federal government to Quebec, instead it is the retrenchment of the federal government that allows Quebec to protect and promote its own goals. For other critics, this containment of the federal government in some policy domains (notably, social policy) under the auspices of open federalism is simply a rebranding of either coordinate federalism[5] or masks a neoliberal approach to governance and welfare policy (Jeffery 2010).

Regardless of one's understanding of open federalism – either a new era in relations with Quebec, or simply a different name for a style of federal-provincial relations that have existed in the past – it is worthwhile to evaluate the performance of the Harper government in regard to open federalism. Writing in 2010, Laforest finds that *fédéralisme d'ouverture* (open federalism) has been an unfulfilled promise: the federal government has not made significant strides in curbing its spending power in areas of provincial jurisdiction, federal government attendance at first ministers' conferences has not been consistent, and the federal government has pursued policies that run counter to the interests of Quebec (Laforest 2010, 18).

An analysis of the Conservative Party's four election platforms (2006, 2008, 2011, and 2015) supports the conclusions of Laforest. While the party's 2006 election platform devoted a large section to defining open federalism, calling for a "Charter of Open Federalism" and explaining some policy implications for this model of federalism, the 2008 platform spent significantly less time discussing open federalism, but still renewed the promise of a Charter of Open Federalism (Conservative Party of Canada 2006, 2008). In comparison, the 2011 and 2015 platforms did not specifically address the demands of Quebec and made

---

5 Coordinate federalism defined here refers to a style of multi-level governance that allows for each order of government to pursue its own policy domains found within its constitutionally defined powers, without interfering with the other order of government. See Cody (2008).

no mention of a Charter of Open Federalism (Conservative Party of Canada 2011, 2015).

A measurement of government priorities through analysis of electoral platforms shows that open federalism fell out of the Harper government's purview, or at least failed to be one of their main priorities (see chapter 13 in this volume). Greater evidence of the lack of action by the federal government on its promises of open federalism was found in the fact that the government never introduced legislation to create a Charter of Open Federalism, nor delivered formal retrenchment of the federal spending power. The lack of action on open federalism and the failure to provide any true incentives to Quebec demonstrated the conclusions of Caron and Laforest: in the Harper government's record on open federalism in relation to Quebec, much of its action remains in the domain of "symbolic multinationalism," and the government made no concrete changes in the way Canadian federalism operates (2009, 45). The symbolic nature of the Conservative Party's action on an open federalism with Quebec was certainly found in its adoption of the "distinct society" motion in Parliament, to be discussed below.

As the prominence of open federalism faded from the rhetoric of the Harper government, the number of Conservative parliamentarians elected from Quebec did not improve. Following the 2008 election, the Conservative Party returned as a minority government, with only ten Quebec MPs, failing to increase their numbers in the province. Although there were many reasons for this result, the decision by the Harper government to cut $45 million in funding to arts and cultural programs was instrumental. The cuts were very unpopular in Quebec among the arts and cultural community, which mobilized against the Conservative Party. Indeed, as the cultural community in Quebec tends to be aligned with the sovereignty movement, the proposed funding cut was used by the Bloc Québécois as evidence that there was a growing divide between Québécois values and Canadian values advanced by the Conservative Party.

This lack of action by the Harper government and its failure to expand its Quebec caucus underlined the notion that the move towards open federalism was largely strategic and did not signal a true shift in the federal conservative parties since 1993 and their relationship with Quebec and its position on federal-provincial relations.

Once the Conservative Party of Canada was able to achieve a majority government without significant support from Quebec, the conversation regarding federal-provincial relations with the province changed.

Open federalism and increasing positive relations with Quebec were no longer priorities of the Conservative Party of Canada. Arguably, this demonstrates that open federalism and support of the distinct society of Quebec was for the most part a pragmatic move, part of a larger election strategy. This assertion will be demonstrated in greater detail in the following section on the federal conservative parties' positions on Quebec identity and the national question, including an analysis of the 1995 referendum.

The National Question and Identity Politics

From the beginning, the Reform Party's roots as a party of the West did not place it in a position to gain mass appeal in Quebec. Indeed, some speculated that if Quebec were to separate, the party would have a much greater chance at forming a majority government in Ottawa (Gibbins 1996). Despite the fact that the party was formed as a party of the West, its actions and statements certainly did not support the notion of a distinct identity, and at times it directly undermined any effort to recognize such an identity. As previously mentioned, the Reform Party campaigned against both the Meech Lake and Charlottetown Agreements and made it known that its opposition was based largely on the portions of the agreements that granted special recognition for Quebec. Moreover, the Reform Party did not promote the federalist side in the campaign leading to the 1995 referendum on sovereignty association. Indeed, for the Reform Party, "their Canada need not include Quebec" (Cody 1998, 458).

In their rejection of the argument that Canada was founded on two cultures of French and English, the Reform Party strongly opposed any measures that granted special powers to Quebec, aimed at protecting their status as forebear of a founding culture. The Reform Party's vision of equality of provinces dictated firm rejection of constitutional recognition of a distinct society for Quebec. In their view, Quebec not only stood in the way of an equal provinces model, it also prevented the achievement of the greater goal of the Reform Party – small government. The distinctive character of Quebec, formally recognized or not, thwarts a "melting pot assimilationist consensus society" that the Reform Party had hoped to achieve (Cody 1998, 458). This core theoretical divide between the Reform Party and the call for a distinct recognition of Quebec meant that the party could never be a true ally for the federalist faction in Quebec politics.

In the fall of 1995, the citizens of Quebec voted for the second time on a referendum on the sovereignty of Quebec. The "yes" to sovereignty campaign was initially led by Jacques Parizeau, the premier and the leader of the Parti Québécois government, who was joined mid-campaign by the leader of the Bloc Québécois, Lucien Bouchard. The "no" side or federalists were officially led by the leader of the Quebec Liberal Party, Daniel Johnston, but saw important leadership provided by Prime Minister Jean Chrétien, and Jean Charest, who led the Progressive Conservative Party. During the 1995 referendum, Chrétien made a series of strategic speeches to appeal to Quebeckers' emotional attachment to Canada, and Jean Charest effectively used the Canadian passport during speeches to reinforce the direct cost to Quebeckers of a victory for the sovereignty option. The two federal conservative parties played very different roles in the referendum campaign – Charest was a strong campaigner for the "no" side and attempted to parlay the media attention he gained during the campaign into future votes within Quebec (Hébert 2014).

Not surprisingly, the Reform Party led by Manning did not play a large role in the referendum, for either the sovereignty or federalist camps. The limited action of the Reform Party was not solely due to its opposition party status in the House of Commons, but rather, was a reflection of weak relations with Quebec and its lack of support for a distinct Quebec. The role played by the party in the referendum campaign was a nuanced position that at times caused the Reform Party to be accused of supporting the separatists. The Reform Party attempted to position itself as the only party that could lead Canada following a successful yes to sovereignty campaign (Flanagan 2009). However, for many in the federalist camp, to suggest a Canada without Quebec was almost sacrilege.

As the referendum campaign continued, Prime Minister Chrétien stated that he would not accept a simple majority of 50 per cent plus one for sovereignty in the referendum as a decisive democratic call for separation. Manning responded that the federal government needed to respect the choice of Quebeckers, arguing that a simple majority was all that was required for separation. In addition, instead of strongly opposing the Quebec sovereignty movement, Manning made it clear that a Reform Party government would take a "yes" vote as an opportunity for constitutional reform. This flicker of support for the sovereignty camp by Manning resulted in Chrétien accusing the Reform Party of being akin to the Bloc Québécois and supporting the breakup of the country (Chrétien 1995). Throughout the lead up to the referendum, the Reform Party was accused of "being in bed with the separatists," for voicing their less than clear support for the federalists. However, when the Reform Party took a step back from the referendum debate, they were accused of not doing enough (Gibbins 1996). The referendum campaign concluded on 30 October 1995, when 50.6 per cent of Quebec voters rejected sovereignty, with 94 per cent of eligible voters participating.

The Reform Party's position on Quebec during the referendum was consistent with its overall approach to the province: "If Québeckers reject ... [its] version of equal provinces, *adieu* and Godspeed" (Cody 1998, 458). The Reform Party refused to acknowledge or treat Quebec as different from other Canadian provinces. Indeed, in its 1997 Blue Book platform following the referendum, any discussion of national unity and secession is done in general terms and makes no mention of Quebec. All of the party proposals put forward in the platform aimed at addressing national unity do so without making any concessions to sovereignty and are centred on decentralization of powers from the federal government, the protection of provincial jurisdiction, and equality of the provinces. Although the leader of the PC party, Jean Charest, made impassioned pleas for Quebec voters to vote against the referendum, the party's 1997 election platform is quite similar to that of the Reform Party and explicitly rejects distinct treatment or special powers for Quebec (Progressive Conservative Party of Canada 1997).

The next major development in the conservatives' approach to Quebec after the 1995 referendum occurred almost a decade later, with Harper's outreach to the province through his pronunciation of open federalism. More than just articulating this vision of federalism, Harper proposed to provide Quebec a seat at UNESCO, a move that would allow the province to engage in relations with other international states, which demonstrated a break with the party's historical approach to Quebec. This promise, however, would never come into full fruition, as the rules of UNESCO preclude Quebec from sending its own delegate separate from Canada. Instead, the province was provided with a greater role within the Canadian delegation (Hueglin 2006). While this may appear as a minor change from the original promise to Quebec, the distinction is important, as the province was not acting in its own capacity in the international organization; instead, it is still very much part of the Canadian delegation and could not be understood to speak only for the Province of Quebec. As a result, in providing the province with a greater voice on the international stage, the actions of the Harper government were limited and largely symbolic.

Symbolically, perhaps the most noteworthy action taken by the Harper government was the recognition of Québécois as a nation. As mentioned previously, the idea of Quebec forming a distinct society within a larger Canadian society has been a theme in Canadian politics since prior to Confederation. Indeed the distinct character of Quebec has been a point of debate and at many times contention since the negotiations on Confederation in the 1860s, through to both the Meech Lake and Charlottetown Accords in the late twentieth century (Russell 2004). While informal recognition of the distinct character of Quebec has been a part of Canadian politics since prior to the foundation of the country, it has never been formally recognized either constitutionally or statutorily. Following his first successful election, with the help of the voters of Quebec, Stephen Harper sponsored a motion in the House of Commons to recognize a Québécois nation. Specifically the motion read, "That this House recognize that the Québécois form a nation within a united Canada" (Government of Canada 2006c). Following the tabling of this motion, Minister of Intergovernmental Affairs Michael Chong resigned from Cabinet, arguing that the motion was akin to acknowledging ethnic nationalism (see chapter 12 in this volume).

At first glance, for the Conservative Party and Harper, the Québécois motion appeared to be a strong break with a conservative tradition beginning with the Reform Party. Certainly, it is very difficult to envisage the Reform Party under the leadership of Manning supporting such a motion. Indeed, instead of following the Reform Party tactic of ignoring the uniqueness of Quebec and pushing for a style of governance that did not result in special or different treatment for any province, this motion appeared to overtly recognize the fact that Quebec is different from other provinces. Upon a closer reading of the motion, this evaluation is premature for three central reasons. First, the motion does not use the phrase *distinct society* that was part of both Meech and Charlottetown. *Distinct society* implies recognition of a distinct culture, history, and legal tradition of the Province of Quebec that is different and separate from the rest of Canada (Russell 2004). Second, this motion is limited to Québécois as a people as forming a nation. It specifically avoids acknowledging that the borders of this nation are congruent with the Province of Quebec. This limits the ability of the Government of Quebec to argue that it is distinct from all other provincial governments, giving it an upper hand in federal-provincial relations and the distribution of constitutional powers. Third, this motion is not a constitutional amendment, nor is it a legal statute. Instead, it is purely a symbolic gesture that is not legally binding on any parties and does not imply any changes in relations with Quebec. While it would be difficult to imagine a government led by the Reform Party passing such a motion, the Québécois motion has no real implications for governance, and its effect remains only symbolic (Caron and Laforest 2009; Laforest 2010).

The Québécois motion remains the high point in relations between the Conservative government of Stephen Harper and Quebec. Following the realization that the party could not expand on its position within the province, its strategy for Quebec noticeably changed. As former party strategist Tom Flanagan explains, with the results of the 2008 election, the Conservative Party realized that Quebec would not be the route towards a majority government and shifted its priorities towards wooing ethnocultural minority voters (2011) (see chapter 5 in this volume). This change resulted in the government pursuing several policy changes that ran directly against the desires of most Quebec voters, such as its law-and-order criminal justice policy agenda that involved changes to the Youth Criminal Justice Act and the dismantling of the long-gun registry. During the debates leading to these changes, Quebec became a vocal opponent to the Harper government, with its minister of justice appearing at parliamentary committees strongly advocating against the changes on behalf of his province.

The disjuncture between the priorities of the Harper government and those of the Province of Quebec became even more pronounced following the adoption of Bill C-10 – Safe Streets and Communities Act, commonly referred to as the omnibus crime bill. This bill amended many aspects of criminal justice policy in Canada, such as increasing the number of offences that carry mandatory minimum sentences, and the reaction from Quebec was both swift and harsh. Liberal member of Parliament and former minister of justice Irwin Cotler declared that the passage of Bill C-10 marked a "sad day for criminal justice." Writing from the perspective of an MP from Quebec, he criticized the lack of consultation with the provinces over the bill and argued that the bill violated the Quebec model of justice, which favours measures aimed at rehabilitation rather than punishment (Cotler 2011). The reaction to Bill C-10 from the pro-sovereignty faction of Quebec was much more dramatic, with members of the Parti Québécois claiming that passage of this bill provides "a very, very strong case for Québec's independence

... It's a defeat for Québec, it's a defeat for our values" (Dougherty 2012, n.p.) The Government of Quebec also rejected the policy shift by the Harper government, by refusing to fund the changes required by Bill C-10, arguing that the premise and goals of the legislation run counter to the interests of Quebec (Fitzpatrick 2011). The policy shift of the Harper government, specifically on criminal justice policy, sent a strong sign to Quebec that it moved on from attempting to foster a relationship between the province and the Conservative Party.

Conclusion

The actions of the Conservative Party of Canada under the leadership of Stephen Harper in the past several years, most pronounced following its election as a majority government without the assistance of ridings in Quebec, signalled an abandonment of the province. While those within the Conservative Party would not label this shift as abandonment, they do acknowledge that the priorities of the party were no longer to secure support from Quebec (Flanagan 2011). Whatever the case, these changes make clear that many attempts by the Conservative Party to improve relations with Quebec were essentially pragmatic and calculated election strategies. Since the party's early roots in the Reform Party, it strongly rejected asymmetrical federal relations aimed at recognizing the distinctiveness of the Province of Quebec. Not only did the Reform Party under Preston Manning's leadership oppose both the Meech Lake and Charlottetown Accords, his rhetoric made it clear that the Reform Party was not only equipped, but also ready to lead a Canada without Quebec. Similarly, during the 1995 referendum on Quebec sovereignty, the Reform Party did not make a strong push on behalf of the federalists, which at times put the leader in conflict with the "no" side of the debate. The other federal conservative party, the PC Party, did play a central role in the 1995 referendum through the participation of its leader Jean Charest in the "no" campaign. Unfortunately for the PCs, this position of prominence did not translate into substantial electoral success in Quebec. Indeed, during the post-1993 era the PCs faced a struggle for power not only within Quebec, but across Canada as well.

With the Reform Party past in mind, it appeared to be a truly great shift in the party strategy when Stephen Harper, as leader of the Conservative Party, offered open federalism and tokens such as the Québécois parliamentary motion. While this change in policy towards *la belle province* helped the Conservative Party breakthrough electorally in Quebec during the 2006 election, the party was unable to capitalize on this growth in Quebec and did not increase its caucus numbers during either the 2008 or 2011 election. Once the Conservative Party realized that it would never be able to woo Quebec to become part of its winning coalition, it reverted to its past approach of either ignoring the desires of the province or directly opposing them and shifted its priorities to other more persuadable constituencies. This strategy may have been premature, however, as despite increasing the number of Conservative members elected in the province to twelve in the 2015 election, the party lost its majority status to the Liberals and demonstrated the difficulty of forming a government in Canada without substantial support from Quebec.

REFERENCES

Anderson, Lawrence. 2007. "Federalism and Secessionism: Institutional Influences on Nationalist Politics in Québec." *Nationalism & Ethnic Politics* 13 (2): 187–211. http://dx.doi.org/10.1080/13537110701293070.

Bélanger, Éric, and Richard Nadeau. 2009. "The Bloc Québécois: Victory by Default." In *The Canadian Federal Election of 2008*, edited by Jon H. Pammett and Christopher Dornan, 136–61. Toronto: Dundurn.

Breton, Raymond. 1988. "From Ethnic to Civic Nationalism: English Canada and Quebec." *Ethnic and Racial Studies* 11 (1): 85–102. http://dx.doi.org/10.1080/01419870.1988.9993590.

Cameron, Barbara. 2008. "Harper, Québec and Canadian Federalism." In *The Harper Record*, edited by Teresa Healy, 419–33. Canadian Centre for Policy Alternatives. https://www.policyalternatives.ca/Reports/2008/09/HarperRecord/index.cfm.

Caron, Jean-Francois, and Guy Laforest. 2009. "Canada and Multinational Federalism: From the Spirit of 1982 to Stephen Harper's Open Federalism." *Nationalism & Ethnic Politics* 15 (1): 27–55. http://dx.doi.org/10.1080/13537110802672370.

Chrétien, Jean. 1995. *Debates (Hansard)*. Parliament. House of Commons. 35th Legislature, 1st Session, 19 September. Ottawa: Queen's Printer.

Clarke, Harold D., Allan Kornberg, Thomas Scotto, and Joe Twyman. 2006. "Flawless Campaign, Fragile Victory: Voting in Canada's 2006 Federal Election." *PS, Political Science & Politics* 39 (4): 815–19. http://dx.doi.org/10.1017/S1049096506060987.

Cody, Howard. 1998. "A Captive Three Times Over: Preston Manning and the Dilemmas of the Reform Party." *American Review of Canadian Studies* 28 (4): 445–67. http://dx.doi.org/10.1080/02722019809481613.

– 2008. "Minority Government in Canada: The Stephen Harper Experience." *American Review of Canadian Studies* 38 (1): 27–42.

Conservative Party of Canada. 2006. "Stand Up for Canada: Conservative Party of Canada Federal Election Platform."

– 2008. "The True North Strong and Free: Stephen Harper's Plan for Canadians."

– 2011. "Here for Canada: Stephen Harper's Low-Tax Plan for Jobs and Economic Growth."

– 2015. "Protect Our Economy: Our Conservative Plan to Protect the Economy."

Cotler, Irwin. 2011. "A Sad Day for Criminal Justice." *Huffington Post*, 6 December.

Dougherty, Kevin. 2012. "Tory Crime Bill a 'Very Strong Case' for Québec's Independence: Parti Québécois Member." *National Post*, 13 March.

Fitzpatrick, Meagan. 2011. "Québec Will Refuse to Pay for Omnibus Crime Bill." CBC News, 1 November.

Flanagan, Tom. 2009. *Waiting for the Wave: The Reform Party and the Conservative Movement*. Montreal and Kingston: McGill-Queen's University Press.

– 2011. "The Emerging Conservative Coalition." *Policy Options* (June–July): 104–8.

Gibbins, Roger. 1996. "Western Canadian Nationalism in Transition." *Constitutional Forum* 7 (2): 52–7.

Government of Canada. 2006a. Agreement between the Government of Canada and the Government of Québec concerning the United Nations Educational, Scientific and Cultural Organization (UNESCO). 5 May.

Government of Canada. 2006b. *Debates (Hansard)*. Parliament. House of Commons. 39th Legislature, 1st Session, 22 November. Ottawa: Queen's Printer.

Government of Canada. 2006c. Speech from the Throne. 39th Parliament of Canada, 1st Session.

Harper, Stephen. 2004. "My Plan for 'Open Federalism.'" *National Post*, 27 October.

Hébert, Chantal. 2007. *French Kiss: Stephen Harper's Blind Date with Québec*. Toronto: A.A. Knopf Canada.

– 2014. *The Morning After: 1995 Québec Referendum and the Day That Almost Was*. Toronto: A.A. Knopf Canada.

Hueglin, Joe. 2006. "Prime Minister Harper's Government Vulnerable on Québec and UNESCO." *Hilltimes.com*, 24 April.

Jeffery, Brooke. 2010. "Prime Minister Harper's Open Federalism: Promoting a Neo-liberal Agenda?" In *The Case for Centralized Federalism*, edited by Gordon DiGiacomo and Maryantonett Flumian, 108–36. Ottawa: University of Ottawa Press.

Laforest, Guy. 2010. "The Meaning of Canadian Federalism in Québec: Critical Reflections," translated by G. Laforest. *Revista d'estudis autonomics i federals* 11:10–55.

Lecours, André, and Daniel Béland. 2010. "Federalism and Fiscal Policy: The Politics of Equalization in Canada." *Publius: The Journal of Federalism* 40 (4): 569–96. http://dx.doi.org/10.1093/publius/pjp030.

Malloy, Jonathan. 2003. "High Discipline, Low Cohesion? The Uncertain Patterns of Canadian Parliamentary Party Groups." *Journal of Legislative Studies* 9 (4): 116–29. http://dx.doi.org/10.1080/1357233042000306290.

Manning, Preston. 1993. "The Case for a New Federalism." Speech presented at the Empire Club of Canada, Toronto, 1 October.

McRoberts, Kenneth. 2001. "Canada and the Multinational State." *Canadian Journal of Political Science* 34 (4): 683–713. http://dx.doi.org/10.1017/S0008423901778055.

Progressive Conservative Party of Canada. 1997. "Let the Future Begin: Jean Charest's Plan for Canada's Next Century." https://www.poltext.org/sites/poltext.org/files/plateformes/can1997pc_plt_en.pdf.

Reform Party of Canada. 1988. "The West Wants In!" Election Platform of the Reform Party of Canada, 14 August.

– 1999. "The Blue Book: Principles & Policies of the Reform Party of Canada – 1999."

Russell, Peter H. 2004. *Constitutional Odyssey: Can Canadians Become a Sovereign People?* 3rd ed. Toronto: University of Toronto Press.

Wells, Paul. 2006. *Right Side Up: The Fall of Paul Martin and the Rise of Stephen Harper's New Conservatism.* Toronto: McClelland & Stewart.

8 Delegating Indigenous Rights and Denying Legal Pluralism: Tracing Conservative Efforts to Protect Private Property Regimes and "Canadian" Territory

MICHAEL MCCROSSAN

In the fields of Indigenous politics and law, the language of "reconciliation" has featured prominently in both the legal and political domains over the course of the past twenty years. Faced with an increasingly broad array of Indigenous claims to land, governance, and calls for historical redress, federal parties have often harnessed the language of "reconciliation" in the context of establishing renewed relationships between Indigenous peoples and non-Indigenous Canadians. Following the Report of the Royal Commission on Aboriginal Peoples (1996), the Jean Chrétien Liberal government issued a "Statement of Reconciliation" in 1998 that acknowledged "mistakes" of the past while simultaneously pointing to a future world in which Indigenous people would be full participants – or "partners" – within the broader political, economic, and cultural community of Canada. Ten years later, when Conservative Prime Minister Stephen Harper issued a historic apology to former students of residential schools, "reconciliation" once again took centre stage in the context of illuminating a dark historical chapter and "moving forward" in a communal spirit of "partnership" and "renewal."

This acknowledgment of the weight of history by political actors is significant, for it is a disagreement about the very nature of Canada's past, present, and future that resides at the heart of Indigenous rights discussions and policy considerations. What meaning does the early treaty-making process between the Crown and Indigenous peoples have for Canada's constitutional order? Are treaties simply historical anomalies that hold little relevance within "modern" Canada? Should Indigenous people be able to claim rights to practices only exactly as they had been performed in the past, or might Indigenous "rights" be capable of evolving to meet the contemporary needs of communities? These are just a few of the questions that political and legal actors have been forced to grapple with in the field of Indigenous politics. In particular, since the constitutional entrenchment of Aboriginal and treaty rights in 1982, a variety of Indigenous claims concerning land and resource rights, sovereignty, and governance have been passionately debated. However, in publicly presenting positions on the nature and meaning of Indigenous "rights," legal and political actors have presented not only alternate understandings of "reconciliation," but also competing conceptions of sovereignty and Canadian identity.

Though both the Supreme Court of Canada and the federal government have recognized "reconciliation" as a framework for responding to Indigenous claims and establishing a renewed relationship, the emergence of new populist political parties on the federal scene in the 1990s called this framework into question. While numerous studies have been written on reconciliation and efforts to renew relationships with Indigenous peoples in the context of governmental policy during this period (see Coulthard 2014, 115–24; Ladner 2001), insufficient attention has been paid to the policies espoused by conservative parties (and their continuing effects). As such, this chapter will explore three thematic questions:

1 Understanding Indigenous claims: How have federal conservative parties since 1993 understood and responded to Indigenous claims?
2 Inherent rights: How receptive have they been to Indigenous claims concerning "inherent" rights to sovereignty and self-government?
3 Reconciliation and Indigenous issues: What underlying framework or vision of reconciliation guides their approach to Indigenous issues?

Through an examination of policy documents, speeches, and debates in the House of Commons, this chapter shows that conservative parties have often expressed a clear commitment and orientation to pan-Canadian visions of citizenship and territory in such a way that pre-existing Indigenous rights to land, sovereignty, and governance are conceptually excluded and discounted from policy consideration. This chapter will begin by providing an overview of the legal basis of Indigenous claims, paying particular attention to how scholars and political actors have understood common law principles of "continuity" and the existence of legal pluralism in Canada. It will then examine conservative approaches to reconciling Indigenous claims while in opposition, contrasting competing conceptions of "inherent" rights expressed by opposition parties and their underlying policy priorities. Finally, the chapter will consider Indigenous policy approaches pursued by the Conservative Party of Canada (CPC) over the last decade and assess the likelihood that Indigenous legal pluralism will be recognized.

Legal Pluralism and "Inherent" Rights

Conventional understandings of Indigenous rights to sovereignty and governance, particularly within introductory political science texts, have a tendency to limit the legal basis for Indigenous claims. For instance, while acknowledging that constitutional documents such as the Royal Proclamation of 1763 "indisputably" recognized Indigenous rights, these rights are often placed within a framework of overarching Crown authority (Brooks 2015, 504, 513). Indeed, as John Borrows (1994) has noted, most interpretations of the proclamation have tended to regard it as a unilateral assertion of Crown sovereignty, as it declares Indigenous territories to be "under our Sovereignty, Protection, and Dominion." However, a key component of the British legal tradition is the doctrine of *lex loci*, which recognizes the continuity of local laws and governing institutions (Barsh 2004). Under British imperial law, Indigenous laws and rights to governance were not automatically displaced upon Crown assertions of sovereignty, but continued to exist in the face of British settlement (ibid.; see also Slattery 1987).

This respect for legal continuity can be partially observed in the Royal Proclamation of 1763 and the Treaty of Niagara, ratified the following year, in 1764. As scholars such as John Borrows (1994) and Peter Russell (2005) have demonstrated, in order to comprehend the true "spirit and intent" of the proclamation, one must move beyond its written terms and incorporate both Indigenous perspectives and consequent actions in relation to the document. One historic event that allows for such dual understandings to emerge is the Treaty of Niagara. The meeting at Niagara, between Sir William Johnson, the British Crown's superintendent of Indian affairs, and approximately two thousand Indigenous chiefs, representing more than twenty-four nations, was one of the largest assemblages of Indigenous nations at the time (Borrows 1994, 22). The treaty set forth an agreement that recognized and affirmed the sovereignty and laws of both Indigenous and settler nations.[1]

While the terms of the Royal Proclamation of 1763 and the Treaty of Niagara have never been formally repealed, Canadian settlers ignored established principles of legal pluralism. As demonstrated by section 91(24) of the Constitution Act, 1867, "Indians" and their reserved "Lands" were simply presented as an additional "class of subjects" under the regulatory control of Parliament (see Jhappan 1995). Harnessing the constitutional authority granted under the section, Parliament passed the Indian Act in 1876, giving the federal executive sweeping powers of control over status Indians and their social and political structures. It is not an exaggeration to say that the Act's leviathanic tentacles touch nearly all aspects of "Indian" existence (Jhappan 1995, 159; Abele 2007). It not only confers extraordinary power in the minister of Indian affairs to determine Indigenous governmental structures and the definition of "Indian" membership, but also provides the Cabinet with the authority to make regulations over an extremely broad variety of policy areas (see Abele 2007, 8). In effect, the Act not only ignored the continuity of Indigenous legal systems, but also directly attempted to undermine traditional political structures by imposing preferred colonial forms of governance (Ladner 2003).

While the federal government historically interpreted its authority under section 91(24) of the constitution as an unbridled power to "civilize" and "assimilate" "Indians" (Tobias 1991), Indigenous people, on the other hand, consistently argued that their inherent rights to sovereignty and self-government had never been surrendered. These competing perspectives came into direct conflict as the Liberal government in the 1960s attempted to dissolve itself of any responsibility for Indian affairs. Building upon Pierre Trudeau's conception of the "Just Society" and "equal rights" for all Canadians, the government's White Paper of 1969 proposed to terminate the "separate legal status" of Indians, dismantle the Indian Act and the Department of Indian Affairs, and

---

1 Indeed, John Borrows notes that after Sir William Johnson had spoken at the gathering, First Nation peoples utilized a two-row wampum belt to reflect their understandings of both the treaty and the Royal Proclamation as symbolizing a "parallel" relationship predicated upon principles of "peace, friendship and respect, where each Nation will not interfere with the internal affairs of the other" (1994, 24).

marshal Indigenous peoples down a "new road" towards full and equal citizenship in Canada (Department of Indian Affairs 1969).

Perhaps not surprisingly, the White Paper was passionately resisted by status Indians, who engaged in protest and mass mobilizations across the country. These tactics not only led to the eventual abandonment of the White Paper, but also to the rise of national Indigenous organizations who continued to mobilize to both protect the constitutional status of Indigenous people and press for recognition of their inherent rights. While Indigenous organizations often mobilized around different interests and concerns, they have nevertheless articulated a common position: the origins of Indigenous rights derive from inherent legal systems that do not depend upon the Canadian constitutional order for existence (Ladner and McCrossan 2009).

This position was forcefully articulated during the constitutional discussions of the early 1980s surrounding constitutional patriation and the proposed Charter of Rights and Freedoms (see Ladner and McCrossan 2009). Under section 35[2] of the Constitution Act, 1982, Indigenous peoples made a breakthrough in securing entrenchment of Aboriginal and treaty rights. Given that Aboriginal and treaty rights were now officially "recognized and affirmed," there was hope that core elements of the common law tradition, such as legal pluralism and "continuity," would be respected as these principles were now further entrenched in the constitution (ibid., 276; see also Henderson et. al 2000).

This acknowledgment can be observed in the final version of the Charlottetown Accord, which proposed the entrenchment of an "inherent right" to self-government and the creation of a third order of government. Though the Charlottetown Accord was ultimately defeated in a national referendum, the recognition of Indigenous "inherency" and broad support for Indigenous perspectives represented a "sea-change" in Indigenous constitutional discourse (Jhappan 1993, 226). While both the Trudeau era (1968–79 and 1980–4) and the Mulroney era (1984–93) were particularly concerned with "rights," Pierre Trudeau's commitment to tenets of liberal individualism and notions of equality caused him to discount collective claims to land and pre-existing Indigenous

---

2 Section 35(1) of the Constitution Act, 1982 reads: "The existing [A]boriginal and treaty rights of the [A]boriginal peoples of Canada are hereby recognized and affirmed," Constitution Act, 1982 being Schedule B to the *Canada Act 1982* (UK), c 11.

rights (Abele, Graham, and Maslove 1999; Jhappan 1993). In contrast, the increased militancy and political mobilization of Indigenous people during the Mulroney era – such as during the Meech Lake Accord and at Oka – not only raised awareness of Indigenous issues, but also produced "an awakening understanding among policy-makers and the general public of the centrality of Aboriginal perspectives on land and governance issues" (Abele, Graham, and Maslove, 276). Though the Progressive Conservative Party (PC) had supported an "inherent" right to self-government during the Charlottetown Accord, its support for Indigenous rights would wane, at times vacillating between recognizing Indigenous peoples as simply just another minority group and/or subsuming Indigenous rights within a pan-Canadian discourse of "equality." Nevertheless, while this discursive "sea-change" would sustain its momentum into the 1990s as the newly elected Liberal government, under Jean Chrétien, formally recognized an inherent right to Indigenous self-government under section 35 (Department of Indian and Northern Affairs 1995), new "populist" voices emerged on the federal scene questioning the legitimacy of the "inherent" rights discourse.

"Conservatives" in Opposition (1993–2006): Privileging Settler Property Regimes

In its early policy literature, the Reform Party articulated a conception of Canada that initially appeared broadly sympathetic to Indigenous claims. For instance, the Reform Party's 1988 Blue Book (its policy platform) stated its opposition to any definition of Canada based upon the notion of "two founding races, cultures and languages" (Reform Party 1988, 3). As Preston Manning would later note, such a vision of Canada fundamentally excluded all those "other Canadians" who were not of English or French origin (Manning 1992, vi). Indeed, scholars have long noted that a "two nations" theory not only undermines Indigenous nationhood, but also explicitly excludes a history of pre-Confederation partnerships and continuing constitutional relations (see Jhappan 1993). However, while the party's first Blue Book paid particular attention to engaging with long-standing national myths, it did not offer particularly detailed prescriptions concerning Indigenous rights. This lack of detail would be rectified in the years preceding the 1993 federal election as a more substantive description of the party's Indigenous policy began to take form.

For instance, in its 1991 Blue Book, the party described its policy concerning Indigenous people as committed to supporting the creation of a "new relationship." This (undefined) "relationship" would emerge through a constitutional convention where Indigenous perspectives on "the nature" and meaning of their rights could be articulated (Reform Party 1991, 32). Although the scope of this relationship was not specifically defined, Preston Manning described the need to establish this new relationship so that "outstanding land claims" and forms of Indigenous economic dependence could be resolved (Manning 1992, 248). Given that one primary failure of the Meech Lake Accord was the exclusion of Indigenous peoples and their concerns, this expressed commitment to holding a "constitutional convention" could be read as a constructive effort to build dialogue regarding land and ongoing territorial entitlements.[3] Perhaps even more significantly, the party's "issue statement" concerning self-government, dated that same year, linked Indigenous "control" over their own affairs to the "new relationship" itself (Reform Party 1992). However, while the party's discourse appeared on the exterior to notionally support claims to governance, its permutations and territorial commitments suggested otherwise.

Though the Reform Party publicly proclaimed its support for increased Indigenous control over their own affairs, it undercut the possibility of realizing forms of Indigenous self-government through strict commitment to pan-Canadian principles and liberal democratic values of individual "equality" (Patten 1999).[4] Given that a fundamental principle underpinning the policy framework of the Reform Party centred on recognition of the "equality" of all Canadian citizens under the law (Manning 1992, 300), it is highly unlikely that forms of self-government that recognized a different set of laws for Indigenous people could ever be fully supported by the party (see also Patten 1999, 40–1). For example, in its early policy literature the party expressed a committed

---

3 Indeed, Manning suggested the need for a constitutional convention so that Indigenous peoples could "define th[e] new relationship from *their* perspective" (1992, 248; emphasis added).

4 It should be noted that in the context of the party's position on multiculturalism, Della Kirkham suggested that by "promoting the equality of all individuals regardless of 'race, language and culture,' the [Reform Party] obscure[d] racial and ethnic differences that [were] still the basis of discrimination" and ultimately "disregard[ed] the realities of racism and discrimination" (1998, 263).

desire to realize a "new definition" (Reform Party 1988, 3) or "vision" of Canadian national identity. While this vision centred on overcoming "old" or outdated conceptions about the foundational interplay of "two nations," the party also offered a definition of "New Canada," which reverberated with pan-Canadian descriptions of citizenship and terri- tory (Reform Party 1991, v). This "new" vision not only invoked the principle of "equality" as a defining characteristic of Canadian citizen- ship, but also engaged in a fundamental flattening of multiple or di- verse territorial claims by defining Canada as a "federation of equal provinces" rather than a federation of founding groups. This flattening of Canadian territory can be further observed in the party's description of the land belonging to Canada: "We believe that Canada's identity and vision for the future should be rooted and inspired by a fresh ap- preciation of 'our land' and the supreme importance to our well-being of exploring, developing, renewing, and conserving our natural resources and physical environment" (Reform Party 1990, 4; 1991, 1; 1995, 6; see also 1988, 22).

In effect, the Reform Party's vision of "New Canada" was predicated upon a naturalized understanding of Canadian territory, which called for continuing efforts to "explore" and "develop" Canadians lands. How- ever, given Manning's previous acknowledgment of the existence of outstanding land claims, this call to further explore and exploit lands belonging to "Canada" could be read as particularly problematic. What territorial rights, for example, might Indigenous peoples possess in the face of exploitation designated for the benefit of all Canadians? Would Indigenous peoples be able to determine how their lands would be de- veloped in a manner that reflected their own traditions?

Though the majority of Reform policy documents referred to building a "next" (Reform Party 1988) or "new" Canada (Reform Party 1990; 1991; 1995), it is within the speeches and writings of Preston Manning where the most detailed description of this vision can be found. In his book entitled *The New Canada*, Manning constructs the Canadian landscape as a space defined by the perpetual settlement of newcomers who have chosen to come to Canada and participate as "Canadians." Indigenous peoples themselves are included in this definition as people belonging to Canada whose own stories relate tales of a "long journey" to a new land (Manning 1992, 352). While this definition was clearly designed to discount the sovereign claims of Quebec and notions of "two founding nations," it also undermines Indigenous claims to land by defining the arrival of Indigenous peoples as simply the first crest of an unending wave of immigration. This representation of Indigenous people as just another settler/immigrant group bears a striking resemblance to representations that would later figure prominently in Tom Flanagan's *First Nations? Second Thoughts*. As Flanagan argued, "Europeans are, in effect, a new immigrant wave, taking control of the land just as earlier [A]boriginal settlers did" (Flanagan 2000, 6). However, this similarity is perhaps not surprising, given that, as Manning acknowledged in the preface to *The New Canada*, Flanagan (who was then the party's director of policy, strategy, and communication) contributed to the third part of the book (along with Stephen Harper), where such representations of Indigenous people can be found (Manning 1992, x). Under the framework advanced by Manning and further developed by Flanagan, Indigenous peoples are simply an additional group of Canadians located within the territorial spaces presently claimed by Canada with little room to assert pre-existing rights outside the purview of the larger "Canadian" community.

In effect, though the Reform Party's discourse may have initially given the outward appearance of supporting forms of Indigenous "control" over their affairs, this support would be further undermined by the party's own commitment to a particular vision of Canadian sovereignty and territory. For instance, Reform policy documents from 1996 to 1997 outlined a far more detailed approach to Indigenous affairs than what the party had previously articulated. In these documents the party defined its position on Indigenous self-government as a "delegated form" within the legal and territorial "borders" of Canada (Reform Party 1996–7, 24). Such a position conceptually excluded any form of "inherent" Indigenous rights. Whereas both the Royal Proclamation and the subsequent Treaty of Niagara established principles and protocols to enable multiple legal orders to coexist and share sovereignty, the Reform Party's discourse, on the other hand, "collapsed"[5] multiple sovereign spaces into a unified vision of sovereignty (ibid., 23). Such adherence to a framework of legal and social unification not only reified Canadian sovereignty as immutable, but also ultimately precluded recognition of Indigenous legal orders and "inherent" rights to government.

---

5 For a detailed discussion of the manner in which the jurisprudence of the Supreme Court has fundamentally "collapsed" Indigenous territories, see McCrossan (2015).

However, what is perhaps most interesting about the Reform Party's discourse in relation to Indigenous people is that it also occurred within the context of openly championing neoliberal principles of privatization, deregulation, and free-market capitalism (Reform Party 1996–7). Under the party's policy framework, continued support for special interests was seen as leading Canada further down a "path" littered with signs of disunity and difference, rather than towards a "new road" built upon individual equality and economic liberation (Manning 1992, 298–9). In order to realize this vision the Reform Party argued that "the creation of wealth and productive jobs for Canadians is best achieved through the operations of a *responsible, broadly-based, free-enterprise economy* in which private property, freedom of contract, and the operations of free markets are encouraged and respected" (Reform Party 1988, 12; emphasis added). As will be discussed below, though the party presented its policies as committed to ending the dependence of Indigenous people, it appeared more concerned with protecting the prevailing property rights of non-Indigenous people at the expense of recognizing pre-existing rights to land and governance.

Likewise, official party platforms of the Progressive Conservative Party during the 1990s also publicly proclaimed a desire to end the economic "dependence" of Indigenous peoples while simultaneously situating them within a pan-Canadian discourse of equal rights. For instance, though the PCs' 1993 electoral platform under Kim Campbell made only brief mention of the rights of Indigenous peoples – listing their interests alongside those of women, minority groups, and persons with disabilities within the context of "justice for all Canadians" (PC Party 1993, 7, 27) – the party's 1997 platform included far more detailed descriptions of its policy proposals concerning Indigenous people.

Under Jean Charest's plan for the "next century," the PC Party vowed to balance the budget within three years through "tough decisions." Some of these proposed decisions, which would directly affect Indigenous people, included a substantial reduction in federal funding and the eventual elimination of the Department of Indian and Northern Affairs (PC Party 1997, 17). However, while the party did invoke the right to self-government and Indigenous self-reliance, the following statement was buried in the platform's appendix: "As we finally move to recognize Canada's Aboriginal people as true equals in our society, it is not unreasonable to ask them to accept their fair share of the costs associated with returning Canada's fiscal state to balance" (PC Party 1997, 59). In effect, though the party continued to publicly support the right to self-government, the right itself appeared constrained by a discourse that situated Indigenous peoples firmly within the larger settler society as "equal Canadians." It is perhaps telling that within this discourse of equality the PC Party made little mention of respecting historic treaty relationships and ongoing obligations.[6]

Though federal conservative parties during the 1990s displayed dwindling support for inherent rights to self-government, the policies of the Reform Party in particular appeared committed explicitly to protecting the prevailing distributions of power and property rights of non-Indigenous people. This position can be most readily observed in the House of Commons debates concerning Bill C-9, an Act to give effect to the Nisga'a Final Agreement. The agreement itself was part of a tripartite treaty that settled a long-standing territorial dispute between the Nisga'a Nation and the governments of Canada and British Columbia in May 1999. The agreement gave the Nisga'a ownership over roughly 2,000 square kilometres of land in the lower Nass Valley of British Columbia and recognized the continuing existence of traditional Nisga'a laws and rights to self-government and jurisdiction. Though the Liberals, Bloc Québécois, NDP, and PC parties all publicly expressed their support for the treaty and provisions for self-government, the Reform Party provided trenchant criticism of the bill and its perceived "negative" impacts. In particular, the Reform Party took great issue with the fact that the bill recognized a different set of laws for the Nisga'a people (as opposed to "one law" for all Canadians). However, what is most interesting about the position advanced by the Reform Party in the House is that it advocated a "new relationship" that denounced the "status quo" while simultaneously grounding its position in a previously defeated policy proposal.

For example, Preston Manning, in a lengthy speech in the House, described Pierre Trudeau's approach to Indigenous affairs under the White Paper of 1969 as emblematic of the "correct" or "proper" way to define new relationships with Indigenous peoples (*House of Commons Debates* 1999). Though Manning often criticized the policy legacies of Trudeau, particularly in relation to Quebec (Manning 1992, 223), Trudeau's approach to individual equality during the time of the White Paper was

---

6 While federal conservative parties may have displayed declining support for "inherent" Indigenous rights, it should be noted that the New Democratic Party explicitly advocated for upholding inherent rights to self-government during this period (see NDP 1997).

invoked by Manning to discount the Nisga'a Treaty. Much like the architects of the White Paper, Manning called for the rapid assimilation of Indigenous peoples into Canadian society as a way to end "separate status" and "dependence" while simultaneously ignoring the broader structures of colonialism that continued to dispossess Indigenous peoples of their lands and rights to governance (*House of Commons Debates* 1999).

Whereas the federal Liberal and PC parties expressed support at times for the "inherent" right to self-government during the 1990s and into the following the decade, the discourse of the Reform Party, on the other hand, (re)opened space for conceptualizing Indigenous rights as "delegated" forms embedded within a framework of individual equality *and* the protection of private property. This framework for assessing Indigenous claims was imported practically wholesale into the policies of the Reform Party's successor, the Canadian Alliance (CA), upon its founding in 2000. For instance, the CA's official "declaration of policy" expressed the party's position on self-government in similar terms of "delegated" rights and "individual equality" under Canadian law (Canadian Alliance 2000a, 6–7). Moreover, in addition to continuing the Reform Party's approach to self-government and orientations towards "individual" equality, the CA also expressed its support for "existing" rights to property (7). It should be noted that this particular policy was framed in the context of land claim "negotiations" where existing rights to property would be "respected." While the Supreme Court of Canada mandated that negotiated land settlements be conducted in "good faith" with "give and take on all sides" (Delgamuukw 1997, para. 186), it is unclear from this policy statement just what weight might be accorded to Indigenous perspectives.

The CA would begin to fill in the specifics of its Indigenous policy with the publication of its federal election platform entitled "A Time for Change." While the party's election platform continued to stress the value of "individual equality" and the importance of "delegated" rights, it also prioritized Indigenous participation in the free market through "direct private ownership" of their lands (Canadian Alliance 2000b, 21). However, the primary concern of the CA's Indigenous policies was to ensure that the rights of "non-natives" or "exiting property holders" be protected during land claim negotiations (ibid.) That is to say that while the right of Indigenous people *to establish* private ownership of reserve lands was protected under the policies of the Reform and CA parties, it was the *already established* and *existing* property interests of non-Indigenous people that were prioritized. In effect, under the

CA's policy framework, Indigenous peoples appear to be able to benefit from – or protect – their lands only if they accept predominant ways of organizing, using, and exploiting land. Much like the earlier policies of the Reform Party (1996–7, 23; 1999), this framework ultimately appears to be an additional way to ensure Indigenous territorial dispossession by making it easier for non-Indigenous people (and third-party interests) to purchase and gain ownership of Indigenous lands.

Though the PC Party did not explicitly situate its policies within a discourse of protecting prevailing property interests, it continued to express its endorsement of inherent rights to self-government "within Canada for Canada's Aboriginal people" (PC Party 2000, 18). This stated placement of self-government "within Canada" – and Indigenous peoples as constitutive components of Canadian identity – was expressed throughout the party's 2000 electoral platform. While the PC Party did declare a commitment to end "paternalistic and colonial approaches," it nevertheless maintained that "in order to ensure fairness and equality, the *Charter* must apply to Aboriginal self-government" (ibid.).

Many of the ideas expressed by the Reform, CA, and PC parties – particularly those regarding the importance of establishing and protecting private property, "delegating" rights to Indigenous people, and locating self-government within the constitutional context of "Canada" – can be seen reflected in the initial policies of the Conservative Party of Canada. Indeed, in the party's first election platform, the discourse of "inherent" rights was notably absent in the document's discussion of self-government. In its place was a position on self-government that was far more neutral and innocuous in tone: "The Conservative Party believes in the principle of self-government within the context of the Constitution of Canada" (Conservative Party 2004, 33). Although it is unclear from this first platform just what "principle" of self-government the party supported, it is significant that the party more forcefully declared that "principles" of the Charter "must" apply to Aboriginal governments (ibid.). Given the highly individualistic nature of the Charter and its expressions of protecting the equality rights of all Canadians, such a requirement could very well undermine respect for Indigenous difference and "collective" claims to land and governance. Nevertheless, the actual policy "plan" outlined in the platform – in which self-government is notably not listed – continued to invoke the importance of developing "property regimes" on reserves. In effect, much like the former policies of the Reform and CA parties, the CPC viewed Indigenous land rights through a framework of individual self-interest. It is telling that this "property regime" was not described as encouraging economic sustainability, or strengthening Indigenous relationships to land, but rather as "encourag[ing] lending for private housing and businesses" (ibid.). Such a perspective seems to view the lands currently held by Indigenous peoples solely as "objects" to be individually demarcated, parcelled out, and exploited.

This statement concerning the development of "property regimes" for Aboriginal reserves remained unchanged in the party's 2006 federal election platform (Conservative Party 2006, 38). However, one notable difference can be observed in the document's treatment of Indigenous governance. According to the platform, if elected, the CPC would "[r]eplace the Indian Act (and related legislation) with a modern legislative framework which provides for the devolution of full legal and democratic responsibility to [A]boriginal Canadians for their own affairs within the Constitution, including the Charter of Rights and Freedoms" (ibid.). While it is unclear from this statement specifically what the "replacement" of the Indian Act and "devolution" of authority might entail, the language used here does evoke the previous aspirations of the White Paper (and former Reform Party policies) to vacate the policy field and disengage from Indigenous affairs. Moreover, the fact that the authority that "Aboriginal Canadians" possess is described as resulting from a process of "devolution" within the Constitution likely means that Indigenous understandings of "inherent" rights and nationhood are discounted in favour of delegated rights under the existing Constitution. Nevertheless, one additional change that can be seen in this platform concerns economic development and opportunities in the North for both "Aboriginal and non-Aboriginal" people (18). In fact, after gaining power in 2006, the Conservative government's first two Throne Speeches would not only present a vision of Canadian identity and territorial sovereignty that directly affected Indigenous rights to land, but also a representation of Canadian history that could undermine Indigenous claims to sovereignty and governance.

Conservatives in Power (2006–2015): Privileging Settler Histories and "Canadian" Sovereignty

Only one specific reference was made to "Aboriginal peoples" in the Conservative government's first Speech from the Throne, delivered on 3 April 2006. This brief reference was made in relation to "improv[ing] opportunity for all Canadians" (Canada 2006). However, while little attention was devoted to Indigenous people outside the interests of the broader Canadian community, the Throne Speech stressed the need to "defend" Canadian sovereignty in the context of a tenuous world order. Both Indigenous people and Canadian sovereignty would be linked in the government's second Throne Speech on 16 October 2007.

Under the heading "strengthening Canada's sovereignty and place in the world," the Conservative government harnessed the North in a way that not only emphasized it as an area of policy priority, but also as a site where Canadian sovereignty itself could be performed and asserted. Not only was the North invoked as part of the lands belonging to – or possessed by – Canada, but also to signify an essential component of "Canadian" identity. In this respect, the Arctic was presented in the Throne Speech as a sovereign "Canadian" space to be continuously explored, used, and mapped (Canada 2007). As Stephen Harper would note later that year, "Canada has a choice when it comes to defending our sovereignty over the Arctic. We either use it or lose it. And make no mistake, this Government intends to use it. Because Canada's Arctic is central to our identity as a northern nation" (Prime Minister's Office 2007).

However, excluded from this discussion is any reference to the historic use and occupation of the North by Indigenous peoples. As Frances Abele has argued, this "use it or lose it" mantra "ignores the 'use' – the long-term habitation – of the Northlands by Canadian Inuit, Dene, Cree and other Aboriginal peoples" (2011, 220). At the same time, the prime minister's Throne Speech and subsequent ruminations on the North can also be understood as doing much more than simply ignoring Indigenous territorial usage. Rather, the speeches themselves can be seen as reasserting "Canadian" sovereignty over Indigenous peoples and their traditional territories (Prime Minister's Office 2007). Such assertions not only ignore diverse relationships to land occurring within those borders, but they also undermine Indigenous rights to sovereignty and governance by recasting Indigenous peoples as "Canadians" firmly situated within the sovereign space of Canada.

Though the Conservative government's discourse tended to locate Indigenous peoples within the context of a unified territorial collectivity, this is by no means to suggest that the government completely ignored Indigenous concerns. On the contrary, the government's second Speech from the Throne made particular mention of providing an apology for Indian residential schools in order to "close this sad chapter in our history" (Canada 2007). The government fulfilled this promise on

11 June 2008, when Prime Minister Harper issued a historic apology in the House of Commons to former students of Indian residential schools. In his apology on behalf of the government and all Canadians, Harper apologized for the physical, sexual, and emotional abuse suffered by former students and the lasting intergenerational effects caused by a "policy of assimilation." Noting that the lack of an apology had hindered efforts to achieve "healing" and "reconciliation," he called for a "new beginning" and relationship based upon knowledge of "our shared history" (*House of Commons Debates* 2008). While Harper should certainly be commended for issuing the apology and raising awareness of the policy's effects, a number of scholars have drawn attention to the form of the apology and its removal of residential schools from a broader history of colonialism. For instance, Jennifer Henderson and Pauline Wakeham note that not only is the term *colonialism* absent from descriptions of past state actions, but by carefully containing mistakes of the past to a discrete moment in time, the apology implied that it was only the history of residential schools that needed to be addressed and overcome (Henderson and Wakeham 2009, 2).

This inability to reconcile with and acknowledge a broader colonial history can be observed in comments made by Harper the following year at the G20 Summit in Pittsburgh. In his remarks at a press conference after the meeting, the prime minister stated that, unlike other political democracies, Canada had "no history of colonialism." While Harper could have been referring to an external history of colonialism beyond Canada's present territorial boundaries, this perspective nevertheless effaced a history of colonial practices within Canada's own borders that have led to the dispossession of Indigenous peoples from their traditional territories (Ladner and McCrossan 2014). Indeed, the Conservative government's approach to history tended to isolate and highlight particular "foundational" events that privilege the actions of settler communities.

For instance, in the 2008 and 2011 federal election platforms, the Conservative government stressed the importance of celebrating the 400th anniversary of French and English settlements (Conservative Party 2008, 28), the bicentennial of the War of 1812 (ibid.; 2011a, 18), and the 150th anniversary of Confederation (Conservative Party 2008, 28; 2011a, 18). While Indigenous peoples are often recognized in relation to their contributions to the War of 1812 (Conservative Party 2011a, 38), the primary focus has been on celebrating the role played by Canada's "two founding nations" in building the existing constitutional structure. Not only does this ignore Indigenous alliances with the Crown and reasons for their involvement in the War of 1812, but also the foundational role played by early peace and friendship treaties. In a manner similar to the previous discourse of the Reform and CA parties, the Conservative government presented a vision of self-government that also discounts "inherent" or "immemorial" rights in favour of *delegated* or "devolved" rights "within our federal system" (Conservative Party 2011b, 24).[7] As such, the possibility of recognizing multiple legal systems or parallel sovereign relationships is conceptually limited under the framework employed by the Conservative party.[8] The effects of this framework for Indigenous affairs could be seen in a range of policy changes and legislative enactments passed in 2012.

For instance, in its March 2012 federal budget, the Conservative government announced its intention "to explore with interested First Nations the option of moving forward with legislation that would allow private property ownership within current reserve boundaries" (Department of Finance 2012a, 165). On the one hand, this "exploration" was consistent with past declarations by both the Reform and CA parties in regards to establishing Indigenous regimes of private ownership (see also *House of Commons Debates* 1999, 1145). However, this push towards "voluntary" ownership appeared to be strongly influenced by the more recent writings of Tom Flanagan and others. As Flanagan argued in his section of *Beyond the Indian Act*, in order to contribute to Indigenous economic advancement and ensure Indigenous participation within the "modern" market economy, the Canadian government should work towards "a regime of fee-simple ownership that First

---

7 Conservative government efforts to ensure further "control" of Indigenous governments can also be seen in the Throne Speech where the government declared that First Nations chiefs and councillors would be "required" "to publish their salaries and expenses" (see Canada 2011). For a detailed discussion of the Conservative government's discourse of "transparency" and the resulting First Nations Transparency and Accountability Act, see Pasternak (2015).

8 While the CPC's framework seemingly discounted inherent Indigenous rights, the NDP continued to support inherent rights to self-government (see NDP 2004, 2006, 2008). In fact, one notable shift occurred in the NDP's 2006 election platform in which the party's discourse not only recognized forms of legal pluralism by advocating for "creating legal space and recognition for the legitimacy and jurisdiction of [I]ndigenous governments," but also implicitly recognized a nation-to-nation relationship by referring to Indigenous peoples as the "Original Nations of Canada" (see NDP 2006, 20–2).

Nations can opt into *voluntarily*" (Flanagan, Alcantara, and Le Dressay 2010, 53; emphasis in original). For Flanagan, this form of voluntary ownership could be realized through the implementation of a First Nations Property Ownership Act – a proposed piece of federal legislation also championed in the book's foreword by former Kamloops Indian band chief C.T. (Manny) Jules – that would not only contribute towards Indigenous self-government by "emancipating" Indigenous people from the Indian Act, but also to greater involvement within the broader Canadian economy. However, it is important to note that there is little discussion of any Indigenous cultural conceptions of land that might eschew forms of "control" or human domination. Instead, these proposals seem designed to ensure that Indigenous lands can be more easily transferred to and exploited by "other Canadians" (29).

Perhaps the most significant developments in relation to land and reconciliation occurred during the Conservative government's final term in office. In 2012 the Conservative government passed two omnibus pieces of legislation that made substantial amendments in a number of policy areas.[9] For instance, Bill C-45 included changes to the Indian Act that directly reflect conservative concerns regarding the leasing of reserve lands in the context of expeditiously reducing "unnecessary costs" and stimulating economic development on reserves (Department of Finance 2012b). In this regard, through changes made to the "voting threshold" surrounding the leasing of lands, the federal government essentially undercut the collective basis of Indigenous rights and relationships to land by unilaterally determining the correct – and least "cumbersome" – way for reserve lands to be cleared for development (ibid.). Additionally, the Conservative government announced in 2014 that it would be "taking action to promote reconciliation" and "developing a new Framework for Addressing Section 35 Aboriginal Rights" (Aboriginal Affairs and Northern Development 2014a). As part of this process, the minister of Aboriginal affairs appointed Douglas R. Eyford[10] as a ministerial special representative to "lead engagement"

---

9 See *Jobs, Growth and Long-term Prosperity Act,* SC, c 19, 29 June 2012; see also *Jobs and Growth Act,* SC, c 31, 14 December 2012 (Bill C-45).

10 While previously appointed as a "special federal representative," Douglas Eyford also submitted a report to the prime minister in 2013 on "west coast energy infrastructure." For further discussion of the underlying logics contained in the reports, see McCrossan (2016).

with Aboriginal peoples and help "renew and reform" Canada's
Comprehensive Land Claims Policy (ibid.). The government released
an "Interim Policy" in this area in September 2014. While the Interim
Policy does reiterate the Canadian government's 1995 recognition and
policy surrounding the inherent right to self-government under section
35 (see Aboriginal Affairs and Northern Development 2014b, 17), it also
advances a number of "principles" of reconciliation that potentially
further undercut Indigenous legal orders and jurisdictions.

For instance, building upon previous Supreme Court jurisprudence surrounding the "purpose" of section 35 and the essential "objective" to "reconcil[e] the pre-existence of Aboriginal societies with
the sovereignty of the Crown" (see Aboriginal Affairs and Northern
Development 2014b, 7), the Interim Policy notes that "[r]econciliation
promotes a secure climate for economic and resource development that
can benefit all Canadians and balances Aboriginal rights with broader societal interests" (ibid., 8). Indeed, the document "recognizes"
that reconciliation necessitates that "any infringement of Aboriginal
rights requires a justification in accordance with standards established
by the Canadian courts" (ibid.). In effect, the "renewal" of Canada's
Comprehensive Land Claims Policy begins by invoking legal principles of reconciliation, which not only conceptually exclude Indigenous
legal orders and jurisdictions by enabling governments to infringe
upon Aboriginal rights in the name of broader economic and developmental objectives (see Delgamuukw 1997, para. 165), but also situates
Aboriginal peoples within an overarching framework of Crown sovereignty. Likewise, while the 2015 report delivered by Douglas Eyford
attempts to move beyond the "legal theory" (2015, 35) of reconciliation
and outline a "new reconciliation framework" (ibid., 36), the report itself is ultimately structured by similar naturalized understandings of
Crown sovereignty. For instance, though the report does acknowledge
that Aboriginal organizations have stressed that "indigenous systems
of governance and laws are essential to the regulation of lands and
resources throughout British Columbia" (ibid., 31), the report then
bluntly states, "Aboriginal representatives need to acknowledge that
their communities are part of the broader Canadian social, political,
and economic community over which the Crown is sovereign" (ibid.,
32). In effect, the fundamental vision of reconciliation found within
the policies and commissioned reports of the CPC appears to be one
that is oriented to both the frameworks of Crown sovereignty and a
"free[ly] competitive market economy" (Conservative Party 2011b) in

such a way that Indigenous legal orders and claims to land are effectively undermined and subsumed within broader Canadian economic and developmental interests.

Conclusion

Though this chapter has focused primarily on "conservative" Indigenous policy discourses emanating from a chain of populist parties speaking on behalf of "all Canadians," it is important to note that Indigenous voices did not passively accept the integrationist measures implemented by the Conservative government. In response to many of the amendments embedded within the Jobs and Growth Act, an Indigenous grassroots social movement known as Idle No More formed to protest the government's policy enactments and to raise awareness of Indigenous concerns surrounding ongoing forms of colonial dispossession and violence. Engaging in demonstrations, hunger strikes, and other forms of resistance across the country (see chapter 4 in this volume), the Idle No More movement called upon the federal government to respect the "spirit and intent" of treaties by recognizing the pre-existing rights to land and sovereignty possessed by Indigenous peoples.

Indeed, the continuing grassroots mobilization of Indigenous communities was also readily apparent in the forty-second Canadian general election. While rates of electoral participation among Indigenous people in Canada have tended to be lower than those of non-Indigenous Canadians – for such reasons as geographic dispersal, political alienation, and conceptions of inherent sovereignty and citizenship (Ladner and McCrossan 2007) – the 2015 federal election resulted in notable differences in relation to both Indigenous policy and Indigenous electoral participation. In particular, the 2015 federal election not only saw the highest number of Indigenous MPs (ten) elected to the House of Commons (see Talaga 2015), but also potentially the largest increase in participation rates among Indigenous peoples in Canada, with turnout in some communities reportedly rising by more than 270 per cent (Puxley 2015). While this was driven partially by a reaction to the Conservative policies canvassed above, as well as by clear efforts to mobilize substantial numbers of Indigenous voters to effect governmental change (Talaga 2015), it is also worthwhile to note some differences in policy discourse during the campaign. Though the federal leaders debates themselves were largely devoid of substantive discussion of Indigenous issues,[11] both NDP leader Tom Mulcair and Liberal leader Justin Trudeau vowed to renew a "nation-to-nation" relationship and achieve "reconciliation" with Indigenous peoples, in speeches given before the annual general meeting of the Assembly of First Nations (CBC News 2015).

In fact, not only did Trudeau repeat this commitment throughout the campaign, but in his speech before the Assembly of First Nations, he also invoked the "two-row wampum" itself in the context of a "renewed relationship" (Liberal Party 2015). As the Two-Row Wampum conveys an understanding of the Haudenosaunee (Iroquois or Six Nations) Confederacy's conception of their treaty relationship with settler nations, or a relationship predicated upon peaceful coexistence where both parties recognized the jurisdictional autonomy of each nation and the possibility for separate legal orders to coexist within a shared "space" (see Asch 2014, quoting Dale Turner at 113), this reference is significant. If, as the new prime minister has stated, he is sincerely committed to establishing a "nation-to-nation" relationship with Indigenous peoples, then Trudeau's invocation of the "two-row wampum" could provide an opening to move away from previous unilateral approaches to "reconciliation" and to begin building upon the principles of legal pluralism embedded within Canada's constitutional foundations.[12]

REFERENCES

Abele, Frances. 2007. *Like an Ill-Fitting Boot: Government, Governance and Management Systems in the Contemporary Indian Act*. National Centre for First Nations Governance. http://fngovernance.org/resources_docs/Analysis_of_Governance_and_Management_Under_the_Indian_Act.pdf.

---

11 At one point during the *Globe and Mail*'s debate on the economy, Liberal leader Justin Trudeau remarked in passing that the leaders "haven't talked about [First Nations issues] enough tonight," but then proceeded to provide very little substantive discussion himself about Indigenous concerns (*Maclean's* 2015).

12 However, it should be noted that the strength of these discursive commitments have been called into question. For instance, commentators have suggested that Trudeau's recent approval of the Kinder Morgan Trans Mountain pipeline expansion perhaps indicates that Trudeau's commitment to establishing a new relationship may be nothing more than a "superficial approach to Indigenous rights and environmental integrity" (Powless 2016).

– 2011. "Use It or Lose It? The Conservatives' Northern Strategy." In *How Ottawa Spends 2011–12: Trimming Fat or Slicing Pork?* edited by Christopher Stoney and G. Bruce Doern, 218–42. Montreal and Kingston: McGill-Queen's University Press.

Abele, Frances, Katherine Graham, and Allan Maslove. 1999. "Negotiating Canada: Changes in Aboriginal Policy over the Last Thirty Years." In *How Ottawa Spends 1999–2000*, edited by Leslie Pal, 251–92. Ottawa: Oxford University Press.

Aboriginal Affairs and Northern Development Canada. 2014a. "Minister Valcourt Announces Measures to Advance Treaty Negotiations and Reconciliation." http://news.gc.ca/web/article-en.do?nid=871349.

– 2014b. *Renewing the Comprehensive Land Claims Policy: Towards a Framework for Addressing Section 35 Aboriginal Rights*. Ottawa: Aboriginal Affairs and Northern Development (Interim Policy). https://www.aadnc-aandc.gc.ca/DAM/DAM-INTER-HQ-LDC/STAGING/texte-text/ldc_ccl_renewing_land_claims_policy_2014_1408643594856_eng.pdf.

Asch, Michael. 2014. *On Being Here to Stay*. Toronto: University of Toronto Press.

Barsh, Russell Lawrence. 2004. "Indigenous Rights and the *Lex Loci* in British Imperial Law." In *Advancing Aboriginal Claims; Visions, Strategies, Directions*, edited by Kerry Wilkins, 91–126. Saskatoon: Purich Publishing.

Borrows, John. 1994. "Constitutional Law from a First Nation Perspective: Self-Government and the Royal Proclamation." *University of British Columbia Law Review* 28 (1): 1–47.

British Columbia. 1999. *Nisga'a Final Agreement Act, SBC 1999*. Victoria: Queen's Printer (Nisga'a Final Agreement).

Brooks, Stephen. 2015. *Canadian Democracy*. Don Mills, ON: Oxford University Press Canada.

Canada. 1996. *Report of the Royal Commission on Aboriginal Peoples*, Vol. 1: *Looking Forward, Looking Back*. Ottawa: Supply and Services.

– 2006. "Speech from the Throne to Open the First Session, Thirty-Ninth Parliament of Canada." http://www.parl.gc.ca/Parlinfo/Documents/ThroneSpeech/39-1-e.html.

– 2007. "Speech from the Throne to Open the Second Session, Thirty-Ninth Parliament of Canada." http://www.parl.gc.ca/Parlinfo/Documents/ThroneSpeech/39-2-e.html.

– 2011. "Speech from the Throne to Open the First Session, Forty-First Parliament of Canada." http://www.parl.gc.ca/Parlinfo/Documents/ThroneSpeech/41-1-e.html.

Canadian Alliance. 2000a. *Canadian Alliance Declaration of Policy*. 1–10. http://web.archive.org/web/20000829033244/http://www.canadianalliance.ca/yourprinciples/policy_declare/acrobat_doc/policydoc.pdf.

194   The Blueprint

- 2000b. *A Time For Change: An Agenda of Respect for All Canadians.* 1–24. https://www.poltext.org/sites/poltext.org/files/plateformes/can2000all_plt_en._14112008_173717.pdf.
CBC News. 2015. "AFN General Assembly: Tom Mulcair, Justin Trudeau Vow to Promote Reconciliation," 7 July. http://www.cbc.ca/news/aboriginal/afn-general-assembly-tom-mulcairjustin-trudeau-vow-to-promote-reconciliation-1.3140885.
Conservative Party of Canada. 2004. *Demanding Better.* https://www.poltext.org/sites/poltext.org/files/plateformes/can2004pc_plt_en._14112008_171920.pdf.
- 2006. *Stand Up for Canada.* https://www.poltext.org/sites/poltext.org/files/plateformes/can2006pc_plt_en._14112008_165519.pdf.
- 2008. *The True North Strong and Free: Stephen Harper's Plan for Canadians.* https://www.poltext.org/sites/poltext.org/files/plateformes/can2008pc_plt_eng._13112008_193556.pdf.
- 2011a. *Here for Canada: Stephen Harper's Low Tax Plan for Jobs and Economic Growth.* https://www.poltext.org/sites/poltext.org/files/plateformes/can2011pc_plt_en_12072011_114959.pdf.
- 2011b. *Policy Declaration* (Amended 11 June 2011). http://web.archive.org/web/20120803173656/http://www.conservative.ca/media/2012/07/20120705-CPC-PolicyDec-E.pdf.
Coulthard, Glen. 2014. *Red Skin, White Masks: Rejecting the Colonial Politics of Recognition.* Minneapolis: University of Minnesota Press.
Department of Finance. 2012a. *Jobs, Growth, and Long-term Prosperity: Economic Action Plan 2012.* Ottawa: Public Works and Government Services Canada. http://www.budget.gc.ca/2012/plan/pdf/Plan2012-eng.pdf.
- 2012b. *Background Document: Bill C-45 – "Jobs and Growth Act, 2012."* Ottawa: Department of Finance. http://www.fin.gc.ca/pub/c45/c45-eng.pdf.
Department of Indian Affairs and Northern Development. 1969. *Statement of the Government of Canada on Indian Policy.* Ottawa: Queen's Printer.
Department of Indian and Northern Affairs Canada. 1995. *The Government of Canada's Approach to Implementation of the Inherent Right and the Negotiation of Aboriginal Self-Government.* Ottawa: Public Works and Government Services.
Eyford, Douglas R. 2015. *A New Direction: Advancing Aboriginal and Treaty Rights.* Ottawa: Aboriginal Affairs and Northern Development. https://www.aadnc-aandc.gc.ca/DAM/DAM-INTER-HQ-LDC/STAGING/texte-text/eyford_newDirection-report_april2015_1427810490332_eng.pdf.
Flanagan, Tom. 2000. *First Nations? Second Thoughts.* Montreal and Kingston: McGill-Queen's University Press.

Flanagan, Tom, Christopher Alcantara, and Andre Le Dressay. 2010. *Beyond the Indian Act*. Montreal and Kingston: McGill-Queen's University Press.

Henderson, James (Sakej) Youngblood, Marjorie L. Benson, and Isobel M. Findlay. 2000. *Aboriginal Tenure in the Constitution of Canada*. Scarborough, ON: Carswell.

Henderson, Jennifer, and Pauline Wakeham. 2009. "Colonial Reckoning, National Reconciliation? Aboriginal Peoples and the Culture of Redress in Canada." *English Studies in Canada* 35 (1): 1–26. http://dx.doi.org/10.1353/esc.0.0168.

House of Commons Debates. 36th Parliament. 2nd Session. No. 011 (26 October 1999) at 1055–155 (Hon. Preston Manning).

– 39th Parliament. 2nd Session. No. 110 (11 June 2008) at 1515–25 (Prime Minister Stephen Harper).

Jhappan, Radha. 1993. "Inherency, Three Nations and Collective Rights: The Evolution of Aboriginal Constitutional Discourse from 1982 to the Charlottetown Accord." *International Journal of Canadian Studies* 7–8:225–60.

– 1995. "The Federal-Provincial Power-Grid and Aboriginal Self-Government." In *New Trends in Canadian Federalism*, edited by Francois Rocher and Miriam Smith, 155–84. Peterborough, ON: Broadview.

Kirkham, Della. 1998. "The Reform Party of Canada: A Discourse on Race, Ethnicity and Equality." In *Racism & Social Inequality in Canada: Concepts, Controversies & Strategies of Resistance*, edited by Vic Satzewich, 243–67. Toronto: Thompson Educational Publishing.

Ladner, Kiera. 2001. "Negotiated Inferiority: The Royal Commission on Aboriginal People's Vision of a Renewed Relationship." *American Review of Canadian Studies* 31 (1–2): 241–64.

– 2003. "Rethinking Aboriginal Governance." In *Reinventing Canada: Politics of the 21st Century*, edited by Janine Brodie and Linda Trimble, 43–60. Toronto: Prentice Hall.

Ladner, Kiera, and Michael McCrossan. 2007. *The Electoral Participation of Aboriginal People*. Ottawa: Elections Canada.

– 2009. "The Road Not Taken: Aboriginal Rights after the Re-imagining of the Canadian Constitutional Order." In *Contested Constitutionalism: Reflections on the Canadian Charter of Rights and Freedoms*, edited by James B. Kelly and Christopher P. Manfredi, 262–83. Vancouver: UBC Press.

– 2014. "Whose Shared History?" *Labour/Le Travail* 73:200–2.

Liberal Party of Canada. 2015. "Remarks by Justin Trudeau at the Assembly of First Nations 36th Annual General Assembly." https://www.liberal.ca/realchange/justin-trudeau-at-the-assembly-of-first-nations-36th-annual-general-assembly.

Maclean's. 2015. "Tale of the Tape: Transcript of the Globe Debate on the Economy," 18 September. http://www.macleans.ca/politics/ottawa/tale-of-the-tape-transcript-of-the-globe-debate-on-the-economy/.

Manning, Preston. 1992. *The New Canada*. Toronto: Macmillan Canada.

McCrossan, Michael. 2015. "Contaminating and Collapsing Indigenous Space: Judicial Narratives of Canadian Territoriality." *Settler Colonial Studies* 5 (1): 20–39. http://dx.doi.org/10.1080/2201473X.2014.925609.

– 2016. "Enduring Eliminatory Logics, Market Rationalities, and Territorial Desires: Assessing the Harper Government's Legacy Concerning Aboriginal Rights." *Review of Constitutional Studies* 21 (2): 187–208.

NDP. 1997. *A Framework for Canada's Future*. https://www.poltext.org/sites/poltext.org/files/plateformes/can1997ndp_convention_en_12072011_124006.pdf.

– 2004. *Jack Layton, NDP: New Energy. A Positive Choice*. https://www.poltext.org/sites/poltext.org/files/plateformes/can2004ndp_plt_en._14112008_171856.pdf.

– 2006. *Getting Results for People: Platform 2006*. https://www.poltext.org/sites/poltext.org/files/plateformes/can2006ndp_plt_en._14112008_165642.pdf.

– 2008. *Jack Layton and the New Democrats: A Prime Minister on Your Family's Side, for a Change*. https://www.poltext.org/sites/poltext.org/files/plateformes/can2008ndp_plt_eng._14112008_160417.pdf.

Pasternak, Shiri. 2015. "The Fiscal Body of Sovereignty: To 'Make Live' in Indian Country." *Settler Colonial Studies* 6 (4). http://dx.doi.org/10.1080/2201473X.2015.1090525.

Patten, Steve. 1999. "The Reform Party's Re-Imagining of the Canadian Nation." *Journal of Canadian Studies / Revue d'études canadiennes* 34 (1): 27–51.

Powless, Ben. 2016. "Trudeau's Contradictions on Environment, Indigenous Rights." *Policy Options* (9 December 2016). http://policyoptions.irpp.org/magazines/december-2016/trudeaus-contradictions-on-environment-indigenous-rights/.

Prime Minister's Office. 2007. "Prime Minister Stephen Harper Announces New Arctic Offshore Patrol Ships." News release, 9 July. http://news.gc.ca/web/article-en.do?crtr.sj1D=&mthd=advSrch&crtr.mnthndVl=&nid=335789&crtr.dpt1D=&crtr.tp1D=&crtr.lc1D=&crtr.yrStrtVl=2008&crtr.kw=&crtr.dyStrtVl=26&crtr.aud1D=&crtr.mnthStrtVl=2&crtr.yrndVl=&crtr.dyndVl=.

Progressive Conservative Party of Canada. 1993. *Making Government Work for Canada: A Taxpayer's Agenda*. https://www.poltext.org/sites/poltext.org/files/plateformes/can1993pc_plt_en_12072011_130659.pdf.

– 1997. *Let the Future Begin: Jean Charest's Plan for Canada's Next Century*. https://www.poltext.org/sites/poltext.org/files/plateformes/can1997pc_plt_en.pdf.

– 2000. *Change You Can Trust: The Progressive Conservative Plan for Canada's Future.* https://www.poltext.org/sites/poltext.org/files/plateformes/can2000pc_plt_en._14112008_173707.pdf.

Puxley, Chinta. 2015. "Voter Turnout up by 270 Per Cent in Some Aboriginal Communities." *Toronto Star*, 25 October.

Reform Party of Canada. 1988. *Platform and Statement of Principles of the Reform Party of Canada.* Calgary: Reform Party (Blue Book]). http://contentdm.ucalgary.ca/cdm/compoundobject/collection/reform/id/197.

– 1990. *Principles and Policies.* Calgary: Reform Party of Canada (Blue Book). http://contentdm.ucalgary.ca/cdm/compoundobject/collection/reform/id/2230.

– 1991. *Building New Canada: Principles and Policies: The Blue Book.* Calgary: Reform Fund Canada. https://www.poltext.org/sites/poltext.org/files/plateformes/can1991r_plt_en_12072011_125340.pdf.

– 1992. *The Green Book: Issues and Answers.* Calgary: Reform Party, Caucus Issue Statement no. 10, 20 November 1991. http://contentdm.ucalgary.ca/cdm/compoundobject/collection/reform/id/713/rec/5.

– 1995. *Building A New Canada: Principles and Policies, The Blue Book 1995.* Calgary: Reform Fund Canada. http://contentdm.ucalgary.ca/cdm/compoundobject/collection/reform/id/2156.

– 1996–7. *A Fresh Start for Canadians: Blue Book: 1996–1997 Principles & Policies of the Reform Party of Canada.* Calgary: Reform Fund Canada. https://www.poltext.org/sites/poltext.org/files/plateformes/can1996r_plt_en_12072011_124840.pdf.

– 1999. *The Blue Book: Principles & Policies of the Reform Party of Canada – 1999 as Authorized by Reform Party Members, Assembly '98.* Calgary: Reform Fund Canada. http://contentdm.ucalgary.ca/cdm/compoundobject/collection/reform/id/2258/rec/31.

Russell, Peter H. 2005. *Recognizing Aboriginal Title: The Mabo Case and Indigenous Resistance to English-Settler Colonialism.* Toronto: University of Toronto Press.

Slattery, Brian. 1987. "Understanding Aboriginal Rights." *Canadian Bar Review* 66:727–83.

Supreme Court of Canada. *Delgamuukw v British Columbia*, [1997] 3 SCR 1010. [Delgamuukw].

Talaga, Tanya. 2015. "Behind the Scenes on the Push to Rock the Indigenous Vote." *Toronto Star*, 23 October.

Tobias, John L. 1991. "Protection, Civilization and Assimilation: An Outline History of Canada's Indian Policy." In *Sweet Promises: A Reader on Indian-White Relations in Canada*, edited by J.R. Miller, 127–44. Toronto: University of Toronto Press.

9 The Message Despite the Media? Conservative Parties' Relationship with the Press

ANDREA LAWLOR

The task of handling the mass media occupies a privileged place on the priority list of political parties. In the case of the Conservative Party of Canada (CPC), privilege, somewhere along the line, has given way to scepticism, peppered with the occasional bout of hostility. Structuring this sometimes-friendly, sometimes-tempestuous relationship are two core questions: How does the CPC view the media, and how do the media view them? As they relate to party politics in general, the roles that media inhabit are many and varied: media are an informational source for the public, a reflection of current events, an investigative force, and occasionally an enthusiastic antagonist. As a result, as far as political parties are concerned, coverage from the media is good when it can be leveraged, but potentially fatal if negative. This chapter explores that relationship from federal conservatives parties' time in opposition (1993–2006) to their days in government (2006–15), addressing three questions that characterize the party–media relationship:[1]

1 Party-side approaches to media: How have federal conservative parties regarded and interacted with media?
2 Media-side approaches to the party: How have the parties been viewed *by* the media and *in* the media?

---

1 The terms *media* and *press* are used interchangeably throughout this chapter and serve as umbrella terms that incorporate both news journalists and editors (unless otherwise specified). This borrows from Donsbach and Patterson (2004), who use the term *journalist* to include those who are involved in editorial decision-making, story selection, presentation, and actual reporting.

3 Media type and influence: How has the party used traditional and new media to build a stronger relationship with voters?

The Evolution of Mass Media in Tory Politics

"Modern politics is media politics," according to political scientist and former Conservative strategist Tom Flanagan (1995, 98). In the twenty-four-hour media market, and the era of the perpetual campaign where image counts for (almost) everything, parties can scarcely afford to be on poor terms with the press. Somewhat paradoxically, however, media, with their trademarked "bad news sells" approach, tend to muddy images of politicians, backroom strategists, and even the party faithful, often rendering them *persona non grata* to parties. Thus, savvy media strategists in the vein of Warren Kinsella, Dimitri Soudas, and James Carville, who can broker relationships between parties and the Fourth Estate, have become the new power-players in the modern era of mediated politics.

The Conservatives have, in some ways, embraced this reality better than other parties. In a culture where media trivialize elections by focusing on the leaders and horserace, rather than substantive policy issues, and where advertising takes on an increasingly negative tone, the modern Conservatives have come out the clear winner in creating a cohesive image with little dissent. But the party's discipline on the subject of media is well rooted in its historical tradition.

From Confederation, federal conservative parties have forged strong relationships with media. During the early days of political media (1867–1930), election campaigns were the primary source of media's interest. Local media reported on local events, therefore platform speeches and stumping were essential, as candidates like John A. Macdonald had to rely on whistle-stop tours and local town halls organized by local party members to get their message out. Politicians lacked the media machines and advertising budget of modern parties, thus candidates were forced to forge positive relationships with (often) highly partisan papers.

The advent of radio in the 1920s represented a tremendous change in the scope and variety of political communications. It increased the power of journalists to demand information from politicians and to reveal more information about parties and politics (Sears 2006). The next two decades were dominated by radio, both through the use of political advertisements and through political radio shows. Alberta Premier

William "Bible Bill" Aberhart, famous for his religious fervour and fiscally conservative nature, "thundered his blending of biblical fundamentalism and Social Credit monetary theories" on his *National Bible Hour*, a program, later taken over by Ernest Manning, father to future Reform leader Preston Manning (Mackey 2005, 84).

Conservative Prime Minister R.B. Bennett notably used radio to address the nation, bypassing the print media, whom he saw as often hostile (Carty, Young, and Cross 2000). Bennett reportedly had a strong mistrust of the media, viewing them as inherently biased against him so much so that in an attempt to avoid being maligned in the press, the Tories established the Standard News Service to produce and distribute news stories favourable to Conservatives to over a hundred local newspapers (Plamondon 2009). From 1929 into the early 1930s, regional newspapers across Canada received news stories free of charge from the Standard News and, in turn, the party received "the kind of political advertising that the party could not have bought" for the money they invested in the service (Levine 1996, 158). This enabled Conservatives to control their own messaging, something that would later become a dominant theme in their media strategy.

It was, however, the advent of television that truly exposed partisan politics to a broader audience, and consequently a larger focus upon candidate and leader image. Diefenbaker's 1957 and 1958 federal campaigns were the first to incorporate formal televised media into their voter outreach strategies. Adopting a friendly attitude towards televised media became an advantage for parties, not only because of the visual nature of the medium, but also because, as of the 1970s, the Canadian Radio-television and Telecommunications Commission (CRTC) required that broadcasters allocate air time to ads for registered political parties during campaigns (Brooks 2007). As a result of this transition to a televised media strategy, parties were able to tailor or "narrowcast" their message to specific socio-demographic groups of voters (Cross 2004).

Since the 1970s, Canadian conservative parties have developed strong party and extra-parliamentary media response units that include press secretaries for the prime minister, directors of communications in the PMO and PCO, as well as a host of media strategists in the party office to handle the twenty-four-hour news media cycle. This has placed politicians in the dubious position of having access to the media at any time, and, reciprocally, the media having access to them. While parties have adopted the essential role of media management as a part of their structure, preparation has not always prevented poor performance. Conservative leaders have had their moments of limelight and their gaffes. The press regarded Prime Minister Brian Mulroney as charming and savvy, but that did not prevent them from playing up negative qualities, portraying him as the ambitious, manipulative salesman (Levine 1996). Perhaps no leader was more maligned by the media than short-term prime minister Kim Campbell, who was alternately perceived as too "soft" or too aggressive in the way she addressed press questioning (Sheckels 2012). Consequently, Conservatives have had to be wary of media, but have nevertheless found ways to leverage their capacity to spread the Conservatives' message.

Conservatives and the Mass Media: Allies or Adversaries? In Opposition, 1993–2006

After a heated 1993 federal election, the Progressive Conservative Party found itself a fractured, if not broken version of its former self. Holding only 2 of the 156 seats the party held at dissolution, the PCs were largely ignored by media (Carty, Young, and Cross 2000). The PCs' use (or abuse) of attack ads levelled against opponent Jean Chrétien during the campaign had decimated their popularity, playing poorly with the Conservative base and undecided voters (Segal 2011). Internally, the party had suffered a great blow, losing a segment of its more right-of-centre wing to the newly formed Reform Party and its charismatic leader Preston Manning, also losing another regionally oriented segment of voters to the Bloc Québécois.

Both the PCs, under new leader Jean Charest, and the Reformers, led by Manning, reached out to voters to build popularity. The Reform Party, with its commitment to populist outreach, took a tele-democratic approach to connecting with voters, using a series of e-town halls to spread their message, particularly outside of their Alberta base (Barney 1996). Although coverage of Manning was generally positive, it was heavily controlled. Like Bennett before him (and Harper after him), Manning liked to be in control of the media message, meticulously crafting his own speeches, sometimes to the chagrin of the party's communications strategists (Flanagan 1995).

After their electoral success in 1993, the party's media strategists had more to contend with than just speech-writing. Fielding a slate of largely inexperienced candidates had generated a lot of negative publicity, some due to controversial stances of candidates and party members.

Gordon LeGrand, elected to the executive of Leeds-Grenville riding association, had publicly demonstrated against bilingualism, stepping on the Quebec flag in 1989. Media also dug up stories of party members' associations with the neo-Nazi Heritage Front, prompting the party to be on guard against media exposure of elements of the membership with controversial views or pasts (Flanagan 1995).

Yet Manning maintained a positive public image in the early days. A skilled rhetorician, Manning appeared to naturally attract press. If anything, it was his tendency towards lengthy, sometimes esoteric responses that created friction with the media's desire for short, pithy one-liners. His academic nature inevitably created a disconnect with the grassroots membership, which press was happy to report (Carty, Young, and Cross 2000). Some of his main challenges with the press came through constitutional issues, including the 1992 Charlottetown Accord and the 1995 Quebec referendum on secession. Even with their platform that proposed substantial constitutional revision, the Reform was critiqued for not having a concise, easy-to-print vision of their party goals.

By the 1997 federal election campaign, the PCs appeared to have rebounded from their dismal 1993 performance. Leader Jean Charest had improved party popularity, polling at approximately 60 per cent for both competence and trustworthiness in Quebec (CROP 1997), and above 40 per cent in the rest of Canada (Environics 1997). Alongside Charest and the Progressive Conservatives, the Reform also benefited from the intense media coverage of the 1997 federal election campaign. While the PCs were successful as the result of Charest's debate performance, the Reform picked up speed because of their use of negative ads to woo support away from their opponents (Nevitte et al. 2000). The media's response to the Reform's performance was somewhat tepid (Winsor 1997).

Despite the positive electoral performance, perceptions of the Reform's more "extreme" positions hindered party growth outside of the West. Manning was viewed as "arrogant" by voters and did not figure well in rankings of leadership acumen (Nevitte et al. 2000). The press were no longer particularly friendly to Manning either. Reports from the *Globe and Mail* highlighted Manning's fractious relationship with the press, as the party leader accused the media of being on a "witch hunt" for racism in the party (*Globe and Mail* 1997), and often reporting on fissures within the party.

By 2000, the Reform, realizing its inability to break out of its Western base, transformed into the Canadian Alliance. Manning bid for the leadership but ultimately lost to media darling Stockwell Day. When he was elected to the House in July 2000, the media appeared alternately enraptured by and antagonistic to Day's flashy persona, pouncing on events such as his Jet Ski arrival at a press conference on Lake Okanagan (Greenspon 2001).

But media popularity was short-lived for Day. He struggled to make a strong enough impression in the 2000 campaign. His overall performance was diminished by the media's focus on two aspects of his campaign: the fear that Day would implement two-tier health care, and his strong Christian fundamentalist religious convictions – especially the suggestion that he supported a creationist view of the world. Concerns over Day's religious beliefs were cemented by the airing of the CBC documentary, *The Fundamental Day*, which reported on Day's strong evangelical views, and by a *Maclean's* cover story with Day's picture and the caption: "How Scary?" Both pieces suggested that Day's fundamentalist views would permeate his public policies, which the press felt obligated to highlight in detail (Haskell 2009).

It was not all bad press for the Canadian conservative movement. The political right had some newfound support in the media. Hollinger Media mogul Conrad Black's creation of the *National Post* in 1998 meant that the 2000 election was fought with a national right-of-centre media outlet voicing a pro-right view. Peter White, Black's partner at Hollinger, the *Post*'s parent company, even served as co-chair of the 2000 Alliance election campaign (Dornan and Pyman 2001). The Sun Media newspaper chain also tended to throw support behind the right, even if a portion of it focused on the trivial.[2]

By 2002, Day's struggle with party leadership had become well documented in the media (Boyle 2002; Laghi 2002). Day lost the 2002 Alliance leadership battle to Stephen Harper, a long-time Reform/Alliance party member and organizer. An MP for Calgary West, Harper was generally friendly towards the media and cultivated a reasonably good relationship with the local papers at the outset of his candidacy for leadership (Flanagan 2007). During the leadership race, however, Harper failed to cultivate a strong media presence in the same way as other candidates such as Day, instead focusing on a grassroots campaign (ibid.), an approach he would advocate throughout his leadership.

2 The paper took to featuring pictures of Catherine Clark, daughter of PC leader (and former prime minister) Joe Clark, with a description of her outfits.

While his modest media profile approach may have worked as a leadership candidate, as leader, some early problems created a rather uneasy relationship between Harper and the press (Paraskevas 2002). But it was not just Harper's choices as leader that prompted media criticism; it seemed that the media had simply not taken a liking to him or his method of communicating with his party and the press. CBC commentator and *National Post* columnist Andrew Coyne referred to Harper as "[Preston] Manning with a mean streak" (Coyne 2002). Don Martin (2002) noted Harper's uncollegial review of his former conservative partners, reporting that Harper did little to prevent negative talk about Joe Clark from within the party. The media appeared to be uneasy with Harper's demeanour and motives, though ultimately regarding him as a competent leader.

The feeling, however, appeared to be mutual. Rarely did there seem to be any love lost between Harper and the press. Long-time advisor Tom Flanagan described Harper's relationship with the media as adversarial (Flanagan 2007). Harper perceived that Day and Manning before him were constantly undersold and often berated by what he perceived to be the "left-wing media," reportedly causing him to question on occasion how long to remain in the political game (Sears 2006, 6). Similar to R.B. Bennett, Harper appeared to hold fast to the notion that there was an anti-Conservative bias embedded in the media's coverage of him and his party. Harper became obsessed with the fact that some former reporters (especially those from the CBC) went to work for Liberals (Martin 2010a; Wells 2006), while his supporters in the party view even generally perceived right-of-centre publications such as *Maclean's* "as part of the 'vast left-wing media conspiracy' because it publishes unflattering cover photos of the PM" (Sears 2006).

Harper contested the June 2004 federal election as Conservative leader, having held the post only since March. As the campaign opened, Harper was off to a fair start in the press. On the day of the Conservative Party's campaign launch, columnist Don Martin referred to Harper as "essentially bulletproof" for his policy proposals and slick presentation (Martin 2004). The *National Post* editorial page called Harper's Conservatives "a modern, moderate, mainstream alternative" that stood in sharp contrast to Paul Martin's floundering Liberals, now weathered by the negative press around the Sponsorship Scandal.

However, heading into a campaign against the well-oiled Liberal election machine would not be without contest. The media had no problem finding their own faults with Harper and the Conservative slate of candidates during the campaign. By the second week of the campaign, the *Globe and Mail* reported on the possibility of the Conservatives re-opening the abortion debate (Sallot 2004). A day later, the press report-ed on Harper's record on support for entering the Iraq war. Widely perceived as a defining moment in Canada's foreign policy, Harper had supported sending troops in with the American allies – a decision that did not sit well with many Canadians, including many on the right.

Despite Harper's attempt to moderate some of the more hard-line Conservatives' opinions on socially and fiscally conservative issues such as same-sex marriage, abortion, and the privatization of health care, the media quickly asserted that Harper appeared to have a "hid-den agenda" (Ivison 2004). Consequently, his desire to talk about tax reform was overshadowed by questions of the level of moral conserva-tism that he would bring to the House of Commons as leader. However, it was not only the media's lack of focus on Harper's policy ideas that taxed the future prime minister's patience with the press. In the wake of an unfortunate comment from Conservative campaign headquarters about Paul Martin allegedly supporting child pornography, the press surrounded Harper's tour bus, refusing to budge until he addressed the allegation. This incited such anger in Harper that he reportedly vowed to never let journalists get the better of him again, foreshadow-ing the years of enmity ahead (Martin 2010a).

The 2004 election was ultimately not as fruitful for the Conservatives as they may have hoped, though they did manage to pick up twenty-seven seats from what the Canadian Alliance and Progressive Conservatives previously held, keeping the Liberals to a minority government. In the nineteen months that intervened before the next election, Harper worked to improve his relationship with the media. In 2004, he gave media scrums that would last the better part of an hour, seeking to appear more transparent. A policy wonk by nature, Harper had no trouble speaking at great length about his party's policy prescriptions. But that openness appeared to do him more harm than good as the press later hounded him for not always maintaining that level of availability (Flanagan 2007).

Harper's negative experiences with the media had scarred him, and he sought to have more control over his interactions with the press. After the 2004 election, he had Press Secretary Dimitri Soudas collect questions from reporters in advance of media scrums. Reporters would be acknowledged only if they had submitted their question in advance and if the question was one Harper wanted to answer (Wells 2006). Media outlets were initially uncertain about agreeing; however, most found that, if one media outlet complied, all had to follow suit or lose a potential scoop to the competition.

Despite a heavy hand with the press, Harper's and the Conservatives' currency was up by the 2006 federal election campaign. Prime Minister Paul Martin was perceived as too closely tied to the corruption around the Sponsorship Scandal, and the government fell to a motion of non-confidence in late November 2005. Harper made immediate use of his improving (if still tenuous) relationship with the media, announcing a policy per day, including the popular, if controversial, cut to the GST and the parent-directed "dollars for daycare" plan for parents with young children. Again Harper found himself defending his party against criticisms of unfettered social conservatism, with abortion, same-sex marriage, and the private delivery of health care on the agenda at points in the campaign. Senior campaign staff including Campaign Director Doug Finley and Director of Operations Jenni Byrne were assigned to keep controversial candidates out of the limelight, preventing missteps that would scare off undecided voters (Flanagan 2007).

There was a clear desire for change from the past decade of Liberal rule, but still some apprehension over who would lead Canadians out of it successfully. According to Strategic Council polling firm chief Allan Gregg, "The population accept[ed] the message, but has some real resistance to the messenger" (Laghi 2005). Nevertheless, by the end of the campaign, the Conservative Party had endorsements from the *Globe and Mail*, *National Post*, the *Economist*, and several local papers. Despite their scepticism, the press perceived Harper to be the most competent leader of the lot.

In Government, 2006–2015

Governing parties have a significant advantage over opposition in attracting media coverage (Hopmann et al. 2012). While the Harper minority government immediately generated interest from the press, the newly installed Prime Minister's Office was not eager to return the favour. Harper wanted greater control over the media's access to the government, both himself and his ministers. In the past, Harper often felt that he received poor treatment from the press when he answered questions, so he effectively just stopped doing it (Martin 2010a). Soon after his election in January 2006, it was widely observed that the prime minister had avoided both print and televised media since taking office. The practice of instituting a list of questions he would answer, which appeared to work during his time as opposition leader, became permanent.

The Harper PMO instituted other practices that challenged the previously unfettered access of the press. Implementing an unofficial media protocol that sought to better control the media's access to the PM, reporters were banned from scrumming in the hallway outside the Cabinet meeting room (Wells 2006; also see chapter 12 in this volume). Harper refrained from making announcements or taking questions in the National Press Theatre, which had been built specifically for simultaneous French-English translation for the press, instead insisting on a PMO-moderated question-and-answer session (O'Malley 2006; Wells 2013).

Announcements on pieces of legislation, including the controversial Federal Accountability Act (2006), were held in the halls of the House of Commons with no notice and few questions taken from the press. Media scrums became the purview of press officers within the PMO, who would take the names of reporters who wanted to ask questions, and call on them if and when it suited the prime minister. This approach engendered a level of hostility in the media that finally boiled over at a Parliament Hill news conference announcing the Conservative government's decision to send $40 million in humanitarian and military assistance to the Darfur region of the Sudan. Press gallery members refused to submit their names to press officer Dimitri Soudas, instead lining up at the microphones to ask questions. When Soudas insisted that the prime minister would not take questions that were not on the list, many reporters left the conference, saying "they could as easily hear Mr Harper read his Darfur statement on TV monitors" (Sallot 2006).

Not to be belittled by the national media's rejection of the Conservative approach to communications management, the PMO reached out to local media and sympathetic right-wing bloggers, and used the party website to release speeches and quotes. In some ways, Harper's communications strategy appeared to be geared more towards the average citizen than that of some of his predecessors. Harper became somewhat Janus-faced with the media, appearing friendly with local reporters days after getting into a verbal row with a CBC reporter (Ibbitson 2006). In the PMO, Harper was reported to pay close attention to local or regional televised news programs, believing that his base and his prospective supporters were likely not subscribing to the mainstream national papers, but small, locally focused news outlets (Martin 2010a).

Harper had selectively included the press in his messaging strategy; consequently, the press has not reacted monolithically to Stephen Harper. While some found themselves in favour with the Conservative PMO, many journalists, particularly those who covered Parliament Hill, bore the brunt of his ire towards media. This antagonism reached new heights in 2010, when the Canadian Association of Journalists wrote an open letter excoriating the government for preventing ministers and civil servants from speaking with the press, and for its propagandistic approach to information distribution.

The PMO found new ways for the prime minister to reach out to the public. Harper saw a market for voter support by targeting ethnic media outlets (see chapter 5 in this volume). While immigrants had typically been viewed as the constituency of the Liberal Party, the Conservatives saw the increasingly diverse Canada (especially in areas such as urban Toronto and Vancouver) as able to be wooed over to the party, given their shared family-oriented, socially conservative values (see chapter 5 in this volume). Stations like southern Ontario's OMNI that featured multilingual news programming were watched attentively. To improve his outreach to the many ethnic communities across Canada, Harper appointed Angelo Persichilli, former editor of the *Corriere Canadese*, a widely circulating Italian language Canadian newspaper, as the communications director for the PMO in August 2011. Persichilli may have lasted only a year on the job, but the signal to the media was clear: Harper valued media outreach that targeted "regular people" over the left-wing elite (Hébert 2011).

Harper was not the only Conservative to view an outreach to ethnic media as essential to success. The Conservative Party paid a media monitoring firm more than $460,000 over two years to track media representations of the party. Citizenship and Immigration Minister Jason Kenney paid the same firm almost $750,000 over three years to monitor how minority groups perceived the minister and his department (LaFlamme 2012). This use of public funds for media analysis, coupled with over $1 million spent to finance an ad campaign promoting immigration reforms, engendered more than modest disapproval from Conservative critics (Greenaway 2008).

A young government, particularly one in a minority position, might be expected to have to troubleshoot their way through the first year or two. But the Conservative government took a particularly hard line against any media that refused to report the sanctioned message. The PMO's crackdown on handling access to information requests, and using the

RCMP to forcibly eject members of the press from the 2007 Conservative caucus meeting, were beyond the run-of-the-mill "media management." Policy discussions turned into one-liners, while most messages responding to reporters' questions or even in Question Period appeared poised to shut down any controversy. Observing the change in Ottawa's approach to media prompted *Globe and Mail* columnist Jeffrey Simpson (2007) to write, "Never in Canada have these approaches been carried to such extremes, backed by such overt hostility toward the media," signalling a palpable shift in the relationship between the executive and the media.

The media also faced radio silence from ministers and backbenchers. Policy announcements were communicated directly by the Prime Minister's Office, often substituting the prime minister himself on larger announcements that would have traditionally been made by a minister. More friendly assessments suggested that the PM was trying to give his inexperienced Cabinet time to learn their files (MacDonald 2006). But Harper was familiar with the media's aggressive questioning of ministers after Question Period and Cabinet meetings and "had to find a way to keep them out of the spotlight, safe from the braying journalistic pack" (Martin 2010a, 20–1). The PMO was aware that media control involved complete consistency to prevent perceptions of government flip-flopping or inexperience. If this was true for ministers, it was even more acutely necessary for green backbenchers.

The Conservative government was not only concerned about media gaffes from its own. The bureaucracy was reported to also have felt a clampdown in speaking to the press. News releases from line departments had to get clearance by the PMO. Reports of muzzled federally employed scientists on issues such as the shutdown of the Experimental Lakes Project and Keystone Pipeline garnered bad press from notables such as environmentalist David Suzuki (Koring 2013). Media bans were reported to extend as far as federal librarians and archivists (McClelland 2013). Much of what the Conservative machine appeared to be doing was related to managing any commentary – good or bad – to come out of the government. Where comments were positive, the government wanted to have their announcement timed when people would notice. Their extensive use of embedding government program advertising (e.g., the widespread advertising of the Canada Economic Action Plan) in their media scrums was leveraged both to stay on message and to positively advertise their record. Where comments were negative, the government appeared to want to spin them as the government making a principled decision on an issue. Outbursts over the widely chastised cancellation of the long-form census were rebranded as the government protecting the rights and privacy of citizens in the face of unwanted government incursion. A new era of mediated politics was well underway.

Perhaps that is why the 2015 campaign appeared to be something of an anomaly for the media-savvy Conservatives. Their tried and true approach of negative campaign ads and a tightly monitored media campaign with little emphasis on individual candidates and a leader-centric style model of messaging did not yield the results that the CPC had become used to. Speculation as to why the Conservatives lost swathes of support across the country pointed to the use of attack ads that were viewed both as distasteful and as having set the bar too low for key opponents (viz. Trudeau) (*Globe and Mail* 2015). Furthermore, after ten years of excluding the media from meaningful policy conversations and replacing them with hostile attacks and negative messaging, media were increasingly challenged to find anything of substance to report on. The Conservative model of flashy policy announcements with great visuals but little content was something that Les Whittington of the *Toronto Star* referred to as "government by photo op" – message delivery by flashy images rather than meaningful dialogue (Whittington 2015). While this tactic may have tidily avoided too many candidate gaffes, it eventually had the effect opposite to what was intended – it made the Conservatives appear distant and remote in their governance – a far cry from their early populist roots and contemporary family-driven policy agenda.

The Conservatives and Media Outlets

The relationship between the Conservative government and the press – as tenuous as it has been – has been characterized not only by interactions with individual reporters or editors. The Conservatives have been unique in their pursuit of actually changing the Canadian media landscape as it relates to politics. From their Reform days, the Conservatives have appeared to have little regard for the country's public broadcaster, the CBC. According to Christopher Dornan (2006), conservatives see it as "an $800-million cash grab to propagandize the country with lefty-Liberal cant using taxpayers' own money." At the 1991 Reform convention, delegates voted in favour of privatizing the CBC (Cross 2004), who wasted no time in lobbing a volley in the party's direction, featuring an unflattering skit about Preston Manning on the comedy program *Double Exposure*.

Perhaps it is unsurprising then that one of Manning's original supporters, Harper, would continue to push back against the CBC's hal-
lowed place in the Canadian media landscape. Wells characterizes the
Conservatives as believing that the public broadcaster is little more than
a "grotesque money pit" (2013, 30). During the 2006 election campaign,
an NDP candidate suggested that a Harper government would end
funding to the CBC. Rather than placating concerns, Heritage Minister
Josée Verner simply responded that it was "not part of the platform,"
but made no attempt to refute the possibility for the future (Gagnon
2008). In the same campaign, Harper cut short CBC access to him during
elections, reducing their usual half-hour year-end interview to fifteen
minutes, while maintaining the time allotted to their chief competitor,
CTV (Taber 2007). In the aftermath of the 2006 in-and-out scandal,[3] the
Conservatives accused the CBC of conspiring with the Liberals to un-
earth the story (Martin 2010a).

As a minority government, the Tories were limited in what they
could do to reduce spending on the public broadcaster. But the power
of majority status increased their freedom to more aggressively attack
the CBC's privileged position. Bill C-60, the Conservative 2013 budget, contained a clause buried in the 111-page bill that would allow the
Cabinet to approve CBC salaries, working conditions, and collective
bargaining, removing the arm's length between the government and
the public broadcaster (*Huffington Post Canada* 2013). At the November
2013 Conservative Party convention, party delegates approved a motion to restructure the CBC, including splitting the TV and radio operations, with the goal of eliminating public funding. While the motion
– passed 596–504 – referred to the CBC "an important part of the broadcasting system in Canada," it ultimately called for changes to a system
that gives public broadcasters an entrenched advantage over privately
owned and operated networks (Wingrove 2013).

Yet the Conservatives have not uniformly fought against all media
outlets. Launched in early 2011 by Quebecor Media, the Sun News
Network appeared to be connected with Conservative Party staffers,

---

3 The "In-and-Out Scandal" refers to the 2006 election campaign controversy surrounding the Conservative Party's transfer of funds between the central party office
and local riding associations. The alleged intent of the practice was to circumvent
Elections Canada's mandated campaign spending limits in the purchase of advertising. Charges against the Conservative Party of Canada pursued by the RCMP were
eventually dropped in 2012.

if not the party itself. Former PMO director of communications Kory Teneycke became Sun TV's VP of development, advocating for a "Fox News North," conservative-styled, twenty-four-hour news network that would provide an opposing opinion to the CBC and a less-moderate right-of-centre view than CTV. While Teneycke ultimately resigned to assuage claims of influence peddling, he was later replaced by another Conservative operative, former Mulroney spokesman Luc Lavoie (Cheadle 2010).

Sun TV's launch was fraught with challenges with or without the Conservatives' help. Originally applying to the CRTC or a Category 1 licence, which would make carriage of the network mandatory for cable and satellite providers in Canada, the network later changed its application and aimed for a Category 2 licence instead, which would mean that Quebecor would have to negotiate carriage with individual cable distributors. Rumours circulated that the Harper government attempted to coerce CRTC Chair Konrad von Finckenstein and remove Vice-Chair Michel Arpin in order to secure Sun TV's spot on mandatory carriage (Martin 2010b), though nothing came of it.

Sun TV's relationship with the Conservatives did not extend only to administrative matters. Sun featured coverage of an October 2011 citizenship ceremony that was, in fact, only a recreation of an actual oath-swearing ceremony. The press might not have reviewed this so harshly if the Canadian Press's Jennifer Ditchburn had not uncovered evidence through access-to-information requests that Citizenship and Immigration Minister Jason Kenney's staff had directed departmental officials to add a citizenship ceremony at Sun TV to their list of scheduled events for Citizenship Week (Ditchburn 2012a). More problematic, the photo-op featured six CIC employees, brought in at the last minute to fill in for new citizens who were unable to attend. The result was the appearance that Sun TV called the shots, and the federal government would comply if reports would appear favourable (Walkom 2012). With the closure of Sun TV in early 2015, it remains to be seen if the party will try to cultivate a new exclusive relationship with another broadcast network, though it seems unlikely given the already small broadcast sector in Canada.

Finally, where news coverage lacked, the Conservatives created their own. The party purchased a television studio outside Ottawa dedicated solely to preparing party-approved news clips for regional broadcasters (who often lack the funds to produce the breadth of coverage that would be appreciated by the PMO). The PMO communications team become responsible for scripting and filming news-style clips posted to a publicly funded website called "24 Seven," which documented Harper's attendance at staged events, offered interviews with him and the occasional minister or a special guest such as Laureen Harper. The goal of 24 Seven was to bypass trouble associated with the "uncontrollable" mainstream televised media and provide stories and images that placed the Harper government in the best possible light. This level of planning and expense was unprecedented in Canadian politics, resulting in some reporters to referring to the Conservatives as a "government obsessed with image" (Simpson 2014).

The Conservatives and Social and Digital Media

The increasing importance of social and other forms of online media to improve public outreach, especially during campaigns, has meant that all parties have had to adopt new strategies in releasing information and communicating with party supporters. Though an essential part of every modern party's platform or outreach strategy, digital media have been used primarily for "outward communications, not real democratic exchange," affording parties the opportunity "to talk the talk of democratic participation and openness online without necessarily having to walk the walk" (Barney 2007, 379).

Conservatives were somewhat late to the digital media game, with one of their first major forays into digital media outside of the standard party website occurring in 2004 in the form of a response to the Liberal attack website, StephenHarperSaid.ca. By the time the Conservatives were in government, digital media outreach had become a well-defined, professional element of political marketing. Blogging became a central component of digital media for parties by 2006, as did Facebook (Small 2008). What parties were still missing, however, were the resources and infrastructure to manage two-way communication. The prime minister's personal Facebook profile did not feature a wall that would allow supporters to communicate with the party (ibid.). Even during the 2008 campaign, when other parties opened up their Facebook walls and YouTube comment fields to public commentary (moderated by the party), the Conservatives still used social media (Twitter, in particular) exclusively for outreach, not bidirectional communication (Small 2012). By the 2011 campaign, the Conservatives had become far more adept at using social media to connect politicians to voters. Even Prime Minister Stephen Harper became active on Twitter and Google+, using the sites to indulge in a rapidly growing pastime for social media users, posting, among other items, photos of his kitten playing with a shoe-lace (Smith 2011).

Public outreach was not the only reason parties sought out social and online media opportunities. All mainstream parties have embraced on-line media as a way to attack their opponents. During the 2008 cam-paign, the Conservatives were forced to respond to a Facebook group that attempted to prevent the party from obtaining a majority, called the "Anti-Harper Vote Swap Canada." Using the popular social media application, the site encouraged voters in electorally close ridings to vote for the party most likely to win against Conservative candidates. Though controversial, the strategy was deemed legal by Elections Canada. But the Conservatives were not a party that would let such a strategy pass; Facebook groups quickly sprouted, including the "Anti-Anti-Harper Vote Swap" and "Voters against Vote Swapping," to coun-ter the movement (Small 2012).

Despite a slow start, the Conservatives themselves quickly carved out a niche in using social and digital media to attack their opponents. One of the most controversial ads the Conservatives ran was a part of their "Not a Leader" website that targeted Liberal leader Stéphane Dion in the 2008 campaign. Other negative online ads included "The Dion Tax Trick" website and radio ads that targeted Dion's carbon tax policy (Small 2012). During the 2011 election, the Conservatives renewed their attack-the-leader strategy with the "Just Visiting" attack ads, followed by "Ignatieff Me!," an anti–Michael Ignatieff Facebook group that ran during the leader's tenure.

If there is one area of social and digital media that the Conservatives have truly embraced, it is the social media or micro-blogging platform, Twitter. Several Conservative ministers (notably former Treasury Board President Tony Clement), as well as the prime minister (or their offic-es, at least) have used Twitter to send out political, and, on occasion, personal information blasts to party members and potential support-ers. Conservative staffers also joined the social media fray in support of the party's objectives with senior aides such as former director of communications Dimitri Soudas, former chief of staff Guy Giorno, and Director of Communications Jenni Byrne, maintaining active Twitter accounts that advertised Conservative policy positions, events, and achievements (Mayeda 2011).

Not all Conservatives have used Twitter as successfully. Days be-fore the 2011 election, Andrew Prescott, deputy campaign manager to Guelph Conservative candidate Marty Burke, sent out a message on

Twitter warning of "voter suppression calls," which later were sus-pected of being associated with alleged (and anonymous) robocaller "Pierre Poutine" (McGregor 2012). Another Conservative, Senator Patrick Brazeau, reacted negatively to a story by Jennifer Ditchburn, of the Canadian Press, on his absences between June 2011 and April 2012, with an uncomplimentary Tweet referencing her last name (Ditchburn 2012b). Brazeau later deleted his Twitter account.

Social media may prove to be the most quickly growing mode of par-ty communication. The introduction of the aforementioned 24 Seven YouTube channel featuring weekly promotional videos about Harper was an example of the Conservatives going on the media offensive and providing content, even if it attracted only a small viewership. The im-mediate nature of the communication and its interactivity broke down formerly (almost) impenetrable walls between parties, the press, and the public – particularly the party brass who provided the party with its core financial support. As much as social media may be targeted as a way to engender new support, it may be that their greatest strength is reinforcing communication with the party membership.

Social media have undoubtedly become a much larger part of par-ties' strategies for voter outreach and mobilization, yet it would be an overstatement to suggest that social media are solely responsible for electoral outcomes. Since 2011, parties have dedicated considerable resources to carefully populating and monitoring their social media profiles, but that is not to suggest that two-way communication with the broader electorate has become the norm. As suggested by Harold Jansen in a 2015 interview with CBC, monitoring social media (viz. Twitter) in the context of a campaign has become a preoccupation for journalists that may not be shared by the wider voting public (Basen 2015). Rather, social media coverage of the campaign, though constant and thorough, appeared to operate in a closed loop of the politically knowledgeable and attentive. This suggests that social media will re-main central to parties' communication strategies, but the motivation for this centrality may be driven as much by a desire to present a differ-ent form of mediated communications (i.e., communicating messages to journalists through Twitter) as it is a form of public outreach.

Conclusion

In 2007, Stephen Brooks noted, "Today, no party ... would think of going into an election campaign without a well-developed media strategy" (355). Any successful media strategy, of course, would include print, television, radio, digital, and social media. The Conservative Party has had its share of run-ins with the media. Though many of those may have been of their own making, media strategy is as important now as it has ever been. Given the run of negative press from several mainstream media sources – print, television, and digital – cultivating a positive relationship with the Fourth Estate ought to be on the Conservative Party's priority list. Indeed, neither the Conservatives nor any other party can afford to make an enemy of the media. It is possible, of course, to circumvent the print and televised media to a certain degree using digital media, blogging platforms, and social media. But where there is a public and commercial press that remains the primary source of news information, parties of all stripes will be forced to play ball.

The media model used by the Conservatives from 2004 onward is being challenged both in form and in content. Party communications are increasingly akin to corporate media strategies that brand parties as if they were products to be sold to the electorate (Marland 2016). In this regard, parties are less reliant on the "free press" of the mass media, at least in part because party communications budgets are increasing. The 2015 election also shook up the content of party communications as mediated through the press: the Conservatives' Liberal challengers openly rejected the style of negative campaigning that had become prominent in Conservative media strategy and Canadian politics more broadly (see Rose 2012). While the strength and longevity of the Liberals' trend towards "sunny ways" may evoke scepticism from hardened political analysts, it is as clear that a negative media strategy can, at least sometimes, be supplanted by more positive discourse.

The Conservatives are challenged to move forward on their media strategy, particularly as they move back into the role of Official Opposition. The challenge will be twofold: first, the media themselves are changing. As Robin Sears (2006) points out, the growth in media has been in non-traditional and non-political news. This style of news does tend to call for a government that can present a coherent, attention-grabbing message, while still engaging with the public on their own terms. The Conservative Party leader that follows Stephen Harper will have to carefully consider what balance to strike between centralized media strategy and letting the members of government connect with their constituents. The second challenge for the Conservative Party is how they will define and deliver a multimedia presence and a multi-strategy approach to getting their message out, not only to partisans but to the ever-present politically undecided. Arguably, it was this group that were responsible for the Liberal majority government elected into office in October 2015. The Conservatives may have successfully mobilized their base, but as core partisans shrink and the politically undecided grow in numbers, the Conservative strategy will have to be as varied as the voters it is trying to attract.

REFERENCES

Barney, Darin. 1996. "Pushbutton Populism: The Reform Party and the Real World of Teledemocracy." *Canadian Journal of Communication* 21 (3).
– 2007. "The Internet and Political Communication in Canadian Party Politics: The View from 2004." In *Canadian Parties in Transition*, edited by Alain G. Gagnon and A. Brian Tanguay, 371–82. Peterborough, ON: Broadview.
Basen, Ira. 2015. "Social Media's Significance Oversold amid Election Hype." CBC News, 16 October.
Boyle, Theresa. 2002. "Alliance Rivals Blast Day 'Threat.'" *Toronto Star*, 1 March.
Brooks, Stephen. 2007. "Television Advertising by Political Parties: Can Democracy Survive It?" In *Canadian Parties in Transition*, edited by Alain G. Gagnon and A. Brian Tanguay, 355–70. Peterborough, ON: Broadview.
Carty, R. Kenneth, Lisa Young, and William P. Cross. 2000. *Rebuilding Canadian Party Politics*. Vancouver: UBC Press.
Cheadle, Bruce. 2010. "Former Harper Spokesman Quits Sun TV amid Controversy." Canadian Press, 15 September.
Coyne, Andrew. 2002. "Manning with a Mean Streak: The New Alliance Leader Shares Traits with Former Mentor." *National Post*, 21 March.
CROP. 1997. "Political Survey 1997–06." Montreal: CROP.
Cross, William P. 2004. *Political Parties*. Vancouver: University of British Columbia Press.
Ditchburn, Jennifer. 2012a. "Federal Bureaucrats Posed as 'New Canadians' on Sun News Citizenship Ceremony." *Toronto Star*, 2 February.
– 2012b. "Youngest Senator Has Worst Attendance Starts Twitter War with Reporter." *Canadian Press*, 26 June.
Donsbach, Wolfgang, and Thomas E. Patterson. 2004. "Political News Journalists." In *Partisanship, Professionalism, and Political Roles in Five Countries*, edited by Frank Esser and Barbara Pfetsch, 251–70. Cambridge: Cambridge University Press.
Dornan, Christopher. 2006. "Harper's Been Mum on the CBC, but His No-Show Drops a Loud Hint." *Globe and Mail*, 14 January.

Dornan, Christopher, and Heather Pyman. 2001. "Newspaper Coverage of the Campaign." In *The Canadian General Election of 2000*, edited by Jon H. Pammett and Christopher Dornan, 191–214. Toronto: Dundurn.

Environics. 1997. "Focus Canada 1997–01." Toronto: Environics.

Flanagan, Tom. 1995. *Waiting for the Wave*. Toronto: Stoddart Publishing.

– 2007. *Harper's Team: Behind the Scenes in the Conservative Rise to Power*. Montreal and Kingston: McGill-Queen's University Press.

Gagnon, Lysiane. 2008. "Insensitivity Sinks Tories in Québec." *Globe and Mail*, 13 October.

Globe and Mail. 1997. "Reform Leader Assails Reporters for 'Witch Hunt': Media's 'Fixation' on Alleged Racism among Party Candidates Detracts from Important Issues, Manning Charges." 4 April.

– 2015. "It Wasn't Just Harper: Why the Conservatives Lost, and How They Can Win Again." 23 October.

Greenaway, Norma. 2008. "Tory Ethnic Media Ads in Contempt, MPs Say; Immigration Reforms Focus of Campaign, but Not Yet Law." *Ottawa Citizen*, 16 May.

Greenspon, Edward. 2001. "Covering Campaign 2000." In *The Canadian General Election of 2000*, edited by Jon H. Pammett and Christopher Dornan, 165–90. Toronto: Dundurn.

Haskell, David M. 2009. *Through a Lens Darkly: How the News Media Perceive and Portray Evangelicals*. Toronto: Clements Publishing Group.

Hébert, Chantal. 2011. "New Harper Communications Aide Will Only Widen Chasm with Québec." *Guelph Mercury*, 3 September.

Hopmann, David N., Christian Elmelund-Praestekaer, Erik Albaek, Rens Vliegenthart, and Claes H. de Vreese. 2012. "Party Media Agenda-Setting: How Parties Influence Election News Coverage." *Party Politics* 18 (2): 173–91. http://dx.doi.org/10.1177/1354068810380097.

Huffington Post Canada. 2013. "Bill C-60: Tories Quietly Taking Control of CBC, Group Alleges." 4 April.

Ibbitson, John. 2006. "The Prime Minister and the Press: Who'll Blink First?" *Globe and Mail*, 13 April.

Ivison, John. 2004. "Harper Hasn't Bested the Fear Factor." *National Post*, 2 June.

Koring, Paul. 2013. "David Suzuki Slams Harper Science Policy in Washington Speech." *Globe and Mail*, 11 October.

LaFlamme, Lisa. 2012. "Harper." CTV News-PM. 14 November.

Laghi, Brian. 2002. "Rivals Accuse Day of Threatening Caucus; Former Leader's Hint That Dissenters Could Face Punishment Suggests 'Purge,' Hill Says." *Globe and Mail*, 1 March.

Laghi, Brian. 2005. "Harper's Negative Image Hurts Positive Message." *Globe and Mail*, 2 December.

Levine, Allan. 1996. *Scrum Wars: The Prime Ministers and the Media*. Toronto: Dundurn.

MacDonald, L. Ian. 2006. "Gag Rule Gives Ministers Time to Learn the Ropes: The Press Doesn't Like It, but Harper Wants the Government to Focus on Five Priorities." *Montreal Gazette*, 20 March.

Mackey, Lloyd. 2005. *The Pilgrimage of Stephen Harper*. Toronto: ECW.

Marland, Alex. 2016. *Brand Command: Canadian Politics and Democracy in the Age of Message Control*. Vancouver: UBC Press.

Martin, Don. 2002. "Harper Opponents: Be Afraid." *Calgary Herald*, 21 January.

– 2004. "Harper Has a Flawless Launch." *National Post*, 24 May.

Martin, Lawrence. 2010a. *Harperland: The Politics of Control*. Toronto: Penguin.

– 2010b. "Is Stephen Harper Set to Move against the CRTC?" *Globe and Mail*, 19 August.

Mayeda, Andrew. 2011. "Tories Warming Up Their Twitter Fingers." *Winnipeg Free Press*, 27 March.

McClelland, Bob. 2013. "No Need for Muzzle on Librarians." *Postmedia Breaking News*, 19 March.

McGregor, Glen. 2012. "Guelph Tory Warned of Robocalls before Vote; Tweets Started after 'Burner Phone' Activation." *Ottawa Citizen*, 9 March.

Nevitte, Neil, André Blais, Elisabeth Gidengil, and Richard Nadeau. 2000. *Unsteady State: The 1997 Canadian Federal Election*. Toronto: Oxford University Press.

O'Malley, Kady. 2006. "Harper and the Media: Former Grit PMO Communications Specialists Offer Some Free Advice." *Hill Times*, 6 February.

Paraskevas, Joe. 2002. "Harper Defends Personnel Moves." *Calgary Herald*, 15 January.

Plamondon, Bob. 2009. *Blue Thunder: The Truth about Conservatives from Macdonald to Harper*. Toronto: Key Porter Books.

Rose, Jonathan. 2012. "Are Negative Ads Positive? Political Advertising and the Permanent Campaign." In *How Canadians Communicate*. Vol. 4, *Media and Politics*, edited by David Taras and Christopher Waddell, 149–68. Athabasca: Athabasca University Press.

Sallot, Jeff. 2004. "Abortion Creeps back on to Political Agenda." *Globe and Mail*, 2 June.

– 2006. "PM Presses On in His Feud with the News Media." *Globe and Mail*, 26 May.

Sears, Robin V. 2006. "Harper vs the Press Gallery: The Frog and the Scorpion." *Policy Options* (July). http://policyoptions.irpp.org/fr/

magazines/border-security/harper-vs-the-press-gallery-the-frog-and-the-scorpion/.

Segal, Hugh. 2011. *The Right Balance*. Toronto: Douglas & McIntyre.

Sheckels, Theodore F. 2012. *Political Communication in the Anglophone World: Case Studies*. Lanham, MD: Lexington Books.

Simpson, Jeffrey. 2007. "PM's Personality + Tory Heritage = Hatred of Media." *Globe and Mail*, 30 October.

– 2014. "A Government Obsessed with Image – 24 Seven." *Globe and Mail*, 9 July.

Small, Tamara. 2008. "The Facebook Effect? Online Campaigning in the 2008 Canadian and US Elections." *Policy Options* (November): 85–7.

– 2012. "E-ttack Politics: Negativity, the Internet & Canadian Political Parties." In *How Canadians Communicate*. Vol. 4, *Media and Politics*, edited by David Taras and Christopher Waddell, 169–88. Athabasca: Athabasca University Press.

Smith, Joanna. 2011. "Social Message: Watch My Kitten Play; Photos of Stanley Prominent on Harper's New Google+ Account." *Toronto Star*, 28 July.

Taber, Jane. 2007. "Stéphane Dion Gives Us Something to Chew On." *Globe and Mail*, 22 December.

Walkom, Thomas. 2012. "Citizenship Ruse Says a Lot about Harper." *Toronto Star*, 8 February.

Wells, Paul. 2006. *Right Side Up*. Toronto: Douglas Gibson Books.

– 2013. *The Longer I'm Prime Minister: Stephen Harper and Canada, 2006–*. Toronto: Random House Canada.

Whittington, Les. 2015. "'Government by Photo Op': How Stephen Harper Froze Out Ottawa's Press Corps." *Toronto Star*, 21 June.

Wingrove, Josh. 2013. "Fifteen Tory Motions to Know About from the Convention." *Globe and Mail*, 3 November.

Winsor, Hugh. 1997. "Election '97 Price Exacted from Liberals for Early Vote." *Globe and Mail*, 3 June.

10 Conservative with the Constitution? Moderation, Strategy, and Institutional Distrust

EMMETT MACFARLANE

The post-1993 period has been described as one where a "constitutional exhaustion" quickly gave way to "constitutional normalcy" (Russell 2004, 228). The difficulties associated with achieving major formal constitutional reform were made apparent by the failure of the Meech Lake and Charlottetown Accords. Canadian constitutional politics since then has, for the most part, been approached on an informal basis. As a result of this contemporary context, much of the focus of governments vis-à-vis the Constitution has been on adjusting and reacting to the requirements of the Charter of Rights and Freedoms and to the corresponding expansion of the power of courts, particularly the Supreme Court, in constraining and shaping public policy through judicial review.

This chapter examines Canada's federal conservative parties and the Constitution, from 1993 to 2015. Specifically, it focuses on how the Reform/Canadian Alliance, Progressive Conservatives (PCs), and the Conservative Party of Canada (Conservative Party) have dealt with constitutional change, the courts, and the Charter of Rights. It is motivated by two questions:

1 Constitutional change: How have the parties approached constitutional change? What are the different approaches adopted by the PCs and the Reform/Alliance? How has the Conservative Party reconciled these approaches in government?

2 The courts and the Charter of Rights: How have the parties approached specific rights issues like abortion and the equality rights of gays and lesbians, the role of courts, judges, and interest groups

in Charter litigation, and the judicial appointments process? How have differences manifested from opposition to government?[1]

The PCs and Reform/Alliance had different perspectives on many of these issues. Reform's western roots meant strong advocacy for the principle of provincial equality, which cultivated its support for Senate reform (see chapter 11 in this volume) as well as a hard-line stance on Quebec's competing constitutional demands (see chapter 7 in this volume). A strong social conservative base in the Reform/Alliance also often meant a critical view of progressive social change resulting from judicial review of the Charter. By contrast, the PCs took an accommodative stance on national unity and often articulated a more progressive policy outlook and supportive view of the Charter project. These diverging attitudes meant that the united Conservative Party, which emerged in 2003, had to approach the Constitution in a moderate, strategic manner – with mixed results – in order to accommodate its dual bases and ensure electoral success.

Constitutional Change

The prevailing post-1993 context had significant implications for how the federal conservative parties approached constitutional change and national unity, and continued to guide the approach taken by the Conservative government from 2006 to 2015. The 1982 Constitution Act, which included the Charter of Rights and Freedoms, recognition of Indigenous and treaty rights, and a domestic amending formula, did not signal an end to the years of "mega constitutional" politics – a series of intergovernmental negotiations on major constitutional reform – that preceded it (Russell 2004). Mega constitutional politics began in earnest in the late 1960s, and the 1982 package that ultimately passed muster bore a deal that was eventually supported by all provinces except Quebec. The belief that Quebec's lack of consent needed to be rectified – that Quebec needed to be "brought back in" to the Constitution – sparked additional attempts at major constitutional reform under the PC government of Brian Mulroney in the late 1980s and early

---

1   As this volume includes chapters of federalism (see chapter 3) and Indigenous Peoples (see chapter 10), I have decided not to include in-depth discussion of the constitutional division of powers or Indigenous and treaty rights.

1990s. These efforts culminated in the Meech Lake and Charlottetown Accords, both of which included, among other items, Senate reform, changes to the Supreme Court appointments process, and a clause that would recognize Quebec as holding distinct constitutional status. Both accords failed, a fact portrayed by Quebec sovereigntists as a rejection of Quebec by the rest of Canada, and support for separation spiked (Young 1999). The subsequent election of a Parti Québécois government and the referendum campaign that quickly followed resulted in a near-victory for separatists in 1995, with 49.4 per cent voting in favour. This aftermath, coupled with the high level of consensus required for major constitutional amendment, has greatly dampened any desire for significant formal constitutional change among most Canadian political elites, something that, as explored below, is particularly evident in the approach of the Conservative government.

In Opposition, 1993–2006

After the failure of the Charlottetown Accord, appetite for major constitutional reform among Canada's political class had almost completely evaporated. Perhaps the one notable exception came in the form of Reform Party support for Senate reform by advocating for a "Triple E" (equal, elected, effective) Senate. Though the idea of a reformed upper chamber that would see senators elected on the basis of an equal provincial distribution emanated from the Canada West Foundation, print media in Alberta, and the provincial legislature during 1980s, according to David Smith, "It was Preston Manning, Reform's founder, who conferred upon Triple E an institutional legitimacy enjoyed by no earlier proposal for upper chamber redesign" (2003, 57). Senate reform remained a major feature of the Reform Party's (and later the Canadian Alliance's) platforms through the 1990s and 2000s. However, with no other major political parties interested (the NDP preferred abolition), little progress on the issue was made, given the party's opposition status. One central difficulty, discussed in more detail below, pertains to the constitutional amending formula: any change to the distribution of seats in the Senate, its powers, or the method of senatorial selection requires the agreement of the federal Parliament and at least two-thirds (seven) of the provinces representing at least 50 per cent of the population. Even informal changes have proven difficult. Attempts to hold advisory senatorial elections in Alberta "fizzled" in the late 1990s when only the Reform Party ran a candidate (ibid.).

The federal conservative opposition parties also adopted different normative positions on what constitutional proposals ought to be advanced in the face of the Quebec secession referendum campaign. In Jean Charest, who took over as leader of the PCs after the 1993 election left him as one of only two remaining PC MPs in the House of Commons, the PCs had a "young, dynamic Québecer who was credible in defending federalism and had a substantial incentive to improve his fortunes and those of his party by doing so" (Young 1999, 11). As such, he was front and centre in continuing the party's support for the distinct society concept and in promising constitutional renewal during the No campaign in 1995, something the prime minister, Jean Chrétien, promised only when polls suggested the Yes side was winning and "near-panic" had struck (35–6).

By contrast, the Reform Party's approach regarding Quebec and the Constitution stemmed from its origins as a western-based protest party. Though Reform would support changes that would result in decentralization, it favoured equality of the provinces and opposed group rights, official bilingualism, and constitutional recognition of Quebec as a distinct society. In fact, certain elements of the Reform Party, including then-MP Stephen Harper, felt Manning's opposition to the Charlottetown Accord was too "lukewarm" (Flanagan 2007, 15; Wells 2006, 13). The Reform Party also advocated taking a tougher stance than other federalists during the 1995 referendum campaign. Manning argued that the rest of Canada needed to make it clear that ripping up the Constitution was not going to be an easy process and that Quebec had no guarantees of an easy economic relationship with the rest of Canada following a Yes vote.

Manning also pushed Chrétien on issues of clarity surrounding secession, which would later be raised as a constitutional question to the Supreme Court in the aftermath of the razor-thin referendum outcome. In the lead-up to the vote, Manning questioned Chrétien on whether the government was prepared to deal with a negative outcome, asking in the House of Commons, "Will the Prime Minister make clear that a yes vote means Québec is on its way out, that a no vote means Québec is in the federation for the long haul, and the 50 per cent plus one is the dividing line between those two positions?" (Young 1999, 55). In Manning's view, separatists believed they could vote for separation and "still enjoy the benefits of federalism," and he pushed Chrétien to repudiate that fact (ibid.). After the referendum, the federal government implemented a dual-track approach to intergovernmental relations.

Plan A would see the government seek accommodation through decentralizing certain responsibilities (like employment training) and asymmetrical federalism. Plan B, the "tough cop" to Plan A's "good cop," would see the federal government set out rules and conditions for a potential future secession gambit (Russell 2004, 240). Part of Plan B included posing a reference to the Supreme Court on the constitutionality of unilateral secession.

Although the questions posed to the Court in *Reference re Secession of Québec* (1998) focused squarely on the legality of unilateral secession, the Court went much further than many observers expected. In a unanimous opinion, the justices ruled that Quebec did not have the ability to secede unilaterally under constitutional or international law. However, the Court also declared that in the event of a "clear majority" of the Quebec population answering a "clear question" on secession in the affirmative, the rest of Canada has a duty to negotiate. The Court did not provide any content to the duty, and so it left the "political" actors to decide a number of crucial issues: What is a clear majority? Who determines what constitutes a clear question? What role, if any, would Indigenous peoples – particularly those in Quebec – have in any negotiations? The Court's decision also implies that the duty to negotiate does not translate into any particular outcome. In effect, the decision leaves unanswered almost all practical questions surrounding the constitutional process and requirements of secession.

In response, the Liberal government introduced a law that attempts to put into effect the Court's reference opinion. The Clarity Act outlines rules dictating the federal government's approach to a potential secession referendum. It includes provisions that state that the House of Commons will determine whether a referendum question is sufficient to result in a clear expression of the will of Quebeckers; if it does not, the government of Canada will not enter into negotiations in the aftermath of an affirmative vote. While not stating a specific threshold, the Act also leaves it to the House of Commons to determine whether a Yes vote is substantial enough to be considered a clear majority. The Act also specifies that any negotiations must be undertaken in the context of an amendment to the Constitution and must consider issues relating to provincial borders, the rights and interests of Indigenous peoples of Canada, division of assets and liabilities, and the protection of minority rights.

Significantly, the Clarity Act was opposed by the PCs (under the leadership of Joe Clark, who did not yet hold a seat) (Russell 2004). Almost half the PC MPs voted against the Clarity Act, while most Reform MPs voted in favour. By contrast, Stephen Harper is credited by Flanagan as having played an important role in the lead-up to the Clarity Act as a Reform MP (2007). Harper's private member's legislation, introduced in 1996, contains elements that eventually were incorporated into the Clarity Act, including provisions on federal assessment of the clarity of a potential referendum question. However, it took a much more hard-line stance, including provisions for the government of Canada to hold its own parallel referendum question in the event the question posed by Quebec was deemed unclear or included the possibility of unilateral secession. According to William Johnson, "The great weakness of the Clarity Act, unlike Harper's Bill C-341, is that it does not deal with the most likely outcome, that is, a unilateral declaration of independence ... Harper's bill indicated precisely what the federal government would do: domestically, it would enforce all its laws and maintain the Constitution before the courts; internationally, it would advise all other countries that Canada did not recognize the independence of Québec" (2005, 278).

Where the PCs advocated accommodation and distinct society status, Reformers advanced a tough federalist line. For the latter, this approach (in addition to earlier party policies such as opposing official bilingualism) created a distinct impression among Quebeckers that the Reform Party was anti-Quebec (Clarkson 2005). From an electoral perspective, this was not a significant problem for the party in the late 1990s; however, it was an image the future united Conservative Party would take pains to address.

In Government, 2006–2015

In government, the Conservative Party's approach to Senate reform focused on informal changes rather than pushing for anything that would require constitutional amendment. This is not only in contrast to the Triple-E proposal advanced by the Reform/Alliance, but is also a step back from an approach advocated by Harper himself. In 2001, as president of the National Citizens' Coalition, Harper signed an open letter to Alberta Premier Ralph Klein that, among other things, suggested a provincial referendum on Senate reform would force the federal government and other provinces to the negotiating table. According to the letter, an interpretation of the Supreme Court's *Secession* reference "is that the federal government and other provinces must seriously consider a proposal for constitutional reform endorsed by 'a clear majority on a clear question' in a provincial referendum" (Harper et al. 2001). This is an adventurous – but dubious – interpretation of the decision, considering that its focus was specifically on the issue of secession.

The Conservative Party's 2006 platform simply promised to create "a national process for choosing elected Senators from each province and territory" and to propose further reforms at some point (Conservative Party of Canada 2006, 44). Unable to pass legislation on reform during its first term, the party's 2008 platform promised to either reform or abolish the Senate. It stated that "as a minimum, a re-elected Conservative Government will reintroduce legislation to allow for nominees to the Senate to be selected by voters, to provide for Senators to serve fixed terms of no longer than eight years, and for the Senate to be covered by the same ethics rules as the House of Commons" (Conservative Party of Canada 2008, 24). The 2011 platform complained that the "Ignatieff-led Coalition with the NDP and Bloc Québécois" had resisted reform efforts, and promised to reintroduce legislation setting term limits for senators, to "establish a democratic process for selecting senators" and appoint those who are selected through such processes (Conservative Party of Canada 2011, 63).

Critics of the Conservative Party approach argued that the changes the government sought – elections and term limits – require formal constitutional amendment, something the Supreme Court confirmed after the government finally referred a set of reference questions on its Senate reform plans (*Reference re Senate Reform* 2014). With regard to "consultative" Senate elections, the government argued that so long as the final decision on appointment remains with the governor general (in practice, by the prime minister) then a formal amendment is unnecessary. The Court made short shrift of this argument, stating the clear purpose of the reform was to give the Senate a popular mandate, making it unlikely the prime minister would routinely exercise meaningful discretion in the selection process (*Reference re Senate Reform* 2014, para. 62). Similarly, the Court ruled that imposing term limits could change the fundamental nature of the Senate and thereby requires the consent of the provinces under the general amending formula. As a result, significant Senate reform is likely off the table (for a critique of the Court's reasoning in the Senate reference, see Macfarlane 2015). The two largest provinces, Ontario and Quebec, have been lukewarm at best on reform, and other provincial governments, like Saskatchewan, prefer abolition (CBC News 2013). Given the Court also affirmed that abolition requires the unanimous consent of all provinces (as removing the Senate necessitates amendment of the amending formula itself, which requires unanimity), that option is unlikely as well. The Conservative government showed virtually no appetite for large-scale intergovernmental negotiations, especially in constitutional change (see chapters 7 and 13 in this volume).

The Conservative Party has shown a similar preference for informal constitutionalism in national unity. After forming his first government in 2006, Harper sought to strengthen the party's standing in Quebec by reaching out. As Flanagan writes, he "advocated dealing with the fiscal imbalance, letting Québec be represented at UNESCO, and recognizing the Québécois as 'a nation within a United Canada'" (2007, 279). The nation motion was passed in the House of Commons on 27 November 2006 with the support of all but a handful of Liberal MPs and Independents, though Harper lost a Cabinet minister, Michael Chong, who resigned in opposition to the motion (Canwest News Service 2006). The nation motion in some ways marked a serious departure from Harper's Reform Party roots. The western contingent of the party's base had long been opposed to special recognition for Quebec. However, a more fundamental aspect of the motion is that Harper learned from the difficulties Mulroney faced when attempting significant formal constitutional change (Wells 2006). The nation motion had the virtue of not only being smart electoral politics, but also of having virtually no constitutional meaning. Unlike a constitutionally entrenched distinct society clause, the recognition of the Québécois as a nation by the House has no impact on judicial enforcement of the Charter of Rights or other aspects of the Constitution. It is thus perfectly in keeping with the 1997 Calgary Declaration agreement reached by all provinces except Quebec, which simultaneously acknowledged the unique character of Quebec society but started from the premise of equality of Canadians and the equal status of all provinces. In that sense, the Conservative government's decision to support the motion was not a repudiation of the Reform Party's long-standing position on Quebec but the end point of a compromise reached almost a decade prior, which both the Progressive Conservatives and Reform Party ultimately (in the case of Reform, tacitly) supported (Young 1999).

The Conservative government also came to the defence of the Clarity Act, which itself had not been supported by Clark's PCs at the time it was passed, when in 2013 it joined the other parties to vote down a Bloc motion to repeal it (Mas 2013). Nevertheless, Harper remained largely silent in a debate spurred by the NDP's assertion that a simple majority was sufficient to constitute a "clear majority." The NDP position was criticized severely by the Liberal Party. The Conservative Party's relative silence over the disagreement is consistent with earlier Reform Party statements that 50 per cent plus one was sufficient and with the private member's legislation Harper himself introduced as an MP in 1996. As columnist Chantal Hébert writes, "Harper is too prudent to discard the possibility that there could be a referendum on his watch. He is unlikely to sacrifice an ounce of political discretion to an opposition cat fight in the House of Commons" (2013).

The Conservative Party's approach to constitutional change is marked by a combination of prudence and strategic thinking. Unwilling to repeat the cacophonous and potentially damaging rounds of large-scale attempts at formal constitutional tinkering the country endured in the 1980s and 1990s, the Conservative government either sought to finesse reforms informally, as it did with the Senate, or walk a careful line on its articulation and approach to issues like national unity. As regards to Senate reform, this approach was unsuccessful. The government's approach to national unity was prudent, in that it avoided adopting positions that might have inflamed separatist passions. With little evident public appetite in Quebec for another referendum on secession, it seems the Conservative Party found a balance between the positions advanced by Reform and the PCs in the immediate post-Charlottetown period.

The Courts and the Charter of Rights and Freedoms

The Charter of Rights has been, in a narrow partisan sense, associated with the Liberal Party. However, in light of its overwhelming popularity with Canadian citizens, as a source of debate or policy disagreement, most political activity surrounding the Charter has normally centred on the manner of its enforcement by courts, the nature of interest group activity, and controversies surrounding particular rights issues rather than the constitutional text itself. Perhaps one exception to this general rule concerns the notwithstanding clause, the existence of which Mulroney once declared meant that the Charter was "not worth the paper it was written on" (Russell 2007, 65). It is noteworthy, however, that this is a position Peter Russell suggests makes Mulroney a "Charter worshipper" rather than critic (ibid.), even though the notwithstanding clause is part of the Charter itself.

Prior to 1993, both Reform and the PCs adopted a position on so-cial issues involving Charter rights, like abortion or gay and lesbian equality, that fundamentally left the issues to individual members. The PCs approached moral questions as non-partisan issues (Farney 2012). Reform's 1990 *Blue Book* took a slightly modified stance, encouraging its MPs to articulate their personal views but also stating that they are expected to "faithfully vote the consensus of the constituency in the appropriate divisions of the House of Commons if such a consensus ex-ists" (101). The early Reform Party also favoured direct democracy ap-proaches and would have been happy to see contentious issues settled via referenda. As social conservatives became more prominent within the party by the mid-1990s, the divisions between the PCs and Reform in these rights areas became more pronounced.

1993–2006

Judicial policy decisions under the Charter have been subject to con-siderable criticism from many on the social conservative side of the Reform, Canadian Alliance, and Conservative parties. As a result of the antipathy many of the parties' members occasionally express in regard to Charter enforcement – and specifically to the approach of the courts on a number of rights issues – respective leaders Manning, Stockwell Day, and Harper each had to withstand attacks that they had a "hid-den agenda" to infringe rights. These concerns typically focused on al-legations they sought to end abortion and same-sex equality rights, but extended to a host of issues including health care, criminal law, and the justice system. Not all criticisms were about a "hidden" agenda; for example, the 2004 Conservative Party platform articulated a plan to withdraw the reference questions posed to the Supreme Court on same-sex marriage (Kheiriddin and Daifallah 2005, 38). As discussed below, however, the Conservative Party has explicitly avoided adopting con-troversial policies like regulating abortion, out of recognition that seek-ing to place limits on certain rights will damage its electoral success.

One major source of intellectual thought on the Charter for the con-servative movement generally was the "Calgary school," a group of University of Calgary academics influential with – and, for some, involved in – the Reform/Alliance and Conservative Party. Among people who work or were educated at Calgary are: Harper; Tom Flanagan, who served as Conservative Party campaign manager in 2004; Ian Brodie, who served as the party's executive director and later as Harper's chief of staff; and Ray Novak, who served as Harper's executive assistant and later as chief of staff. Among the most influential academic work on the Charter that emanates from the Calgary school is Ted Morton and Rainer Knopff's "Court Party Thesis," which reflects conservative sentiment regarding social change wrought by the Charter. These changes are described as the result of judges wielding excessive discretionary power, supported by a Court Party comprising predominately left-wing interest groups organizing around national unity, civil libertarianism, equality seeking, social engineering, and post-materialism (Morton and Knopff 2000). Groups like the Women's Legal Education and Action Fund (LEAF), the Canadian Civil Liberties Association, and Equality for Gays and Lesbians Everywhere (EGALE) advance litigation tactics that differ from "ordinary" litigation activity – the latter of which involves individuals or groups seeking to protect themselves from unreasonable rights infringement by the state – by striving to change constitutional rules and affect broader policy outcomes in a manner they view as socially desirable.

Brodie's academic work extends the Court Party thesis by examining the nature of interest group litigation. He argues that by adopting a theory of "disadvantaged groups" into its jurisprudence, the Court gained these groups as allies (2002, xvii). Particularly troubling for Brodie was the state-sponsored nature of many of these efforts, in the form of programs like the Court Challenges Program (CCP). Initially established in 1978 to assist groups that might battle provincial language laws (in the wake of the Parti Québécois' agenda in Quebec), the CCP was expanded to include funding for equality rights challenges (ibid.). As Brodie describes the key problem with this dynamic, "The contribution governments have made to the growth of interest group litigation in Canada forces us to reconsider the ideas underlying the traditional views of interest group litigation and judicial review. This conclusion is analytical, not ideological. The new judicial involvement in the policy process is sometimes the result of the state working through interest groups. The Court Challenges Program represents the embedded state at war with itself in court" (2000, 122).

Nevertheless, it is not difficult to see why the state providing funds for challenges to its own laws might be particularly offensive from a conservative perspective. Further, that the groups comprising the Court Party tend to be socially progressive rather than conservative also explains why the social conservative elements within the Reform/Alliance were most critical of judicial review under the Charter. As Farney notes, the considerable role played by the courts in effecting social change helped to make the populist wing of the Reform Party natural allies of social conservatives on this front (2012).

By the mid-1990s, abortion had fallen from the legislative agenda (the last major attempt to replace Criminal Code restrictions on abortion after the Supreme Court's 1988 decision in *R v Morgentaler* was introduced in 1989 and eventually failed on a tie vote in the Senate). At the same time the rights of gays and lesbians soon became the most hotly contested social issue in Canada (Farney 2012, 106). Reform assemblies began passing resolutions declaring the party's support for the traditional definition of marriage, and Reform MPs were almost unanimously opposed to adding sexual orientation to the protected grounds of the Canadian human rights code (ibid.). It seemed as though social conservatives dominated the party, although much of the concern they articulated was also institutional, as it was aimed squarely at the fact that courts, rather than Parliament, were setting policy. The institutional concerns translated into very vocal support by the Reform Party for changes to the Supreme Court appointments process, with Manning citing the enhanced policymaking powers of the Court under the Charter as grounds for a more transparent and accountable system. As Crandall notes, this view was later carried by the Canadian Alliance and the Conservative Party (2013).

Farney writes, "On gay rights, unlike abortion, the Reform Party developed a clear position. Its ambiguity on abortion meant some significant tension with the pro-life movement initially, but as the debate became more defined in terms of gay rights, the Reform Party became the Canadian party with the most room for social conservative activism" (2012, 110). By contrast, the PCs of the mid- to late 1990s began to distinguish themselves from the populism and social conservatism of the Reform/Alliance by emphasizing their progressive, Red Tory roots. In a 2000 debate on a bill extending rights and benefits to same-sex couples, PC MP Peter MacKay (who would later become the Conservative government's justice minister) argued in support of the law on the basis of equality and fairness (121).

Harper, who won the leadership of the unified Conservative Party in 2004, had to approach controversial social rights issues with tremendous care. At the party's 2005 policy convention, Harper and his inner circle determined that the best strategy was to allow full debate and also to permit the "silent majority" to win. On abortion and official bilingualism, an overall moderate agenda – votes on party policy to not support any legislation that would regulate abortion and to support the Official Languages Act – emerged (Wells 2006, 142; Kheiriddin and Daifallah 2005). On the issue of same-sex marriage that year, Harper allowed a free vote, although Conservative Party MPs voted overwhelmingly in favour of preserving the traditional definition (Farney 2012).

It is noteworthy the extent to which Harper managed to effectively sideline (yet placate) social conservative members of his party and caucus. Controversial rights issues had severely hampered the Conservative Party during the 2004 campaign, particularly when it was revealed the party's justice critic, Randy White, conducted an interview stating his belief the notwithstanding clause should be invoked to protect the traditional definition of marriage (Clarkson 2005), and Conservative Party MP Cheryl Gallant compared abortion to murder and equated gays with criminals (Kheiriddin and Daifallah 2005). In part, Harper's approach stems from his own policy preferences. In contrast to former Canadian Alliance leader Stockwell Day, who was openly pro-life and evangelical in his beliefs, Harper is arguably not best described as a social conservative. His approach has led some commentators to suggest his principal goal is incremental rather than sweeping change, coupled with a primary ambition to ensure long-term conservative governance (Wells 2006). Regardless of whether Harper's approach stems from sincere or strategic preferences, restricting abortion rights and attempting to roll back language policy are not amenable to electoral success in Canada, something the Conservative leader clearly recognized.

This moderate approach to certain rights issues was one of several factors explaining Conservative Party success in the 2006 campaign. During the campaign, Liberal leader Paul Martin had been so desperate to stoke fears that a Conservative government would violate Charter rights that in the middle of a leaders debate he promised to pass a constitutional amendment banning federal use of the notwithstanding clause (Russell 2007). Ironically, it was only when Harper, responding to media questions about a potential majority government, attempted to quell such fears that they actually materialized: polls suggesting a Conservative Party majority deflated after he stated that "Liberal courts" (along with a Liberal Senate and a Liberal civil service) would act as a check against a Conservative Party majority (Wells 2006, 231). Ultimately the Conservative Party emerged from the 2006 campaign with a minority government, one that, as it pertains to the Charter, would adhere to a largely moderate approach in relation to those core social conservative issues, but with much less moderation on others.

2006–Present

Since its first policy convention in 2005, the Conservative Party under Harper remained steadfast that it would not introduce or support any legislation restricting abortion in Canada – a promise the media asked the prime minister to repeat during every subsequent election campaign. This has not meant the Conservative Party has shied away from advancing and defending policies that come up against rights claims, particularly when "law and order" or national security are implicated. On a handful of prominent issues, the government acted with a conservative ideological consistency: passing mandatory minimum sentencing laws; attempting to shut down the supervised drug injection facility (Insite) in Vancouver by enforcing the Controlled Drugs and Substances Act (CDSA); and refusing for many years to seek the repatriation of Omar Khadr, the lone Canadian held at Guantanamo Bay on terrorism charges. In each of these areas, the government suffered losses at court. Mandatory minimums have been found to constitute "cruel and unusual punishment" (Canadian Press 2012). In *Canada (Attorney General) v PHS Community Services* (2011), the Supreme Court ruled that the health minister's decision to refuse to extend an exemption under the CDSA for Insite violated the rights of those using the service. Finally, in *Canada (Prime Minister) v Khadr* (2010) the Court ruled that Khadr's continued detention constituted a violation of his Charter rights (Macfarlane 2012).

The Conservative government also cancelled the Court Challenges Program in 2006, although it restored some funding two years later to support official minority language claims (*Montreal Gazette* 2008). The cancellation of the CCP was strongly criticized by rights organizations, though the decision was of little surprise, given Brodie's role as chief of staff and his earlier writing on the program. Further, the government was met with criticism for its lack of interest in celebrating the twenty-fifth and thirtieth anniversaries of the Charter (*National Post* 2007; Bryden 2012). The government came under fire for spending more money on the anniversary of the War of 1812 and the Queen's Diamond Jubilee celebrations. This manifestation of symbolic politics suggested to critics that the government has disdain for the Charter itself.

Despite these cases and policy decisions, a strong case can be made that the Conservative government was often moderate in its overall approach to the Charter, at least outside of the "law and order" context. First, despite the fears of the Conservative Party's loudest critics, the government avoided forays into controversial social policies like abortion or attempts to roll back same-sex equality rights. Second, even where the Supreme Court's jurisprudence has been favourable to more conservative approaches in particular policy areas – such as its 2005 decision striking down Quebec's prohibition on the purchase of private medical insurance (*Chaoulli v Québec (Attorney General)*) – the government did not move to take advantage in an ideological way, such as by encouraging more private delivery of health care via changes to the Canada Health Act. Another example involves third party spending limits, a policy challenged by the National Citizens' Coalition when Harper was president but upheld by the Court (*Harper v Canada (Attorney General)* 2004). Upon forming government, Harper was free to seek repeal of the law but chose not to.

Third, successful Charter challenges to legislation passed by governments of all stripes have been the norm since 1982. Various elements of the Liberal government's anti-terrorism legislation, including those relating to investigative hearings and security certificates, were either altered or invalidated by the Supreme Court (Macfarlane 2012). The courts have applied the Charter to institute a host of protections for the criminally accused throughout the 1980s and 1990s (Roach 2007). As government losses have been common in these areas, the Conservative government's record is not by itself sufficient evidence that the Conservative Party has been particularly ideological or anti-Charter.

Finally, and perhaps most importantly, until controversy emerged over a 2013 appointment to the Supreme Court, Harper's appointments had not been partisan or particularly ideological. While he has avoided appointing judges who could be remotely identified as "liberal" in outlook, he clearly refrained from stacking the bench with conservatives. Of the eight justices he (successfully) appointed, all were lauded as well qualified by the legal community. There has been a sense that the Court has been more cautious and moderate under Chief Justice McLachlin (Macfarlane 2013), but this is a trend that began early in her tenure and is therefore something Harper's appointments continued rather than instigated (Tibbetts 2013).

Unfortunately, the government's appointment of Marc Nadon in 2013 resulted in controversy over the eligibility requirements of Federal Court judges from Quebec, leading to a Supreme Court reference opinion effectively undoing the appointment (Section 6 of the Supreme Court Act lays out specific eligibility requirements for appointees to the three seats designated for Quebec) (*Reference re Supreme Court Act* 2014).

The Court concluded that the Supreme Court Act's eligibility rules are part of the Constitution, and so any changes to them requires unanimous provincial consent. Critics argued the appointment was an attempt to get a conservative voice on the Court, particularly in light of a deferential decision by Nadon in the Khadr case (Hopper 2014). Even more criticism emerged after the Prime Minister's Office (PMO) and the Supreme Court engaged in an unprecedented public spat, in which the government implied the chief justice acted inappropriately by phoning the PMO to warn about the potential eligibility issue before Nadon was named to the bench (Cheadle 2014).

In the eyes of critics, the government's behaviour during this controversy confirmed its disdain for the Supreme Court itself. The Nadon saga also highlights the lack of transparency surrounding the judicial appointments process. Although more modest than earlier Reform Party proposals, which included a parliamentary ratification process (Crandall 2013), the government adopted a committee process to narrow a long-list of candidates to a short-list, and held public interviews in Parliament with most new appointees. These modest reforms were ultimately not successful. First, the parliamentary interviews with appointees did not generate particularly good questions from MPs, in part because they were often held only days after the appointment was announced, leaving members very little time to prepare. Rather than focus on the appointees' perspectives on their role or the functioning of the Court, the questions posed were rarely edifying. The committee interview of Justices Andromache Karakatsanis and Michael Moldaver arguably descended into farce, with NDP MP Joe Comartin repeatedly questioning Moldaver on his lack of proficiency in French (Macfarlane 2011). Comartin's questions were about the government's choice in selection, which Moldaver could hardly be expected to speak to. Second, the problematic nature of the secrecy of the short-list committee's work was highlighted during the institutional spat over the process leading up to Nadon's failed appointment. Members of the bipartisan committee were not able to divulge anything about the deliberations, including and extending to whether the short-list produced received all-party support. The incident illustrates that even though the Conservative government approached certain policy areas with moderation, its general attitude toward institutions like the Court reflects distrust. As a result of the fallout of the Nadon appointment, the government rescinded these minor reforms and reverted to the opaque, closed-door process of judicial selection.

Overall, the Conservative Party's approach to the Charter reflected ideological imperatives tempered in some contexts by strategic behaviour. The government, for the most part, avoided entangling itself in rights controversies pertaining to social policies or deeply divisive issues (even while some members of its caucus pursued private member's legislation or motions on topics like abortion) (see chapter 2 in this volume). Where the government itself pursued policies that come up against Charter claims, it was often where the rights claimants were not especially sympathetic from a public opinion standpoint: the criminally accused, drug addicts, or prisoners. Even the decision to cancel the Court Challenges Program likely entailed a certain political calculus, as it is a relatively modest program (with a budget of less than $6 million) and one with minimal public visibility. This paints a picture of a government that preferred incremental change with minimal political cost rather than sweeping or divisive policy measures as it pertains to the Charter. If the government's overall approach to the courts did not reflect the more critical and ideological stance the Reform/Alliance adopted while in opposition, its confrontation with the Court over Nadon underscores the limits of that moderation. Moreover, some of the policies and rhetoric emanating from the Conservatives in the 2015 federal campaign – in which they lost power – belied this previous moderation. The attempt to ban the wearing of niqabs at citizenship oath ceremonies, and the passing of a law to revoke citizenship of dual citizens in terrorism cases were both widely criticized as unconstitutional by experts.

Conclusion

The patterns of behaviour exhibited by federal conservative parties in opposition, and the Conservative Party in government, invite a number of conclusions. First, in addition to the normal governing pressures that produce a less ideological and more moderate and strategic approach to policy issues than a party might adopt while in opposition (brokerage politics being the norm in a country as diverse and regional as Canada), the Conservative government had the added task of governing while maintaining the support of previously separate party bases. It is also more intuitive for a regional protest party to act in an ideologically "pure" manner; once the Reform/Alliance had clear national ambitions it was necessary to adjust some of its attitudes toward constitutionally entrenched principles (or even reverse them, as it did in the case of its opposition to official bilingualism). Second, a culture of leader dominance of political parties in Canada is strikingly evident from this analysis. It is difficult to imagine Stockwell Day carving as moderate a path, or Joe Clark maintaining the support of the social conservative part of the Conservative Party base, as Stephen Harper did. The approach the Conservative government took on the Constitution was not just strategic electoral calculus but was also a careful balance and prioritization of existing policy preferences. Harper was central to the Conservative Party's success in that regard.

Finally, any analysis of a "conservative" record vis-à-vis the Constitution must be measured against previous governments and contemporary context. The parties' approaches to the Constitution, whether in opposition or government, are not formed in a vacuum. On this point it is important to bear in mind that some of the moderation of the Conservative Party's approach in certain areas was shaped and constrained by institutional culture and path dependency. For example, it was much more difficult for Harper to "stack the bench" of the Supreme Court with conservative appointments because his predecessors, Chrétien and Mulroney, refrained (for the most part) from overly partisan or ideological appointments. The failed Nadon appointment underscores the point that institutional and constitutional restraints are important in this regard as well.

A further contextual factor must be noted to underscore the provisional nature of this analysis: for only part of the Conservative government's time in power was it free from the shackles of a minority Parliament. It is unclear whether a second majority mandate would have encouraged an even more assertive form of constitutionalism from the Conservative Party, although its obsession with the niqab during the 2015 campaign suggests it might have. Nevertheless, with almost a decade in government and four of those holding a majority of Parliament, the Conservative government maintained a relatively steady, prudent hand on the constitutional wheel when it comes to social policy, and a testy, more political approach on institutional politics around the Constitution. On the latter, it bumped up against the Court itself, usually to end up on the losing side, and whether this confirms for critics that the Conservative government gave in to an ideological approach to the Constitution, or for supporters that the Supreme Court was a "Liberal" check on the Conservative Party, depends on one's perspective.

REFERENCES

Brodie, Ian. 2002. *Friends of the Court: The Privileging of Interest Group Litigants in Canada*. Albany: State University of New York Press.

Bryden, Joan. 2012. "Charter Anniversary Party Turns Partisan." *Metro News*, 17 April. http://metronews.ca/news/canada/107396/charter-anniversary-party-turns-partisan/.

Canadian Press. 2012. "Mandatory Gun Sentence Struck Down by Ontario Court." CBC News, 13 February. http://www.cbc.ca/news/canada/toronto/mandatory-gun-sentence-struck-down-by-ontario-judge-1.1170188.

Canwest News Service. 2006. "Harper Government Loses Minister over Québec 'Nation Resolution.'" Canada.com, 27 November. http://www.canada.com/vancouversun/news/story.html?id=9726530a-3a94-4f9b-9c7c-3eefda47ab6b.

CBC News. 2013. "Saskatchewan Premier Restates Call to Abolish the Senate," 24 May. http://www.cbc.ca/news/canada/saskatchewan/saskatchewan-premier-restates-call-to-abolish-senate-1.1305245.

Cheadle, Bruce. 2014. "Supreme Court Chief Justice Denies Contacting PM." CTV News. 2 May. http://www.ctvnews.ca/politics/supreme-court-chief-justice-denies-contacting-pm-harper-says-he-did-nothing-wrong-1.1803052

Clarkson, Stephen. 2005. *The Big Red Machine: How the Liberal Party Dominates Canadian Politics*. Vancouver: UBC Press.

Conservative Party of Canada. 2006. *Stand Up for Canada: Conservative Party of Canada Federal Election Platform*. Ottawa: Conservative Party of Canada. https://www.poltext.org/sites/poltext.org/files/plateformes/can2006pc_plt_en._14112008_165519.pdf.</other>

– 2008. *The True North Strong and Free: Stephen Harper's Plan for Canadians*. Ottawa: Conservative Party of Canada. https://www.poltext.org/sites/poltext.org/files/plateformes/can2008pc_plt_eng._13112008_193556.pdf.

– 2011. *Here for Canada: Stephen Harper's Low-Tax Plan for Jobs and Economic Growth*. Ottawa: Conservative Party of Canada. https://www.poltext.org/sites/poltext.org/files/plateformes/can2011pc_plt_en_12072011_114959.pdf.

Crandall, Erin. 2013. "Intergovernmental Relations and the Supreme Court of Canada: The Changing Place of the Provinces in Judicial Selection Reform." In *The Democratic Dilemma: Reforming Canada's Supreme Court*, edited by Nadia Verrelli, 71–86. Montreal and Kingston: McGill-Queen's University Press.

Farney, James. 2012. *Social Conservatives and Party Politics in Canada and the United States*. Toronto: University of Toronto Press.

Flanagan, Tom. 2007. *Harper's Team: Behind the Scenes in the Conservative Rise to Power*. Montreal and Kingston: McGill-Queen's University Press.

Harper, Stephen, Tom Flanagan, Ted Morton, Rainer Knopff, Andrew Crooks, and Ken Boessendool. 2001. "An Open Letter to Ralph Klein." *National Post*, 24 January. http://www.cbc.ca/canadavotes2004/leadersparties/leaders/pdf/firewall.pdf.

Hébert, Chantal. 2013. "NDP May Be Mirroring Public Opinion on Quebec." *Chronicle Herald*, 3 February. http://thechronicleherald.ca/opinion/621107-hebert-ndp-may-be-mirroring-public-opinion-on-Québec.

Hopper, Tristin. 2014. "Marc Nadon Caught Stephen Harper's Attention with Dissent Khadr Ruling in 2009." *National Post*, 21 March. http://news.nationalpost.com/2014/03/21/marc-nadon-caught-stephen-harpers-attention-with-dissent-khadr-ruling-in-2009/.

Johnson, William. 2005. *Stephen Harper and the Future of Canada*. Toronto: McClelland & Stewart.

Kheiriddin, Tasha, and Adam Daifallah. 2005. *Rescuing Canada's Right: Blueprint for a Conservative Revolution*. Mississauga, ON: John Wiley & Sons Canada.

Macfarlane, Emmett. 2011. "Why Public Hearings with Supreme Court Nominees Should Mean Something." *Maclean's*, 6 March. http://www.macleans.ca/politics/why-public-hearings-with-supreme-court-nominees-should-mean-something/.

– 2012. "Failing to Walk the Rights Talk? Post-9/11 Security Policy and the Supreme Court of Canada." *Review of Constitutional Studies* 16 (2): 157–79.

– 2013. *Governing from the Bench: The Supreme Court of Canada and the Judicial Role*. Vancouver: UBC Press.

– 2015. "Unsteady Architecture: Ambiguity, the Senate Reference, and the Future of Constitutional Amendment in Canada." *McGill Law Review* 60 (4): 883–903. http://dx.doi.org/10.7202/1034056ar.

Mas, Susana. 2013. "MPs Reject Clarity Act Repeal in 283–5 Vote." CBC News, 6 March.

Montreal Gazette. 2008. "Tories Restore Parts of Scrapped Court Challenges Program." 19 June.

Morton, F.L., and Rainer Knopff. 2000. *The Charter Revolution and the Court Party*. Peterborough, ON: Broadview.

National Post. 2007. "PM Passes on Marking Charter Anniversary." 11 April.

Roach, Kent. 2007. "Is There a Tyranny of the Charter in Criminal Justice and Security Policy?" *Policy Options* (February): 94–8.

Russell, Peter H. 2004. *Constitutional Odyssey: Can Canadians Become a Sovereign People?* Toronto: University of Toronto Press.

– 2007. "The Notwithstanding Clause: The Charter's Homage to Parliamentary Democracy." *Policy Options* (February): 65–8.

Smith, David E. 2003. *The Canadian Senate in Bicameral Perspective.* Toronto: University of Toronto Press. http://dx.doi.org/10.3138/9781442680609.

Tibbetts, Janice. 2013. "Building Consensus." *Canadian Lawyer,* July. http://www.canadianlawyermag.com/4710/building-consensus.html.

Wells, Paul. 2006. *Right Side Up: The Fall of Paul Martin and the Rise of Stephen Harper's New Conservatism.* Toronto: Douglas Gibson.

Young, Robert A. 1999. *The Struggle for Québec.* Montreal and Kingston: McGill-Queen's University Press.

CASES CITED

Canada (Attorney General) v PHS Community Services Society, 2011 SCC 44, [2011] 3 SCR 134

Canada (Prime Minister) v Khadr, 2010 SCC 3, [2010] 1 SCR 44

Chaoulli v Québec (Attorney General), [2005] 1 SCR 791, 2005 SCC 35

Harper v Canada (Attorney General), [2004] 1 SCR 827, 2004 SCC 33

R v Morgentaler, [1988] 1 SCR 30

Reference re Secession of Québec, [1998] 2 SCR 217

Reference re Senate Reform, 2014 SCC 32

Reference re Supreme Court Act, ss 5 and 6, 2014 SCC 21

11 More Than a Terrain of Struggle: Parliament as Ideological Instrument and Objective under Conservatism

JONATHAN MALLOY

At first glance, a comparison of how Canadian conservatives approached parliamentary institutions between 1993 and 2015 seems to reveal a sharp contrast between conservatives in opposition and conservatives in government. In the 1990s, the Reform Party and its leader Preston Manning promoted and to some degree followed an idealized view of the House of Commons, with individual MPs responsible to constituents above all, and placed a strong initial emphasis on institutional reforms, particularly Senate reform. But the Conservative Party in power under Stephen Harper followed a disciplined and confrontational approach that left little room for autonomous MPs and took an incremental and ultimately failed approach to Senate reform. Furthermore, while Manning and the Reform Party promoted a highly idealized vision of parliamentary democracy, the Conservatives showed a clear willingness to bend and challenge unwritten parliamentary traditions. In short, while all parties' and leaders' attitudes to Parliament are determined to some degree by whether they sit in opposition or in government, Reform and the Conservatives appear to have approached Parliament from strikingly opposite paradigms (with the Progressive Conservative Party presenting a third, middle-ground approach).

However, common to both major phases of conservatism – Reform in opposition and the Conservatives in power – is the manner in which they incorporated Parliament into their ideological paradigms and objectives. Traditionally, Canadian brokerage parties saw Parliament as a relatively neutral terrain of struggle – a space for political jockeying and advantage, but not itself associated with any particular end or ideological objective. Parties played predictable government and opposition positions and reliably switched their tune as they went in and out of power, while MPs perpetually struggled to find roles within the framework of party discipline and the ever-increasing complexity of governance. The House of Commons underwent occasional bouts of reform, especially in the 1960s and 1980s. But for both the Liberals and Progressive Conservatives, the basic questions, themes, and norms of Parliament remained largely the same and perpetually familiar. In contrast, the Reform Party and the Conservative Party of Canada presented distinctly different orientations and paradigms that attempted to shift understandings and practice of how Parliament works, as part of each party's larger ideological and strategic goals. Thus, despite the contrasts between the two, we see a unique and shared orientation that views Parliament not merely as the terrain or host of political and ideological struggle, but an *object of struggle itself.*

Parliament is a puzzling institution, and legislatures in general are paradoxes (Malloy 2010; Loewenberg 2011). The Parliament buildings in Ottawa stand as the most physical representations of our democracy. But Parliament is also a void that symbolizes frustration and cynicism with the Canadian political system. Parliamentary debate and voting are highly scripted and predictable, especially under majority governments. The relationship of Parliament to either representation or policymaking is subtle and rarely linear, which frustrates citizens and legislators alike and leads to perennial calls for reform (Mallory 1979; Axworthy 2008).

The paradox of Parliament can be understood through two competing logics – a logic of representation (also known as the Whig or legislator-centred approach) and a logic of governance (also known as the Tory or executive-centred approach) (Birch 1964; Franks 1987). The first logic focuses on Parliament as a representative body and MPs as the voice of Canada, either as vehicles of direct delegate-style representation or trustees exercising their judgment on behalf of Canadians. In contrast, the logic of governance emphasizes Parliament – and specifically the House of Commons – as the body from which government draws its power and to which it is responsible. It sees MPs primarily as part of this larger process, organized into government and opposition blocs and playing roles within these as part of the "mobilization of consent" (Franks 1987, 217). This approach does not dismiss the individual roles of MPs but emphasizes their *collective* function, closely linked to political parties and party leaders. Both these logics have a sound basis but compete against each other to produce the puzzle and paradox of legislatures. As we will see, the Reform Party tended to emphasize the first logic, while the Conservative Party in power was more associated with the second.

Historically, Canadian scholarship on Parliament has had a strong normative undertone, often emphasizing the logic of governance and downplaying the logic of representation (Malloy 2002), and extolling Parliament's ambiguity as a virtue that provides flexibility and adaptability over time (J. Smith 1999). However, a more recent approach suggests that the pendulum has swung too much in favour of the logic of governance. This work focuses particularly on the apparent decline in agreed conventions surrounding parliamentary institutions under recent minority governments of both parties but especially the Conservative party (Aucoin, Jarvis, and Turnbull 2011; Russell and Sossin 2009). Significantly, the normative concerns of both approaches were driven partly in reaction to the ideas and actions of conservatives since 1993 – first, Reform's strong embrace of the logic of representation, and then the Conservative preference for a truncated and extreme logic of governance.

As mentioned, parliamentary research has historically leaned to the normative, and often engaged in circular, never-ending debates upon these themes. A more recent wave of empirical research is helping us move beyond the circular debates to inform us more on how Parliament actually works. But this does not erase the basic paradoxes and questions of Parliament itself, and the tension between the logics of representation and governance. Hence, in this chapter we will focus on those tensions and how conservatives in opposition and government approached them, through three questions:

1 Role of the member of Parliament: How did party discipline operate in conservative parties, in theory and in practice?
2 Unwritten conventions: How did conservative parties approach and interpret unwritten conventions and norms of Parliament?
3 The Senate: How did conservative parties view the Senate and what priority did they place on its reform?

Understandings of Parliament have always been animated by the above themes. But as stated, historically the two major brokerage parties approached them in broadly similar ways, differing largely by whether they were in or out of power. In contrast, federal conservative parties after 1993 posed distinct and often novel approaches, and while the Reform and Conservative attitudes may initially seem polar opposites, we will see how they both viewed Parliament as part of their overall ideological strategy. We will now explore these questions, first by conservatives in opposition, and then by conservatives in government.

In Opposition, 1993–2006

To understand how conservative parties in opposition approached these perennial questions of Parliament, we must first contrast the experience of the traditional Progressive Conservatives with the very different paradigm offered by the Reform Party.

Prior to 1993, the Progressive Conservative approach to Parliament was, in broad terms, similar to the other brokerage party, the Liberals. Interest in Parliament and enthusiasm for parliamentary reform was determined less by party principles and more by circumstances. While the twentieth-century Progressive Conservatives were perhaps more prone to general laments about the decline of Parliament, this was probably largely a function of their long stretches out of office. It was also fuelled by the particular inclinations of leaders like John Diefenbaker, whose oratorical commitment to Parliament was not always accompanied by practice in their prime ministerships. While paying lip service to the supremacy of Parliament, the PCs often opted for opportunism over principle, such as Joe Clark's failure to summon Parliament for 142 days after winning power in 1979, the longest ever such stretch (Aucoin, Jarvis, and Turnbull 2011).

Brian Mulroney produces a slightly more complex picture. His approach to Parliament included managing the largest ever parliamentary caucus in his first term, and then maintaining that caucus amid terrible political conditions in the second. Mulroney created the special McGrath reform committee in 1984 and implemented many of its recommendations, such as election of the Commons Speaker by secret ballot. He is also notable for a remarkably persuasive power of caucus management, managing to keep the ranks solidified in the party's darkest hours. But this remained driven by circumstances, expediency, and tactical calculations, and Parliament was a terrain of struggle, and not an end in itself. The same general style is seen in the Progressive Conservative Party after 1993. While its devastating reduction to two MPs made House of Commons matters largely moot for the party, it retained a large Senate caucus that served as the party's parliamentary flagship from 1993 to 1997 (Franks 1999). These Senators used their majority to block several government bills, much as Liberal senators had blocked key Mulroney government bills. Like the Liberals, the post-1993 PC party displayed no particular interest in Senate reform; rather it saw the Senate as part of the overall parliamentary battlefield and the means to keep the party alive. After 1997, with a renewed Commons caucus of twenty MPs and the shift in Senate power back to the Liberals, the PCs reverted to the traditional opposition role of expedient opposition sniping and scrutiny in the Commons. Throughout, parliamentary institutions remained a terrain of struggle – the space in which parties played their given roles and furthered their objectives. Parliament was not an objective itself.

In sharp contrast, parliamentary reform and direct democracy were at the heart of the Reform Party project, and primary objectives in their own right. Preston Manning wrote in 1992, "To get on the road to New Canada we need a fundamental reform of our democratic processes" (P. Manning 1992, 321). But in Manning's populist vision, parliamentary reform was practically a destination in its own right. The 1988 Reform Party *Platform and Statement of Principles* begins first with sections titled "Constitutional Reform" (including a Triple-E Senate) and "Political Reform" (parliamentary reform and direct democracy measures), before moving to economic and social reform (Reform Party of Canada 1988). The "Statement of Principles" in the 1991 *Reform Party of Canada Principles and Policies* pamphlet lists twenty-one principles; the very first is a Triple-E Senate (Reform Party of Canada 1991). Principles 12 through 15 also address parliamentary and direct democracy initiatives. In short, institutional and democratic reforms were priorities and ends in themselves, not just expedient means by which to further other party objectives. To understand and analyse this approach, very different from that of the Progressive Conservatives, we will now look at how the Reform Party approached the chapter's three guiding questions.

The first question asks, *How did party discipline operate in conservative parties, in theory and in practice?* Party discipline and the role of individual MPs is a central tension between the logics of representation and governance, and it dates back to Burke's delineation of "delegates" (MPs responsible to constituents) versus "trustees" (MPs exercising their own judgment). Twentieth-century Canadian MPs and parties lurched primarily between the trustee orientation and a third role that privileged party discipline above all. But the Reform Party brought a fresh, intense focus on the constituency-driven delegate role, in theory and to some degree in practice. In his 1992 autobiography Manning identifies three theories of representation closely correlating to the above:

- A *delegate* theory of representation in which "Canadians want their members of Parliament to faithfully and accurately represent their views on a major issue when a clear consensus on that issue can be determined in the riding" (321).
- A *mandate* theory in which "Canadian voters also want their representatives to practice the principles, implement the platforms, and keep the promises on which they were elected to Parliament. In other words, voters not only expect, but will demand, that on many occasions their elected representatives 'vote the party line' because that's what they promised to do if elected" (ibid.).
- And finally a *trustee* theory: "At the same time, most Canadians are prepared to respect the judgment, conscience and experience of their individual elected member, particularly if that member shows respect for the judgment, values and experience of constituents" (ibid.).

Manning then says, "The Reform Party has drawn on all three models to develop what I, as a former physics student, like to call a 'unified field' theory of representation" (Manning 1992, 321; see also Laycock 2002, 102–3). Manning suggested that the three models could be reconciled in a democratic, equal parliamentary caucus, while leaving open the possibility that Reform MPs could occasionally exercise their own judgment and openly break from the party line if they could demonstrate a strong base in constituency opinion.

Prior to 1993, Manning and the party's ideas on representation were entirely theoretical, save for the party's lone MP Deborah Grey. Even after 1993 they were seen only in an opposition context, where the party did not have the obligations of a government to maintain the confidence of the House and implement its policies. The "unified field" theory was further mediated by Manning's early eschewal of traditional opposition partisanship. Manning in his early Commons years had an exaggerated respect for the dignity of Parliament and an abhorrence of the traditional clash between government and opposition.

Manning's theory was put to the test in two significant ways: parliamentary voting and caucus behaviour. One of the first and most prominent challenges to the Reform commitment to placing constituents first was in 1995 with Bill C-68, establishing the long-gun registry. While the party as a whole opposed C-68, three MPs from urban ridings voted for the legislation because of its popularity within their constituency. The issue "provided the party with an opportunity to show

how it differed in style from the governing Liberals" (Docherty 1997, 165). While rural Liberal MPs voting against the bill were punished to varying degrees, Manning and Reform praised one dissenting MP in particular – Jim Silye from Calgary Centre, who ran an opinion poll to gauge constituents' views – as an example of the virtue of their flexible system. However, while the party made a point of celebrating such moments of constituency-based dissention, they were in fact sporadic and unusual. Godbout and Hoyland (2011) find that in the Thirty-Fifth Parliament of 1993–97, Liberals were in fact slightly more likely to dissent against their own party compared to Reform. Dissent for Reform was thus more *ceremonial* than truly *substantial*, and the party could afford to celebrate and showcase occasional examples without much consequence. For example, Manning had earlier announced in 1994 that after having polled constituents on assisted suicide, he would reverse his personal position and vote for such legislation if it came forward. But this commitment never came to a test with actual legislation (Carty, Cross, and Young 2000).

The larger difficulty of balancing party, constituency, and personal views within the party caucus was seen in 1996 with Bill C-33, extending human rights legislation to include sexual orientation. Sentiment in the party was clearly against the bill, but one MP, Silye again, voted for the legislation, citing a poll of his riding, and was not disciplined. However, two other MPs, Bob Ringma and Dave Chatters, were reported as having made derogatory comments about gays (one an older quote that was resurrected); a third MP, Jan Brown, then publicly criticized these comments. Manning reprimanded Brown and temporarily suspended all three members, and Brown soon left to sit as an independent. According to Docherty, this showed that "within the Reform party, members were more free to vote against their party than they were to speak against it" (1997, 168). The discipline against Brown showed the limits of the Manning/Reform approach, which allowed for occasional ceremonial dissensions like Silye's but could not tolerate larger, public displays of dissension and unrest in any direction. This controlling approach was not unlike other parliamentary parties; indeed, "in punishing the individuals who spoke against the party or brought the party unwelcome publicity, Reform Leader Preston Manning displayed a classical understanding of legislative traditions and folkways" (170). Dissenting votes were thus more ceremonial than regularized, and this was not expanded into a more robust and general sense of freedom for MPs.

The second question in our analysis asks, *How did conservative parties approach and interpret unwritten conventions and norms of Parliament?* Parliament, like other political institutions descending from the British Westminster model, relies on a mix of written rules and unwritten conventions and norms. Written rules include the standing orders of the two chambers, along with subsequent interpretations, rulings, and other constitutional acts and documents. Unwritten conventions and norms range from issues of decorum in the chamber – e.g., traditional Commons-style heckling is less acceptable in the Senate – to central facets like the confidence convention. Many important aspects like ministerial responsibility involve a mix of written and unwritten rules. In a category of its own is the third component of Parliament, the Crown, in which formal and written de jure rules differ greatly from the unwritten de facto conventions.

The Reform Party and its leader present a certain irony here. Manning was effusive in his praise for democratic institutions and traditions, but arguably had a weak command of the realities of Westminster-style parliamentary democracy. Tom Flanagan wrote in 1995, "Unfortunately, [Manning] is not particularly well-prepared for the task [of opposition leader]. He comes out of the non-partisan tradition of Alberta, in which all successful premiers have acted as if the opposition were irrelevant ... Reinforcing this personal experience is Manning's conception of the role of the opposition, which he describes as putting forth 'constructive alternatives'" (Flanagan 1995, 167).

In challenging what they saw as deficiencies of the House of Commons, Manning and his party somewhat paradoxically and unintentionally undermined many of the actual unwritten conventions and norms of the chamber, especially the conception that the opposition's job is indeed to oppose. The "constructive alternatives" approach led to a number of unusual behaviours in 1994 (Flanagan 1995; D. Smith 2013, 85). The Reform caucus was seated alphabetically, with Manning in the third row. Instead of a frontbench shadow cabinet of critics, the caucus was divided into issue committee "clusters" with no single spokesperson (see chapter 12 in this volume). MPs avoided heckling and noisy displays, and delivered longwinded questions and statements. Hence, says Flanagan, in its initial months Manning "did not lead the Reform caucus in a coordinated way to embarrass, hinder or otherwise influence the government" (Flanagan 1995, 167). Even if driven by sincerity and goodwill, Manning's exaggerated and idealistic sense of Parliament arguably was undermining its real traditions, especially for those of an opposition leader in a parliamentary system, and thus ultimately not contributing to good representation and good parliamentary government.

However, these practices, especially the seating plan, lasted only a few months, and by the fall of 1994, the party began to conform to more standard opposition behaviours. The general explanation from Flanagan and others is that Manning and the party realized their "constructive" behaviour was yielding little fruit and especially media coverage; the poor seating imagery, lack of a clear frontbench of spokespeople, and lack of succinct messages meant the party struggled for notice. David Smith persuasively argues that "the resulting policy confusion and lack of prominence encouraged the party to conform to accepted practice in the new Parliament elected in 1997" (2013, 85). Manning also relaxed other supposedly hard principles. He originally pledged not to move into the opposition leader's residence of Stornoway if he became eligible (joking about turning it into a bingo hall) but changed his position after the 1997 election when he did qualify. In 1999, Reform led a notable delay of the Nisga'a treaty bill, forcing hundreds of amendments – an action that the Preston Manning of early 1994 would surely have deemed "unconstructive" – and by this time, there were fewer constituency-based dissenting votes to celebrate. The party appeared cohesive and similar to other opposition parties, including the renewed Progressive Conservatives under Joe Clark, as it evolved into the Canadian Alliance and Manning lost the leadership to Stockwell Day. While the Reform Party as a whole continued to embrace ideas of institutional reform and direct democracy to a greater extent than other parties, especially at the grassroots, its parliamentary arm under the close control of Manning appeared to have largely conformed to the existing rules and norms of the House.

The third question considers, *What is the role of the Senate?* In Reform's early years the Triple-E Senate was perhaps the single greatest objective of the party, and we saw earlier that it sat at the top of their 1991 pledge list. But Preston Manning's true focus was gaining power through the House of Commons, and Senate reform was less significant for the party leadership, though it remained extremely popular at the grassroots. Faron Ellis (2005) documents this divide in the run-up to the 1992 Charlottetown Accord, when Manning supported a preliminary accord that included Senate reform that did not meet Triple-E standards. In so doing, "Manning abandoned his previous Triple-E rigidity for a more immediate short-term agenda" (82) that was not acceptable to large swathes of current party members. A survey at the 1992 party convention found that 96.3 per cent of delegates favoured a Triple-E Senate (113). However, the end of mega-constitutionalism after the collapse of the Charlottetown Accord allowed Manning to downplay the issue entirely, and while Reform continued to pay homage to Triple-E, it invested little in the idea. In Manning's 2002 memoir, he says somewhat curiously that he had long wanted to give a speech in the Commons "outlining in detail the defects of the Canadian Senate" but had been unable to until 1998 for lack of procedural openings and the custom of not criticizing "the other place" (Manning 2002, 208–9) – a reason that does not explain his lack of enthusiasm for talking about it elsewhere. In the meantime, as mentioned, the Senate became the primary base of operations for the rump Progressive Conservative Party, harassing and delaying the Chrétien government until the Liberals gained a majority in the upper house in early 1997 and the PC party reasserted itself with twenty Commons seats in the 1997 election.

While Reform under Manning had become comfortable with its parliamentary role by the end of the decade, the change to the Canadian Alliance under Stockwell Day brought a new set of challenges. As a former Alberta MLA and Cabinet minister, Day was even more closely associated than Manning with the executive-dominated Alberta legislative scene of the time and showed a clumsy touch as opposition leader. Internal dissent grew against Day's leadership style, and several members led by Deborah Grey and Chuck Strahl left the caucus and/or were expelled, eventually forming the Democratic Representative Caucus (DRC) and a loose coalition with the Progressive Conservatives, though it was unable to gain recognition as a full parliamentary party.

The DRC faction was driven by a mix of personalities and the complicated "unite the right" context of the early 2000s, and did not necessarily pose a different understanding of two of the overall questions that animate this chapter – the role of individual MPs or the Senate. However, the unique entity did touch on unwritten or partly written parliamentary conventions. A faction breaking away from one party and then entering a loose coalition with another could be seen as following the occasional tradition of floor-crossing by individual MPs, or as something not seen since the conscription crisis of 1917 and formation of the Unionist Party by Conservatives with disaffected Liberals, a different arrangement that was accompanied and ratified by a general election. Stephen Harper stayed relatively silent on the DRC, which was associated with Manning loyalists, and Harper appears to have said nothing at the time about the general principle of whether MPs elected under a party label could later repudiate that banner, and/or join a (opposition) coalition with another party, though he later expressed very definite opinions about such matters, as we see below.

In 2002–3, both conservative parties were consumed with leadership succession and then reunification. This allowed for some streamlining and sorting out of individual dissenting MPs in all directions. Scott Brison and Keith Martin left the PC and Alliance parties respectively to join the Liberals, John Bryden crossed over to join the new Conservative Party (but was unable to win a subsequent Conservative nomination), and Joe Clark and a few other MPs and senators refused to join the new Conservative Party and continued to identify as Progressive Conservatives, though without legal rights to the party name. The result of this sorting (followed later by Belinda's Stronach's crossing to the Liberals in 2005) was a highly unified Conservative party, while the Liberals, consumed by the Martin-Chrétien civil war, were more in disarray. Perhaps unsurprisingly, Godbout and Hoyland (2011, 377) find that in the Thirty-Eighth Parliament of 2004–6, the Conservatives, BQ, and NDP all displayed similar high levels of unity, while the Liberals were the most divided (though still 95 per cent unified).

Stephen Harper showed far less fascination than Preston Manning with democratic structural reforms, even in theory, and this apparent disinterest may have assisted the eventual merger of the PC and Alliance parties. For example, Harper acceded to the PC request to conduct leadership campaigns on an equal-riding basis rather than a single mass vote. In the run-up to the 2004 election, the party repeated old Reform promises like fixed election dates and Senate reform but, as Flanagan notes, "conspicuously absent … was any mention of direct democracy, which had caused so much trouble in the Canadian Alliance campaign of 2000" (2007, 157). But while it was clear that the approach of conservatives in power under Stephen Harper towards Parliament would be different from the initial, if later watered-down, approach of Reform under Preston Manning, it was not clear whether the party would follow the more traditional parliamentary ways of the Progressive Conservatives or chart a new course entirely.

In Government, 2006–2015

The Conservative Party of Canada's approach to Parliament during its time in power from 2006 to 2015 can be understood in several ways.

Most immediately, we can identify several incidents where the Conservatives challenged parliamentary traditions and unwritten conventions. This was typically for immediate political advantage, but was also driven by a larger and particular interpretation of the logic of governance that gave considerable discretion to the right of governments to have their way, subject only to periodic elections. We can also see a pattern of party discipline that, while not necessarily greater than that of other parties, was accompanied by a much greater silencing of caucus members and a further decline in autonomy by backbenchers. We also see a lurching and ultimately futile Senate reform agenda.

As mentioned above, Stephen Harper and his Conservatives did not replicate the Reform priority of direct democracy, parliamentary reform, and other process issues. Focused more on Liberal missteps and on convincing Canadians the party did not stand for radical policy changes, the Conservatives limited themselves in the 2006 election to a few discrete institutional pledges within the larger framework of a promised new accountability act, such as fixed election dates and the creation of a parliamentary budget officer. Both of these were implemented soon after the party came to power, though neither developed exactly as intended. However, the Conservatives in power soon demonstrated a distinct new approach to Parliament, one that challenged traditional norms and saw Parliament as an *instrument*, not just a terrain of struggle, to be used to further their overall strategic goals. To understand these dynamics, we will turn again to the three overall questions about (1) the role of individual MPs and party discipline, (2) unwritten norms and conventions, and (3) the Senate.

The first question again is, *How did party discipline operate in conservative parties, in theory and in practice?* While Preston Manning saw constituency-empowered MPs and his "unified field" vision as the best check on executive power, Peter Russell (2008) has argued that the better check is minority government. As he argues, the first Harper term in office was characterized by messy but reasonably productive bargaining between parties. This was very different from the Manning/Reform theoretical vision of democracy, rooted in the logic of representation and the power of individual MPs and constituencies. Instead, individual MPs were less significant in minority government bargaining, and the Thirty-Ninth Parliament (2006–8) saw very limited dissent, especially in the government ranks. Again we can refer to Godbout and Hoyland's findings (2011) that the Conservatives, NDP, and Bloc were all very highly unified in their parliamentary voting in 2006–8, while the Liberals displayed the greatest tendency towards dissent (see also Curry and Thompson, 2013).

The Conservatives' expedient approach to constituency opinion was revealed early with the naming of David Emerson, newly re-elected as a Liberal, to the Conservative Cabinet, with no requirement he resign and run again until the next general election. This was a shocking contrast to the Reform vision that placed constituents above all else (as well as later Conservative attacks against dissenters like Brent Rathgeber in 2013[1]). More broadly, while Garth Turner emerged as an early superficial gad-fly, few substantive dissenters or alternative sources of power emerged in the Conservative ranks, either in the trustee or delegate model. A pos-sible exception was Michael Chong who, after resigning from Cabinet on principle in 2006, later emerged as a champion of modest parliamen-tary reforms to Question Period in 2009 (which were never passed) and party caucus structures in 2013, including an option for MPs to enact a mechanism at the beginning of each Parliament to allow leadership challenges. However, Chong's proposals never directly threatened the existing Conservative structure and Harper's leadership, nor did MPs in any party opt to enact the mechanism after the 2015 election.

All parties seek to minimize public dissent in their ranks. But the Conservatives enforced a particularly strong culture of disciplined and centralized communications, making it even less likely that indepen-dent-minded backbenchers or committees would emerge in the public eye. Media revelations in 2007 about a party obstruction manual for committees suggested the party actively kept MPs under tight control as loyal party soldiers, rather than allowing committees to develop as a place of partial autonomy for backbench MPs, as Brian Mulroney did (though see Wilson 2016). Conservative MPs did enjoy influence behind the scenes through the party's own internal system of backbench con-sultations (Wilson 2015) but the significance of this is difficult to assess. A particularly Orwellian incident occurred in 2012 when backbencher

---

1   Conservative MP Brent Rathgeber left the Conservative caucus in June 2013 to sit as an independent, citing excessive centralization and control of MPs. On 6 June 2013, in response to an NDP question on floor-crossing, Conservative Minister Rona Ambrose said in the House, "We do think he should do the right thing by him and by his constituents: run in a by-election as an independent" (House of Commons 2013).

David Wilks was filmed expressing opposition to a government budget bill, only to repudiate his remark in a written statement a day later. And as mentioned, in 2013, Alberta MP Brent Rathgeber resigned from the caucus, complaining about excessive and controlling discipline. But such incidents are not unusual for a mature majority government, and they more or less follow the familiar patterns and paradoxes between the two logics of representation and governance. Overall, despite their iron image, the Conservatives in power were not terribly dissimilar from predecessor governments in their use of party discipline.

A more interesting test of the Conservative approach to individual MPs' roles was its evolving attitude to anti-abortion private members' bills and motions. Both before and during his time in power, Stephen Harper said he did not want to reopen the abortion debate in Canada. But many of his backbenchers and Conservative party members did. This led to several private members' bills and motions in the government's early years, most notably Rod Bruinooge's "Roxanne's Law" (a bill that would make it a crime to coerce a woman into having an abortion). Harper made clear these were not government policy and personally voted against Bruinooge's bill, but also did not openly discipline backbenchers who introduced or supported such bills and motions. The Conservatives appeared willing to make some accommodation for MPs based on conscience – a variation on the constituency-based dissents of the Reform era. However, over time the government became less tolerant. In 2012, Conservative whip Gordon O'Connor delivered a strong attack in the Commons on Stephen Woodworth's motion to revisit the question of when life starts, and in 2013 the government actively blocked Mark Warawa's bill on sex selection. The latter led to further government controls over Standing Order 31 statements, the time before Question Period when backbenchers can make short speeches on any topic, which some Conservatives were using for abortion-related issues. This suggests that government patience had worn thin and pro-life backbenchers were becoming too distracting, necessitating a tighter grip on them as individual MPs and shutting down an area of independent backbench activity.

Overall, the attitude of the Conservatives in power towards party discipline and the role of MPs was firmly biased towards parties and a logic of governance, with little or none of the legislator-centred rhetoric of the Reform era. The greater control of Conservative communications meant dissenters and flashes of independence were less likely to emerge visibly than in previous eras. But while the government was more openly controlling than its predecessors, MPs voted much as they did in previous Parliaments.

Where we do see greater difference and a distinct Conservative style is in the second question: *How did conservative parties approach and interpret unwritten conventions and norms of Parliament?* The Conservative Party in power showed that it was willing to severely bend unwritten conventions in the service of its immediate political and policy interests. While these actions have been roundly criticized by a wide range of expert observers, scholars are in less agreement over their impact. For some, they represent an unprecedented abuse of power by Stephen Harper that goes well beyond any acts of his predecessors; for others, they are merely the latest developments in an ongoing deterioration of Canadian parliamentary norms and traditions.[2] These actions can be grouped into three general categories: manipulation of the parliamentary calendar; access to documents; and a general mischaracterization of the Westminster model. The first category includes the breaking of the spirit, if not the letter, of the fixed election date law in 2008, the manipulation of the parliamentary calendar to avoid the scheduled non-confidence vote of 1 December 2008, and the subsequent sudden prorogation of Parliament that week and again in December 2009. The second includes the Afghan detainee documents showdown of April 2010 and the finding of contempt over the government's failure to produce documents in March 2011 (as well as a separate issue of a minister refusing to apologize for misleading the House). The third covers the repeated Conservative attempts to delegitimize "unelected" coalitions and other questionable assertions such as its call for Brent Rathgeber to resign and run to retain his seat; as noted, a requirement not placed on David Emerson in 2006.

These incidents need not be detailed at length here and, as noted, have sparked considerable scholarly and popular debate (Russell and Sossin 2009; Aucoin, Jarvis, and Turnbull 2011). The interesting focus here is how the Conservatives justified their actions. In some cases, the party defended itself by pointing to Liberal parallels, such as the sudden prorogation of November 2003 by Jean Chrétien, and Liberal evasion of confidence votes in May 2005 and in 1968 in the last days of the Pearson

2 For an authoritative scholarly discussion of this debate, see Aucoin, Jarvis, and Turnbull (2011).

government. But we also see a repeated and striking indifference by the Conservatives to even keeping up the appearance of following traditional conventions, and an occasional willingness to mislead and mischaracterize basic aspects of the parliamentary system. On more than one occasion, Stephen Harper and others argued erroneously that coalition governments were incompatible with the Westminster model (e.g., saying at the height of the 2008 constitutional crisis when the Liberals and NDP attempted to form a coalition government with parliamentary support from the Bloc Québécois that "Stephane Dion does not have the right to take power without an election" (Laghi 2008). Instead, the party based its arguments and legitimacy on electoral mandates – arguing that no party can govern without one, and that parliamentary conventions can be bent and broken because the only true arbiter is the electorate.

This interpretation of the logic of governance – that parliamentary actions are either wholly justified or illegitimate, depending on the presence of an electoral mandate – is consistent with what Pond (2005) identifies, in a study of Mike Harris's Ontario, as the neoliberal theory of parliamentary representation. Like Harper, Harris displayed little interest in the deliberative functions of the legislature, to the point of reducing its seats by a quarter in the "Fewer Politicians Act." Instead, Harris justified his actions through his electoral mandate and repeatedly tried to play that mandate as a trump card whenever legislative obstacles arose. Harper followed a similar path, and in this way his Conservatives in power approached Parliament not as a neutral field or terrain of struggle, but an institution to be itself reshaped through a particular ideological approach.

The third question asks, *How did conservative parties view the Senate and what priority did they place on its reform?* The Reform Party made Senate reform a key objective and initially an outright obsession, though Preston Manning was less committed than grassroots members. The Conservative Party did not place the same premium on Senate reform, especially once in power, but did embark on a drawn-out and ultimately futile incremental reform agenda.

After taking power, Harper appointed an elected senator-in-waiting from Alberta, while refusing to fill other provincial vacancies. Instead, the Conservatives pursued an incremental strategy, proposing term limits and mechanisms to allow provincial elections (J. Smith 2009) rather than attempting a total overhaul. However, this became bogged down with reforms repeatedly reintroduced but encountering various obstacles, leading to dwindling government interest. The Conservatives eventually began appointing batches of new senators, who were noticeably deferential to the government (in contrast to others like Hugh Segal, a Conservative appointed by Liberal Paul Martin). But the party was subsequently embarrassed by its own appointees Mike Duffy, Pamela Wallin, and Patrick Brazeau, who became enmeshed in expense controversies and other matters, damaging any Conservative claim to have made the second chamber better. After years of futile attempts, the government finally asked the Supreme Court of Canada to rule on the constitutionality of its incremental reforms; the Court ruled in 2014 that such changes could not proceed without provincial approval (unlikely, given the varying provincial stances on the Senate), effectively ending the Harper government's Senate reform agenda. By 2015, Harper wanted nothing to do with the Senate at all, refusing to fill any more vacancies and pledging he would not make any future appointments, though leaving unclear whether this was even constitutionally possible.

Thus, while ultimately failing, the Conservative attempt to reform the Senate – like the more radical ideas of Reform before it – challenged traditional understandings of Parliament, treating the institution as an object to be reshaped in its own right rather than a neutral terrain of struggle. Even more clearly, the Conservatives were willing to confront unwritten norms and traditions of Parliament, and whether this was only a continuation of past practices or something wholly different, they largely justified their actions through their electoral mandate. In doing so, they have may have permanently shifted understandings of parliamentary institutions and aspects such as coalition governments, access to documents, and other previously accepted norms.

Less clear is the purpose that these Conservative manipulations of Parliament were to serve. While Reform's attitude to parliamentary institutions was driven by Manning and the party's populist and idealistic visions of New Canada, what were the ideological ends for the Conservative government? To some degree the goals of Stephen Harper's manipulations of Parliament can be seen as consistent with Pond's "neoliberal" model and serving particular right-wing objectives, such as the refusal to release military documents. But unlike the Harris Conservatives in Ontario, for example, we do not see quite the same close alignment between an ideological policy agenda and its implementation through an aggressive parliamentary agenda – at least, no more than most other majority governments.

One explanation is circumstantial and path-dependent – that Harper's controlling ways stemmed from the circumstances of the first Conservative minority, with an inexperienced government and the perpetual threat of another election, and then never changed to accommodate new circumstances. This theory was noticeably advanced by some Conservatives after the 2015 defeat to explain where the party had gone wrong. In the words of one PMO staffer, "A lot of trust was placed in Stephen Harper and his staff's ability to navigate [the] uncertain Parliamentary waters [of minority government]," and this minority mentality of tight solidarity and central control continued even after the 2011 majority victory: "By then habits were too old and loved to die hard" (MacDougall 2015). Control no longer served the ends of power; it had become an end in itself. Another possible goal of the Conservative ideological reshaping of Parliament may have been to squeeze out the Liberal Party and realign Canadian politics into a two-party, left-right polarization (a long-time if ephemeral goal of both Preston Manning and his father Ernest Manning [Manning 1967]). For much of the Conservative era, the Liberals seemed less equipped to compete in the new, more confrontational and ideological sphere. In contrast, the NDP generally kept up with the Conservative approach. The New Democrats have long demonstrated high levels of party discipline and have historically been far less tormented than either the Liberals or conservatives (of all varieties) by the paradoxes of the logics of representation and governance. New Democrats appear to struggle far less with the dilemma of the individual MP than do members in other parties and have long called for abolishing the Senate entirely. The Conservative approach thus seemed to box the Liberals into a corner, with their more traditional approach to Parliament. Yet it was ultimately counterproductive, with Justin Trudeau's Liberals coming to power in 2015 in part through a backlash against the Conservatives' controlling ways.

The approach of Conservatives in power to Parliament remains, as with all elements of the Harper government, difficult to explain conclusively and open to various interpretations. Still, while its approach seems much more driven by the logic of governance rather than the Reform Party's logic of representation, both parties – conservatives out of power and in power – demonstrated a shared belief that Parliament was not just neutral terrain with predictable roles, as it was viewed by the Progressive Conservatives. Rather, Parliament was itself an objective to be reshaped in the party's own image and world view, and used as an ideological instrument to further the party's overall goals.

Conclusion

The future direction of Conservative approaches and attitudes to Parliament is difficult to discern. The above analysis has rested heavily on party leaders Manning and Harper (along with PC leaders and the interregnum under Stockwell Day). The question is, what will develop with the departure of Stephen Harper?

Will a new leader bring a new approach to the question of MPs and party discipline? It is unlikely that subsequent leaders will enjoy the re-markable loyalty and powers of control possessed by Stephen Harper, co-founder of the party and the leader who brought them out of the electoral wilderness. The stresses of a leadership race and years in op-position may lead to a more heterogeneous and open parliamentary caucus closer to the earlier brokerage era, and a return to the more tra-ditional discussion and agonizing over party discipline and the role of the individual MP (which of course has never gone away entirely). But serious enthusiasm for Reform-style direct democracy has dwindled to negligible levels in the party, though a leadership transition and re-building in opposition may provoke new interest.

More interesting will be future approaches to unwritten conven-tions. Most of the Conservative actions described above were driven by the minority government situation and being outnumbered in the House; fewer crises developed in the majority era. But it will be inter-esting to see, for example, whether future Conservative leaders (and those of other parties) are more willing to support the initiatives that have emerged arguing that Canada should follow the lead of other Westminster systems and codify previously unwritten conventions (Aucoin, Jarvis, and Turnbull 2011; Russell 2009). Harper and senior Conservatives displayed no interest in these movements to write rules down, but this may change. Less clear is whether Parliament has been permanently damaged by the abuse of prorogation, blocking of access to documents, and other problems – notwithstanding the Trudeau gov-ernment's promises of restoration.

Finally, while Preston Manning was not necessarily as committed as grassroots members were to the Triple-E formula, Senate reform was fundamental to the Reform Party program and identity. Stephen Harper delivered at least partly on this with his incremental proposals, though he was clearly unwilling to pursue them at any cost, and he offered no concrete solutions in the 2015 election. While the Trudeau government has pursued its own Senate reform agenda, the upper chamber no longer occupies the same primacy for conservatives that it did in the Reform or initial Conservative years. And overall, conservatives in both eras showed a striking willingness to use and reshape Parliament as an ideological instrument in which to further their long-term objectives, rather than a neutral terrain of struggle in which government and opposition have always known and played their roles.

REFERENCES

Aucoin, Peter, Mark D. Jarvis, and Lori Turnbull. 2011. *Democratizing the Constitution: Reforming Responsible Government.* Toronto: Emond Montgomery.

Axworthy, Thomas. 2008. *Parliamentary Reform: Everything Old Is New Again.* Kingston: Institute of Intergovernmental Relations.

Birch, Anthony. 1964. *Representative and Responsible Government: An Essay on the British Constitution.* Toronto: University of Toronto Press.

Carty, R.K., William Cross, and Lisa Young. 2000. *Rebuilding Canadian Party Politics.* Vancouver: University of British Columbia Press.

Curry, Bill, and Stuart Thompson. 2013. "Conservative MPs Break Ranks More Often Than Opposition." *Globe and Mail*, 3 February.

Docherty, David C. 1997. *Mr Smith Goes to Ottawa: Life in the House of Commons.* Vancouver: University of British Columbia Press.

Ellis, Faron. 2005. *The Limits of Participation: Activists and Leaders in Canada's Reform Party.* Calgary: University of Calgary Press.

Flanagan, Tom. 1995. *Waiting for the Wave: The Reform Party and Preston Manning.* Toronto: Stoddart.

– 2007. *Harper's Team: Behind the Scenes in the Conservative Rise to Power.* Montreal and Kingston: McGill-Queen's University Press.

Franks, C.E.S. 1987. *The Parliament of Canada.* Toronto: University of Toronto Press. http://dx.doi.org/10.3138/9781442678262.

– 1999. "Not Dead Yet But Should It Be Resurrected? The Canadian Senate." In *Senates: Bicameralism in the Contemporary World*, edited by C. Samuel Patterson and Anthony Mughan, 120–61. Columbus: Ohio State University Press.

Godbout, Jean-Francois, and Bjørn Hoyland. 2011. "Legislative Voting in the Canadian Parliament." *Canadian Journal of Political Science* 44 (2): 367–88. http://dx.doi.org/10.1017/S0008423911000175.

House of Commons. 2013. *Debates* (June 6). Ottawa.

Laghi, Brian. 2008. "Harper Buys Time: Coalition Firms Up." *Globe and Mail*, 29 November.

Laycock, David. 2002. *The New Right and Democracy in Canada: Understanding Reform and the Canadian Alliance*. Toronto: Oxford University Press.

Loewenberg, Gerhard. 2011. *On Legislatures: The Puzzle of Representation*. Boulder, CO: Paradigm Publishers.

MacDougall, Andrew. 2015. "Putting the PMO in Its Place." *Ottawa Citizen*, 30 October. http://ottawacitizen.com/opinion/columnists/macdougall-putting-the-pmo-in-its-place

Mallory, J.R. 1979. "Parliamentary Reform: Every Solution Creates a New Problem." *Journal of Canadian Studies / Revue d'études canadiennes* 14 (2): 26–34.

Malloy, Jonathan. 2002. *The "Responsible Government Approach" and Its Effect on Canadian Legislative Studies*. Ottawa: Canadian Study of Parliament Group.

– 2010. "The Drama of Parliament under Minority Government." In *How Ottawa Spends 2010–2011: Recession, Realignment and the New Deficit*, edited by G. Bruce Doern and Christopher Stoney, 31–48. Montreal and Kingston: McGill-Queen's University Press.

Manning, Ernest. 1967. *Political Realignment: A Challenge to Thoughtful Canadians*. Toronto: McClelland and Stewart.

Manning, Preston. 1992. *The New Canada*. Toronto: Macmillan.

Pond, David. 2005. "Imposing a Neo-Liberal Theory of Representation on the Westminster Model: A Canadian Case." *Journal of Legislative Studies* 11 (2): 170–93. http://dx.doi.org/10.1080/13572330500158599.

Reform Party of Canada. 1988. *Platform and Statement of Principles*.

– 1991. *Reform Party of Canada Principles and Policies*.

Russell, Peter H. 2008. *Two Cheers for Minority Government*. Toronto: Emond Montgomery Press.

– 2009. "Learning to Live With Minority Governments," in Russell and Sossin, *Parliamentary Government in Crisis*, 136–49.

Russell, Peter H., and Lorne Sossin, eds. 2009. *Parliamentary Government in Crisis*. Toronto: University of Toronto Press.

Smith, David E. 2013. *Across the Aisle: Opposition in Canadian Politics*. Toronto: University of Toronto Press.

Smith, Jennifer. 1999. "The Canadian House of Commons at the Turn of the Millennium." *Canadian Public Administration* 42 (4): 398–421.

– 2009. *The Democratic Dilemma: Reforming the Canadian Senate*. Kingston: Institute of Intergovernmental Relations, School of Policy Studies, Queen's University.

Wilson, Paul. 2015. "Minister's Caucus Advisory Committees under the Harper Government." *Canadian Public Administration* 58 (2): 227–48.

– 2016. "Harper and the House of Commons: An Evidence-Based assessment." In *The Harper Factor*, edited by Jennifer Ditchburn and Graham Fox, 27–43. Montreal and Kingston: McGill-Queen's University Press.

12 A Wolf in Wolf's Clothing: The Stephen Harper Ministry

J.P. LEWIS

After the swearing-in of his new Cabinet, in the fall of 2015 new Liberal Prime Minister Justin Trudeau proclaimed "Government by cabinet is back" (Authier 2015). Trudeau's declaration reflected a common sentiment of the almost decade of Conservative government where power was increasingly centralized in the Prime Minister's Office and Cabinet ministers were increasingly marginalized. However, Stephen Harper did not introduce centralization of power in the Prime Minister's Office to Canadian politics. Dating back to John A. Macdonald, all of Canada's prime ministers have been accused of centralization and control. Political historians, for example, routinely refer to an old political cartoon depicting Depression-era Prime Minister R.B. Bennett holding a Cabinet meeting by himself. Most observers argue that, all too often, Canadian prime ministers have assumed control over ministerial portfolios and provided Cabinet with "consensus" decisions, while keeping the majority of their ministers at arm's length; their closest unelected, political staffers, meanwhile, are always in the loop (Aucoin 1986; Bakvis 2000; Matheson 1976; Savoie 1999a; White 2005). Previous prime ministers have been compared to both presidents (Smith 1971) and dictators (Simpson 2001). Consequently, it is nothing new for detractors to point out the tendency for control and centralization under Harper. What is new is the *extent* of control and centralization. This chapter will discuss the prime minister and Cabinet in the former Conservative government with special attention to three questions:

1 Prime ministerial power: How did Stephen Harper centralize power in the Conservative government?

2 Ministerial power: How influential were Cabinet ministers in the
  Conservative government?
3 The political Cabinet: How did Stephen Harper use his Cabinet
  politically?

In the tradition of other long-serving contemporary Canadian prime
ministers (Trudeau, Mulroney, Chrétien), Stephen Harper has been
mythologized by exaggerating his most caricature-like traits. For his
admirers, he is the "Great Right Hope," the architect of the merged
Conservative Party, and the one responsible for bringing down the federal Liberal juggernaut. For his critics, he is a robotic, controlling ideo-
logue who made Canada unrecognizable by his style of government
and policy decisions. While neither of these portrayals is entirely ac-
curate, the popular depictions of Harper in his time as prime minister
have focused on control, paranoia, and increased partisanship (Harris
2014; Martin 2010; Wells 2013). As they did with his boyhood idol (and,
later, his political foil) Pierre Trudeau, most Canadians have a love-hate
relationship with Harper; for his opponents, he was not just viewed as
the leader of the party they did not support, he was the enemy and a
bully – an aggressor. He was seen not as a wolf in sheep's clothing like
previous long-serving prime ministers such as Jean Chrétien or Brian
Mulroney, whose autocratic ways were more nuanced, but as a wolf in
wolf's clothing – wearing his agenda and his choice for political practice openly for all to see. In fact, Harper was forthright about his philosophical approach to leadership: "'We obviously do want our team to
act together to inform each other of what we're saying and doing so
we're not caught by surprise. My 20 years in this business convinces me
that there are only two kinds of prime ministers, prime ministers that
are in control of their government and those that aren't. In either case
you're criticized but I'd rather be criticized on leading from strength
than leading from weakness'" (Doyle 2008b).
  The perception of a controlling centre was greatly helped by the
Conservative government's unprecedented approach to message control (see chapter 2 in this volume). The mainstream media were caught
in the crosshairs of this approach, and much of the Harper story was
played out through his office's ongoing battles with the parliamentary
press (see chapter 9 in this volume). In recent years, greater attention
has been paid to the centralization of power in Canadian politics, especially with former Liberal leader and prime minister Paul Martin,

and his pledge to battle the "democratic deficit" in the wake of the sponsorship scandal. While Martin never fulfilled his pledge and had his attempts hampered by the Liberals' minority government status, Harper quickly appeared to revert to the control-and-command model attached to Martin's predecessor, Jean Chrétien.

For early Reform Party supporters, it was not supposed to be this way. In the late 1980s and early 1990s, the party represented a break from the establishment Liberal and Progressive Conservative governments, which had held power since Confederation. The Reform Party proposed radical democratic additions to the Canadian polity, from an elected Senate to member recall to national referenda; many of the initial institutional policy ideas of the party challenged the power of the Canadian political executive and the appointment and law-making ability of the prime minister.

While Stephen Harper was a key player in the federal conservative movement before becoming leader of the Conservative party in 2003, Preston Manning was the driving force during the early Reform years. However, once Manning found himself in elected office, it was a struggle to stay true to his populist, anti-establishment roots while fulfilling the roles of party leader and leader of the official opposition. Manning's goal of reforming Canadian political institutions was quickly challenged. He attempted to construct the first Reform shadow cabinet after the 1993 federal election – an election that sent fifty-two Reform MPs to Ottawa. Manning wanted to do away with the idea of a shadow cabinet with traditional party critics and instead create committees of several members of Parliament to scrutinize the government on policy issues. The Reform's changes did not last long. By June 1994, the party had reverted to the traditional party critic system. The failure of the Reform Party's institutional reform attempts would foreshadow the party's gradual retreat from democratic and populist priorities. Eventually, as this chapter argues, this retreat would be complete, with the Conservative government abandoning most ideas that had led to the creation of the Reform Party in the first place.

While Preston Manning was the founding figure and enjoyed healthy support during the first decade of the party's existence, Stockwell Day, the first leader of the Reform Party's successor, the Canadian Alliance, was at the centre of a case study in a political party turning against its leader. In April 2001, less than a year after winning the party's leadership, thirteen members left the Canadian Alliance caucus in a major revolt against Day's leadership; together, the renegade group established the Democratic Representative Caucus (see chapter 11 in this volume) and eventually Harper defeated Day at a subsequent party leadership election in the spring of 2002. Two years later Harper was elected leader of the Conservative Party of Canada, a party created by the merger of the Canadian Alliance and the Progressive Conservatives. Unlike Day, Harper would never fall victim to inter-party strife, even though he led a party that was a merger of two distinctly separate political organizations. After an early conflict with Peter MacKay over rules governing the representation of riding associations from former Canadian Alliance and Progressive Conservative members, a relative calm between the two camps emerged (Johnson 2005). Both Day and MacKay would end up as key ministers in Harper's Cabinet.

Throughout the 1990s the Progressive Conservative Party also followed a populist approach to the Canadian political executive. After its defeat in 1993, the party proposed reforms to the Prime Minister's Office. Part of Jean Charest's platform during the 1995 PC leadership race included a renewal to democracy and accountability within the party, turning the page on the years of Mulroney's "unaccountable, uncommunicative advisors" (Gessell 1995). The PCs' attempt to reinvigorate their brand was introduced at the party's 1995 convention "Jump Start," and was based on the familiar Reform mantra of bottom-up policymaking (Blanchfield 1995).

Throughout the 1990s and early 2000s, both federal conservative parties attempted to capitalize on populist sentiments by introducing platform proposals that challenged the power of the prime minister. The ideas expressed in the Reform Party's 1993 federal election platform are found throughout PC, Reform, and Canadian Alliance and Conservative parties' platforms up to the 2006 federal election, when the Conservatives eventually took office. Table 12.1 presents the parties' positions on five proposals that challenge the powers of the first minister.

As table 12.1 shows, while divided on issues of referenda, fixed election dates, and an elected Senate, the federal conservative parties pre-merger supported curtailing the prime minister's appointment powers and giving more votes to members of Parliament. Nevertheless, once in power, the Conservative government did little to challenge prime ministerial power. The government unsuccessfully pursued reform to judicial and Senate appointment processes. As well, while the government passed fixed election date legislation, the government broke this law in 2008 and again in 2011 when Harper forced an election before the

Table 12.1. Party Platform and Challenges to PM Power

	PM appointment power	Referendum	Free votes / more power to MPs	Fixed election dates	Elected Senate
Reform 1993		•	•	•	•
PC 1993	•		•		
Reform 1997	•	•	•		•
PC 1997	•				
CA 2000	•	•	•	•	•
PC 2000	•		•		•
Conservative 2004	•		•	•	•
Conservative 2006	•		•	•	•

fixed date. Finally, in October 2015, the government would follow the legislated fixed election date.

While Canadian prime ministers enjoy astonishing power, it is hedged by a moderate Canadian political culture and a prime minister's desire to be re-elected; exhibiting dictatorial behaviour can sour the electorate against an incumbent party. With the power to appoint judges, ministers, senators, the governor-general, deputy ministers, and ambassadors, combined with the ability to whip their caucus into passing any bill into law, prime ministers could all act like dictators, but significantly, they do not. Donald Savoie (2005), an expert on executive power in Canada, observed, "Like tigers that do not easily part with their stripes, those who hold effective power see little reason to part with it or even attenuate its scope" (17). In many ways, Harper kept those traditional stripes as he retained and gained his prime ministerial power.

Prime Ministerial Power: How Did Stephen Harper Centralize Power in the Conservative Government?

As the previous section has outlined, the office of the prime minister provides a number of tools to centralize power in the Prime Minister's Office (PMO) and marginalize the influence of other political actors, including members of Parliament, Cabinet ministers, and the public service. Harper changed a number of the common practices abided by previous prime ministers in their approach to the political executive. Internal institutional reforms under the Conservative government include abandoning the designation of a deputy prime minister, drop-ping Senate representation in Cabinet, and expanding what is cov-ered under Cabinet confidences. Most prime ministers have included deputy prime ministers in their Cabinets (e.g., Donald Mazankowski – Mulroney Cabinet; Sheila Copps – Chrétien Cabinet), and the lead-ers of the government in the Senate (e.g., Lowell Murray – Mulroney Cabinet; Jack Austin – Martin Cabinet). Harper did not name a deputy prime minister in his first Cabinet and never subsequently assumed the practice. He initially appointed senators to Cabinet, including the powerful Marjory LeBreton, but ended the practice soon after the Mike Duffy/Pamela Wallin/Patrick Brazeau Senate spending scandal be-gan. Ending previous practices that may have shared decision-making and influence with other political actors reflects indications that power is centralizing. While the internal reforms were significant, Harper's changes to external communications and access have received the most attention. Harper and the PMO implemented a number of communica-tion control policies, including withholding Cabinet meeting schedules and removing the microphone outside the Cabinet meeting room for press availability of ministers. Even when the press discovered when Cabinet was meeting, there was no opportunity to ask questions of ministers when their discussions had ended. Previous governments not only provided the press with Cabinet meeting schedules, they also pro-vided opportunity for media scrums, a practice that the new Trudeau government quickly resumed. Beyond avoiding spontaneous press questioning, under Harper, ministers were expected to vet national me-dia interview requests with the PMO.

Communications management was a central theme of the Harper Cabinet from the beginning. The elevated levels of message control were introduced by the PMO during the first few months in govern-ment – ministers were directed to focus on the five priorities from the election campaign and vet media contact and public statements with the PMO. Other actions were considered to be crucial to avoiding mes-saging mistakes experienced by the Reform Party and Canadian Alli-ance. Early in the first mandate, Harper sent a warning through his Chief of Staff, Ian Brodie, that sanctions would be levied against mem-bers who contradicted or embarrassed the government (Panetta 2006).

Harper's approach to political communications was formed by ob-serving the gaffes, media leaks, and problematic statements made by the Reform and Canadian Alliance parties. Before taking office, Harper witnessed numerous attempts by leaders to control their caucuses and the party's message. Of all the leadership examples he drew on, Harper followed the path of Liberal Prime Minister Jean Chrétien and aimed to avoid the political management issues that plagued Manning, Day, and Martin. Paul Martin's struggle to clearly communicate his agenda to the public (the *Economist* referred to him as "Mr Dithers" [2005]) would directly inform the approach of the Conservative government. As one former PMO staffer noted, "In opposition we [were] watching Martin's cabinet meetings and the ministers [were] scrumming after cabinet meetings and whatever message the government had that day [was] gone by the time the media [got] a hold of it." The staffer went on to say, "I remember sitting with Harper and saying 'If we form government or when we form government this is never going to happen. We are going to be in control of the message to the extent a government can'" (interview with author). Much of the message control was done by exempt staff in the PMO. Exempt staff provide ministers with political advice, do not play a role in the operations of the minister's department, and are "exempt" from controls dictated by the Public Service Commission (Privy Council Office 2011).

The exempt, unelected, partisan staff in the Prime Minister's Office are the target of much of the centralization criticism. Donald Savoie (1999a, 1999b, 2008, 2013) has argued that PMO staff have an influential role in government – in many cases more powerful than most of the Cabinet. Harper was no exception. Political advisors within the PMO played a major role in shaping the politics and policy of the Conservative government. Director of Communications Dimitri Soudas was noted for not only ending media access to Cabinet ministers before and after Cabinet meetings, but also playing a major role in advocating for the government's targeting of ethnic media (Persichilli 2011). Chief of Staff Guy Giorno was especially important in implementing disciplined government. He had a history with some ministers because of his previous work in the same role for Ontario Premier Mike Harris. Harris's Cabinet included influential Harper ministers Jim Flaherty, Tony Clement, and John Baird. In Ontario, Giorno had run a disciplined office; Flaherty and others were thus accustomed to (and approved) his style, making it easier to adopt this same approach in the Conservative government (Naumetz 2009).

The disciplined approach routinely marginalized Cabinet ministers. PMO communications officers became integral players in the Conservative government. As one former minister noted, "[The] PMO controls everything – you have a press conference [planned] for weeks and it can be cancelled the day before because Harper wants to make an announcement" (interview with author). As mentioned earlier, the government's strict communications approach began as soon as the party took power. Soon after the Conservatives formed government in 2006, a leak to the *Globe and Mail* disclosed a communications plan that included the policy that all communications must get PMO approval (Campbell 2006). The PMO's omnipresence in the lives of Cabinet ministers quickly became the norm. Government officials referred to "The Full Langevin" (a reference to the Ottawa building where the PMO offices are found), to describe when a minister is in enough trouble that the PMO and Privy Council Office (PCO) take over the file from the minister and his department (Wells 2009). At times, the PMO's control spilled over into more trivial or meddling concerns, including encouraging ministerial staff to not join Facebook and stay away from the popular Ottawa pub known for political gossip and gadflies, D'Arcy McGee's (Rana 2007). Adding to the centralization has been the increased involvement of the Privy Council Office (PCO), the secretariat to Cabinet and the coordinating department for all of federal government. Some suggest that, under Harper, the PCO moved from a simple supportive role to one that was much more involved (Harris 2014).

While guiding ministers and staff is one method of control and discipline, a more direct method involved the PMO simply staffing the ministers' offices themselves. Most power struggles and conflicts take place between staff in different offices, rather than politicians, and having one of your own (a PMO-appointed staffer) in a minister's office makes this process much more seamless for the PMO (interview with author). Adding to the difficulty of being out of power for so long and the fragility of job security in a minority government, the ministers also had to negotiate the new Federal Accountability Act, which made it more difficult to convince individuals to take a job knowing there was a waiting period of five years to take on work lobbying the government. After the 2011 federal election, the Conservative staff pool was down to around 200 to fill 400 to 500 positions (Shane 2011). Still, while previous PMOs have had some involvement in ministerial staff hiring, the Conservative PMO not only vetted most hires, but also placed a number of former PMO staff in ministerial offices (especially after the 2011 federal election), and in some cases the PMO threatened ministers to either find new chiefs of staff or resign from Cabinet (Devlin Marier 2007). By February 2014, 75 per cent of ministers had former PMO staff working in their offices. PMO deputy chief of staff for issues management, Keith

Beardsley, called it an "operational advantage" (Ryckewaert 2014b). One specific example of the PMO staffing a minister's office occurred when Rona Ambrose encountered problems as environment minister and the PMO replaced her chief of staff with Harper's legislative assistant Bruce Carson (Simpson, Jaccard, and Rivers 2008). When ministers were not being controlled by staffing decisions, they were most likely controlled by decisions from staff. Few federal governments have been as branded or scripted as the Conservative government under Stephen Harper, and much of this approach was implemented by PMO and ministerial staff (Marland and Flanagan 2013). Much of the branding and scripting was achieved through unprecedented control over the media's access to ministers.

The theme of restricting access also extended to Cabinet meetings. Previous governments have generally always allowed the media time with ministers, particularly after meetings of the full Cabinet. Harper was quick to put an end to this practice, arguing that "meetings of cabinet are private. It's a constitutional thing" (Doyle 2006). The press routinely complained that any information requests directed at ministers' offices were met with no response by phone or email, and that ministers routinely declined phone, television, or in-person interviews. As Michael Harris notes in his book on Harper and the Conservative government, "It [the government's media strategy] came down to three words: less is more. 'No comment' was often a winning strategy" (2014, 77).

The Conservative government restricted access to the political executive in a number of other ways as well, including:

- Harper did not use the MPs' front entrance to the Centre Block of Parliament, as has been the tradition of other prime ministers.
- Harper did not use the National Press Theatre for press conferences (as of 2015, he had not used it for five years) (Ryckewaert 2014a).
- On trips abroad, Harper stopped holding regular scrums with the travelling press.
- Harper stopped the tradition of the PM attending the Annual Press Gallery Dinner when the Conservatives formed government in 2006.
- The PMO introduced a list system where reporters would put their name on a list and the PMO would decide what questions to take (leading to a May 2006 walkout of reporters from a press conference).

- The PMO did not issue an official press release or provide media availability in March 2014 when three Cabinet ministers were sworn into new positions, instead circulating footage of the event on the PMO's "24 Seven" YouTube channel (see chapter 9 in this volume).

Many observers suggest that the disciplined approach to government was simply an extension of Harper's personality (Martin 2010; Harris 2014). Harper defended his media strategy: "They [the public] expect the Prime Minister to do his job. They don't expect the Prime Minister to aspire to be a media star as an end in itself" (Harper 2007). Other factors help explain this atypical approach to political communications by the government. Two major ones were the inexperience of Harper's front bench and the advent of governing in a Web 2.0 environment, defined by twenty-four-hour news cycles, new social media, and ever-changing communications technology. A disciplined strategy may be the only choice for governments who hope to sustain their message to voters and implement their agenda in this new technological landscape. In the communications strategy the Conservative government adopted, power was more centralized and ministers became more marginalized. The following section will discuss ways in which Conservative Cabinet ministers lost power and influence in the federal government.

Ministerial Power: How Influential Were Cabinet Ministers in the Conservative Government?

While a few high-profile ministers played significant policy and po-litical roles in the Conservative government, for the most part Cabinet ministers were rarely visible on the public stage, except to make strate-gically planned policy and spending announcements. Reporter Jacques Bourbeau described the Cabinet ministers who never walked the pub-licly accessible hallways in Centre Block and avoid being scrummed as "the ghosts of Parliament Hill" (*Hill Times* 2014). The "ghosts" of Harper's Cabinet also followed an increasing trend of decreasing min-isterial influence. While academics have been concerned about the marginalization of ministers before Jean Chrétien (Smith 1971; Aucoin 1986), Donald Savoie's research in the 1990s on Chrétien's Cabinet placed new attention on the phenomenon. In his 1999 *Governing from the Centre*, Savoie compared Cabinet to a focus group. Two prime min-isters later, Savoie argued, "Cabinet decision making is dead" (in Doyle

2008a); "How does cabinet now operate? It is no longer clear that it has much standing even as a focus group" (Savoie 2013, 75).

Unbeknownst to most Canadians, the Conservative Cabinet almost never held meetings. The full ministry did not hold weekly meetings like previous federal Cabinets (e.g., the full Chrétien Cabinet met for two hours every week). These were abandoned soon after the Conservatives formed the government in 2006 (Doyle 2006). Demonstrating the importance of communications strategy and management to the government, the times when the most Cabinet ministers congregated was during the PMO-led preparation in the hour before Question Period. When the full Cabinet did meet, it was normally at "retreats" or for tasks such as approving appointments. The part of Cabinet that did meet every week was the powerful Priorities and Planning (P&P) Committee, which was chaired by Harper. At P&P, decisions made by the rest of the Cabinet committee system were ratified by select groups of Cabinet ministers who held committee membership.

The Conservative government also made Cabinet meetings less meaningful in other, more inconspicuous ways. The government made changes to the Memoranda to Cabinet (information packages provided to ministers on issues at hand) by eliminating the background/analysis sections of the documents (Rubin 2014). The removal of this information denied Cabinet ministers additional content that can contribute to debate and discussion at Cabinet meetings. Another document the Conservative government changed was the ministers' mandate letters. Mandate letters are written by the PMO and signed by the prime minister and act as a task list for ministers. Under Harper, mandate letters provided much more detailed lists of what ministers need to accomplish (Ivison 2007). The more specific the mandate letter, the less policy freedom and political manoeuvring a Cabinet minister will enjoy.

A common complaint about autocratic governance is the act of prime ministers undercutting their Cabinet ministers. A classic example and often-told tale was Pierre Trudeau's significant economic announcement at a 1978 conference in Bonn without Minister of Finance Jean Chrétien's knowledge. Later, Chrétien did it himself when he announced his own national emissions target after sending Environment Minister Christine Stewart and Natural Resources Minister Ralph Goodale to the Kyoto conference on climate change. Harper's own move came when he announced the government's intention to support the Bloc Québécois motion to recognize Quebec as a nation without informing his minister of intergovernmental affairs, Michael Chong, about the position. Chong disagreed with the decision and resigned from Cabinet – the only resignation on a matter of principle that Harper would have to confront. In fact, the number of public disagreements and mixed messaging between Harper and his ministers is short enough that they can be listed here:

- Peter MacKay: Criticized the Conservative Party's handling of Brian Mulroney in 2009 when caucus members were told to cut ties to the embattled PM
- Jim Flaherty: Publicly supported disgraced Toronto Mayor Rob Ford in 2013 as the Conservative Party distanced itself, disagreed with Harper on the government's income-splitting tax policy in 2014
- Jason Kenney: Spoke publicly in support of Nigel Wright in 2013 after he was fired for his involvement in alleged payments to Senator Mike Duffy to cover expense costs

Other public disagreements seem to fall into Harper's strategic handling of moral issues files, where he allowed ministers to vote with their conscience on bills or motions the prime minister knew would not pass (Restoration of Traditional Marriage, December 2006 – six ministers; studying the point at which a fetus becomes a human being, September 2012 – eight ministers).

MP Brent Rathgeber who left the caucus to sit as an independent argued, "In recent years, cabinets, ceasing to be deliberative bodies, have become increasingly merely ornamental. The members are chosen because of the demographic they represent and their role is reduced to the equivalent of the prime minister's cipher" (2014, 99). In terms of individual ministers' influence, in Harper's Cabinet there were two types of ministers. There were substantive, influential, and visible ministers and there were representative, marginal, and relatively unknown ministers. Since 2006, the latter group has been much greater in number than the former. In the early days of the Conservative government an unusual mix of former PCs, Red Tories, and fiscal conservatives were described as powerful ministers – Jim Prentice, Jim Flaherty, John Baird, Rob Nicholson, Maxime Bernier, Peter Van Loan, and Senator Marjory LeBreton. This "inner circle" remained relatively unchanged. While Prentice left for the private sector in 2010 and Flaherty and Baird resigned in 2014 and 2015, the elevation of ministers Tony Clement, Jason Kenney, and Rona Ambrose seamlessly filled the roles as the public faces of Cabinet. Not surprisingly, because of his portfolio, Minister of

Finance Jim Flaherty was regularly viewed as the most powerful minister. In fact, Flaherty may not have become the third longest-serving finance minister had he not threatened to quit Cabinet in 2007 when Harper wanted to move him to the Industry portfolio (Carson 2014).

One of the more public examples of Cabinet ministers' diminishing influence was in Question Period, where ministers increasingly did not answer questions from the opposition. While the House of Commons Procedures Compendium does give ministers the option to "provide an answer, defer an answer, explain briefly why an answer cannot be provided at that time or say nothing," the Conservative government was especially reluctant to let ministers stand and respond in the House. The government's strategy was to designate one point person to answer questions, even if it did not apply to his responsibilities or himself individually. During the week that Foreign Affairs Minister Maxime Bernier was called to resign and grilled for leaving sensitive documents behind at a girlfriend's apartment, House leader Peter Van Loan took the brunt of the fire, answering 129 questions (Wherry 2008). In June 2008, the *Hill Times* completed an analysis of Question Period from 1 May to 10 June – House Leader Van Loan answered 244 of 933 questions asked by the opposition (Doyle and Thompson 2008).

While the public presence of Cabinet ministers may clearly be on the wane, there may be hope for powerful ministers behind closed doors in the unsung Cabinet committee system. Cabinet committees are permanent or ad hoc groups created by the prime minister to support Cabinet planning and decision-making. Regular use of the committee system began in the 1940s, but it was not until the 1970s when Pierre Trudeau experimented with a complex committee system (White 2005). Since Trudeau, each prime minister has continued with the Cabinet committee system to varying degrees. For Stephen Harper, his committee system was dominated by the familiar faces of ministers the Conservative government allowed to develop public personas. The two committees of consequence were Priorities and Planning (P&P) and Operations. P&P included the chairs of all the lower committees with the big picture direction of the government. The Operations Committee was also seen as powerful and dealt with legislative affairs, daily communications, and issues management. As one former PMO staffer noted, "His [Harper] P&P committee is his Cabinet. The full formal Cabinet only meets rarely and only mainly to approve appointments or have some sort of round table to discuss where we are – I would say it meets every second or third month, mainly to deal with appointments" (interview with author). While Chrétien had dropped the Priorities and Planning Committee, Harper followed Martin's reintroduction of the powerful Cabinet committee. As table 12.2 shows, Harper's Priorities and Planning Committee was dominated by familiar faces. Considering the marginalization of Cabinet, this is an especially exclusive club: between 2006 and 2015 only twenty-seven of sixty-seven ministers served on P&P and only five of eighteen female Cabinet ministers. In addition to P&P, the powerful Operations Committee was chaired by three powerful ministers – Jim Prentice (February 2006 to November 2010), John Baird (November 2010 to April 2011), and Jason Kenney (April 2011 to October 2015).

While Stephen Harper's predecessors contributed to the centralization of power in the Canadian political executive, changes he and his government made increased this centralization. Ending regular full Cabinet meetings and placing an emphasis on the Priorities and Planning Committee reduced the majority of ministers' roles as decision-makers for the government. As well, under the Conservative government, institutional checks on power such as Question Period were relegated to a communications exercise where ministers were less and less responsive to the questions of the opposition. The accumulation of these changes was damaging to Cabinet as an institution, but as the following section will explain, follow a clear political strategy of Stephen Harper and the Conservative government.

The Political Cabinet: How Did Stephen Harper Use His Cabinet Politically?

From the outset, Harper used Cabinet, its internal construction and external presentation, as a political tool to internally manage the challenges of a newly merged party and externally to continue to steal electoral support from the hegemonic Liberal Party. For example, in 2006 Harper's first Cabinet included appointments that surprised long-time political observers and frustrated Reform-era Conservatives. To address his shortage of big city ministers, Harper appointed Liberal MP David Emerson (Vancouver) as minister of international trade, and campaign co-chair (and unelected) Michael Fortier (Montreal) as minister of public works. The appointments were in direct contrast to the populist values, including opposition to government floor-crossing and unelected senators, that the Reform Party was built on. While Emerson's floor-crossing and Fortier's appointment to Senate and Cabinet drew a lot

Table 12.2. Priorities and Planning Committee Membership

February 2006	January 2007	August 2007	October 2008	May 2011	July 2013
John Baird	John Baird	John Baird	John Baird	John Baird	*Rona Ambrose*
Maxime Bernier	Maxime Bernier	Maxime Bernier	Lawrence Cannon	Tony Clement	John Baird
Lawrence Cannon	Lawrence Cannon	Lawrence Cannon	Tony Clement	**John Duncan**	Tony Clement
Stockwell Day	**Tony Clement**	Tony Clement	Stockwell Day	*Diane Finley*	Ed Fast
Jim Flaherty	Stockwell Day	Stockwell Day	Jim Flaherty	Jim Flaherty	*Diane Finley*
Marjory LeBreton	Jim Flaherty	**David Emerson**	*Marjory LeBreton*	**Jason Kenney**	Jim Flaherty
Peter MacKay	*Marjory LeBreton*	Jim Flaherty	Peter MacKay	Denis Lebel	***Shelley Glover***
Jim Prentice	Peter MacKay	*Marjory LeBreton*	**Christian Paradis**	*Marjory LeBreton*	Jason Kenney
Chuck Strahl	**Rob Nicholson**	Peter MacKay	Jim Prentice	Peter MacKay	Denis Lebel
Vic Toews	Jim Prentice	Jim Prentice	Chuck Strahl	**James Moore**	*Marjory LeBreton*
	Chuck Strahl	Vic Toews	Vic Toews	Christian Paradis	Peter MacKay
	Vic Toews		*Josée Verner*	Vic Toews	James Moore
					Rob Nicholson
					Christian Paradis
					Gerry Ritz
					Bernard Valcourt
		June 2008, Bernier leaves Cabinet, ***Josée Verner*** joins and **Michael Fortier** joins until October 2008	August 2010, ***Diane Finley*** joins November 2010, Prentice leaves Cabinet	February 2013, Duncan leaves Cabinet and **Ed Fast** joins	July 2013, *LeBreton* leaves Cabinet March 2014, Flaherty leaves Cabinet and **Joe Oliver** joins February 2015, Baird leaves Cabinet

Source: "Cabinet Committees 1979 to Date," Parliament of Canada, http://www.parl.gc.ca/ParlInfo/compilations/FederalGovernment/CommitteeCabinet.aspx

Note: **Bold** denotes new addition, *italic* denotes female minister

of attention, many long-time Western MPs from the Reform/Canadian Alliance days were left out in favour of Central Canadian MPs who had just recently joined the federal conservatives – bypassing former Reform/Canadian Alliance stalwarts Jay Hill and Diane Ablonczy and handing significant portfolios to former provincial Progressive Conservatives Jim Flaherty and John Baird. Harper placated some of the concerns of the old guard with Cabinet appointments – appointing eight of the thirty-three members of his first Canadian Alliance shadow cabinet to the front benches at some point in the Conservative government (Diane Ablonczy, Stockwell Day, John Duncan, Rob Merrifield, James Moore, Gerry Ritz, Monte Solberg, and Vic Toews).

Harper's initially trimmed thirty-member Cabinet (nine fewer than Martin's Cabinet) was a nod to populist concerns about government size and followed a tradition of PMs naming small first Cabinets (Mulroney – twenty-eight; Campbell – twenty-five; Chrétien – twenty-two, with eight secretaries of state). The idea of a small Cabinet is sold mainly on its political merits and it is difficult to assess whether a small, medium, or large Cabinet leads to more effective governance. Still, a common trend is that Cabinets grow as governments remain in power, in response to new representational concerns and restless backbenchers waiting for promotion. As figure 12.1 shows, on this front Harper was no different.

Contributing to the growth of Harper's Cabinet was the somewhat enigmatic position of secretary of state/minister of state. Harper initially continued the Chrétien practice of naming secretaries of state, but in December 2008 Harper named eleven ministers of state – not full members of Cabinet, but still members of the ministry. While not a member of full Cabinet, the minister of state is still a perk for MPs, as it comes with a better salary, office budget, car allowance, and driver (Macleod 2008). For a PM, these peripheral Cabinet appointments allow for more cover from collective Cabinet responsibility, creating an even more disciplined caucus and belief from backbenchers that someday, they too could end up as a minister. After Harper's 2013 Cabinet shuffle he could lay claim to having the most women in Cabinet in history (twelve). However, many of these appointments were to marginal Cabinet portfolios.

Within this larger Cabinet, Harper was politically strategic with his promotions, demotions, and overall Cabinet composition. As the previous section suggested, Harper definitely had his favourites, and these favourites were used as fixers through targeted Cabinet appointments.

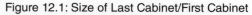

Figure 12.1: Size of Last Cabinet/First Cabinet

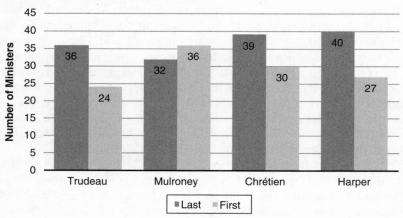

While Jim Flaherty was Harper's steady hand at finance for eight years (he was the longest-serving minister in one portfolio in Harper's Cabinet and the third-longest-serving finance minister after William Fielding and Paul Martin – eight years, one month, and twelve days), John Baird and Jim Prentice in the early years and Jason Kenney in the later years were key ministers assigned to deliver policies or clean up troubled portfolios. Baird began his time in Cabinet as president of the Treasury Board, ushering through the new Federal Accountability Act, only to be moved to the Environment portfolio to replace what was viewed as an ineffective Rona Ambrose. In Environment, Baird led the government's opposition to the Kyoto Protocol and then moved to Transport, Infrastructure, and Communities to help with implementation and communications on the government response to the 2008 global recession, "Canada's Economic Action Plan." Jim Prentice filled a similar fixer role. Starting his time in the contentious portfolio of Aboriginal Affairs, Prentice played a significant part in the government's reversal of the previous Liberal government's Kelowna Accord. After his time in Aboriginal Affairs, Prentice was strategically moved to Industry and then Environment in efforts of the government to demonstrate policy priorities. While it was difficult to be elevated to be one of Harper's rising Cabinet stars, oddly it was equally difficult to end up in Harper's public doghouse.

While many rightfully accuse Harper of controlling or silencing ministers, his nine-year record as Cabinet boss suggests he gave ministers a relatively long leash. Of course, this forgiveness can easily be seen as protecting the government's brand rather than defending government ministers. A number of senior ministers emerged unscathed from political scandal: Peter MacKay (government helicopter ride from a private salmon camp in Newfoundland), Lisa Raitt (describing the isotope shortage crisis as a "sexy story" because it involved cancer), John Baird (connections with embattled Ottawa Mayor Larry O'Brien), Jason Kenney (questionable fundraising letter), Tony Clement (comments on Sudbury's Inco and G20 spending in his Muskoka-area riding). Others have been returned to Cabinet after previous Cabinet resignations from scandals (Maxime Bernier and John Duncan).

Harper's first Cabinet firing over a political scandal was Maxime Bernier and came after almost two and a half years in government in May 2008. Table 12.3 displays the Conservative government's political scandal Cabinet resignations in comparison to the Mulroney and Chrétien governments. Bernier's fatal mistake was embarrassing the government by leaving sensitive Cabinet documents at the home of a former girlfriend who had ties to the Hells Angels. Oddly, another high-profile exit from Harper's Cabinet involved links to shady individuals. In April 2010, Harper not only removed Helena Guergis from Cabinet and caucus but also called in the police. Harper was responding to allegations (of which the specifics were never revealed) that allegedly implicated herself and husband, former member of Parliament Rahim Jaffer, to unseemly behaviour. Guergis would eventually be cleared of any wrongdoing (LeBlanc 2010).

Even though the Bernier and Guergis affairs were filled with lurid details of sex and a criminal underworld, the Bev Oda resignation could have contributed most to damaging the Conservative brand. For a party whose initial success was built on promoting accountability in Ottawa and fighting government waste, Oda's stories of $1,000 per day luxury cars and $16 glasses of orange juice were troubling for Conservative supporters. As an example of what type of behaviour could bring a minister down in the Conservative government, it was the spending scandal and not a more policy-related scandal that led to Oda's resignation. In 2009, Bev Oda altered documents concerning the funding of a church-based aid group, Kairos, by the Canadian International Development Agency. Oda added the word *not* to a document that had

Table 12.3. "Scandal" Resignations

Mulroney (1984–93)		Chrétien (1993–2003)		Harper (2006–15)	
1985	Robert Coates John Fraser Marcel Masse	1998	Andy Scott	2008	Maxime Bernier
1986	Sinclair Stevens	2002	Art Eggleton Lawrence MacAulay	2010	Helena Guergis
1987	Andre Bissonnette Roch La Salle			2012	Bev Oda
1988	Michel Côté			2013	John Duncan Peter Penashue
1989	Bernard Valcourt				
1990	Jean Charest				
1991	Alan Redway				

Source: "Ministerial Resignations," Parliament of Canada,
http://www.parl.gc.ca/parlinfo/Compilations/FederalGovernment/MinisterialResignations
.aspx

already been signed and approved. This incident was let pass, while Oda's expenses were not.

While Harper was reluctant to let ministers resign, he did demote ministers who had been perceived to be struggling in their portfolios: January 2007, Rona Ambrose was demoted from Environment to Intergovernmental Affairs and Western Diversification; August 2007, Gordon O'Connor from Defence to Revenue; October 2008, Gary Lunn from Natural Resources to minister of state for sport; and Julian Fantino from Veterans Affairs to associate minister of defence in January 2015.

Based on polling around Cabinet scandals in the Conservative government, it could be argued that the resignations did not damage support for the government. Table 12.4 shows the trace amounts of change found in support for the government in opinion polling before and after Cabinet scandal resignations.

From these polling numbers, one might conclude that Harper handled his worst cases of Cabinet controversy, where there was no option but ministerial resignation, with reasonable success. Even in the latter half of the Conservative government's third mandate, political scandal did not befall Conservative Cabinet ministers but rather Conservative senators and staff. As the final section will discuss, the political success

Table 12.4. Polling after Cabinet Scandals

Minister	Date of resignation	CPC support before (%)	CPC support after (%)	Change (%)
Maxime Bernier	26 May 2008	34.0	32.0	-2.0
Helena Guergis	9 April 2010	33.2	31.5	-1.7
Bev Oda	3 July 2012	32.6	35.4	+2.8
John Duncan	15 February 2013	35.1	31.3	-3.8
Peter Penashue	14 March 2013	31.5	30.2	-1.3
AVERAGE CHANGE				-1.2

Sources: Numbers for support before and after from "Federal Monthly Poll Averages," 308.com, except for Bernier where Strategic Council polls are used.

of Harper's Cabinet management rarely coincided with democratic improvement to these institutions. Conventions such as ministerial responsibility will continue to erode as long as prime ministers' political choices to not abide by these conventions are politically successful. As political success is found in these precedents, long-term damage to political institutions such as Cabinet is unavoidable.

Conclusion

In 1997, while heading the conservative advocacy group the National Citizens Coalition, Stephen Harper co-wrote an essay with University of Calgary political science professor and Reform Party strategist Tom Flanagan. In "Our Benign Dictatorship" the authors lamented the decline of Canadian political institutions under the federal Liberal government: "Although we think of ourselves as living in a mature democracy, we live, instead, in something little better than a benign dictatorship, not under a strict one-party rule, but under a one-party-plus system beset by the factionalism, regionalism and cronyism that accompany any such system" (Harper and Flanagan 1997, 34). Ten years later, *Globe and Mail* columnist Jeffrey Simpson wrote, "Ask yourself this: How many ministers can I name? If you get above three, you receive a medal" (2007). Simpson's question reflects the view that Harper did not depart much from his predecessors and in many cases heightened autocracy and centralization in federal politics. Outside of Cabinet management, Harper added to Simpson's view, being accused of abusing his power as prime minister by proroguing Parliament in 2008 and 2009, and calling a snap election in 2008 after having introduced fixed-date election legislation the previous year. As mentioned earlier in the chapter, Harper is not the only prime minister to be accused of abusing the office's tremendous powers. One of Harper's recent predecessors, Jean Chrétien prorogued Parliament in 2003 and called snap elections in 1997 and 2000. Still, few of the directions in which Harper has taken the office of the prime minister or the Cabinet would have been popular with the Reform, Canadian Alliance, or even Progressive Conservative opposition caucuses and leadership. While in the aftermath of the 2015 Conservative defeat many inside the party complained that the tone of the government had led to their downfall, Harper still had come close to a fourth government mandate. If the further growth of power in the Prime Minister's Office and marginalization of Cabinet and Cabinet ministers is true, then the important question that emerges is "How did Harper get away with it?" Although there is no single answer to this question, there are a few reasons why this trend continues, regardless of increased attention, scrutiny, and criticism. The reasons are listed below.

The Political Capital of Stephen Harper

As is mentioned often in this book, at the very least Stephen Harper has been an exceptionally successful politician. Harper's undeniable success was built on a series of achievements: (1) merging the Canadian Alliance and Progressive Conservative parties, (2) reducing the Liberal Party to a minority government, (3) forming a Conservative minority government, and (4) forming a Conservative majority government. Since Harper ran a "hub and spoke" operation, he was the face and rightful claimant to the party's success and its subsequent failures. The achievements of the Conservative Party were made without a clear lieutenant (no Paul Martin who served as Jean Chrétien's powerful finance minister) or formidable caucus or advisor (in almost a decade as prime minister, Harper had four chiefs of staff and nine directors of communications). Notwithstanding branding efforts, the Conservative Government *was* the Harper Government. Harper could pull power and influence to the centre because his political success supported his institutional actions to those most directly affected – his caucus and Cabinet.

The Evolution and Triangulation of Political Communication in Canada

In their 2014 edited collection, *Political Communications in Canada*, Alex Marland and colleagues argue that a "triangulation of political communication" has taken place. The triangulation includes: (1) the intensity of partisanship found in the communications of Canadian political institutions, (2) the new 24/7 news cycle's impact on communication, and (3) the effect of Canada's regional dimension on messaging. The three developments lead to new tactics and strategies of political communication that are best suited to message control, which leads to the concentration of power in a central place – the Prime Minister's Office. The often-noted Message Event Proposal (the communications tool that helped the government vet and script public events to help them stay on message [Blanchfield and Bronskill 2010]) and vetting of Cabinet minister press conferences, interviews, and media availability were products of new communication strategies built in response to the changing environment of Canadian politics. The courtiers who surround prime ministers once described by Donald Savoie are now less about presenting policy advice and more about delivering public relations strategies.

The Rise of the "One Member, One Vote" Leadership Convention

By embracing the leadership selection of "one member, one vote," most political parties in Canada have removed an important line of accountability from the leader to the caucus. Without the need for caucus support to become leader, he or she is answerable to party members at large instead of elected legislators in their caucus (Carty, Cross, and Young 2000). Because the party leader is now less answerable to the caucus, she or he is less responsive to complaints concerning party discipline or autocratic decision-making. With the Conservative party embracing this method of leadership selection, risks surrounding Harper's approach to message control and the marginalization of Cabinet did not threaten his leadership, because he owed his job to the party membership and not the parliamentarians and ministers he was controlling. As long as the membership-paying base is happy, it is difficult to remove the sitting leader of a party.

Considering why Stephen Harper was able to increase the centralization of power in the political executive, what does the future hold for this Canadian political institution? What may prove to be the greatest scandal of the Conservative governments' three mandates is the Mike Duffy/Pamela Wallin/Patrick Brazeau Senate scandal that began in 2013. Notably, the scandal had ties directly back to the PMO and the outcomes of centralized power. As Andrew Coyne suggests in his foreword to Brent Rathgeber's book *Irresponsible Government*, "The Wright-Duffy affair, in which a sitting legislator was paid tens of thousands of dollars to keep quiet about a matter that was embarrassing to the government: the logical consequence of a system where all power resides in the Prime Minister's Office" (Coyne 2014, 13). While the Westminster system is susceptible to powerful first ministers, other jurisdictions such as New Zealand, Australia, and the United Kingdom have all put in place mechanisms to curtail the powers of the PM. In recent years, critics have suggested that reforms to political parties, Parliament, and the Constitution could curtail the centralization of power (Aucoin, Jarvis, and Turnbull 2011).

It is useful to consider Stephen Harper's legacy to the political executive and Cabinet government in Canada in two different ways: first the health of Canadian democracy, and second the success of political practice. First, in terms of how Harper's approach to the political executive contributed to the health of Canadian democracy, most would argue that the so-called democratic deficit has widened as the result of the Conservative government's strict communications management, dismissive approach to full Cabinet as a consultative/decision-making body in any form, and marginalization of most Cabinet ministers as significant political actors on the national stage. In light of this, one could argue that Harper was politically successful through tight control of Cabinet communications and ministers' profiles, resulting in relative party harmony and electoral success. In both 2008 and 2011, despite early concerns with how Harper was using his Cabinet, the Conservative party's standing improved in the House of Commons. As well, despite the relative newness of the Conservative Party of Canada, Harper kept his Cabinet and caucus together with few episodes of dissension and no leadership challenges.

The initial approach of Liberal Prime Minister Justin Trudeau to Cabinet – mainly on availability to the media – generated substantial excitement and the impression that decision-making power and authority is being shared by Cabinet. Yet the lure of message control, particularly with a relatively inexperienced Cabinet, may be strong, and we are left waiting to see whether Harper's contribution to centralization of power and marginalization of ministers has created an irreversible "democratic deficit" for his successors to overcome.

REFERENCES

Aucoin, Peter. 1986. "Organizational Change in the Machinery of Canadian Government: From Rational Management to Brokerage Politics." *Canadian Journal of Political Science* 19 (1): 3–27. http://dx.doi.org/10.1017/S0008423900057954.

Aucoin, Peter, Mark Jarvis, and Lori Turnbull. 2011. *Democratizing the Constitution: Reforming Responsible Government.* Toronto: Emond Montgomery.

Authier, Philip. 2015. "Quebec Back in the Action: Six Spots in Trudeau's Cabinet Mean Increased Clout in Ottawa." *Montreal Gazette*, 5 November.

Bakvis, Herman. 2000. "Prime Minister and Cabinet in Canada: An Autocracy in Reform?" *Journal of Canadian Studies / Revue d'études canadiennes* 35 (4): 60–79.

Blanchfield, Mike. 1995. "Tories Trying to Rise from Ashes." *Montreal Gazette*, 29 April.

Blanchfield, Mike, and Jim Bronskill. 2010. "Documents Expose Harper's Obsession with Control." *Toronto Star*, 6 June.

Campbell, Clark. 2006. "Harper Restricts Ministers' Message." *Globe and Mail*, 17 March.

Carson, Bruce. 2014. *14 Days: Making the Conservative Movement in Canada.* Montreal and Kingston: McGill-Queen's University Press.

Carty, R. Kenneth, William Cross, and Lisa Young. 2000. *Rebuilding Canadian Party Politics.* Vancouver: UBC Press.

Coyne, Andrew. 2014. "Foreword." In *Irresponsible Government: The Decline of Parliamentary Democracy in Canada*, by Brent Rathgeber, 11–13. Toronto: Dundurn.

Devlin Marier, Rita. 2007. "Shuffle Forces Out Ministerial Staffers, Brings Dispute with PMO to the Fore." *Hill Times*, 20 August.

Doyle, Simon. 2006. "Full Cabinet Meeting Irregularly, Every Two Weeks to a Month." *Hill Times*, 26 June.

– 2008a. "'Cabinet government, as we knew it, is dead,' Says Author Savoie." *Hill Times*, 2 June.

– 2008b. "PM's Tight Control on Government a Weird Strategy Say Some Experts." *Hill Times*, 28 January.

Doyle, Simon, and James Riley Thompson. 2008. "Cabinet Ministers Should be Defending Policies, Not Just House Leader Van Loan, Say Experts." *Hill Times*, 23 June.

Economist. 2005. "'Mr Dithers' and His Distracting 'Fiscal Cafeteria,'" 17 February.

Gessell, Paul. 1995. "Charest Bid to Be Top Tory Includes Effort to Forget Role in Bad Old Days." *Ottawa Citizen*, 10 March.

Harper, Stephen. 2007. "Interview." CTV with Lloyd Robertson and Bob Fire, 22 December.

Harper, Stephen, and Tom Flanagan. 1997. "Our Benign Dictatorship: Canada's System of One-Party-Plus Rule Has Stunted Democracy." *Next City* 2 (2): 34.

Harris, Michael. 2014. *Party of One: Stephen Harper and Canada's Radical Makeover*. Toronto: Viking.

Hill Times. 2014. "Cabinet Ministers Should Be More Accessible," 16 June.

Ivison, John. 2007. "With a Fistful of Power: Criticized as Controlling, Harper May Turn His Governing Style into a Winning Strategy." *National Post*, 1 September.

Johnson, William. 2005. *Stephen Harper and the Future of Canada*. Toronto: McClelland and Stewart.

LeBlanc, Daniel. 2010. "RCMP Clears Helena Guergis and Rahim Jaffer." *Globe and Mail*, 21 July.

Macleod, Harris. 2008. "PM Harper Opts for More Costly Minister of State Positions in Bigger Cabinet." *Hill Times*, 1 December.

Marland, Alex, and Tom Flanagan. 2013. "Brand New Party: Political Branding and the Conservative Party of Canada." *Canadian Journal of Political Science* 46 (4): 951–72. http://dx.doi.org/10.1017/S0008423913001108.

Marland, Alex, Thierry Giasson, and Tamara Small, eds. 2014. *Political Communication in Canada: Meet the Press and Tweet the Rest*. Vancouver: UBC Press.

Martin, Lawrence. 2010. *Harperland: The Politics of Control*. Toronto: Viking Canada.

Matheson, W.A. 1976. *The Prime Minister and the Cabinet*. Toronto: Methuen.

Naumetz, Tim. 2009. "PM Harper's Iron Message Control Working." *Hill Times*, 16 November.

Panetta, Alexander. 2006. "Gaffes Could Cost Job, Tory Cabinet Warned." *Montreal Gazette*, 15 April.

Persichilli, Angelo. 2011. "Soudas Helped Kenney Change His Approach with Ethnic Media." *Hill Times*, 6 June.

Privy Council Office. 2011. Accountable Government: A Guide for Ministers and Ministers of State. http://www.pco-bcp.gc.ca/docs/information/publications/aarchives/ag-gr/2011/docs/ag-gr-eng.pdf.

Rana, Abbas. 2007. "PMO's Order to Get Off Facebook Angers Some Cabinet Staffers." *Hill Times*, 4 June.

Rathgeber, Brent. 2014. *Irresponsible Government: The Decline of Parliamentary Democracy in Canada*. Toronto: Dundurn.

Rubin, Ken. 2014. "Harper's Cabinet Need Not Have Any Background Facts, Reinforces Greater Cabinet Secrecy." *Hill Times*, 14 April.

Ryckewaert, Laura. 2014a. "Aglukkaq, Ambrose, Nicholson Least Accessible Cabinet Ministers, Say Hill Reporters." *Hill Times*, 9 June.

–   2014b. "Hill Climbers: Lots of Former Prime Minister's Office Staffers Now Working in Ministerial Offices." *Hill Times*, 3 February.
Savoie, Donald. 1999a. *Governing from the Centre: The Concentration of Power in Canadian Politics*. Toronto: University of Toronto Press.
–   1999b. "The Rise of Court Government in Canada." *Canadian Journal of Political Science* 32 (4): 635–64. http://dx.doi.org/10.1017/S0008423900016930.
–   2005. "The Federal Government: Revisiting Court Government in Canada." In *Executive Styles in Canada: Cabinet Structures and Leadership Practices in Canadian Government*, edited by Luc Bernier, Keith Brownsey, and Michael Howlett, 17–46. Toronto: University of Toronto Press.
–   2008. *Court Government and the Collapse of Accountability in Canada and the United Kingdom*. Toronto: University of Toronto Press.
–   2013. *Whatever Happened to the Music Teacher? How Government Decides and Why*. Montreal and Kingston: McGill-Queen's University Press.
Shane, Kristen. 2011. "Inside the PMO: Harper's Not the Dictator He's Made Out to Be." *Hill Times*, 4 April.
Simpson, Jeffrey. 2001. *The Friendly Dictatorship*. Toronto: McClelland & Stewart.
–   2007. "It's All about Harper, and That's the Political Beef." *Globe and Mail*, 7 July.
Simpson, Jeffrey, Mark Jaccard, and Nic Rivers. 2008. *Hot Air: Meeting Canada's Climate Change Challenge*. Toronto: Emblem Editions.
Smith, Denis. 1971. "President and Parliament: The Transformation of Parliamentary Government in Canada." In *Apex of Power: The Prime Minister and Political Leadership in Canada*, edited by Thomas Hockin, 308–25. Toronto: Prentice Hall.
Wells, Paul. 2009. "The Real Shame in the Raitt Scandal." *Maclean's*, 12 June.
–   2013. *The Longer I'm Prime Minister: Stephen Harper and Canada, 2006–*. Toronto: Random House Canada.
Wherry, Aaron. 2008. "The Man Who Ate Question Period." *Maclean's*, 11 June.
White, Graham. 2005. *Cabinets and First Ministers*. Vancouver: UBC Press.

13 Federal Feet and Provincial Pools: The Conservatives and Federalism in Canada

ANNA ESSELMENT

Federal-provincial relations in Canada are constantly evolving. A glance through books on Canadian politics will show that federalism has been broadly characterized as "classical," "cooperative," "competitive," and "collaborative." Each categorization tries to capture the essence of federal-provincial interactions during a certain period in Canadian history. The nature of federalism in Canada is driven by several key questions: Should Canada be more or less centralized? Should the federal government limit the use of its spending power in areas of provincial jurisdiction? What is the right balance between respect for the constitutional division of powers and the need for federal government assistance in providing key social and economic programs?

Parties assuming power at the federal level have as often been determined to centralize the federal system as they have been to respect the constitutional division of jurisdictional responsibilities. This chapter will demonstrate that most iterations of post-1993 federal conservative parties have had a surprisingly consistent approach to federalism in Canada. The natural position for the federal conservative parties since 1993 has been to emphasize the constitutional division of powers and a retrenchment of the federal government from provincial spheres of power.[1] An examination of aspects of fiscal federalism (describing the financial relations between the federal, provincial, and territorial

---

1 After enjoying majority governments in 1984 and 1988, the Progressive Conservative Party of Canada held just two seats after the 1993 federal election. The PC platforms in 1997 and 2000 indicate the party's preference for a strong role for the federal government in health care, post-secondary education, and interprovincial trade, thus separating this party from the more strict view of constitutional divisions espoused by the Reform, Alliance, and later the Conservative Party.

governments) demonstrates that the Conservative government under Stephen Harper followed through with its intended objective of disentangling federal from provincial responsibilities, primarily through its more limited use of federal spending power.

This disentanglement is also evident in the evolving practice of executive federalism – no longer did the prime minister gather the first ministers together to discuss matters of national importance. Instead, Stephen Harper preferred what I call "individualized executive federalism," where he limited opportunities to be collectively pushed by provincial leaders by substituting first ministers' meetings with one-on-one conversations over the phone or in person with individual premiers and territorial leaders. In short, and with a few notable exceptions, traditional stances and the practices in power by Conservatives on federalism appeared to converge.

While diminishing the role usually played by the central government in Canada's federation may reflect constitutional principles, it also invites questions about the future ability of the federal government to effectively tie the nation together. With retrenchment of federal leadership in areas of health care and social policy, for example, how would national priorities be set? Could effective economic strategies be forged when the prime minister refused to meet with the premiers as a group? How would Harper's return to the classical view of federalism affect the future of intergovernmental relations in Canada? After providing a review of the federal principle in Canada and a select history of conservatism and federalism, this chapter will focus on the Conservative Party of Canada and its approach to federal-provincial relations through two themes:

1 Open federalism: How has the idea of open federalism affected fiscal arrangements between the federal and provincial governments?
2 Executive federalism and intergovernmental relationships: How has executive federalism evolved during the Harper government?

The chapter will conclude by examining exceptions to the preferred approach to federalism by the Conservative government under Stephen Harper's leadership.

The Federal Principle in Canada

In federal systems, constitutional authority is divided between two levels of government. It is often embraced in countries where there are divisions based on territory, language, religion, ethnic diversity, or combinations thereof. Federalism fits where, as A.V. Dicey noted, two or more entities desire union, not unity (Dicey 1961). Each level of government is considered equal or "coordinate" (Watts 1999) and neither is subordinate to the other (Wheare 1964).

At the time of Confederation in Canada, the founders were "reluctant federalists" (Smith 2004, 41). While they were most familiar with the British and French tradition of strong unitary governments, the delegates at the Charlottetown and Quebec conferences in 1864 wisely agreed to create a system in which there would be two levels of government: federal and provincial. The combination of shared and local rule meant that laws over general matters could be created for the whole of Canada (such as monetary policy, national defence, trade and commerce, and the criminal law), while provincial governments would have constitutional jurisdiction over matters of a more local nature, such as education, health, and property and civil rights. The British North America Act set out the constitutional heads of power for each level in sections 91 (federal) and 92 (provincial).

The constitutional listing of responsibilities, while certainly helpful, did not deter conflict over the division of powers in Canada. The judicial system has been a prominent player in Canadian federalism and, since Confederation, has been called upon many times to resolve disputes between the levels. Scholars have noted the important impact of judicial decisions on the development of Canadian federalism. Both the Judicial Committee of the Privy Council (the British court that served as Canada's highest tribunal until 1949) and, later, the Supreme Court of Canada have decided division-of-powers cases that have strengthened the hand of either the federal or provincial governments. The consensus is that the provinces benefited most from early judicial decisions, and Canada became much more decentralized as a result (Vipond 1985).

While the significance of constitutional cases is undisputed, the approach of the governing party in Ottawa to issues of federalism is of particular interest here. Some parties, for example, have viewed their role primarily as nation-builders, using the federal government's power to spend to help create or maintain national programs and set policy objectives that have often overlapped areas of exclusive provincial legislative responsibility (many Liberal governments have been partial to this course of action). Other parties, particularly the Conservatives in the last decade, but also the Reform and Canadian Alliance, have taken the opposite view: the constitutional division of powers should be respected, the federal spending power should be used sparingly and only with the consent of the provinces, and the setting of public priorities for programs receiving federal funding should be tasked to the provinces themselves.

There is no "correct" approach to federal-provincial relations in Canada. The preference of the federal government of the day is often determined by myriad factors, including (but not limited to) the issue at hand, the ideological perspective of the governing party regarding proper federal arrangements, the fiscal capacity of the government, the demands from the provinces, and public opinion.

Federalism and the Conservatives

The twentieth century witnessed the Conservative Party in government only intermittently, punctuated by long periods out of power. When there have been Conservative prime ministers, the general tendency has been to respect provincial spheres of power. Progressive Conservative Prime Minister John Diefenbaker was an exception; he used the federal spending power to greatly increase payments to individuals for welfare, unemployment insurance, veterans' pensions, and family allowances (Newman 1973). Diefenbaker presided as the Canadian welfare state was steadily expanding, so perhaps other Conservatives would forgive his federal largesse at the time.

Save for Joe Clark's short time in power in 1979, another twenty-two years would pass until Brian Mulroney's Progressive Conservative victory in 1984. Mulroney was determined to undo a number of Liberal Prime Minister Trudeau's initiatives that he believed undermined the federal principle in Canada. The first of these was to dismantle the National Energy Program (NEP), a mix of grants, taxes, and natural resource revenue-sharing with the federal government that had caused vitriolic uproar among the western provinces, particularly Alberta (Mulroney 2007). The NEP was replaced with provincial energy accords, which essentially returned control over natural resources to the provinces. As noted by Hugh Segal, "Those energy accords helped cement the fact that the Conservatives as a party, unlike the Liberals, actually believed in Sections 91 and 92 of the *BNA Act*" (2011, 83).

Mulroney also moved to reduce the amount of money the federal government transferred to the provinces for health and social programs. The cost-shared formula that provided 50-cents for every provincial dollar spent in these areas was no longer considered feasible, since growth in federal program spending was based on decisions by the provincial governments. Pierre Trudeau's government had, in fact, recognized the folly of the scheme on the national budget, and in 1977 the health transfer plan was restructured to combine both cash and tax points; federal tax points were ceded to provincial governments so they could raise replacement revenue. The Mulroney government pursued a similar reform and put a cap on the Canada Assistance Program (a federal program created in 1966 to transfer funds to the provinces for social assistance and welfare services), since that too was becoming costly for federal coffers. While the government noted it had a role to play in ensuring the maintenance of established programs, it clearly wanted to reduce provincial expectations of the federal government to divide delivery costs equally between them.

The Progressive Conservative government's approach to federalism was also evident in the two major attempts to renegotiate Canada's Constitution. In several respects, both the Meech Lake and Charlottetown Accords reflected a more classical approach to federal-provincial relations. Both deals, for example, entrenched greater provincial input on Supreme Court appointments. While Meech Lake also offered the provinces a say on who would be appointed to the Senate, the Charlottetown Accord went further by permitting either the province-wide elections of Senators or the election of Senators by the provincial assembly (Canada 1992). This would have given the sub-national level much more power over the central institutions of government. Furthermore, both constitutional proposals would also entrench limits to the federal spending power and, where new national cost-shared programs were developed in areas of exclusive provincial jurisdiction, provide compensation to those provinces that opted out of the federal or joint program and established their own (provided the province's program was compatible with "national objectives").

These two initiatives alone – strengthening intrastate federalism (the representation of the provinces within federal institutions) and constitutionally limiting federal intrusions in provincial spheres – exhibit a return to the watertight compartments era of Canadian federalism. A third initiative, the constitutional entrenchment of annual first ministers' conferences (FMCs), could also be viewed as respecting the division of powers, since its purpose was to gather the prime minister and premiers together at least once a year to discuss the state of the federation and, one presumes, to air any grievances about federal feet in provincial pools. While the entrenchment of FMCs might also be seen as an invitation to grandstanding and discord among first ministers, it would also force the prime minister to sit down with his provincial and territorial counterparts. Since FMCs can, by convention, be called only by the prime minister, entrenchment would go some way to assure provincial leaders that time with the PM to discuss matters as a group would be a regular occurrence.[2] The existence of the FMC itself may have had an impact on the behaviour of federal governments, such as depressing any unilateral actions that could affect federal-provincial relations. The lack of meetings between Stephen Harper and the provincial and territorial leaders could be heralded as the ultimate respect for jurisdictional separation (no need to get together since responsibilities are so clearly demarcated), but it also meant that federal "pronouncements" on intergovernmental policy became increasingly commonplace.

The fourth major constitutional proposal concerned Quebec. Both the Meech Lake and the Charlottetown Accords provided for the recognition of Quebec as a "distinct society" within Canada. While the distinct society clause was placed more discreetly in a broader "Canada clause" in the Charlottetown Accord, its inclusion raised the ire of a number of conservatives, particularly in the West. The impetus for the creation of the Reform Party was the result of numerous Liberal transgressions in provincial areas of concern (such as the National Energy Program and the Charter of Rights and Freedoms), but its organization was also spurred by what it viewed as the ceaseless and unnecessary pandering of the Mulroney government to the government and people of Quebec. The first brazen act was the Progressive Conservative government's decision in 1986 to award a contract for building and maintaining a fleet of CF-18 jets to a firm in Montreal, despite a lower bid from a competing company in Winnipeg. The second disappointment was conveying distinct society status on Quebec; for party leader Preston Manning and members of his Reform Party, Canada was a country of equal provinces. No province, or people, should be bestowed with a status that elevates it, or them, above their fellow Canadians. "Regional fairness"

---

2 Since Brian Mulroney and the prime ministers who preceded him were disposed to having gatherings of the first ministers anyway, this section of the Meech Lake and Charlottetown Accords may have seemed redundant. Given Prime Minister Harper's penchant to avoid group meetings, the constitutional forethought in 1987 and 1992 was prescient.

was a core founding principle of the new, populist party (Reform Party of Canada 1988, 6–8).

The Reform Party took its mantra "The West Wants In," its hatred for the Mulroney government, and its vision for a new Canada, and campaigned vigorously in the 1993 and 1997 federal elections, losing both times to the Liberals under leader Jean Chrétien. Despite becoming the Official Opposition in 1997, electoral growth for the Reform Party stalled. Preston Manning was an effective leader of the opposition but took the helm at a time when the Liberal government was actually exemplifying behaviour numerous Reformers would find desirable: the 1995 budget folded Established Programs Financing and the Canada Assistance Plan into the Canada Health and Social Transfer and drastically reduced the funding provided to the provinces. The near-death experience of Canada during the 1995 Quebec referendum meant that Ottawa would get serious with Quebec by devising legislation on constitutional amendments that effectively gave each region a veto over future constitutional change (see chapter 7 in this volume). The Reform Party supported that legislation and also, later, the Clarity Act, 2000, which forbade the Quebec government to unilaterally secede from the federation, as well as the Calgary Declaration, which included a statement about the equality of the provinces in the federation (Manning 2002). The Chrétien Liberals, along with their provincial counterparts (save Quebec), also moved on the matter of the federal spending power by approving the Social Union Framework Agreement (SUFA), which prevented the federal government from introducing new Canada-wide initiatives in social policy without first securing the agreement of a majority of the provinces (Lazar 2000). The Reform Party supported the SUFA and had been urging the government to draft such an agreement for at least a year in advance of the final 1999 agreement (Manning 2002, 187–212). With general agreement about the direction the government was taking on federal-provincial relations, Manning and his caucus pivoted to pressure the Liberals to pay off the deficit and debt more quickly, to ensure greater tax relief for Canadians, and to get serious about democratic reform (ibid.).

This approach to intergovernmental relations shifted in the early 2000s when the surpluses created by the Liberal government's financial prescriptions in the 1990s, combined with the revenue from Brian Mulroney's Goods and Services Tax (GST), began paying huge dividends. Chrétien's successor as Liberal prime minister, Paul Martin, used parts of the federal government's surplus on new social initiatives that rightly belonged within the purview of the provinces. It should be noted that the provinces raised few objections to the federal government's new spending initiatives on health care, cities, pharmacare, and childcare. As Tom Courchene (2008) presciently noted, the provinces were cash starved and willing to take any money on the table, and the Martin government was careful to secure provincial agreements to the funding boosts in existing and new programming, often through striking bilateral federal deals.

Opposition leader Stephen Harper, however, was not pleased with the federal government's "fiscal cafeteria" (*Economist* 2005). Harper's dispute with the actions of the Liberal government was twofold. First, they clearly betrayed his sense of appropriately separate constitutional jurisdictions and his preference for using the federal spending power sparingly. Likewise, the Conservative party leader was wary of the number of one-off deals struck with different provinces over equalization. Harper preferred revising the equalization formula that would eliminate the need for specialized side deals (Conservative Party of Canada 2006). Second, Harper's own ideological predilection was to have a restrained rather than activist state. As a university student, Harper greatly admired the work of Friedrich Hayek, a free-market economist who advocated for smaller government, low taxes, deregulation, and a limited (if any) welfare state (Harris 2014). Liberal policies were clearly trending in the opposite direction. In 2006, when the Conservative Party won a minority government against a beleaguered and scandal-plagued Liberal Party, Harper was determined to return the country to more respectful federal arrangements that also reflected his ideological inclinations. While mostly successful, the Conservatives faced two challenges: first, respecting constitutional boundaries occasionally *required* the use of the spending power and, second, electoral imperatives – particularly in a time of minority governments – compromised even the most fervent ideological adherence.

Stephen Harper's "Open Federalism" (2006–2015)

The newly minted Conservative Party of Canada approached federal-provincial relations in much the same way as their conservative party predecessors; as noted above, it was their belief that former Liberal governments had waded too deeply into provincial spheres of power, and the time had come to make a hasty retreat wherever opportunities could be found, particularly if it required rolling back new or expanded social programs. Conservative Party leader Stephen Harper had made this clear in the 2004 election campaign, although at that time no creative moniker was attached to his view of the proper arrangements in Canada's federal system (Conservative Party of Canada 2004). In the subsequent 2006 election, Harper sharpened his position in the party's platform by labelling his approach "open federalism" (Conservative Party of Canada 2006, 42–3). In a major speech to the Chamber of Commerce in Quebec City in December 2005, and then again in Montreal in 2006, Harper laid out his vision of what open federalism meant: respect for the constitutional division of powers, limits to federal spending power, provincial input where its jurisdictions may be affected, and a role for Quebec in the United Nations Educational, Scientific and Cultural Organization (UNESCO), which the province had been demanding for many years (Government of Canada 2006).

In short, a Conservative government would embrace a classical approach to federal-provincial relations; only with relatively watertight compartments between the levels would the ship of the state stay afloat. Respect for the proper legislative heads of power would, the thinking went, minimize conflict between the provinces and the federal government, reduce the burden on the federal budget to fund expensive social programs, and allow the federal level to concentrate on matters that had, to that point, been neglected – defence, infrastructure, and tax reductions for Canadians. The newly negotiated Child Care Agreements between former Liberal prime minister Paul Martin and each of the provinces were an early casualty of the open federalism approach; it was the sort of program the Conservative government was loath to take on because it so flagrantly violated the open federalism concept: new, expensive, and properly the responsibility of the provinces themselves to create and fund if they so desired. Instead, Harper opted to send monthly cheques directly to Canadian families with children aged six and under to help cover the costs of childcare. While certainly stemming from the federal power to spend, direct deposits to parents was a more legitimate use of funds, since they did not blatantly transgress constitutional lines, and credit could be given where it was due – the Conservative government. Other aspects of fiscal federalism were soon reflected through the open federalism approach.

Fiscal Federalism and the Harper Doctrine

The Conservative government's spring 2007 budget set out what some have called the "Harper Doctrine" (Norquay 2012). The budget made clear that Quebec would receive its own seat at UNESCO, that all provinces should be fully responsible for labour market training,[3] and that formal, legislated limits should be placed on the federal spending power. That budget also embraced open federalism in other ways.

The first was the Conservative government's recognition of a fiscal imbalance in the federation. The government of Ontario, in particular, had pushed the argument that there was a fiscal gap of $23 billion between what its residents were paying into federal revenue streams and what they received back in federal services (Government of Ontario 2005). The 2007 budget attempted to address some of this imbalance by first revising the equalization formula. To curb the practice of making equalization side deals, the federal government would revise the formula and base calculations on a ten-province standard that allowed for either full or partial exclusion of natural resource revenue, including offshore resources. The government expected this would result in an enriched program that would resolve any previous inequities.

The second measure was to provide longer-term funding predictability in health and social transfers by basing them more fully on equal per capita grants. The Conservatives honoured the Health Accord struck between the Liberals and the provincial governments in 2004, and pronounced in 2011 that it would continue to provide 6 per cent increases until 2017 (Ibbitson 2011). The Canada Social Transfer would increase by 3 per cent annually, with additional funding earmarked for post-secondary education and childcare spaces over five years. A third measure was to provide Canadians with tax relief through changes to the tax structure, including another 1 per cent reduction in the Goods and Services Tax (the GST received a 1 per cent cut in the 2006 budget, reducing the total GST from 7 to 5 per cent by 2007).

---

3 At that point, BC, Newfoundland and Labrador, Nova Scotia, PEI, and Yukon had only partially devolved Labour Market Development agreements with the federal government. The federal Conservatives wanted those provinces to assume full responsibility for the delivery of labour market training.

Because of these revisions to the fiscal structure, the government of Quebec received an additional $2.3 billion in transfers, which included a $700 million boost to its equalization payment. While not all provinces were pleased with Harper's budget (Bryden 2007), the government's changes certainly had the effect of lowering the "fiscal gap" rhetoric between the federal government and Ontario and Quebec; this suggested that both provinces were largely satisfied with federal fiscal plans moving forward.

While the Conservative government's initial foray into clarifying roles and jurisdictions, creating greater "fairness" in intergovernmental transfers, and promising to limit the use of the federal spending power was generally well received at the provincial level, the concept of "open federalism" in the field of fiscal federalism did present some drawbacks. Where provincial governments were used to some federal leadership in policy fields – health, for example – the Harper Tories proved less willing to set priorities and national objectives. To be fair, the federal government was certainly concerned about wait times for certain procedures in the health care system, and made this one of their "five promises" in the 2006 campaign on which they wanted to deliver (Esselment 2012). But that one health policy priority would be the last time the federal government would attempt to set national objectives. Instead, the government would use the Harper Doctrine to assert the argument that the provinces should be taking the lead on health care policy because it was their constitutional responsibility to do so. The 2011 Conservative Party platform devoted only a few lines to health care, promoting a collaborative approach with the provinces to "renew the Health Accord," to emphasize the importance of accountability, and to note that "health care is an area of provincial jurisdiction and [we] respect limits on the federal spending power" (Conservative Party of Canada 2011, 30). The 2015 platform was quite similar. The Conservatives highlighted the "right of the provinces to deliver health care within their jurisdictions" and made commitments to provide research into palliative care, to study the Supreme Court decision on assisted suicide, and to renew funding for the Canada Brain Research Fund and cancer research (Conservative Party of Canada 2015, 134–8). Overall, aside from the provision of intergovernmental transfers and ensuring the principles of the Canada Health Act were followed, the Conservatives saw very little role for the federal government in health care writ large.

It was with issues like this that the terms of the Harper Doctrine presented a double-edged sword. Provincial premiers were not necessarily displeased with the federal nod to differentiated constitutional jurisdictions. The Conservative government addressed the fiscal imbalance, made changes to equalization, and lent greater credence to the notion of "fairness" in the distribution of public funds. At the same time, the use of the federal spending power is juxtaposed within the concept of open federalism itself.

Open federalism portends to embrace a limited use of the federal spending power. Time and again, Prime Minister Harper suggested to Canadians that the central authority's ability to spend money on anything it wants, in any jurisdiction it wants, should be severely limited. He went as far as to suggest, in fact, that the federal spending power should be limited through law, although nothing of this sort has been implemented (the constitutional entrenchment of the federal spending in the Meech and Charlottetown Accords may have been the only aspects of the constitutional deals of which Harper actually approved). The juxtaposition is that *it is only through the spending power that the Conservative government was able to pursue open federalism*. The Child Care Agreements negotiated by the former Martin government were quashed because the provision of child care (certainly within the Liberal-drawn parameters as providing "the first social program in a generation") was not a federal responsibility. To ensure the concept of open federalism was realized (but without paying the electoral price of angering parents), Harper used the federal spending power to implement a direct-to-citizen payment of $100 per child, per month, to parents with children aged six and under. This is consistent with the Hayekian view of allowing individuals (in this case, parents) the freedom to make their own choices in the marketplace, but it also requires major unilateral spending by the government in order to respect the country's constitutional boundaries.

Likewise, to avoid a protracted discussion with the premiers and to assert that health care and its program priorities were the purview of the provinces, in 2011 the federal government used its spending power to unilaterally announce a funding formula for the accord until 2017. The formula continued the 6 per cent a year increases until 2017, where funding escalators would reflect GDP growth, but guaranteeing a floor growth of at least 3 per cent of GDP. The premiers were not consulted; no national priorities were set; no national health strategy was discussed. The Conservatives announced the funding and then left the table before anyone had a chance to sit down – not that they were even invited to a discussion, as detailed below (*Huffington Post* 2013).

Executive Federalism and the Harper Doctrine

The classical approach to federalism was not the only aspect of federal-provincial relations that shifted with the Conservative government; it informed other practices and altered what has been otherwise expected behaviour. Executive federalism is an example here. Executive federalism is defined as "the relation between elected and appointed officials of the two orders of government" (Smiley 1980, 91). This could involve meetings and discussions between senior bureaucrats, or meetings of provincial ministers and their federal counterparts who manage similar departments, or both. Of particular interest here are the meetings and/or conferences between the prime minister and premiers. In the past, the meetings of first ministers in Canada have been a prominent site for constitutional negotiations, the setting of national priorities, and the wrangling over funding arrangements for shared programs. The practice of prime ministers regularly bringing together the heads of government in Canada took root in the 1930s. It flourished under Pierre Trudeau, who held fourteen first ministers' conferences (Cohen 1991, 132). Mulroney met with the premiers as a group on twenty-one occasions (ibid.), and Jean Chrétien seven. Paul Martin, while prime minister for two short years, still managed to convene the premiers each year (in 2004 to discuss health care and in 2005 to confer on equalization). Prime Minister Harper had little appetite for calling first ministers' meetings, presiding over just one while he held power (in January 2009 to discuss the global financial crisis and its impact on Canada) (Government of Canada 2009b). Harper was far more comfortable having individual discussions with the premiers rather than gathering them together as a group. This is far different from what Progressive Conservative Prime Minister Brian Mulroney had advanced in the Meech Lake Accord; if the accord had passed, first ministers' conferences would be held at least once a year, as mandated by the Constitution (Privy Council Office n.d.).

One could advance the argument that first ministers' meetings tend to dissolve into opportunities for grandstanding or, worse for the prime minister, the chance for premiers to gang up on the sole federal representative. We expect there have been many meetings where, at their conclusion, the prime minister has felt rather battered and bruised. Even supporters of the Meech Lake Accord thought the idea of forcing annual first ministers' conferences was not in the country's best interest (Cohen 1991). The bilateral approach of *individualized executive federalism*, on the other hand, offered Harper several advantages, such as eliminating the 13 to 1 odds that a first ministers' meeting produces. This approach also keeps the premiers guessing about what the prime minister might be sharing with other premiers, akin to a "divide and conquer" strategy. Finally, to some extent individualized executive federalism cultivates the opportunity for the federal leader to have closer relationships with provincial counterparts, because they occur in private, either in person or over the phone; that type of environment is more amenable for honest and candid conversations.

Norquay (2012) has suggested this practice helped limit, or at least depress, federal-provincial conflict.[4] He may very well be right. At the same time, numerous issues demand collective leadership and agreement on policy direction. Health care is one such area, but so are the economy and infrastructure investments. While the Council of the Federation (the organization that represents Canada's provincial and territorial leaders) continued to meet twice a year to discuss challenges facing the federation, there was increasing concern about federal reluctance to engage with the premiers as a group, particularly as decisions and announcements by the Conservative administration affected the policies and budgets of Canada's provinces (Babbage and Loriggio 2013; Canadian Press 2015).

Exceptions to the Harper Doctrine

The Conservative government remained committed to open federalism in the areas of social policy and executive relations, but provincial jurisdiction over particular economic fields did not receive the same respect. While the federal government has a major role to play in shaping the country's economy, several actions taken by the Conservatives in the wake of the 2008 global economic collapse transgressed the spirit of open federalism. What's more, two successive minority governments, combined with the number of votes and seats in provinces

---

4 A glaring exception would be Stephen Harper's year-long refusal to meet with Ontario Premier Kathleen Wynne (Mas 2014).

like Ontario, meant that many of the Harper Doctrine "exceptions" noted below were driven by an electoral imperative. Put another way, since citizens take financial conditions into account when they vote, the Conservatives required a more "flexible" view of the constitutional separation of responsibilities in order to be viewed as good economic managers (Clarke and Stewart 1994; Lewis-Beck and Paldam 2000).

Consider, for example, Stockwell Day's campaign pledge in the 2000 federal election to eliminate the "alphabet soup" of regional economic development (Canadian Alliance 2000, 7). For Day and his party, tax reductions and other investments would spur the necessary growth for job creation, rendering the "handouts" from regional funding agencies superfluous. To be fair, the new Conservative Party did not specifically mention its plans for regional funding agencies in its 2004 and 2006 platforms. But the Harper government did not dismantle the Atlantic Canada Opportunities Agency, the Canada Economic Development for Quebec Regions, or the Western Economic Diversification Canada. Nor did it jettison the Federal Economic Development Initiative in Northern Ontario. Instead, in 2009 the Harper government created a *new* regional funding agency, this time for southern Ontario, one of the hardest hit areas from the 2008 economic crisis (Government of Canada 2009a). Funding for FedDev Ontario was renewed in 2013, with a plan to inject close to a billion dollars over the ensuing five years to further assist the economic recovery in that region. The large investment in southern Ontario likely contributed to the Conservative party's electoral dividends in that province. In the 2008 election, its share of the province's seat count increased from 40 (in 2006) to 51. In 2011, the Conservatives won 73 of Ontario's 106 seats.

A second counter to the open federalism approach was the federal push to install a national securities regulator to administer and enforce securities law. Each province has its own framework of rules overseeing the trading of stocks and bonds and protecting investors from fraudulent trading practices. In 2013, Finance Minister Jim Flaherty surveyed the cumbersome provincial and territorial patchwork of securities legislation and pressed to create one regulator that would limit inefficiencies, streamline processes, provide better security surveillance, and open Canada's doors to greater investment by simplifying the system of capital markets (Chase 2013). A happy by-product of this action would be the greater sense of economic well-being by Canadians, particularly if they felt their investments were more secure (*Toronto Star* 2014). The push for a national approach is not new; a number of federal governments have tried to cajole the provinces into forming an over-arching commission. In this case provincial resistance was bolstered by an important Supreme Court ruling in 2011 that clearly noted securities law was within provincial jurisdiction (*Reference Re Securities Act,* 2011 SCC 66, [2011] 3 SCR 837). Because of the constitutional division of powers, provincial governments did not have to cede their legislative authority to the federal level. The hard push in 2013 to create a single regulator for the provinces was a centralizing action by the Conservative government, and it certainly did not fit into their classical view of respecting the different heads of power articulated in the Constitution. But the move to capture provincial regulatory schemes and revise them into a broader, country-wide framework did fit with the Conservative government's national economic strategy; strict adherence to the Harper Doctrine would thwart that goal.

Labour market development training was a third area where the Conservative government decided that more national involvement was better, despite the decision of previous federal governments to deliberately download that particular responsibility to the provinces. Placing labour market development under the purview of the provinces was a critical part of Liberal Prime Minister Jean Chrétien's "Plan A" to manage relations with Quebec during the critical sovereignty referendum in 1995 (Bakvis 2002). The Quebec government had long argued that labour market training should be the responsibility of the provinces, since they were already delivering primary, secondary, and post-secondary education; it made sense that training related to the development of provincial labour markets should also be locally controlled and delivered. Worried about the outcome of the sovereignty vote, Chrétien's government agreed and began the process of transferring programs and personnel to the provincial level through labour market development agreements (LMDAs) (ibid.).

Until the 2013 federal budget, the Conservative government appeared to agree that the appropriate place for labour market training was at the provincial level (Government of Canada 2007). But the federal government announced major changes to the program that reflected a broader, national imperative of improving the ability to match skills with employers. Ensuring that the unemployed in Canada were reliably retrained with skills that could actually fill gaps in areas of labour shortages was, like a national securities regulator, a critical part of Stephen Harper's national economic recovery strategy and a key campaign platform plank that emphasized the Conservatives' skill as

sound economic managers and job creators. The central piece of the
redesigned labour market strategy was the Canada Job Grant. The federal government promised employers a grant of $15,000 per worker in
the program, but that money would be equally divided among the two
levels of government and the employer ($5,000 each). The twist in the
Conservative plan was that the federal share would come from money
already being transferred to provinces for existing training programs
(Government of Canada 2013). In other words, the provinces would either have to find new funding for the Job Grant from their own budgets
(approximately $300 million), or eliminate training programs currently
in place.

The way the revised LMDAs were announced was consistent with
an open federalism approach, as provinces were not consulted on the
change or the effects the change would have on their existing programs.
The Canada Job Grants strategy is inconsistent with open federalism,
however, since the federal government attempted to implement major
change in an area that, since 1995, had been considered an area of exclusive provincial responsibility. Not surprisingly, the provinces balked
at the proposal; it took several concessions by the federal government
over the course of a year before most of the provinces agreed to strike
bilateral deals on Job Grants (Payton 2014). This suggests that a consultative role for the provinces before the budget was announced, or even
a meeting between the premiers and prime minister, may have resulted
in an easier – and earlier – implementation of the new Canada Jobs
Grants (Geddes 2013).

Conclusion

Provincial governments were familiar with the approach to federalism preferred by the Stephen Harper Conservative government. Brian
Mulroney attempted to extract the federal government from the provincial sphere, but so did Jean Chrétien during the 1990s. Mulroney tried
to constitutionally entrench that approach; Chrétien agreed to put it in
a framework agreement, using good faith as the guiding enforcement
mechanism. So what is the difference between then and now? Why
should Canadians have been concerned about the Harper Doctrine and
not the Chrétien or Mulroney "doctrines"? Two factors stand out.

The first is that the concept of open federalism led to an absence of
federal leadership in key social policy matters that affect all Canadians. Even though the Conservative government did not have explicit

jurisdiction over health, the federal government, in consultation with the provinces, has a tradition of collaboration in order to set out common national objectives. Whether this be, among many others, patient wait times, senior care, mental health, vaccinations, or screening and diagnostic tests, the federal government can play a role by galvanizing the provinces and setting out a national strategy together. Where provinces are left on their own to devise health funding priorities, Canada may end up with an augmented patchwork of health services that could actually detract from the system as a whole. The Conservative government's lack of involvement in strategic consultations on this file was somewhat curious, since a majority of Canadians (54 per cent) continued to cite health care as their number one issue of concern (CBC News 2015).

What is interesting to point out about Harper's open federalism approach was that it tended to be honoured on social policy, but less so on economic matters. Few would suggest that the federal government has no role to play in the country's economy; in fact, the opposite is true. But it is interesting that elements of the Harper Doctrine – even those that were based on the prime minister's own ideological preferences – were overlooked in the government's pursuit to be viewed as a good economic manager pursuing long-term prosperity for Canadians. These transgressions can be linked to electoral strategy: whereas all Canadians want a strong economy, injecting major investments (such as those emanating from regional economic agency funding) into a province where parliamentary seats are coveted, can have a large pay-off. Likewise, a national securities regulator, labour market training development, and (though not discussed here) tax harmonization are all centralizing actions that transgressed the spirit of open federalism, but were pursued nonetheless because they fit the narrative of economic leadership.

The second factor that evokes some concern was the unwillingness of the Harper government to play a role in the federation by bringing together provincial premiers and territorial leaders for consultations, discussions, and the general soliciting and giving of advice on different issues affecting their mandates. While prime ministers may feel outnumbered in these meetings, the point of past gatherings was that Canadian leaders were meeting and talking *together*. A federal system like Canada's, with vast geography and notable fissures along linguistic, economic, and social lines, demands a continuing conversation among those who are trusted with the public's money. While scholars may not be enamoured with executive federalism, the concept at least includes the notion of ensemble gatherings. Individualized executive federalism, on the other hand, has an even darker undertone, since prime ministers can efficiently divide, conquer, undermine, and even ignore provincial premiers by agreeing only to one-on-one discussions.

In summary, there was a slow turn to the right in federal-provincial relations when the Conservatives came to power in 2006. Two key elements of this evolution were open federalism and individualized executive federalism. Open federalism has at its foundations a healthy respect for classical federalism, but another key pillar is the ideological perspective that espouses small government, minimized budgets, and individual choice in the private marketplace. What becomes glaringly apparent, however, is that the desire to keep (or grow) power will demand the sacrifice of ideological leanings in favour of electoral imperatives. The federal spending power will, paradoxically, be wielded to both uphold open federalism *and* to make amends with voters for its deleterious side effects. It is perilous campaign strategy to anger parents by withdrawing the promise of childcare assistance without somehow replacing those funds. Deficit spending in Ontario through a new regional funding agency betrays conservative values, but injecting billions of government investments in a vote-rich province is quite valuable when attempting to win more seats. A "national" labour training strategy grates against the concept of open federalism, but goes a long way to demonstrate the federal government's commitment to job creation.

Despite the exceptions to the Harper Doctrine, Canadian federalism was fundamentally changed under Stephen Harper's government. It was much different from the approach of Paul Martin, Jean Chrétien, and Brian Mulroney in terms of leadership in the area of social policy and within the federation as a whole. Early indications suggested that Prime Minister Justin Trudeau will embrace the role of national leader in Canada's federal system. Less than a month after the 19 October election, Trudeau announced a November meeting of first ministers to discuss climate change (Fekete 2015). This was part of the larger invitation to all premiers and territorial leaders to accompany him to Paris for a major conference on climate change, one they readily accepted (Cheadle 2015). It is noteworthy, however, that Justin Trudeau's government has also made pronouncements akin to those in the Harper era. The demand that all provinces adopt a carbon price plan by 2018 is one example (Harris 2016). The Liberals have also signalled their intention to forge a new, collaborative relationship with the premiers on other issues, especially health care (Liberal.ca 2015). Unlike their predecessors, the Liberal government has clear federal priorities in the health field, particularly for home care and mental health. New health-care funds are conditional on provincial agreement with those key areas (Curry 2016). Perhaps because there have been so few strings attached to the health-care budget in recent years, collective agreement by the premiers with the Government of Canada proved unreachable. The federal government has instead engaged in bilateral negotiations with the provinces on health care (Galloway 2016).

The Liberal approach to executive federalism is already more inclusive than the doctrine followed by the Harper era, and Justin Trudeau is willing to wade into the social policy jurisdiction of the provinces with the promise of new money. While the shape of federal-provincial relations under the Liberals is still unfolding, it is likely that open federalism will become a relic of the Harper administration.

REFERENCES

Babbage, M., and P. Loriggio. 2013. "Canada Job Grant: Premiers Want Meeting with Harper Government over Controversial Plan." Canadian Press, 25 July. http://www.huffingtonpost.ca/2013/07/25/canada-jobgrant_n_3650556.html.

Bakvis, Herman. 2002. "Checkerboard Federalism? Labour Market Development Policy in Canada." In *Canadian Federalism: Performance, Effectiveness, and Legitimacy*, edited by Herman Bakvis and Grace Skogstad, 197–219. Don Mills, ON: Oxford University Press.

Bryden, J. 2007. "Provinces Slam Tories' Fiscal Cure." *Canadian Press*, 20 March. http://www.thestar.com/news/2007/03/20/provinces_slam_tories_fiscal_gap_cure.html.

Canada. 1992. *Consensus Report on the Constitution, Charlottetown Accord*, 28 August. Ottawa: Supply and Services Canada. https://www.saic.gouv.qc.ca/documents/positions-historiques/positions-du-qc/part3/Document27_en.pdf.

Canadian Alliance. 2000. *A Time for Change*. https://www.poltext.org/en/part-1-electronic-political-texts/electronic-manifestos-canada.

Canadian Press. 2015. "Premiers to Gather Friday in Harper's Backyard, but PM Not Taking Part," 28 January. http://www.squamishchief.com/news/

national/premiers-to-gatherfriday-inharper-s-back-yard-but-pm-not-taking-part-1.1745387.

CBC News. 2015. "Top Issues for Canadians," 21 January. http://www.cbc.ca/player/News/Politics/Power+%26+Politics/ID/2649250980/.

Chase, S. 2013. "Ottawa Plans National Securities Regulator." *Globe and Mail*, 21 March. http://www.theglobeandmail.com/report-on-business/economy/ottawa-plans-nationalsecurities-regulator/article10112074/.

Cheadle, Bruce. 2015. "Premiers Agree to Attend Paris Climate Summit with Trudeau." *Globe and Mail*, 22 October. http://www.theglobeandmail.com/news/politics/premiers-agree-to-attend-paris-climate-summit-with-trudeau/article26945307/.

Clarke, Harold, and Marianne Stewart. 1994. "Prospections, Retrospections, and Rationality: The 'Bankers' Model of Presidential Approval." *American Journal of Political Science* 38 (1): 104–23.

Cohen, Andrew. 1991. *A Deal Undone: The Making and Breaking of the Meech Lake Accord*. Vancouver: Douglas & McIntyre.

Conservative Party of Canada. 2004. *Demanding Better: Federal Election Platform*. http://www.cbc.ca/canadavotes2004/pdfplatforms/platform_e.pdf.

– 2006. *Stand Up for Canada: Federal Election Platform*. https://www.poltext.org/en/part-1-electronic-political-texts/electronic-manifestos-canada.

– 2011. *Here for Canada*. https://www.poltext.org/en/part-1-electronic-political-texts/electronic-manifestos-canada.

– 2015. *Protect Our Economy: Our Conservative Plan to Protect the Economy*. https://www.poltext.org/en/part-1-electronic-political-texts/electronic-manifestos-canada.

Courchene, Thomas. 2008. "Reflections on the Federal Spending Power: Practices, Principles, Perspectives." *Queen's Law Journal* 34:75–123.

Curry, Bill. 2016. "Liberals Fail to Clinch 10-Year Health Deal with Provinces." *Globe and Mail*, 19 December. http://www.theglobeandmail.com/news/politics/no-deal-yet-as-ottawa-and-the-provinces-talk-health-transfers/article33365578/.

Dicey, Albert Venn. 1961. *Introduction to the Study of the Law of the Constitution*. 10th ed. London: Macmillan.

Economist. 2005. "'Mr Dithers' and His Distracting 'Fiscal Cafeteria.'" 17 February. http://www.economist.com/node/3669408.

Esselment, Anna. 2012. "Delivering in Government and Getting Results in Minorities and Coalitions." In *Routledge Handbook of Political Marketing*, edited by Jennifer Lees-Marshment, 303–15. London: Taylor and Francis Group. http://dx.doi.org/10.4324/9780203349908.ch23.

Fekete, Jason. 2015. "Trudeau to Meet Premiers on Nov. 23 to Talk Climate Change." *Ottawa Citizen*, 12 November. http://ottawacitizen.com/news/national/trudeau-to-meet-premiers-nov-23-to-talk-climate-change.

Galloway, Gloria. 2016. "New Brunswick, Feds Reach Separate Agreement on Health-Care Funding." *Globe and Mail*, 22 December. http://www.theglobeandmail.com/news/politics/new-brunswick-reaches-separate-agreement-with-feds-on-health-care-funding/article33409785/.

Geddes, John. 2013. "Premiers vs PM on Job Training." *Maclean's*, 25 July. http://www.macleans.ca/politics/ottawa/the-premiers-unite-against-ottawas-job-training-push-a-tough-test-for-jason-kenney/.

Government of Canada. 2006. "Prime Minister Harper Outlines His Government's Priorities and Open Federalism Approach." News release, 20 April. http://nouvelles.gc.ca/web/article-en.do?crtr.sj1D=&mthd=advSrch&crtr.mnthndVl=&nid=207889&crtr.dpt1D=&crtr.tp1D=&crtr.lc1D=&crtr.yrStrtVl=&crtr.kw=tax%2B&crtr.dyStrtVl=&crtr.aud1D=&crtr.mnthStrtVl=&crtr.yrndVl=&crtr.dyndVl=.

– 2007. "Aspire to a Stronger, Safer, Better Canada: Budget 2007." Department of Finance. http://www.budget.gc.ca/2007/pdf/bp2007e.pdf.

– 2009a. "Canada's Economic Action Plan: Budget 2009." Department of Finance. http://www.budget.gc.ca/2009/pdf/budget-planbugetaire-eng.pdf.

– 2009b. "Prime Minister and Premiers Agree on Action for the Economy." News release, 16 January. http://www.ait-aci.ca/wp-content/uploads/2015/08/action_en.pdf.

– 2013. "Jobs, Growth, and Long-term Prosperity: Economic Action Plan 2013." Department of Finance. http://www.budget.gc.ca/2013/doc/plan/toc-tdm-eng.html.

Government of Ontario. 2005. "McGuinty Renews Campaign to Narrow $23 Billion Gap." News release, 2 June. https://news.ontario.ca/opo/en/2005/06/mcguinty-renews-campaign-to-narrow-23-billion-gap.html.

Harris, Kathleen. 2016. "Justin Trudeau Gives Provinces until 2018 to Adopt Carbon Price Plan." CBC News, 3 October. http://www.cbc.ca/news/politics/canada-trudeau-climate-change-1.3788825.

Harris, Michael. 2014. *Party of One*. Toronto: Viking.

Huffington Post. 2013. "Roy Romanow Urges PM to Meet with Premiers on Health Care," 24 July. http://www.huffingtonpost.ca/2013/07/24/roy-romanow-harperpremiers_n_3643048.html.

Ibbitson, J. 2011. "By Attaching No Strings, Flaherty Binds Irate Provinces to Health Plan." *Globe and Mail*. http://www.theglobeandmail.com/news/

politics/by-attaching-no-strings-flaherty-binds-irate-provinces-to-health-plan/article1360375/.

Lazar, H. 2000. "The Social Union Framework Agreement: Lost Opportunity or New Beginning?" Working Paper 3, August. Queen's School of Policy Studies. http://qspace.library.queensu.ca/handle/1974/14909?show=full

Lewis-Beck, Michael, and Martin Paldam. 2000. "Economic Voting: An Introduction." *Electoral Studies* 19 (2): 113–22.

Liberal.ca. 2015. "A New Health Accord." http://www.liberal.ca/realchange/a-new-health-accord/.

Manning, Preston. 2002. *Think Big: My Adventures in Life and Democracy.* Toronto: McClelland and Stewart.

Mas, Susana. 2014. "Kathleen Wynne Makes Full Court Press for Meeting with PM." cbcnews.ca. http://www.cbc.ca/news/politics/kathleen-wynne-makes-full-court-press-for-meeting-with-pm-1.2869822.

Mulroney, Brian. 2007. *Memoirs.* Toronto: McClelland and Stewart.

Newman, Peter. C. 1973. *Renegade in Power: The Diefenbaker Years.* Toronto: McClelland and Stewart.

Norquay, Geoff. 2012. "The Death of Executive Federalism and the Rise of the 'Harper Doctrine': Prospects for the Next Health Care Accord." *Policy Options* (December): 46–50.

Payton, Laura. 2014. "Canada Job Grant Deal Reached with Quebec, Says Jason Kenney." CBC News, 4 March. http://www.cbc.ca/news/politics/canada-job-grant-deal-reached-with-quebec-says-jason-kenney-1.2559653.

Privy Council Office. n.d. *1987 Constitutional Accord.* http://www.pco-bcp.gc.ca/aia/index.asp?lang=eng&page=hist&doc=meech-eng.htm.

Reference Re Securities Act, 2011 SCC 66, [2011] 3 SCR 837.

Reform Party of Canada. 1988. *Blue Book: Platform and Statement of Principles.* https://www.poltext.org/en/part-1-electronic-political-texts/electronic-manifestos-canada.

Segal, Hugh. 2011. "The Conservative Continuum: From Stanfield to Mulroney." *Policy Options* (April): 79–85.

Smiley, Donald. 1980. *Canada in Question: Federalism in the Eighties.* 3rd ed. Toronto: McGraw-Hill Ryerson.

Smith, Jennifer. 2004. *Federalism.* Vancouver: UBC Press.

Toronto Star. 2014. "Canada Needs a National Stock Market Regulator: Editorial," 10 July. https://www.thestar.com/opinion/editorials/2014/07/10/canada_needs_a_national_stock_market_regulator_editorial.html.

Vipond, Robert C. 1985. "Constitutional Politics and the Legacy of the Provincial Rights Movement in Canada." *Canadian Journal of Political Science* 18 (2): 267–94. http://dx.doi.org/10.1017/S0008423900030250.

Watts, Ronald L. 1999. *Comparing Federal Systems*. 2nd ed. Montreal and
    Kingston: McGill-Queen's University Press.
Wheare, K.C. 1964. *Federal Government*. 4th ed. New York: Oxford University
    Press.

14 Stephen Harper and the Radicalization of Canadian Foreign Policy

SHAUN NARINE

After coming to power in 2006, the Conservative government of Stephen Harper pursued an ideologically driven foreign policy to a degree unprecedented in modern Canadian history. While Harper was willing to put aside ideology for the sake of domestic political gain, the government's fundamental goals were defined by a form of neoconservatism that had detrimental implications for Canada's role in the world.

The key questions of Canadian foreign policy are: How does Canada define its interests? How does Canada advance its interests and values in the world? How does Canada manage its relationship with the United States? What is the nature of Canada's relationship with the larger international community? Canadian governments have traditionally pursued a "special relationship" with the United States but have also supported multilateral institutions as a way to balance American influence. By contrast, the Harper government was hostile to most multilateral organizations, even as it strengthened Canada's ties to security-oriented multilateral organizations, notably NATO. Under the Conservative government, Canada drew strong lines between countries it favoured and those it considered to be enemies, or at least not part of the cultural, political, and economic bloc to which it "belongs." The Conservative government, like all previous governments, emphasized Canada's economic global priorities. However, it made Canadian global economic initiatives subject to narrow economic goals, all but dismissing the value of a Canadian interest in development.

This chapter argues that there were three distinct but complementary and overlapping factors that defined the Conservative government's foreign policy:

1 Domestic political calculations and considerations of partisan political gain: How have domestic political calculations and partisan considerations influenced the foreign policy of the Conservative government?
2 Neoconservative ideology: How has neoconservatism influenced the Conservative Party's approach to the world?
3 Economics and trade: How has the Conservative Party's commitment to economics and trade, especially the energy resource sector, influenced foreign policy?

This chapter is divided into three parts. Part 1 develops the theory underpinning the CPC foreign policy. Part 2 illustrates the many ways in which the Harper government seriously altered Canadian foreign policy in accordance with its electoral strategy and ideology. Part 3 discusses these changes and their implications for Canada's domestic politics and foreign policy.

The Conservative Party of Canada: A Radical Approach to Canadian Foreign Policy

Since the end of the Second World War, a consensus has governed Canadian foreign policy, regardless of the political party in power. As part of the Western alliance, Canada was committed to a strong relationship with the United States. However, Canadian politicians also saw Canada as a middle power with limited resources. Canada benefited from the effective operation of multilateral institutions and international law. Unlike many other Western states, Canada did not have a history of colonial expansion abroad. Its ability to wield influence in multilateral institutions was enhanced by having strong and sensitive relationships with the states of the developing world. Canada invested in the development of multilateral organizations such as the United Nations. This dual approach enabled Canada access to the leading councils of the West as well as the councils of the larger international community and afforded Canada a level of global respect that its material power alone did not merit (Clark 2013; Keating 2013).

The Conservatives under the leadership of Stephen Harper represented a radical departure from the historical norm in Canadian foreign policy, particularly in their hostility towards global multilateralism. Three factors underpinned Harper's approach to foreign policy. First were domestic political considerations. The government saw foreign policy as a useful tool for furthering its electoral strategy by appealing to different ethnic and religious constituencies within Canada. The Conservatives built a multi-ethnic voting bloc by targeting Canada's immigrant communities (and some established ethnic/religious communities) (see chapter 5 in this volume). Foreign policy also helped placate the right-wing political and religious base, which had been unhappy with the government's approach to major domestic social issues. At times, the government adopted ideological positions internationally that it was unwilling to push at the domestic level. Taking a hard, moralistic line at the international level allowed the government to look "tough" and "principled" to its base (Nossal 2013; Gecelovsky 2013).

A second factor shaping Conservative foreign policy was economic advantage, especially the desire to sell Canadian natural resources around the world. Furthering Canadian economic interests has been a goal of every Canadian government, but the Conservatives emphasized this objective to the exclusion of most other considerations. Canadian development and aid policies, for example, were subsumed by the pursuit of Canadian economic objectives (Mackinnon 2013).

These first two factors are not new to Canadian politics. Historically, Canadian political parties have catered to ethnic communities in a search for votes, though the Harper government carried this to a new extreme. Advancing Canadian business has always been a core interest of Canadian governments. What made the Conservatives' approach to foreign policy truly distinctive was their ideological content. The CPC followed a foreign policy ideology that is based in Canadian right-wing conservatism and is heavily influenced by American foreign policy neoconservatism.

Foreign policy "neoconservatism" originated in the United States and is based on a particular understanding of American exceptionalism.[1] McGlinchey explains the foundational ideas of neoconservatism:

---

1 *Neoconservatism* is a term that expresses many different meanings. For this chapter, it is referring to the particular *foreign policy* approach described here. However, the CPC is also neoconservative in the domestic political and economic senses. To confuse things further, neoconservative economic policies are often called *neoliberal*. See Patten (2013).

Irving Kristol [the father of American neoconservatism] describes three central pillars: a strong idea of patriotism, a round rejection of anything resembling or pointing towards a world government, including a round rejection of the United Nations and NATO … and … the view that statesmen should clearly distinguish friends from enemies. These pillars are fused with a strong Manichaean morality … the foreign-policy of a country must represent its internal moral character. Maintaining alliances with dictators and unfavorable regimes is … abhorrent … Neo-conservatism holds the domestic and international sphere to a clear moral and ideological standard and champions the use of militarism to further that standard globally. (McGlinchey 2009)

Neoconservatism was founded by Jewish American intellectuals who were disillusioned by what they felt were the damaging effects of liberalism on American culture and foreign policy in the 1960s and 1970s (Friedman 2005). They opposed American efforts to accommodate the Communist bloc. With the end of the Cold War, neoconservatives demanded that the United States reshape the world to advance American interests. They advocated the overthrow of Saddam Hussein and war against Iran. After 9/11, neoconservatives became more strident in their belief that the world was divided into confrontational cultural blocs and that the Islamic world represented the greatest threat to Western dominance. Iran was the most viable leader of such a bloc (a position that ignores the many sectarian divisions within Islam). They saw "Islamofascism" as the newest manifestation of the totalitarian enemy of the twentieth century – a strange position, given the many philosophical and material differences between the two philosophies (McGlinchey 2009). Neoconservative policies towards the Middle East are intimately tied to the security of Israel, supported by the idea that Israel is the only democratic nation in the region surrounded by hostile dictatorships. Protecting Israel by destroying the threat of Iran is a major preoccupation of neoconservative thinking (ibid.; Boettner 2009). Most of these ideas were manifested in the Harper government's foreign policy. But how did a chauvinistic American ideology become the key to Canadian foreign policy?

Massie and Roussel (2013) describe Harper's world view as that of "neocontinentalism," an extension of the Canadian version of neoconservatism practised by the Reform/Alliance Party and philosophically part of the right-wing political movement that gained influence in the Western world through the 1980s (Patten 2013). They credit the

"Calgary school" of political science with fuelling Canada's neocon-servatism and articulating its core principles. Foremost among these principles was a "commitment to tax reductions and limitation of the role of the state as an economic and social agent" (40). Religious values were present in some debates, such as gay marriage and abortion. Most noteworthy, neoconservatism puts forward the idea that "evil" exists and that it is the duty of citizens and their leaders to act according to "what is right" (40). "At the international level, Canadian neoconser-vatives express distrust towards international organizations (especially the UN), moral fanaticism against threats to Western liberal democracy and Christian values, unqualified belief in the benefits and benevo-lence of US hegemony, as well as faith in the use of force as a legitimate tool of statecraft ... neoconservatives advocate a specific foreign policy objective for Canada: that of achieving the status of being the United States' closest partner and most reliable ally" (41).

Harper and his closest colleagues had very little knowledge of, or experience with, foreign affairs before coming to power (Nossal 2013; Ibbitson 2014a; Harris 2014). American foreign policy neoconservatism was ascendant in U.S. foreign policy at the time of Harper's rise to pow-er and provided an interpretation of reality that aligned perfectly with the Conservatives' predispositions.

After forming a majority government in 2011, Stephen Harper articu-lated his foreign policy in a speech to the Conservative Party. According to Harper, Canada would "no longer just go along and get along with everyone else's agenda. It is no longer to please every dictator with a vote at the United Nations ... We know where our interests lie, who our friends are. And we take strong, principled positions in our dealings with other nations – whether popular or not ... and that is what the world can count on from Canada!" (qtd in Bloomfield and Nossal 2013, 139). Shortly thereafter, Harper was interviewed by *Maclean's* maga-zine: "In this interview Harper persistently articulated a Manichaean vision of global politics: 'a struggle between good and bad, and of moral clarity as the greatest asset and most reliable guide to foreign-policy.' Harper claimed, 'We take stands that we think reflect our own interests but our own interests in a way that reflects the interests of the wider community of nations, or particularly the wider interests of those nations with whom we share values and interests'" (Bloomfield and Nossal 2013, 139). Harper also emphasized the need for military power and the need to "take a side" in the "big conflicts" of the world.

Harper was willing to compromise on ideology when faced with the political imperative of building an electoral coalition. But the government had an ideological agenda and world view to which it was fully committed. When pragmatic politics combined with the ideological convictions of neoconservatism, the Conservatives were uncompromising in pursuing their foreign policy.[2]

The Conservative Government's Radical New Foreign Policy

Between 1993 and 2003, Canada's "conservative" parties followed very different foreign policies (Welsh 2003). The Progressive Conservatives under Jean Charest advocated Canada's "Pearsonian" international ideals more clearly than the governing Liberals, which had made foreign policy continuity secondary to budgetary concerns. The Charest PCs, like Harper's Conservatives, emphasized the need for Canadian foreign policy to value human rights (*Globe and Mail* 1997). However, the image of the world embraced by Charest was much more expansive than that embraced by Harper. Under Joe Clark, who had served as minister for external affairs in the Mulroney government, the PCs continued to adhere to a nuanced and internationalist foreign policy. The Reform Party and its successor, the Canadian Alliance, addressed foreign policy in only cursory ways, focusing mostly on trade and support for the United States.

In opposition, the Canadian Alliance followed a neoconservative foreign policy that mirrored the neoconservatism dominant in the United States. Harper's first major speech to Parliament emphasized his belief that Canada needed to unequivocally support the United States and rejected Canada's focus on multilateralism, particularly multilateral initiatives that put it at odds with the United States (Laghi 2002). In March 2003, Harper and Stockwell Day (the party's foreign affairs

---

2 Nossal argues that the Conservatives were driven primarily by domestic political calculations, not ideology (Bloomfield and Nossal 2013). He acknowledges that Harper had a "Manichaean" world view but feels that this was not a "clear alternative strategic foreign policy perspective" (Nossal 2013, 29). This chapter disagrees. The CPC used foreign policy primarily as a domestic political tool, but its Manichaean world view was strongly held and did reflect a particular conservative philosophical perspective.

critics) wrote an editorial in the *Wall Street Journal* decrying the Liberal government's decision not to join the American invasion of Iraq:

> For the first time in history, the Canadian government has not stood beside its key British and American allies in their time of need. The Canadian Alliance ... supports the American and British position because we share their concerns, their worries about the future if Iraq is left unattended to, and their fundamental vision of civilization and human values. Disarming Iraq is necessary for the long-term security of the world, and for the collective interests of our key historic allies and therefore manifestly in the national interest of Canada. Make no mistake, as our allies work to end the reign of Saddam ... the Canadian Alliance will not be neutral ... we will be with our allies and friends ... Modern Canada was forged in large part by war – not because it was easy but because it was right. In the great wars of the last century ... Canada did not merely stand with the Americans, more often than not we led the way. We did so for freedom, for democracy, for civilization itself. These values continue to be embodied in our allies and their leaders, and scorned by the forces of evil, including Saddam Hussein and the perpetrators of the attacks of Sept. 11, 2001. That is why we will stand – and I believe most Canadians will stand with us – for these higher values which shaped our past. (Harper and Day 2003)

The highly moralistic tone, the allusions to civilizational struggle, the division of the world into friends and enemies based on cultural affinity, an appeal to common military and, more subtly, historical ethnic bonds, illustrate neoconservative themes that remained consistent in Harper's thinking.

In the early 2000s, Harper recognized that new immigrants to Canada were primarily Asian and that they held fiscally and socially conservative views (Ibbitson 2014a, 7). The CPC targeted these voters, using the 2004 redefinition of marriage to include same-sex marriage as a wedge issue to inspire socially conservative immigrants to vote Conservative (see chapter 5 in this volume). Since that time, the CP has made extraordinary efforts to build ties with new Canadian ethnic and religious communities (Nossal 2013; Ibbitson 2014a; Tolley in this volume).

After coming to power in 2006, the Harper government unveiled a foreign policy in keeping with the neoconservative ideology. The Conservative government ignored the advice of the professional diplomats in the Department of Foreign Affairs (Clark 2013). However, it sometimes found that its preferences conflicted with its domestic political goals. Under these conditions, domestic politics took priority.

The strongest example of politics taking precedence over principle was the government's approach to China. The Conservatives "brought to office a mindset and suspicions about the Beijing government that were almost pre-Nixonian" (Clark 2013, 77). For two years, the government followed a policy of "cool politics, warm economics" where Canada continued trade with China while insulting it politically (Lui 2013). Canada suspended its bilateral human rights dialogue with China; it sent Cabinet ministers to celebrate Taiwan's independence day; Stephen Harper met with the Dalai Lama and conspicuously placed the flag of Tibet on his desk; key Conservatives emphasized the importance of building relations with a democratic country like India rather than maintaining them with "a godless totalitarian country with nuclear weapons aimed at us" like China (Clark 2013, 77). When questioned about Canada's cooling relationship with China, Harper responded, "I don't think Canadians want us to sell out … our belief in democracy, freedom, human rights … to the almighty dollar" (ibid). Harper skipped the opening ceremonies of the Summer Olympics in Beijing in 2008. This approach reflected the neoconservative aversion to Communist and "immoral" states. By 2008, however, Harper realized that his other political and economic goals were threatened by his approach to China.

The Canadian business community was upset with the government, and new Chinese immigrants, a key target demographic of the CPC, were angry at seeing their country of origin besmirched. The government set about rebuilding the relationship with China. In 2009, Harper met Chinese Premier Wen Jiabao. The Chinese made it clear they were willing to let bygones be bygones (Mackinnon 2013). However, there remained indications that the Harper government could not let go of its aversion to China. The Canada-China Investment Treaty was signed in 2012, but the government did not ratify it until September 2014, apparently because of continuing opposition within the CPC to closer relations with China (Simpson 2013; Gamache 2014).

A policy area wherein the Conservative government's domestic political goals and foreign policy ideology complemented each other was its approach to Israel. Historically, Canada tilted towards Israel in its foreign policy. Beginning in the 1980s, Canadian policy towards the Israeli-Palestinian conflict became more balanced. Canada recognized that its support of international law and global multilateralism required it to be more critical of Israeli actions and policies. At the UN, Canada voted in favour of measures that condemned Israel's violations of international law and supported the right to Palestinian self-determination (Barry 2010; Clark 2013). Nonetheless, Canada's support of Israel was never in doubt, even as approximately 57 per cent of the Canadian public have a negative view of that country (BBC 2013). Canada's efforts to be balanced meant that it enjoyed credibility with both sides of the Arab-Israeli conflict.

The Conservative government strongly condemned past Canadian efforts to be "fair-minded" and "even-handed" in the Arab-Israeli dispute as demonstrations of moral failure. The government stated unequivocally that it was on "Israel's side" in the conflict and set out to be the most "pro-Israel" state in the world. As Joe Clark, a former Conservative prime minister and minister of foreign affairs noted, "Canadian ministers are more categorical about their commitment to Israel than any other international issue" (Clark 2013, 84). Officially, Canada still supported the creation of a Palestinian state beside Israel and considered East Jerusalem and the West Bank as occupied territory. It regarded Israeli settlements in those areas as illegal under international law. In practice, however, Canada's policy on the conflict changed dramatically. The government protected Israel from any criticism and supported the ambitions of the Likud government of Benjamin Netanyahu.

The extent to which the Conservative government was dedicated to supporting Israel and attacking Israel's perceived enemies within and outside Canada was extraordinary. Some examples of this radical shift in policy were that Canada was the first country in the world, after Israel, to cut funding to the Palestinian Authority in 2006 after parliamentarians from Hamas won an electoral victory, and some were sworn into the Palestinian Cabinet. In that same year, the Canadian government backed Israel's assault on Lebanon, which killed more than 1,000 Lebanese, mostly civilians. Harper opposed a G8 call for an immediate end to the fighting. In 2010, Minister of State of Foreign Affairs Peter Kent implied Canada would go to war on behalf of Israel, claiming he was basing his views on Harper's stated position (Chase 2010). In 2011, Harper prevented the G8 from issuing a statement supporting President Obama's call for a peace between Israel and Palestine based on the 1967 borders, despite this being the foundation of Canada's official policy towards the conflict. This was a rare case of Canada putting its relations with the United States after its relations with another state. Reports in *Ha'aretz* – denied by Harper and Netanyahu's offices – claimed that Harper blocked the G8 statement at the behest of Netanyahu (Ravid 2011; Haaretz Service 2011).

In September 2012, Foreign Minister John Baird unexpectedly closed Canada's embassy in Tehran and expelled Iranian diplomats from Canada. Baird gave no reason for this act, though he expressed the Canadian government's dislike for Iran, primarily because of Iran's antagonism towards Israel (Greenwood 2012). Canadian experts criticized the move for shutting down Canada's eyes in that part of the world (Saunders 2012a). On 29 November 2012, the United Nations General Assembly voted to accord Palestine non-member observer status. The vote was 138–9 in favour, with 41 abstentions. Canada voted against Palestinian observer status. Before the vote, John Baird contacted his counterparts around the world and tried to convince other states to vote against the Palestinians or abstain (Clark and Ling 2012; Clark 2012a; Blanchfield 2013b). Canada threatened the Palestinians with unspecified consequences if they went ahead with their efforts at international recognition (Clark 2012b). On 9 April 2013, Baird met Israeli Cabinet Minister Tzipi Livni in occupied East Jerusalem, something no Canadian minister had done before. The Palestinians interpreted the act as a "deliberate attempt to change the international consensus" on Jerusalem (Ashrawi, cited in Clark 2013, 84). In 2014, Canada threatened to scuttle an international treaty protecting small-scale fisheries that had been in negotiation for five years, and of great benefit to Canadian fishers. The reason: the treaty included a clause protecting the rights of fishers living in occupied territories, an allusion to Palestinians (Bull 2014).The same year, Harper appointed Vivian Bercovici, a pro-Israel political commentator, as Canada's ambassador to Israel. During the Gaza War of 2014, which caused massive Palestinian civilian deaths, Ms Bercovici and the Canadian government expressed no concern about those deaths and moved in lockstep with the Israeli government (Clark 2014). On 18 January 2015, Baird visited the Palestinian Authority in Ramallah. His car was pelted with eggs by an angry crowd (Canadian Press 2015). Baird later demanded that Palestinian spokesman Saeb Erekat apologize for equating violent Jewish settlers with the Islamic State (IS). This prompted Erekat to demand an apology to the Palestinian people from Baird for his unequivocal support of illegal Israeli policies (Erekat 2015). Most tellingly, the Conservative government denounced the Palestinian effort to take Israel to the International Criminal Court. Canada was instrumental in creating the court and, as Heinbecker noted, the government's aversion to using the instruments of international law to address the Arab-Israeli dispute undermined Canada's traditional commitment to international law and deprived the disempowered Palestinians of peaceful means through which to seek their rights (Heinbecker 2015).

The Harper government's antagonism to Israel's critics spilled over into other facets of Canadian politics. The government's ideological hostility to the United Nations was reinforced by its anger over the UN's treatment of Israel. Canadian NGOs were defunded by the government because they were critical of Israel (Clark 2011). The government interfered in the funding of academic conferences in Canada that Israel's Canadian supporters found threatening (Naaman 2009). Within Canada, all political parties made an effort to censor the academic discourse concerning Israel (Abu-Laban and Bakan 2012). The government was condemned by the courts for preventing British politician George Galloway, a critic of Israel, from entering Canada. Rights and Democracy, a federally funded institution established by the Mulroney government to promote human rights and democracy around the world, was destroyed when the Harper government appointed radically pro-Israel academics to its board of governors, and its president, Remy Bureaugard, died of a heart attack after a confrontation with those members (Wells 2010; CBC News 2010). In 2006 a Canadian peacekeeper was killed when the Israeli military attacked a UN outpost in Lebanon over a period of several hours. A Canadian military review panel found the attack to be deliberate. The Canadian government demanded no explanation from Israel (Day 2013; National Defence and the Canadian Forces 2006). Most dramatically, in 2015, the government declared its intention to use Canada's hate speech laws against any person or organization advocating for the Boycott, Divestment, and Sanctions (BDS) movement against Israel. The proponents of BDS include Independent Jewish Voices, the United Church of Canada, and Canadian Quakers. Civil libertarians believe such a use of Canada's hate speech laws would not survive a Charter of Rights challenge; even so, the threat was clearly meant to intimidate and silence criticism of Israel in Canadian civil society (Macdonald 2015).

In January 2014, Harper made his first visit to Israel. He took with him the largest ever delegation of Canadians on a government-sponsored visit (Goodman 2014). Harper's speech to the Knesset emphasized his personal commitment to Israel and essentially claimed that almost any criticism of Israel is anti-Semitic (Akin 2014). He emphasized that "Canada supports Israel because it is right to do so" (S. Harper 2014).

Harper expressed his admiration for Israel, his sympathy to the Jewish people and their suffering, and his conviction that Israel stands at the front lines of a civilizational struggle with fundamentalist Islam that is intolerant and hateful of anything different from itself. He related the Arab-Israeli conflict directly to the 11 September attacks and, in his few comments about the Palestinians, implied that the failure to make peace in the region was attributable to them. Harper insisted that he would never criticize Israel in public. He claimed that "Israel is the only country in the Middle East, which has long anchored itself in the ideals of freedom, democracy and the rule of law" (ibid.). These comments underlined Harper's lack of sympathy for the Palestinians and his selective understanding of history.

The Conservative government's devotion to Israel had international consequences. In 2010, Canada withdrew its campaign for an elected seat on the UN Security Council when it became clear that it would be soundly defeated. To that point, Canada had lost a bid for the UNSC only once before, in 1946. The reasons for Canada's unpopularity in 2010 included international displeasure on the reduction in Canadian development assistance, Canada's obstructionist approach to the international environment, and Canada's "ostentatious" support for Israel (Stairs 2011, 10). Harper emphasized the Israel factor as an example of Canada paying a price for its principled support of Israel and following a "moral" foreign policy.

The government's approach to Israel was the most powerful example of a confluence in the domestic political and ideological factors defining its foreign policy. By unequivocally supporting Israel, the Conservatives successfully appropriated the loyalty of many Jewish Canadians. In the 2011 election, around 52 per cent of Jewish Canadians voted Conservative (Simpson 2011). Though fewer in number than Canadian Muslims, the Canadian Jewish community is far better established, organized, politically engaged, and wealthier (Sasley 2011). It has the potential to be an invaluable asset to the party, especially as the Harper government phased out public subsidies to political parties. In an effort to win back its Jewish support, the Liberal Party sent its leader on a pilgrimage to Israel to establish his loyalty to the Jewish state. The Conservatives' commitment to Israel also appealed to its Christian Zionist evangelical base. Harper's policy on Israel allowed the government to take an unambiguously moral position on a controversial international situation, despite the criticism of Canada, and reinforced Canada's role in fighting on the "right side" in a "big conflict." However, such a simplistic view of such a complex conflict can be explained only if considerations of religious and cultural affinity are brought into play rather than a fair assessment of the merits of the case (MacDonald 2011; Heinbecker 2015).

Other examples of the conjunction between domestic political strategy and a neoconservative/"moral" foreign policy include the government's reactions to Sri Lanka and Russia. In 2013, Harper boycotted the annual meeting of the Commonwealth to protest the treatment by Sri Lanka (the host country) of its Tamil population. Canada suspended its contribution to the funding of the Commonwealth Secretariat for the remainder of Sri Lanka's term as chair. These actions appealed to the more than 300,000 Canadian Tamils, living mostly around Toronto (Bascaramurty and Ibbitson 2013). Harper took a particularly aggressive stance towards Russia's annexation of Crimea and the continuing instability in Ukraine (S. Harper 2014). Canada expelled a Russian military attaché from the embassy in Ottawa, and Harper and John Baird rushed to Kiev to show their support for the new government. Canada sent an election observer force of more than 500 people to observe the Ukrainian presidential election of May 2014. Canada has the largest population of ethnic Ukrainians outside the Ukraine in the world. This response to the Russian actions attempted to consolidate the CPC voting base of ethnic Ukrainians in Western Canada. But it also demonstrated the neoconservative aversion to morally suspect states. Harper considered Russia and Vladimir Putin to be outside the values that bind the states of the G8 and was vociferous in his personal attacks on Putin (T. Harper 2014; Perkel 2014). The Conservatives damaged Canada's relationship with Vietnam by passing a bill commemorating the fall of Saigon to communist forces and declaring 30 April 30 "Journey to Freedom Day" to appeal to Vietnamese refugees in Canada (Mackrael 2015).

Harper used foreign policy to placate the CPC's evangelical Christian base, which was angry at Harper's adamant refusal to reopen the abortion debate inside Canada (Carrier and Tiessen 2013, 190; Gecelovsky 2013). The Muskoka Initiative was introduced by Harper in January 2010 at the G8 summit. It championed the health of women and children at the international level. However, Canada insisted the Initiative would not include family planning and reproductive health. In particular, the government refused to pay for contraception and abortion. American Secretary of State Hillary Clinton attacked the Canadian proposal, stating, "You cannot have maternal health without reproductive health. And reproductive health includes contraception and family planning and access to legal, safe abortion" (Carrier and Tiessen 2013, 185). Under pressure, Harper allowed for family planning but refused to budge on abortion. In 2014, Harper announced an additional $3.5 billion in funding for the maternal health initiative, but reiterated his refusal to allow any funding for abortions, arguing that the issue was too divisive within Canadian society.

Domestic ideological convictions also defined the government's environmental policies. In December 2012, Canada withdrew from the Kyoto Protocol on Climate Change, the first signatory country to formally do so, after years of undermining the climate change regime (Smith 2009). In 2013, Canada became the only country in the United Nations to withdraw from the UN Convention to Combat Desertification, a convention that previous Canadian governments had championed (Blanchfield 2013a). Ostensibly, Canada abandoned the treaty because, according to Harper, it was "not an effective way to spend taxpayer money" (*Globe and Mail* 2013). The Harper government's decision fit with its opposition to research on climate change in Canada and its efforts to silence Canadian scientists (Renzetti 2013; Greene 2014; Liss and Langille 2013). The scepticism towards climate change and science accorded with the government's neoconservative ideology and Christian fundamentalist beliefs. Neoconservatism opposes government regulation and activism; Christian fundamentalism sees environmentalism as a left-wing ideology (Crews 2013). Climate change science also undermined the government's economic objective of making Canada an "energy superpower," based largely on the exploitation of oil. These decisions further damaged Canada's reputation in the developing world. Canada also obstructed international efforts to control the use of asbestos (Ruff and Calvert 2014).

In 2013, the government folded the Canadian International Development Agency (CIDA) and the Department of Foreign Affairs into the Department of Foreign Affairs, Trade and Development (DFATD). This consolidated a government decision to significantly reduce the extent of Canadian aid and link it directly to the promotion of Canadian business. CIDA's activities, which had been heavily concentrated on reducing poverty, building sustainable development, and developing social capital were no longer government priorities (Ibbitson 2013). The emphasis on Canadian trade gained momentum after the 2008–9 global financial crisis demonstrated the dangers of focusing too intently on the United States as Canada's primary trading partner. From 2010 on, the Harper government pursued numerous trade agreements with other economies. It announced an agreement with the European Union in October 2013 and South Korea in March 2014. In 2015, Canada negotiated the Trans Pacific Partnership and is discussing bilateral trade with India, Thailand, and Japan.

On the military front, the Harper government emphasized the need for Canada to pull its weight within its military alliances. Canadian troops were active in Afghanistan for many years, and the government committed to rebuilding the Canadian Navy and Air Force. However, Afghanistan exhausted and depleted the military, and the economic crisis further undermined the government's ability to refurbish it. Canada gained respect from its allies in NATO, especially the Americans and British, and was rewarded by being given command of the NATO interventionary force in Libya. However, the Canadian military is largely incapable of carrying out substantial military engagements. Canada sent six fighter jets and one frigate to Eastern Europe as part of NATO's effort to reassure Eastern European allies nervous about Russian intervention. But the Canadian planes were not armed; the gesture was entirely symbolic. This obvious weakness undermined the government's focus on hard power (Pugliese 2014). The Harper government later resisted NATO pressure to increase Canadian military spending as part of NATO's response to Russian actions in the Ukraine. Finally, Canada joined the United States and Britain in bombing the Islamic State in Iraq and sent Canadian soldiers to train anti-IS forces in the region (CTV News 2015).

Discussion and Analysis

The Conservative government saw Canada as part of a Western bloc of like-minded nations. It was sceptical of the value of diplomacy and multilateralism and emphasized hard power. It believed that Canada advances its interests by playing a valuable role within established Western military alliances. The government preferred to follow the leadership of the United States, though it was generally more hawkish on issues of international conflict than the Obama administration. However, foreign policy was ultimately at the service of the Conservative Party's domestic political goals. The CPC had to win elections in order to fulfil its domestic agenda; foreign policy was one formidable tool to secure votes from specific groups.

Ibbitson argues that the Conservative Party came to power in 2006 with no real foreign policy, but it did have five principles that shaped its approach:

1 Conservative foreign policy reflects the values and interests of the Conservative coalition.
2 Canada's military will be a source of pride, not embarrassment.
3 Canadian foreign policy will bolster patriotic pride.
4 Canada will contribute to multilateral institutions only to the extent they advance Canadian interests.
5 Trade is job one. (Ibbitson 2014a, 12)

Ibbitson's principles accord with the general argument of this chapter: the Conservative government based its foreign policy on parochial conservative principles, rather than any sophisticated understanding of the international system. Foreign policy is about conservative values, patriotism, and militarism; the interests of other countries do not matter. The first four principles relate to the use of foreign policy to shape or transform Canadian national identity, underlining the extent to which the CPC saw foreign policy as an extension of domestic political objectives. The effort to link Canadian patriotism to military action attempted to change Canadians' self-perceptions and encourage a rejection of the long-established Canadian internationalist approach to the world (Galloway 2013; Mahoney 2013). The focus on trade was necessary if any other parts of the political project were to succeed.

The CPC appeal to Canada's new immigrant communities was in contrast to the inclinations of most right-wing, conservative political parties in the Western world. The Reform Party was far more sceptical of "new Canadians" than its present incarnation as the CPC. Conservatives had not entirely abandoned their historical opposition to Canadian multiculturalism, however. The new Canadian citizenship handbook emphasized the British military history of Canada and tried to create an impression of the Canadian identity as one rooted in the colonial past. The government cracked down on refugees and made it more difficult to become a Canadian citizen (Marwah, Triadfilopoulos, and White 2013).

In its outreach program the CPC targeted a wide variety of Canadian ethnic communities, the main targets being "Chinese, Korean, Hindu, Jewish, Persian, Italian, and Vietnamese communities" (Barry 2010, 192). Conspicuously absent was the Canadian Muslim community. Canadian Muslims would seem to be an ideal electoral target for the CPC. They are generally socially conservative and distrustful of government. Many come from countries where expectations of the government are very limited (Ross 2007–8). There are at least 940,000 Muslims in Canada and their numbers are expected to triple by 2030 (Lewis 2011). Nonetheless, the CPC explicitly rejected any outreach to the mainstream Muslim community. Conservative Party workers were instructed to never include photographs of Muslims in campaign literature (Martin 2010, 201). The connections that Harper has to the Muslim community are with smaller and oppressed groups within Islam, such as the Ismaili Muslims (represented by the Aga Khan) and the Ahmadiyya, groups who share values that the government deemed acceptable and/or whose experience of oppression drew attention to the failings of mainstream Islam, reinforcing the idea of Muslims as outside the Canadian consensus. Harper said that the number one threat to Canada and the world was fundamentalist Islam (CBC News 2011). The Canadian government targeted a number of Muslim men for exclusion and harassment, in particular Omar Khadr and Abousfian Abdelrazik (Paris 2011; Saunders 2012b). In December 2011, Immigration Minister Jason Kenney announced that Muslim women would be banned from wearing face coverings when swearing the Canadian oath of citizenship (Marwah, Triadfilopoulos, and White 2013, 110). When this measure was struck down in court, Harper personally promised to appeal (Lowrie 2015). When the court dismissed the appeal during the 2015 election campaign, the Harper government made the niqab issue a core part of its message. Besides the citizenship ceremony, Harper indicated the government was considering banning the niqab from the federal government service. The government used Bill C-24, a law designed to strip Canadians with dual citizenship convicted of terrorism of their Canadian citizenship, to remove the citizenship of convicted terrorist Zakaria Amara. It announced a telephone "hotline" that citizens could call if they suspected their neighbours of "barbaric cultural practices." The government's opponents accused it of sowing division within Canadian society. The government's positions on the niqab were supported by a majority of Canadians. However, by the time the hotline was announced, many Canadians had become uncomfortable with the government's focus on demonizing a specific religious group at the expense of other issues important to the electorate (Wells 2015).

Fundamentalist Islam does pose a threat to the Western world, though this is greatly exaggerated.[3] It is hardly comparable to the Communist bloc of the Cold War. Nonetheless, Conservatives often made this comparison, suggesting (as do the American neoconservatives) that there

---

3 The tendency to exaggerate threats is another neoconservative trait (Boettner 2009).

is continuity between the totalitarian enemies of the Cold War and the Islamic terrorism of today. In the Manichaean world view of the Conservative government, mainstream Islam is the culture of the enemy. This emphasizes the extent to which cultural and religious factors were dividing lines in the Conservatives' world view, both inside and outside Canada. In his criticism of American neoconservatism, Ikenberry notes that that the ideology is profoundly ethnocentric (2004). This is readily apparent in the Harper government.

The government was inconsistent in its application of its "principled" and "moral" foreign policy. In keeping with its Cold War mind-set, the government appeared to be comfortable with undemocratic authoritarian regimes. But it regarded Communist (or even former Communist) and many Islamic governments as enemies (Perkel 2014). To illustrate, Harper's concern with democracy and human rights did not extend to Colombia, despite its human rights abuses (Lui 2013). The Conservatives seemed comfortable with the military government of Egypt, despite the fact that government overthrew a democratically elected – but Islamic – government and sentenced its political opponents to death by the hundreds even as it cracked down on the media. The government had no difficulty with the dictatorship in Bahrain (Paris 2013). Canada sold $15 billion worth of weapons to Saudi Arabia, despite that country's atrocious human rights record.[4] Canada refused to attack Saudi Arabia's human rights record and was the only G7 country not to sign the Arms Trade Treaty that could restrict such a sale on the basis of human rights concerns (Chase 2015a, 2015b). Saudi Arabia was an ally in the fight against Iran and, ironically, Islamic terrorism.[5] Harper was enraged by Russia's illegal occupation and annexation of the Crimea, but refused to publicly criticize Israel's far longer and more brutal occupation of Palestine (T. Harper 2014). The government argued that Canada had no interest in taking a position on possible genocide in the Central African Republic because it could not justify the expense to taxpayers – a curiously cold-blooded position from a government that claimed to follow a "moral" foreign policy. From these

4 The new Liberal government followed through on this sale, tarnishing its image of being respectful of human rights.
5 This is ironic, since so much Islamic fundamentalist terrorism has its roots in Saudi Arabia's Salafist orientation.

examples, it appears that the Harper government first determined whether or not a country was a friend or enemy before it applied moral principles to the relationship. That determination was largely made on religious, cultural, and ideological grounds (Heinbecker 2014).

Harper's contempt for the United Nations, including its efforts to address climate change and environmental issues, indicated a rejection of the wider world community. In a recent book Joe Clark (2013) noted that many countries are attempting to survive and prosper within an international system that is weighted against them. These are barriers that Canada never had to face or overcame in an earlier time when racism, colonialism, and the abuse of human rights were normal practices for Western powers. Understanding the considerable difficulties faced by the countries of the world requires the willingness to listen, understand, and make allowances for their different stages of development. Canada must be willing to engage diplomatically with the rest of the world. These qualities were entirely alien to Harper and the Conservatives' approach to foreign policy. Indeed, after more than eight years in power, Clark was struck by Harper's apparent lack of interest in learning anything of the conditions of other countries, despite Harper's many opportunities to do so. Clark argued that the Harper government "talks more than it acts" and adopts an "adolescent" tone when dealing with the international community, preferring the satisfaction of condemning others to doing the hard work of diplomacy and political engagement that is necessary to bring about real global change (Clark 2013, 100). This behaviour alienated Canada from the rest of the world.

Conclusion

Domestic political/electoral considerations were the most important factors shaping the Conservative government's foreign policy. The Conservatives knew that very few Canadians pay attention to foreign policy, let alone vote on its basis. The few communities that do are diaspora communities of recent immigrants or those who have, like many Jewish Canadians, powerful attachments to a particular foreign country. Foreign policy was useful in building the domestic political coalition that the Conservatives needed to change the nature of Canadian society. The Harper government opened the door on diaspora politics in Canadian foreign policy in a way no previous government had; closing that door may be very difficult. Foreign policy experts are concerned that Canadian diaspora communities may undermine the creation of a coherent and sensible Canadian foreign policy in the future (Carment and Samy 2012; Gurcu 2011). Some commentators believe that pandering to diasporas is an inevitable part of Canada's new politics (Ibbitson 2014a; 2014b). If so, this is a profoundly dangerous development for a multicultural country such as Canada, as illustrated in the Gaza War of the summer 2014. The CPC used the war as an opportunity to raise money by putting up a webpage entitled "Stand with Israel" with the option of donating to the party. The CPC criticized the other major political parties for not being sufficiently pro-Israel. The Liberals eventually offered virtually unqalified support for Israel; the NDP were more nuanced, but their reluctance to criticize Israel for its disproportionate use of force against Palestinians led to conflict within the party (Paris 2014; Yakabuski 2014; Bolen 2014).

Harper's pragmatic focus on electoral politics should not blind us to the fact that, where possible, the CPC foreign policy was driven by ideological goals and dispositions. The Harper government used foreign policy in this way because it believed that much of the traditional trappings of foreign policy, with their focus on diplomacy, do not matter. Hard power and maintaining good relationships with a few Western states matter, but there are no costs involved to Canada of alienating most of the rest of the world. Harper is on record as having said that Canada, in the past, has been ineffectual in the Middle East (Brynen 2007, 78). If so, then there was no harm done to Canada in simply taking a side in the conflict. The government did not seem to care about world opinion. It did not value Canadian "soft power." This was a mistake.

Canada's traditional approach to foreign policy was based on a hard-headed assessment of what Canada could achieve in the world and how it could make its presence felt with the limited resources at its command. Canadian leaders believed that a small power such as Canada increased its global influence by having its voice heard in the councils of the world community. The Conservative government had a very limited view of what councils matter and dismissed the efficacy of being heard. As Joe Clark noted, the Conservatives were ideologically opposed to the idea of an active government; diplomacy requires active engagement from the state (Clark 2013, 103–4). But the government found that pursuing its economic agenda required old-fashioned diplomacy to open the necessary doors.

As the world becomes more complex and the diffusion of global influence creates more centres of power, there will be a greater need for effective multilateral institutions to manage the changing global structure. The Conservative government's aggressive responses to Sri Lanka and Russia may have cheered diaspora communities in Canada, but they also meant that Canada had no influence with those two countries (Heinbecker 2014; Jones 2014). In the Middle East, Canada rendered itself irrelevant. This inability to productively engage with states with which Canada may disagree, and the associated rejection of global multilateralism, meant Canada had no role to play in the world, except as a willing appendage to American power. Neoconservative foreign policy led the United States into some of the worst foreign policy disasters in its history and seriously damaged its international power and prestige. Neoconservatism did not work any better for Canada.

REFERENCES

Abu-Laban, Yasmeen, and Abigail Bakan. 2012. "After 9/11: Canada, the Israel/Palestine Conflict and the Surveillance of Public Discourse." *Canadian Journal of Law and Society* 27 (3): 319–39. http://dx.doi.org/10.1017/S082932010001053X.

Akin, David. 2014. "The Harper Doctrine: You're All Anti-Semites." *Toronto Sun*, 20 January. http://www.calgarysun.com/2014/01/20/stephen-harper-argues-criticizing-israel-is-anti-semitic.

Barry, Donald. 2010. "Canada and the Middle East Today: Electoral Politics and Foreign Policy." *Arab Studies Quarterly* 32 (4): 191–217.

Bascaramurty, Dakshana, and John Ibbitson. 2013. "Scarborough Tamils Elated about Harper's Commonwealth Boycott." *Globe and Mail*, 15 November. http://www.theglobeandmail.com/news/toronto/scarborough-tamils-elated-about-harpers-commonwealth-boycott/article15467105/#dashboard/follows/.

BBC. 2013. "Country Rating Poll." http://www.globescan.com/images/images/pressreleases/bbc2013_country_ratings/2013_country_rating_poll_bbc_globescan.pdf.

Blanchfield, Mike. 2013a. "Canada First Country to Pull Out of UN Drought Convention." *Globe and Mail*, 27 March. http://www.theglobeandmail.com/news/politics/canada-first-country-to-pull-out-of-undrought-convention/article10475872/.

– 2013b. "John Baird Cut Pro-Palestinians Remarks from His UN Address." *Globe and Mail*, 19 February. http://www.theglobeandmail.com/news/politics/john-baird-cut-pro-palestinian-remarks-from-his-un-address/article547382/.

Bloomfield, Alan, and Kim Richard Nossal. 2013. "A Conservative Foreign Policy? Canada and Australia Compared." In *Conservatism in Canada*, edited by James Farney and David Rayside, 139–64. Toronto: University of Toronto Press.

Boettner, Ted. 2009. "Neo-conservatism and Foreign Policy." MA thesis, University of New Hampshire.

Bolen, Michael. 2014. "NDP Youth Wing Chides Mulcair for Not Condemning Israeli Attacks in Gaza." *Huffington Post Canada*, 1 August. http://www.huffingtonpost.ca/2014/08/01/ndpyouth-gaza-letter_n_5642345.html.

Brynen, Rex. 2007. "Canada's Role in the Israel-Palestine Peace Process." In *Canada and the Middle East*, edited by Paul Heinbecker and Bessma Momani, 73–89. Waterloo, ON: Wilfrid Laurier University Press.

Bull, Arthur. 2014. "Small Scale Fisheries Have a Big Problem: Canada." *Telegram*, 3 May. http://www.theglobeandmail.com/news/politics/john-baird-cut-pro-palestinian-remarks-from-his-un-address/article547382/.

Canadian Press. 2015. "Palestinians Protest Baird's Visit by Hurling Eggs, Shoes at Convoy." *Globe and Mail*, 18 January. http://www.theglobeandmail.com/news/politics/palestinians-protest-bairds-visit-by-hurling-eggs-shoes-at-convoy/article22508699/.

Carment, David, and Yiagadeesen Samy. 2012. "The Dangerous Game of Diaspora Politics." *Globe and Mail*, 6 September. http://m.theglobeandmail.com/globe-debate/thedangerous-game-of-diaspora-politics/article544912/?service=mobile.

Carrier, Krystel, and Rebecca Tiessen. 2013. "Woman and Children First: Maternal Health and the Silencing of Gender in Canadian Foreign Policy." In *Canada in the World*, edited by Heather A. Smith and Claire Turenne Sjolander, 183–99. Don Mills, ON: Oxford University Press.

CBC News. 2010. "Rights and Democracy Torn by Dissent," 4 February. http://www.cbc.ca/news/canada/story/2010/02/03/rights-democracy-dissent.html.

– 2011. "Harper Says 'Islamicism' Is the Biggest Threat to Canada," 6 September. http://www.cbc.ca/news/politics/harper-says-islamicism-biggest-threat-to-canada-1.1048280.

Chase, Steven. 2010. "An Attack on Israel Would Be Considered an Attack on Canada." *Globe and Mail*, 16 February. http://www.theglobeandmail.com/news/politics/ottawa-notebook/an-attack-on-israel-would-be-considered-an-attack-on-canada/article4187892/.

– 2015a. "Canada Not Tracking Saudi Human Rights Record Despite $15 Billion Arms Deal." *Globe and Mail*, 20 May. http://www.theglobeandmail.com/

news/politics/canada-not-tracking-saudi-rights-record-despite-15-billion-arms-deal/article24506186/.

– 2015b. "Human Rights Advocates Blast Arms Deal with Saudi Arabia." *Globe and Mail*, 20 May. http://www.theglobeandmail.com/news/politics/arms-deal-with-saudi-arabia-exposes-flaws-of-ottawas-export-control/article24536304/.

Clark, Campbell. 2011. "Speaker Rebukes Bev Oda over Document in Kairos Case." *Globe and Mail*, 10 February. http://www.theglobeandmail.com/news/politics/speaker-rebukes-bev-oda-over-document-in-kairos-case/article566676/.

– 2012a. "Harper Took Steps to Stifle Palestinian Statehood Bid." *Globe and Mail*, 26 November. http://www.theglobeandmail.com/news/politics/harper-took-steps-tostifle-palestinian-statehood-bid/article5655676/.

– 2012b. "Ottawa Softens Position on Palestinian Aid." *Globe and Mail*, 4 December. http://www.theglobeandmail.com/news/politics/canadas-300-million-in-humanitarian-aid-to-palestinians-now-under-review/article5964306/.

– 2014. "Conservatives Opt for Twitter Diplomacy in the Gaza Conflict." *Globe and Mail*, 24 July. http://www.theglobeandmail.com/news/politics/globe-politicsinsider/conservatives-opt-for-twitter-diplomacy-in-the-gaza-conflict/article19735604/.

Clark, Campbell, and Justin Ling. 2012. "Baird Lobbied Hard against Palestinian Bid for Statehood." *Globe and Mail*, 10 April. http://www.theglobeandmail.com/news/politics/baird-lobbied-hard-against-palestinian-bid-for-statehood/article4106351/.

Clark, Joe. 2013. *How We Lead: Canada in a Century of Change.* Toronto: Random House Canada.

Crews, Chris. 2013. "Contesting the Anthropocene: Fundamentalism, Science and the Environment." Presentation to Western Political Science Association, Hollywood, CA, 29 March.

CTV News. 2015. "Canadian Warplanes Conduct First Airstrikes in Syria against Isis," 8 April. http://www.ctvnews.ca/canada/canadian-warplanes-conduct-first-airstrikes-in-syria-against-isis-1.2317911.

Day, Adam. 2013. "One Martyr Down: The Untold Story of a Canadian Peacekeeper Killed at War." *Legion Magazine*, 2 January. http://legionmagazine.com/en/2013/01/one-martyr-down-the-untold-story-of-a-canadian-peacekeeper-killed-at-war/.

Erekat, Saeb. 2015. "It Is John Baird Who Needs to Apologize to the Palestinian People." *Globe and Mail*, 16 January. http://www.theglobeandmail.com/

globe-debate/it-is-john-baird-who-needs-to-apologize-to-the-palestinian-people/article22488148/.

Friedman, Murray. 2005. *The Neoconservative Revolution: Jewish Intellectuals and the Shaping of Public Policy.* New York: Cambridge University Press. http://dx.doi.org/10.1017/CBO9780511818721.

Galloway, Gloria. 2013. "War of 1812 Extravaganza Failed to Excite Canadians, Polls Show." *Globe and Mail,* 21 February. http://www.theglobeandmail.com/news/politics/war-of1812-extravaganza-failed-to-excite-canadians-poll-shows/article8906910/.

Gamache, Nick. 2014. "Jean Charest Critical of Canada-China Deal Delays." CBC News, 16 May. http://www.cbc.ca/news/politics/jean-charest-critical-of-canada-china-deal-delays-1.2644346.

Gecelovsky, Paul. 2013. "The Prime Minister and the Parable: Stephen Harper and Personal Responsibility Internationalism." In *Canada in the World,* edited by Heather A. Smith and Claire Turenne Sjolander, 108–24. Don Mills, ON: Oxford University Press.

Globe and Mail. 1997. "Conservatives Abroad," 26 March.

Globe and Mail. 2013. "Why Canada Chose to Leave a Global Fight against Desertification," 28 March. http://www.theglobeandmail.com/news/world/why-canada-chose-to-leave-aglobal-fight-against-desertification/article10547365/.

Goodman, Lee Anne. 2014. "Harper and His Sizable Entourage Head to the Middle East." *Globe and Mail,* 18 January. http://www.theglobeandmail.com/news/politics/harper-and-his-sizable-entourage-head-to-middle-east/article16398522/.

Greene, Trevor. 2014. "How the Harper Government Committed a Knowledge Massacre." *Huffington Post,* 3 January. http://www.huffingtonpost.ca/capt-trevor-greene/science-cutscanada_b_4534729.html.

Greenwood, Faine. 2012. "Canada Closes Its Embassy in Iran and Will Expel All Iranian Diplomats." *Global Post,* 7 September. http://www.globalpost.com/dispatch/news/regions/americas/canada/120907/canada-closes-its-embassy-iran-and-will-expel-all-irani.

Gurcu, Anca. 2011. "How Diaspora Politics Are Beginning to Drive Canadian Foreign Policy." *Embassy Magazine,* 16 March. http://www.embassynews.ca/news/2011/03/16/how-diaspora-politics-are-beginning-to-drive-canadas-foreign-policy/39996.

Haaretz Service. 2011. "Lieberman Thanks Canada PM for Objection to 1967 Borders at G8," 27 May. http://www.haaretz.com/news/diplomacy-defense/lieberman-thanks-canada-pmfor-objection-to-1967-borders-at-g8-1.364502.

Harper, Stephen. 2014. "Full Text of Historic Speech to Israel's Knesset." *Globe and Mail*, 20 January. http://www.theglobeandmail.com/news/politics/read-the-full-text-of-harpershistoric-speech-to-israels-knesset/article16406371/.

Harper, Stephen, and Stockwell Day. 2003. "Canadians Stand with You." *Wall Street Journal*, 28 March. http://online.wsj.com/news/articles/SB104881540524220000.

Harper, Tim. 2014. "Stephen Harper Has Harsh Words for Putin on Historic Visit to Ukraine." *Toronto Star*, 22 March. http://www.thestar.com/news/canada/2014/03/22/stephen_harper_has_harsh_words_for_putin_on_historic_visit_to_ukraine_tim_harper.html.

Harris, Michael. 2014. *Party of One: Stephen Harper and Canada's Radical Makeover*. Toronto: Viking.

Heinbecker, Paul. 2014. "Harper's Cold War Mindset Diminishes His Global Credibility." *Globe and Mail*, 1 April. http://www.theglobeandmail.com/globe-debate/harpers-coldwar-mindset-diminishes-his-global-credibility/article17754286/.

– 2015. "Canada's Bluster over Palestinian ICC Bid Betrays Its Principles." *Globe and Mail*, 28 January. http://www.theglobeandmail.com/globe-debate/canadas-bluster-over-palestines-icc-bid-betrays-its-principles/article22672289/.

Ibbitson, John. 2013. "Tories' New Foreign-Affairs Vision Shifts to 'Economic Diplomacy.'" *Globe and Mail*, 27 November. http://www.theglobeandmail.com/news/politics/tories-new-foreign-affairs-vision-shifts-focus-to-economic-diplomacy/article15624653/.

Ibbitson, John. 2014a. "The Big Break: The Conservative Transformation of Canada's Foreign Policy." *CIGI Papers*, 29 April. https://www.cigionline.org/sites/default/files/cigi_paper_29.pdf.

– 2014b. "Justin Trudeau Can't Ignore Domestic Concerns in Foreign Policy." *Globe and Mail*, 22 May. http://www.theglobeandmail.com/news/politics/justin-trudeaucant-ignore-domestic-concerns-in-foreign-policy/article18792207/.

Ikenberry, John. 2004. "The End of the Neoconservative Moment." *Survival* 46 (1): 7–22.

Jones, Peter. 2014. "Canada's Bitter, Small-Minded Foreign Policy." *Globe and Mail*, 2 January. http://www.theglobeandmail.com/globe-debate/canadas-bitter-small-minded-foreignpolicy/article16147665/?ts=140602163139&ord=1#dashboard/follows/.

Keating, Tom. 2013. *Canada and World Order*. 3rd ed. Don Mills, ON: Oxford University Press.

Laghi, Brian. 2002. "Harper Adopts Strong Stance in Favour of US." *Globe and Mail*, 29 May.

Lewis, Charles. 2011. "Number of Muslims in Canada Predicted to Triple over Next 20 Years: Report." *National Post*, 31 January. http://life.nationalpost.com/2011/01/31/number-of-muslims-in-canada-predicted-to-triple-over-next-20-years-study/.

Liss, Ryan, and Joanna Langille. 2013. "It's Not Just the Drought Treaty: In International Law, Canada Has Withered." *Globe and Mail*, 29 March. http://www.theglobeandmail.com/commentary/its-not-just-the-drought-treaty-ininternational-law-canada-has-withered/article10549743/.

Lowrie, Morgan. 2015. "Harper Says Ottawa Will Appeal Ruling Allowing Veil during Citizenship Oath." *Globe and Mail*, 12 February. http://www.theglobeandmail.com/news/national/harper-says-ottawa-will-appeal-ruling-allowing-veil-during-citizenship-oath/article22979142/.

Lui, Andrew. 2013. "Sleeping with the Dragon: The Harper Government, China and How Not to Do Human Rights." In *Canada in the World*, edited by Heather A. Smith and Claire Turenne Sjolander, 90–107. Don Mills, ON: Oxford University Press.

MacDonald, Marci. 2011. *The Armageddon Factor: The Rise of Christian Nationalism in Canada*. Toronto: Vintage Canada.

Macdonald, Neil. 2015. "Ottawa Cites Hate Crime Laws When Asked about Its 'Zero Tolerance' for Israel Boycotters." CBC News, 11 May. http://www.cbc.ca/news/politics/ottawa-cites-hate-crime-laws-when-asked-about-its-zero-tolerance-for-israel-boycotters-1.3067497.

Mackinnon, Mark. 2013. "How Harper's Foreign Policy Evolved from Human Rights to the 'Almighty Dollar.'" *Globe and Mail*, 27 November. http://www.theglobeandmail.com/news/world/how-harpers-foreign-policy-focusevolved-from-human-rights-to-the-almighty-dollar/article15631389/.

Mackrael, Kim. 2015. "April 30 to Mark Boat People 'Acceptance' in Canada." *Globe and Mail*, 27 April. http://www.theglobeandmail.com/news/politics/april-30-to-mark-vietnamese-boat-people-acceptance-in-canada/article24148249/.

Mahoney, Jill. 2013. "Five Ways Harper Is Rebranding the Government." *Globe and Mail*, 13 March. http://www.theglobeandmail.com/news/politics/five-ways-harper-isrebranding-the-government/article9710708/.

Martin, Lawrence. 2010. *Harperland: The Politics of Control*. Toronto: Viking Canada.

Marwah, Inder, Triadafilos Triadfilopoulos, and Stephen White. 2013. "Immigration, Citizenship and Canada's New Conservative Party." In *Conservatism in Canada*, edited by James Farney and David Rayside, 95–119. Toronto: University of Toronto Press.

Massie, Justin, and Stephane Roussel. 2013. "The Twilight of Internationalism? Neocontinentalism as an Emerging Dominant Idea in Canadian Foreign Policy." In *Canada in the World*, edited by Heather A. Smith and Claire Turenne Sjolander, 36–52. Don Mills, ON: Oxford University Press.

McGlinchey, Stephen. 2009. "Neoconservatism and American Foreign Policy," E-International Relations, 1 June. www.e-ir.info/2009/06/01/neo-conservatism-and-american-foreign-policy/.

Naaman, Dorit. 2009. "Coordinated Campaign Aimed to Stifle Academic Discussion about Israel Raises Critical Questions." *CAUT Bulletin*, October. https://www.cautbulletin.ca/en_article.asp?articleid=2908.

National Defence and the Canadian Forces. 2006. "Death of Major P. Hess-Von Kruedener," 13 September. http://www.crs.forces.gc.ca/boi-ce/rp/von-kruedener/index-eng.aspx#archived.

Nossal, Kim Richard. 2013. "The Liberal Past in the Conservative Present: Internationalism in the Harper Era." In *Canada in the World*, edited by Heather A. Smith and Claire Turenne Sjolander, 21–35. Don Mills, ON: Oxford University Press.

Paris, Erna. 2011. "The New Solitudes." *Walrus*, March. https://thewalrus.ca/the-new-solitudes/.

Paris, Max. 2014. "John Baird Condemns Hamas Rejection of Ceasefire with Israel." CBC News, 15 July. http://www.cbc.ca/news/politics/john-baird-condemns-hamas-rejection-ofceasefire-with-israel-1.2707646.

Paris, Roland. 2013. "Canada's Tough Talk on Human Rights Rings Hollow in Bahrain." *Globe and Mail*, 10 December. http://www.theglobeandmail.com/news/world/world-insider/bairds-tough-talk-on-human-rights-rings-hollow-in-bahrain/article15839860/#dashboard/follows/.

Patten, Steve. 2013. "Triumph of Neoliberalism within Partisan Conservatism." In *Conservatism in Canada*, edited by James Farney and David Rayside, 59–76. Toronto: University of Toronto Press.

Perkel, Colin. 2014. "Harper Goes on Full-Scale Verbal Attack against 'Evil' Communism." *Globe and Mail*, 31 May. http://www.theglobeandmail.com/news/politics/harper-goes-on-full-scale-verbal-attack-against-evil-communism/article18938819/#dashboard/follows/.

Pugliese, David. 2014. "Unclear Whether CF-18s Canada Is Sending to NATO Units in Show of Force over Ukraine Crisis Will Be Armed." *National Post*, 1 May. http://news.nationalpost.com/news/Canada/Canadian-politics/unclear-whether-cf-18s-canada-is-sending-to-nato-units-in-show-of-force-over-ukraine-crisis-will-be-armed/.

Ravid, Barak. 2011. "Netanyahu Asked Canada PM to Thwart G8Support for 1967 Borders." *Haaretz*, 29 May. http://www.haaretz.com/print-edition/

news/netanyahu-asked-canada-pm-to-thwart-g8-support-for-1967-borders-1.364635.

Renzetti, Elizabeth. 2013. "Censorship Is Alive and Well in Canada – Just Ask Government Scientists." *Globe and Mail*, 22 February. http://www.theglobeandmail.com/commentary/censorship-is-alive-and-well-in-canadajust-ask-government-scientists/article8996700/.

Ross, L.R. 2007–8. "Canadian Muslims and Foreign Policy." *International Journal (Toronto, Ont.)* 64 (1): 187–205.

Ruff, Kathleen, and John Calvert. 2014. "Rejecting Science-Based Evidence and International Co-operation: Canada's Foreign Policy on Asbestos under the Harper Government." *Canadian Foreign Policy Journal* 20 (2): 131–45.

Sasley, Brent. 2011. "Who Calls the Shots?" *Literary Review of Canada*, May. http://reviewcanada.ca/magazine/2011/05/who-calls-the-shots/.

Saunders, Doug. 2012a. "By Cutting Ties with Iran, We Just Shot Ourselves in the Foot." *Globe and Mail*, 8 September. http://www.theglobeandmail.com/opinion/by-cutting-tieswith-iran-we-just-shot-ourself-in-the-foot/article4527936/.

Saunders, Doug. 2012b. "Canada's Treatment of Omar Khadr Should Be a Source of National Embarrassment." *Globe and Mail*, 1 October. http://www.theglobeandmail.com/commentary/canadas-treatment-of-khadr-should-be-asource-of-national-embarrassment/article4579178/.

Simpson, Jeffrey. 2011. "How the Political Shift among Jewish Voters Plays in Canada." *Globe and Mail*, 28 September. http://www.theglobeandmail.com/opinion/how-the-political-shift-among-jewish-voters-plays-in-canada/article4199522/.

Simpson, Jeffrey. 2013. "We Have Pandas, but No Trade Deal with China." *Globe and Mail*, 3 July. http://www.theglobeandmail.com/globe-debate/we-have-pandas-but-no-tradedeal-with-china/article12936621/#dashboard/follows/.

Smith, Heather. 2009. "Unwilling Internationalism or Strategic Internationalism? Canadian Climate Change Policy under the Conservative Government." *Canadian Foreign Policy* 15 (2): 57–77. http://dx.doi.org/10.1080/11926422.2009.9673487.

Stairs, Denis. 2011. "Being Rejected in the United Nations: The Causes and Implications of Canada's Failure to Win a Seat in the UN Security Council." Canadian Defence & Foreign Affairs Institute. https://d3n8a8pro7vhmx.cloudfront.net/cdfai/pages/43/attachments/original/1413677044/Being_Rejected_in_the_United_Nations.pdf?1413677044.

Wells, Paul. 2010. "A Losing Battle." *Maclean's*, 12 February. http://www.macleans.ca/authors/paul-wells/a-losing-battle/.

Wells, Paul. 2015. "The Making of a Prime Minister: Inside Trudeau's Epic Victory." *Maclean's*, 22 October. http://site.macleans.ca/longform/trudeau/index.html.

Welsh, Jennifer. 2003. "'I' is for Ideology: Conservatism in International Affairs." *Global Society* 17 (2): 165–85. http://dx.doi.org/10.1080/136008203 2000069073.

Yakabuski, Konrad. 2014. "What Gaza Tells Us about Canadian Politics." *Globe and Mail*, 7 August. http://www.theglobeandmail.com/globe-debate/what-gaza-tells-us-aboutcanadian-politics/article19946283/.

15 Conclusion: A Moderate Turn to the Right with At Least One Enduring Consequence

PETER H. RUSSELL

This volume charts the impact that federal Conservative parties have had on Canadian politics over the last twenty years. The story that these chapters tell adds up to a moderate turn to the right in some areas and a more significant turn in others. It is too soon to determine the lasting effect of these changes on Canadian politics; however, it is clear that change has occurred. As a number of the authors observe, the Conservative Party that emerged in 2003 from a merger of the Progressive Conservatives and the Canadian Alliance (the successor to the Reform Party) is a new right-of-centre "brokerage" party. Brokerage in this context means a combining of ideological tendencies that must soften their edges in order to accommodate one another. The driving force in this accommodation has been the logic of electoral competition that drives the competitors for power in democracies toward the centre.

What I find so interesting in this account is the discussion of the factors that pull conservatives who want to govern toward the centre. Identifying these factors illuminates enduring and distinctive features of the Canadian body politic. The elements that stand out pertain to constitutional politics, and indeed to the very structure of the country. To begin with, the Conservatives have learned the fundamental lesson about Canadian constitutional politics that the Mulroney Progressive Conservatives learned the hard way: stay away from them. The major reform of the Senate, a Triple-E Senate (elected, equal representation of the provinces, and effective), which the Reform Party, the Canadian Alliance, and Mr Harper all hungered for, was off the table. Why? Because the Conservatives realized that opening up the constitutional process to achieve that goal would plunge the country into another divisive round of mega-constitutional politics. So when the Supreme

Court told Mr Harper's government that it could not unilaterally establish a Senate based on provincial elections (already a retreat from a Triple-E Senate), the Conservatives folded their Senate reform tent. As Emmett Macfarlane puts it, the Conservatives remained uncomfortable in their constitutional harness, with remnants of its Reform/Alliance roots giving it some "indigestion." But the depth of Canada's societal divisions remain an obstacle to fundamental restructuring of Canada's founding Constitution.

The deepest of these divisions are French Canada and Indigenous Canada, the "nations within" whose enduring strength make Canada a multinational country. This was a fact about Canada that Preston Manning's Reform Party could not accept. Its vision of Canada was similar to the one that most Americans hold of their country: a single nation of equal citizens. In this vision there is no room for recognizing particular groups of citizens as having distinct and special constitutional status. It is a vision close to that of Pierre Elliott Trudeau, except he sought a Canada of equal rights-bearing citizens, including the right to be served by a national government and to have one's children educated in either of Canada's two official languages, English or French. It is instructive to see how the Conservatives have moved away from the Reform Party's ideas about Canada.

First with respect to French Canada, the Harper Conservatives, like the Mulroney Progressive Conservatives, rejected Reform Party and western Canadian views and left Canada's official bilingualism intact. As for Quebec, the Conservatives' policy of "open federalism," the strict observance of the constitutional division of powers, and minimal use of the spending power in areas of provincial jurisdiction is a natural product of their own ideology and a good fit with Quebec opinion. So there was no need for accommodation on this point. However, as Anna Esselment points out, there were significant limits to how far the Conservatives would decentralize Canadian federalism, especially in economic policy. Stimulus funding of local infrastructure, pressing for a national regulator of the financial securities industry, and pushing the provinces to accept Ottawa's lead in labour-market training were significant centralizing efforts under the Conservatives. Although the Conservatives' style in the funding of health care was brusque and uncooperative, their pledge to increase provincial grants by 6 per cent a year until 2017, and a guarantee of a floor growth of at least 3 per cent of GDP showed that they were not exactly penny-pinchers in maintaining this pillar of the Canadian welfare state.

In 2006, Stephen Harper, fresh from his first election victory, sponsored a motion in the House of Commons that read, "That this House recognize that the Québécois form a nation within a united Canada." This was the Conservative government's most dramatic move toward accommodating Quebec nationalism. Kate Puddister and James Kelly acknowledge that while it would be difficult to imagine the Reform Party sponsoring such a motion, "the Québécois motion does not have any real implications for governance, and its effect remains only symbolic." Nevertheless, it did mark a step toward Conservatives accepting the multinational nature of Canada. Electorally, the Québécois motion was more than offset by Conservative policies such as cutting back on arts and cultural funding, and a foreign policy that downplayed international cooperation, that went down badly with Quebec voters.

In its relations with Indigenous peoples, again the Conservative Party of Canada moved away from the Reform Party's position, but not far. Preston Manning's Reform Party was totally assimilationist in its approach to Indigenous peoples. Like the Chrétien/Trudeau White Paper of 1969, its message to Indigenous peoples was, Forget about your traditions, your history, and your treaties, and we will work with you to enjoy the life of ordinary Canadians. When the First Nations' leaders rejected that approach, Canada's political parties, left, right, and centre, moved on, as did the country. In 1982, with all-party support, a section was added to Canada's Constitution formally recognizing the "existing aboriginal and treaty rights of Canada's aboriginal peoples." So, unless Prime Minister Harper was prepared to tear up the Constitution, some accommodation with Indigenous Canada was mandatory.

Michael McCrossan's chapter traces how minimal this accommodation was. Its most dramatic measure was Prime Minister Harper's apology in the House of Commons to former students of Indian residential schools. Harper was clearly moved by the destructive impact of the residential school program on the family life of Indians, Metis, and Inuit. It is doubtful that he thought of this in terms of its being one of the consequences of imposing British and Canadian rule on Native peoples. Harper said how proud he was that Canada had "no colonial history." This meant he was insensitive to British and Canadian efforts to colonize Indigenous peoples and the potential of treaty relations to form the basis for a more respectful and mutually beneficial relationship. In responding to the Idle No More movement, Harper committed his government to renewing treaty relations, but made no effort to lead his government in that direction. His government's Indigenous policy initiatives, as McCrossan reports, took the form of top-down, take-it-or-leave-it, federal legislation.

The other dimension of Canadian diversity where the new Conservatives moved some way from their Reform party roots is multiculturalism. Erin Tolley reminds us that the Reform Party and the Canadian Alliance harboured xenophobic, redneck fears of the flow of non-Caucasian immigrants into the county. Far from seeing that flow of immigration reversed, under the Conservative government we witnessed immigration rising to its highest levels in fifty years. Tolley suggests that rather than altruism, this reflected shrewd electioneering. Certainly there was evidence of targeting immigrant groups for electoral advantage in the suburbs of Canada's big cities. Rather than a full-fledged commitment to multiculturalism, the Conservatives, to use Bricker and Ibbitson's phrase, were "resolutely principled when convenient." Certainly the CPC's support for immigration came with a heavy conservative tinge: decreasing the proportion of family class immigrants in favour of those meeting economic criteria, and toughening up the treatment of refugees. One does not find a celebration of "multiculturalism" or a commitment to combatting racial discrimination in the citizenship literature favoured by the modern Conservative Party. And while, as with the Liberals, the Conservatives were keen to integrate immigrants into Canadian society, among the Canadian achievements that immigrants were invited to share, in the Conservative government's literature, were Canada's military glories and British heritage, rather than the Charter of Rights and Freedoms or publicly funded health care.

Another area in which accommodation related to constitutional values took place is the potential clash of the social conservatism in the CPC's roots with the principles enshrined in the Canadian Charter of Rights and Freedoms. Emmett Macfarlane shows how the Conservatives decided they had to swallow the Christian fundamentalism and social conservative activism so prominent among Reform Party members. A pro-life stance on abortion is as incompatible with securing plurality support from Canadian voters as opposing official bilingualism. Similarly, whatever qualms the Conservatives may have had about supporting gay marriage, following the example of Paul Martin – the Catholic Liberal leader who preceded Harper as PM – they did not fight the Canadian courts mandating of same-sex marriage. Here we can also see evidence of the CPC's "Red Tory" roots: Peter MacKay who served for a time as Harper's justice minister, Macfarlane reminds us, argued in favour of the same-sex marriage legislation on the basis of its equality and fairness.

A lingering element of conservative ideology marked the CPC's handling of women's issues. Indeed, as Melanee Thomas explains, "Conservatives simply do not engage with women as a political category." After 2006, the party attracted a higher percentage of women candidates than either the Progressive Conservatives or Reform Party did. But this was done under the banner of "equality of opportunity," not as a reach-out-to-women program. The women Conservative strategists targeted were stay-at-home married women who do not do yoga or eat organic foods. The policy issue most clearly influenced by their anti-feminist ideology was childcare, where the Conservatives brought forward the Reform Party's and Canadian Alliance's tax expenditure program supposedly giving families the choice of how to look after their children, rather than subsidizing day care centres for working moms. Given the economic circumstances of most Canadian women, it is not surprising that there continued to be a gender gap in the Conservatives' voting base.

The policy area in which the Conservatives in office clashed most directly with Charter rights was criminal justice. The Supreme Court found elements of its hard-line "law and order" approach in violation of the Charter. These include mandatory minimum sentencing laws, attempting to close a supervised drug-injection site, and keeping Omar Khadr in Guantanamo Bay. The Conservatives clearly believed that pushing an unambiguous right-of-centre criminal justice policy would pay off electorally. The opposition they encountered here came from the judiciary.

Herein lies an important institutional dimension of the Conservatives' rise to power. Once the Conservatives established a majority government, with their party in control of both Houses of Parliament, the courts, and above all the Supreme Court of Canada, emerged as the most important check and balance on them. Besides their setbacks in the criminal justice area, the Supreme Court overruled the Conservative government's attempt to fill a Quebec vacancy on the Supreme with a Federal Court judge, its plan to change the method of selecting Senators and Senators' terms of office without provincial consent, and, most recently, its attempt to roll back the Supreme Court's earlier jurisprudence on Aboriginal title. It is remarkable that these losses suffered by the Conservatives were delivered by a court that, except for one dissent in the judicial appointment case, was unanimous, with a majority of its members appointed by the Harper government.

Let me add that Canada stands out among the world's constitutional democracies in having no significant checks and balances on the prime minister's judicial selections. Emmett Macfarlane comments that Harper "clearly refrained from stacking the bench with conservatives." That may well be true. But then it would seem that the well-qualified justices Harper has appointed, while not known to be strong liberals, are strong centrists when interpreting the Canadian Constitution. This should be born in mind in considering the democratic legitimacy of the Court blocking questionable institutional changes initiated by a government that never won the support of more than 40 per cent of the Canadian electorate.

No chapter in this volume deals directly with Conservative fiscal and economic policy, but Eric Bélanger and Laura Stephenson's investigation of whether there was a conservative turn among the electorate is instructive. They show that among Conservative supporters there was little change in the gap between hardcore free enterprisers and those who favour a more interventionist government. As they put it, the Conservatives are a "big tent" party on economic issues. This reflects the agreement between Progressive Conservative leader Peter MacKay and Canadian Alliance leader Stephen Harper, on the principles of the Conservative Party they were founding: a belief that it is the responsibility of individuals to provide for themselves, their families and their dependents, was to be balanced by recognizing that government must respond to those who require assistance and compassion. This is surely the basis of a bigger tent than American Republicans can tolerate.

The most distinctive development in domestic policy under the three Conservative-led governments we had in the Harper era was environmental policy. Under the Conservative government, Canada became the only country that signed the Kyoto agreement on climate change to withdraw from that agreement and the only UN member to withdraw from the UN Convention to Combat Desertification. With the Conservatives in control of Parliament, the Environment Assessment Act was replaced by legislation that eliminated smaller assessments, shortened the period for assessments and downloaded additional assessments to the provinces and territories, and the National Round Table on the Environment and the Economy – established by a Progressive Conservative government – was dismantled. Nicole Goodman's chapter on interest groups provides the key to understanding this Conservative retreat from responsible environmentalism. Goodman shows how the oil and gas lobby became the most influential interest group under Conservative rule. She reports that in response to a letter sent to the Conservatives' environment and natural resource ministers from members of this group complaining of restrictive environmental legislation, the Conservative government introduced legislation to repeal or weaken the targeted Acts.

The flip side of the Conservatives' alliance with the petroleum industry was its attack on environmental organizations. This was part of a larger program of discrediting an array of human rights groups as "special interest" groups. Apparently, there was nothing special about the interests of the oil and gas industry. Helping them was simply helping the Canadian economy grow. The ideological premise here – though it was not advanced for public discussion – is that long-run threats to the environment, including global warning, must not stand in the way of short-run measurable economic gains.

The Conservatives' environmental policy cannot be described as a sharp shift, because the Liberals, despite the efforts of their erstwhile leader Stéphane Dion, were not robustly green. But the Conservatives' foreign policy does mark a sharp departure from Liberal and Progressive Conservative governments. Shaun Narine writes, "The Conservative government under Stephen Harper pursued an ideologically driven foreign policy to a degree unprecedented in modern Canadian history." The new direction was away from the internationalism of an honest-broker middle power to a more narrowly Western policy, vigorously supporting the United States, giving unqualified support to Israel, and linking foreign aid to Canadian business promotion. Narine believes that the Conservatives' foreign policy was driven as much by the party's neoconservative ideology as by seeking electoral advantage. Jewish voters' support for the Conservatives certainly rose, but this may have been at the expense of losing support among Muslims. But, as Narine notes, unlike most conservative parties in the Western world, the Conservatives have not been anti-immigrant. Trade diversification has emerged as a priority of the Conservatives' foreign policy, in the case of China trumping Harper's hardline opposition to that country's abuse of human rights.

It remains to be seen whether this foreign policy shift is a built-in, fixed feature of a new conservative ideology or whether it had more to do with Harper's style and personality. Canada's unqualified support for Israel led to its withdrawing its candidacy for a seat on the

United Nations Security Council. Will this anti-UN stance of a country renowned for building up the UN's peacemaking and peacekeeping capacity become a permanent feature of Canadian foreign policy? There are already signs that the new Liberal government will not continue this turn away from internationalism.

Canada's basic institutional framework is that of a parliamentary democracy in a federal state. The Conservatives in power had distinctive approaches to both elements of this framework. Again, the question arises of whether these tendencies were mainly emanations of Harper's personality or were enduring features of contemporary Canadian conservatism.

I have already commented on how the Harper government's policy of "open federalism," a strict observance of jurisdictional boundaries, had some appeal to Quebec and on how, especially on economic matters, the Conservative government was a centralist practitioner of federalism. In her chapter on federalism, Anna Esselment also points out that the Conservatives did not dismantle the "alphabet" soup of regional funding agencies that Stockwell Day as the Canadian Alliance leader proclaimed against. The distinctive feature of the Harper Conservative government's treatment of federalism was its style more than its substance. Prime Minister Harper, as Esselment bluntly puts it, "had little appetite for calling first ministers' meetings." Whereas Mulroney met with the premiers on twenty-one occasions, and Chrétien on seven, Harper presided over only one. Harper preferred bilateral, one-on-one meetings with the provincial premiers, rather than exposing himself to the risk of getting outmanoeuvred by the group.

This move away from the process of co-operative federalism may not prove to be permanent. It is questionable whether a federation like Canada's, with powerful governments at both levels and, despite the ideology of classical federalism, many areas of overlapping responsibilities, can be effectively managed by government-to-government bilateralism. The stumble-bum way in which the Harper government was forced by the provinces into modifying its Jobs Canada program suggests that, without an effective forum for the provinces in the federal Parliament, the machinery of co-operative federalism might make a comeback. This already appears to be happening under the Trudeau Liberal government.

To say the least, Stephen Harper was not a fan of deliberative democracy. The chapters in this book on party organization and Parliament show how far he moved the Conservative Party from its populist

Reform Party roots. As James Farney and Royce Koop show, there was no trace of populism in the command-and-control structure of the Harper Conservative Party. Under his leadership, the CPC became, to use Tom Flanagan's phase, a Garrison party, fusing party organization into non-stop, continuous campaigning. A party structured to serve as the base for a permanent campaign has no room for auxiliary organizations such as a youth wing. In that sense the CPC took on a flat organizational structure. It became highly centralized, with government and party fused at the top. More than ever before, government bore the name of the governing party's leader. Government policy became the leader's and his party's brand. And, as we know from the corporate world, brands are not subject to debate and discussion. They are simply promoted to consumers.

Similarly, there was no trace of Preston Manning's Reform Party ideal of the MP as a delegate of her constituents. This is clear in Jonathan Malloy's discussion of Parliament under the Conservatives. Even in opposition the Reform Party members were freer to vote against their party than to speak against it. But once the Conservatives gained office, there was "a much greater silencing of caucus members and a further decline in autonomous activity by backbenchers." In Malloy's view, while overall voting discipline was not significantly tighter than in previous governments, the Conservatives used other means of controlling backbenchers. For example, the possibility of MPs having some autonomy in their committee work that developed under the Mulroney and Martin governments was closed down under Harper. Indeed, when the Conservatives were in a minority situation. their MPs were instructed how to make committees dysfunctional. The Conservative government's use of omnibus bills demonstrated the same disdain for the deliberative role of Parliament. As Goodman points out in her chapter, much of the legislation emasculating environmental protection was enacted under the omnibus budget bill C-38, thus minimizing the exposure of the legislation to parliamentary and public debate.

As J.P. Lewis notes in his chapter, throughout the mandate of the Harper government, the PMO, by not giving advance notice of Cabinet meetings, made it more difficult for the media to interview ministers. On the politically important files, under Harper, as has been the case since Pierre Trudeau's first government, young, unelected political staffers often controlled what Cabinet ministers (or indeed backbench MPs) could say in public. Nor did Harper retain the zeal he expressed in opposition for making government more accountable. He dropped his proposal for a parliamentary Public Appointments Commission like a hot potato once the opposition expressed doubts about the suitability of his candidate for commission chair. He refused to extend the tenure of an activist parliamentary budget officer, and he was the first prime minister in Canadian history to be found in contempt of Parliament when he refused to comply with a Speaker's ruling to hand over to a House committee information about the treatment of prisoners by Canadian forces in Afghanistan.

The Harper-led Conservatives' treatment of the media was an essential part of their disdain for deliberative democracy. As a rising star in Canadian politics, Stephen Harper had reasonably good relations with the media. But once in power, he and his administration were extremely hostile to the mass media. Andrea Lawlor catalogues measures taken by the PM and his office to control media access to the Conservative government. Jeffrey Simpson, a veteran columnist, says never before have these efforts to control the government's message been carried to such extremes. Among other things, this resulted in a muzzling of the scientists employed by government, cutting back support for the country's National Library and Archives, and reductions of funding to Canada's public broadcaster, the CBC. The Conservatives embraced social media, in particular the micro-blogging platform Twitter. While this enabled them to direct information blasts at their core supporters, it did not contribute to deliberative democracy.

Stephen Harper delivered his most disturbing and dramatic blow to parliamentary democracy in the constitutional crisis of 2008, when he sought a prorogation of Parliament in order to avoid a non-confidence vote in the House of Commons. On this occasion, the Conservatives branded coalition governments as illegitimate unless approved in advance by the electorate. As Jonathan Malloy observes in his coverage of this episode, the party rested its case on electoral mandates. Under this view, it is the electorate, not Parliament, that decides who governs. Were this view to prevail, parliamentary democracy in Canada would simply amount to rule by the least unpopular party for four years, unless the governing party decides to call an election earlier. Harper demonstrated in 2008 that he did not feel bound by the fixed election date legislation of which he had been such an eloquent champion in opposition. It is difficult to explain why he observed the legislated date of the 2015 election so religiously when it would have been so advantageous for him to have the election before the Duffy trial.

It would appear from a reading of this book that a lasting legacy of the dynamic developments on the right of the political spectrum over the last two decades is a sharper contest of left versus right in Canadian federal politics. The right united. The 2015 election answered the question of whether the left – the Liberals and the NDP – would unite. At the federal level, Canadian politics seems to have recovered its classic "two and a half" party form – the two strong "old line" parties plus an important third party. There is no evidence that the Canadian electorate as a whole has turned to the right. After the 2011 election, the Conservatives core support fell to around 30 per cent and remained near that level all the way through the long 2015 election campaign. While Conservative Party governments did not turn out to be a long-term dynasty, the CPC emerged from the 2015 election as the official opposition and the party most likely to succeed the Liberals in government. This book shows that a Conservative return to power will happen only if the party can shed some of Stephen Harper's tendencies and be truly a big tent party of the right.

Contributors

Éric Bélanger is professor in the Department of Political Science at McGill University and is a member of the Centre for the Study of Democratic Citizenship. His research interests include political parties, public opinion, and voting behaviour, as well as Quebec and Canadian politics. He has published more than fifty articles on these topics in scholarly journals such as *Comparative Political Studies*, *Political Research Quarterly*, *Electoral Studies*, *Publius: The Journal of Federalism*, the *European Journal of Political Research*, and the *Canadian Journal of Political Science*. He is also the co-author of five books, including one on Quebec politics, *Le comportement électoral des Québécois* (winner of the 2010 Donald Smiley Prize).

Anna Esselment is an associate professor and associate chair of the Department of Political Science at the University of Waterloo. Her research interests include Canadian institutions, political parties, campaigns and elections, and political marketing. Her work has appeared in the *Canadian Journal of Political Science*, *Publius: The Journal of Federalism*, and *Canadian Public Administration*, and she is a co-editor of a new volume, *Permanent Campaigning in Canada*.

Joanna Everitt is a professor of political science in the Department of History and Politics at the University of New Brunswick (Saint John) and a former Visiting Fellow with the Women and Public Policy Program at Harvard University's Kennedy School of Government. Along with producing four books, she has published dozens of articles in national and international journals and edited collections. Her research specifically examines gender differences in public opinion, media coverage of male and female party leaders and its impact on leadership evaluations, and advocacy organizations and social capital. She was the lead investigator for the 2014 New Brunswick Election Study and was part of the team of scholars that produced the 2004, 2006, and 2008 Canadian Election Studies.

James Farney is an associate professor of politics and international studies at the University of Regina. He researches and teaches in party politics, education policy, and religion in Canadian politics. His work on conservatism includes *Social Conservatives and Party Politics in Canada and the United States* and (edited with David Rayside) *Conservatism in Canada*.

Nicole Goodman is director of the Centre for e-Democracy and has a concurrent appointment with the Munk School of Global Affairs at the University of Toronto. Her current research examines the impacts of technology on political behaviour and public policy in an election context in Canada and comparatively. She has recently published articles in *Environment and Planning C: Government and Policy*, the *International Indigenous Policy Journal*, *Journal or Public Deliberation*, and *Studies in Public Choice*. Her research interests are political institutions, digital technology, elections and political parties, political participation, political behaviour, and public policy.

James B. Kelly is professor of political science at Concordia University. His research focuses on the judicialization of politics associated with the introduction of the Charter of Rights and Freedoms in 1982. He is the author of *Governing with the Charter*, co-editor (with Christopher P. Manfredi) of *Contested Constitutionalism*, and co-author (with Janet L. Hiebert) of *Parliamentary Bills of Rights: The Experiences of New Zealand and the United Kingdom*.

Royce Koop is head and associate professor in the Department of Political Studies at the University of Manitoba. His research focuses on representation, political parties, and grassroots democratic engagement. He is the author of *Grassroots Liberals: Organizing for Local and National Politics* and, with Amanda Bittner, co-editor of *Parties, Elections and the Future of Canadian Politics*.

Andrea Lawlor is an assistant professor of political science at King's University College, Western University. Her research focuses on the role of media in the policy process, Canadian public policy, particularly immigration policy and election finance policy, and political institutions. Her work can be found in the *Canadian Journal of Political Science, Journal of Ethnic and Migration Studies, Election Law,* and *Review of Policy Research,* among other journals. She holds a SSHRC Insight Development Grant for her comparative work on third party spending in Canada and the United Kingdom (with collaborator Erin Crandall).

J.P. Lewis is an assistant professor of political science in the Department of History and Politics at the University of New Brunswick (Saint John). His major research interests are in Cabinet government and citizenship education, with a focus on Canada. His work has appeared in *Governance,* the *Canadian Journal of Political Science, Canadian Public Administration,* the *Journal of Political Science Education,* the *British Journal of Canadian Studies,* and the *Canadian Parliamentary Review.*

Emmett Macfarlane is an associate professor of political science at the University of Waterloo. His research focuses on constitutional politics, public policy, and institutions. He is the author of *Governing from the Bench: The Supreme Court of Canada and the Judicial Role* and the editor of *Constitutional Amendment in Canada.* He has published in the *Canadian Journal of Political Science, International Political Science Review,* the *McGill Law Journal,* and the *Supreme Court Law Review,* among others.

Jonathan Malloy is chair of the Department of Political Science at Carleton University. His research and teaching focus on Canadian political institutions, and he is a former president of the Canadian Study of Parliament Group. He is also the co-editor, with Cheryl Collier, of *The Politics of Ontario.*

Michael McCrossan is an assistant professor in the Department of History and Politics at the University of New Brunswick (Saint John). His research and teaching interests focus on Indigenous constitutional politics, reconciliation, and judicial narratives of sovereignty and territorial space. His work has been published in the *Windsor Yearbook of Access to Justice, Settler Colonial Studies,* and the *Canadian Journal of Political Science.*

Shaun Narine is an associate professor of political science/international relations at St Thomas University. His major area of specialization is the institutions and international relations of the Asia Pacific region, especially the Association of Southeast Asian Nations. He has also written on Canadian foreign policy, with a focus on Canada in the Middle East, and human rights in international relations. He is working on a new project critically examining the foreign policy of the Harper government.

Kate Puddister is an assistant professor in the Department of Political Science at the University of Guelph. Her research and teaching focuses on Canadian politics, judicial politics, and criminal justice policy. Her current work considers the interaction between political actors and the judiciary, the litigation behaviour of governments, and the reliance on the courts to make political and normative decisions.

Peter H. Russell is emeritus professor of political science and principal of Senior College at the University of Toronto. His research and writing have focused on judicial, constitutional, and Aboriginal politics, and more recently on parliamentary democracy. His books include *The Judiciary in Canada*, *Constitutional Odyssey*, *Recognizing Aboriginal Title*, and *Two Cheers for Minority Government*. Russell is an Officer of the Order of Canada and a Fellow of the Royal Society of Canada.

Laura B. Stephenson is an associate professor of political science at Western University. She specializes in political behaviour, both Canadian and comparative. Her research focuses on understanding how institutions and context influence attitudes, electoral preferences, and engagement with politics. She is the co-editor of *Voting Behaviour in Canada* and the co-author of *Fighting for Votes*.

Melanee Thomas is an associate professor in the Department of Political Science at the University of Calgary. Her research and teaching focus on gender and politics, political behaviour and psychology, and Canadian politics. Her work appears in *Politics & Gender*, *Electoral Studies*, and the *Canadian Journal of Political Science*. She is the co-editor (with Amanda Bittner) of *Mothers & Others: The Role of Parental Life in Politics*.

Erin Tolley is an assistant professor of political science at the University of Toronto. Her research focuses on race and gender in Canadian politics, and she is particularly interested in questions of representation. She is the author of *Framed: Media and the Coverage of Race in Canadian Politics*, and the co-editor of five books on immigration, multiculturalism, and diversity.

Index

Page references in *italics* indicate a figure; page references in **bold** indicate a table.

orientations, 26; "Our Benign Dictatorship," 283; parliamentary policy, 19, 252, 258–9, 352; personality, 273; on political advertising, 115; political career, 41, 83, 206–7, 252, 284; political views, 30, 317; public image of, 204, 206, 265; Quebec policy, 150–1, 166, 168–9, 345; on Senate reform, 226–7; use of digital media, 213–14; vision of federalism, 7, 291, 297–8; visit to Israel, 324–5; women's evaluations of, 144

"Harper Doctrine," 299–308

Harper government: 2006 Speech from the Throne, 185–6; access to political executive, 272–3; Air India tragedy inquiry, 110; citizenship policy, 109, 111, 330; communication policy, 19–20, 207, 208, 265, 269–70, 352; comparison to Liberals, 111; constitutional crisis of 2008 and, 352; criminal justice policy, 347; engagement of ethnic voters, 112–16, 116n3; environmental policy, 327; federal-provincial relations, 295, 302, 307–8; fiscal policy, 110, 299–300, 301, 302; health care policy, 300, 326–7; immigration policy, 104–8, 346; Indigenous policy, 17–18, 345–6; labour market strategy, 305–6; media relations with, 203–10, 216–17, 352; multicultural initiatives, 109–11; niqab issue, 111–12, 330; open federalism, 15, 159, 162, 165–6, 303–4, 350; securities legislation, 304–5; social policy, 232–3, 298;

treatment of women's groups, 90–1. *See also* Conservative Cabinet ministers; foreign policy

HarperPAC, 95

Harris, Michael, 272

Harris, Mike, 207, 257, 270

Hayek, Friedrich, 297

Health Accord, 299

Hébert, Chantal, 229

Heinbecker, Paul, 323

Henderson, Jennifer, 187

Hill, Jay, 279

Hoyland, Bjorn, 248, 252, 253

Human Rights Act (Bill C-33), 248

Ibbitson, John, 4, 329, 346

Ikenberry, John, 331

immigration: in Canadian politics, 102–4; Conservative policy on, 107–8; distribution of new immigrants, *109*; family class, 108; Liberal government policy on, 106; rise of, 107; super visa restrictions, 108; Syrian refugee claims, 108

Indian Act (1876), 175, 185, 189

Indigenous people: 2015 federal election and, 191; apology to former students of residential schools, 172, 187; Arctic sovereignty and, 186; conservatives in opposition and, 177–85; conservatives in power and, 185–91; constitutional provisions on, 176; electoral participation, 191; Idle No More movement, 18, 191; inherent rights of, 172–3, 175, 177, 187; inquiry of missing and murdered women, 90; land claims, 179–80, 184–5, 186, 189,

minority members, **119**, 119–21;
Sponsorship Scandal, 206;
"statement of reconciliation,"
172; women candidates, 139
Lim, Janice, 113
Livni, Tzipi, 323
lobbyism, 92
long-gun registry bill (Bill C-68),
247–8
Lunn, Gary, 282

Macdonald, John A., 6, 26, 199, 264
Macfarlane, Emmett, 15–16, 344, 346,
348
MacKay, Peter: disagreements with
Harper, 267, 275; founder of
Conservative Party of Canada, 49;
political scandal, 281; political
views, 30; support of same-sex
marriage legislature, 232, 346–7
Malloy, Jonathan, 18, 351, 352
Manning, Ernest, 200
Manning, Preston: attempt to unite
conservatives, 49; conception of
opposition, 249; criticism of, 16;
idea to reform political institutions, 266; interest group and,
88; leadership style, 266; *The
New Canada*, 179; opposition
to Charlottetown Accord, 224;
on parliamentary representation,
246–7; political career, 83; political views, 30, 177, 253; public
image, 201–3; on Quebec secession, 154, 155, 157, 158, 164, 224;
on Reform Party, 81–2; Senate
reform and, 223, 250–1, 260;
view of Indigenous policy,
178n3, 179–80, 182–3
Manning, Sandra, 132n2

Marland, Alex, 285
Martin, Don, 204
Martin, Keith, 252
Martin, Paul: 2006 election campaign, 233; Cabinet appointments,
120, 121n5; Child Care Agreements, 298; communication
problems, 270; fall of government
of, 206; ministerial career, 280;
negative publicity, 205; pledge to
battle "democratic deficit," 265–6;
social initiatives, 296–7
Martin, Yonah, 121
Massie, Justin, 317
mass media: "24 Seven" website,
213; advent of radio, 199–200;
Conservative parties and, 198–9,
201–10; definition, 198n1; democratic deficit, 204; election
campaigns and, 199, 203, 216;
licensing, 212; negative publicity
of politicians, 202–3; OMNI
television, 208; political shows
and advertising, 199–200; Sun
News Network, 211–12; televised
media strategy, 200; Tory politics
and evolution of, 199–201; voter
outreach strategies through, 200.
See also social and digital media
McCoy, Elaine, 50n6
McCrossan, Michael, 13, 18, 345
McDonald, Marci, 88
McGlinchey, Stephen, 316
McGrath reform committee, 245
McGuinty, Dalton, 84
McLachlin, Beverley, 19, 235
Meech Lake Accord, 154, 155, 166,
177, 221, 223, 294, 295, 302–3
Meisel, John, 26
Message Event Proposal, 285

Perlin, George, 25

Persichilli, Angelo, 208

Plett, Don, 38, 40

Political Communications in Canada (Marland), 285

political parties: brokerage parties, 26–7, 51; cadre parties, 38; franchise parties, 27; identification of, 52–3; leaders' accountability, 285; mergers of, 46–7

Pond, David, 257

Porter, John, 102

Prentice, Jim, 275, 277, 280

Prescott, Andrew, 214

pressure groups. *See* interest groups

prime ministerial power, 264, **268,** 268–73, 286

Prime Minister's Office (PMO): centralization of power, 264–6, 284; communication control, 200, 269, 270–1, 272–3, 285; media protocol, 207, 208–9, 210; ministerial staffing, 271–2; outreach to right-wing bloggers, 207; policy announcements, 209; power and influence, 268, 270; response to access to information requests, 208–9; Syrian refugee claims processing, 108

Priorities and Planning (P&P) Committee, 274

Privy Council Office (PCO), 200, 271

Progressive Conservative (PC) Party: 1993 elections, 5, 34, 140, 201, 202; academic literature on, 10; approach to federalism, 294; attitudes towards Indigenous Canadians, *58*; Canada-U.S. ties attitudes, 54, *56*; CF-18 jets contract, 295; challenges to prime ministerial power, 267, **268;**

childcare policy, 135; Clarity Act and, 225–6, 228; Commons seats, 251; constitutional politics and, 221–3, 294; electoral success in Quebec, 156; foreign policy, 319; formation of, 3; free enterprise attitudes, 54, *55*; immigrants and racial minorities attitudes, *57*; Indigenous policy, 181–2, 184; left-right placement attitudes, 54, *55*; members' ethnic origins, 117, **118**; merger with Canadian Alliance, 46, 49, 267; moral attitudes, *56*, 59; parliamentary policy, 245; partisans, 53–4, **68**, 69, **70, 71**; political platform, 30, 267; Quebec policy, 159, 228; Quebec question attitudes, *58*, 59–60; regional alienation attitudes, *59*; social issues policy, 230, 232; women attitudes, *57*; women candidates, 139, 140, **140**

Puddister, Kate, 11, 15, 345

Putin, Vladimir, 326

Quebec: in Canadian politics, 152–3; Conservative policy towards, 153–6, 162–3, 168–9, 300; constitutional status of, 228, 295; federal relations with, 156–63; labour market training program, 305; Liberal influence in, 150; nationalism, 152–3; as nation within Canada, 166–7, 228; open federalism policy and, 160–1, 165–6; private health care issue, 235; secession referendum, 164, 224–6, 296; social debates in, 154n3; UNESCO partnership proposal, 160, 165

Quiet Revolution, 153